Thriving in the Community College and Beyond

Strategies for Academic Success
and Personal Development

◆ **Joseph B. Cuseo**
Emeritus, Marymount College

◆ **Aaron Thompson**
Eastern Kentucky University

◆ **Julie A. McLaughlin**
Cincinnati State Technical and Community College

◆ **Steady H. Moono**
Montgomery County Community College

Kendall Hunt
p u b l i s h i n g c o m p a n y

Book Team

Chairman and Chief Executive Officer   Mark C. Falb
President and Chief Operating Officer   Chad M. Chandlee
Vice President, Higher Education   David L. Tart
Director of Publishing Partnerships   Paul B. Carty
Editorial Manager   Georgia Botsford
Editor   Lynnette M. Rogers
Vice President, Operations   Timothy J. Beitzel
Assistant Vice President, Production Services   Christine E. O'Brien
Senior Production Editor   Charmayne McMurray
Permissions Editor   Renae Horstman
Cover Designer   Suzanne Millius

Cover image © Shutterstock, Inc.

Kendall Hunt
publishing company

www.kendallhunt.com
Send all inquiries to:
4050 Westmark Drive
Dubuque, IA 52004-1840

Printed in the United States of America
10 9 8 7 6 5 4 3 2 1

Brief Contents

Contents

1   Touching All the Bases   1

An Overview and Preview of the Most Powerful Principles of Community College Success   1

2   Goal Setting, Motivation, and Character   39

3   Managing Time and Preventing Procrastination   79

4   Strategies for Deep Learning and High-Level Thinking   109

5 Strategic Studying and Test Taking 143

6 Diversity and the College Experience 185

Appreciating the Value of Human Differences for Promoting Learning and Personal Development 185

7 Managing Money and Minimizing Debt 219

Balancing Saving, Spending, Learning, and Earning 219

8 Social and Emotional Intelligence 251

Relating to Others and Regulating Emotions 251

9   Health and Wellness   287

10   Educational Planning and Decision Making   331

Making Wise Choices about Your Courses, Major, and Degree Plans   331

11   Career Exploration, Planning, and Preparation   375

Welcome to Our Book

What do you think are the characteristics or features of a textbook that:

1. Make you *want* to read it;

_____

_____

_____

2. Enable you to *learn the most* from it?

_____

_____

_____

_____

◆ Plan and Purpose of This Book

The primary purpose of this book is to help you make a smooth transition to college and equip you with strategies for success in college and beyond. The book is designed to promote the academic excellence and personal development of all students—whether you are a student transitioning directly from high school or an older student transitioning from a full-time or part-time job, living on or off campus, or attending college full or part time. Whatever your previous educational record may have been, college is a new ballgame played on a different field with different rules and expectations. If you haven't been a successful student in the past, this book will make you a successful student in the future; if you have been a successful student, it will make you an even stronger student.

The book's major goal is to help you put into practice one of the most powerful principles of human learning and personal success: *mindfulness*. When you're mindful, you remain aware of what you're doing while you're doing it to be sure that you're doing it effectively and to the best of your ability. Self-awareness is the critical first step toward self-improvement and achieving success in any aspect of your life. If you can develop the habit of watching yourself do college and maintain awareness of whether you're doing it effectively (e.g., using the key strategies identified in this book), you will have taken a huge step toward college success.

> "More than 30 years of research has shown that mindfulness is figuratively and literally enlivening. It's the way you feel when you're feeling passionate."
>
> –Dr. Ellen Langer, mindfulness researcher and author of *The Power of Mindful Learning*

ix

Rather than trying to figure out the most effective way of doing college through trial and error, hoping you'll eventually discover what works best, this book gives you a game plan for getting it right from the start. It provides a plan that's built on a solid foundation of research and equips you with well-documented strategies for doing college strategically and successfully.

Specific, action-oriented strategies make up the heart of this book. However, you'll find that these practical strategies aren't presented to you in the form of a laundry list of isolated and disconnected tips. Instead, strategies are accompanied by a research-based rationale for *why* they are effective and specific practices are linked into broader *principles*, which tie the tips together and make them meaningful. It's not only important to *know* what you should do in college, but also *why* you should do it. If you understand the reason behind a suggested strategy, you're more motivated to take it seriously and take action on it. Furthermore, when specific strategies are organized into general principles, they become more powerful because you're able to see how the same principle may be generalized and applied across different subjects and situations. When you understand a principle, you're also empowered to create specific strategies of you own that flow or follow from the same general principle. Learning the underlying reasons a specific strategy works, and learning how specific strategies are embedded in larger principles, is a more challenging task that represents deeper learning than simply reading statements about what you should or shouldn't do to succeed in college. We believe that you're ready and able to meet this challenge of deeper learning and will find it more stimulating than reading compilations of tips and warnings.

Since the strategies we recommend are research-based, you'll find references cited regularly throughout all the chapters and a sizable reference section at the end of the book. You'll also find that the references cited represent a balanced blend of older, "classic" studies and more recent "cutting-edge" research. This highlights the contemporary relevance of the ideas being discussed and their power to withstand the test of time. It also underscores that the subject of college success, like any other subject in the college curriculum, is a scholarly field of study that rests on a solid body of knowledge research, which spans from the past to the present.

◆ Preview of Content

Introduction

In the introduction to this book, you'll find strong evidence why your college experience has the potential to be the most enriching experience of your life and one that will reap you multiple benefits throughout life. The first year of college, in particular, is a critical stage during which students undergo the greatest amount of learning and personal development. It's also when students experience the greatest challenges, the most stress, the greatest academic difficulties, and the highest dropout rate. This highlights the importance of the first-year experience, the importance of first-year courses designed to promote your college success, and the importance of this book. As documented in the Introduction, numerous studies show that new students who participate in first-year seminars or college-success courses are more likely to continue their enrollment in college, complete their college degree, and get the most of their college experience.

Chapter 1. Touching All the Bases

The first chapter provides an overview and preview of the most powerful principles of college success. Its major goals are to equip you with the big-picture principles that you can use to promote your own success in college and raise your awareness of the range of campus resources available to you that you can use to support your quest for success. The chapter describes what services provided by each of these different resources, why they're worth using, and how you can best capitalize on them during your first year and throughout your college experience.

Chapter 2. Goal Setting, Motivation, and Character

The road to success starts with identifying a desired outcome (an end goal) and then continues with finding the means (succession of steps) to reach that goal. Studies show that setting goals is a more effective way to achieve success than simply telling yourself that you're going to try hard or do your best. This chapter identifies the key steps involved in setting and reaching personal goals, self-motivational strategies for staying on track and moving toward your goals, and the inner qualities (virtues) associated not only with being successful but also with being a person of character.

"Watch your thoughts. They become words. Watch your words. They become deeds. Watch your deeds. They become habits. Watch your habits. They become character. Character is everything."

–Ralph Waldo Emerson, famous philosopher, public speaker, and advocate for the abolition of slavery

Chapter 3. Managing Time and Preventing Procrastination

You will encounter an academic calendar and class schedule in college that differs radically from those of your previous years of schooling. You'll be surprised at how much "free time" you have because you'll be spending less time sitting in class; however, you'll be expected to spend more time outside of class on work related to class. Learning to use your out-of-class work time strategically and productively is critical to ensuring academic success in college, and ways to do so are examined in this chapter. Furthermore, time is a valuable personal resource; if you gain greater control of it, you can have greater control of your life. Managing your time well not only enables you to get your work done on time but also enables you to attain and maintain balance in your life. This chapter offers a comprehensive set of strategies for managing time, combating procrastination, and ensuring that your time-spending habits are aligned with your educational goals and personal values.

Student Perspective

"In high school, a lot of the work was done while in school, but in college all of your work is done on your time. You really have to organize yourself in order to get everything done."

–First-year student's response to a question about what was most surprising about college life (Bates, 1994)

Chapter 4. Strategies for Deep Learning and Higher-Level Thinking

The fourth chapter is intended to help you apply research on human learning and the human brain to become a more effective and efficient learner. It takes you through three key stages of the learning process: from the first stage of acquiring information through lectures and readings, through the second stage of studying and retaining that information in your brain, to the final stage of retrieving (recalling) the information you've studied on your exams. The ultimate goal of this chapter is to supply you with a set of powerful strategies that you can use to promote learning that is *deep* (not surface-level memorizing), *durable* (not short term but long lasting), and retrievable (accessing it when you need it).

What would you say is the difference between *learning* and *memorizing*?

_____

_____

_____

_____

_____

_____

Chapter 5. Strategic Studying and Test Taking

The fifth chapter supplies you with effective study strategies that are derived from research on human learning and the human brain. These strategies which will enable you to learn and understand what you're studying more deeply, retain it longer, and recall it at test time. The chapter also supplies a set of strategies that you can use before, during, and after tests to improve your performance. You'll acquire strategies for answering different types of test questions, for becoming more "test wise" and less "test anxious," and for using your test results as feedback to improve performance on future tests.

Chapter 6. Diversity and the College Experience

Chapter 6 clarifies what diversity means, demonstrating how experiencing diversity can deepen learning, promote critical and creative thinking, and contribute to your personal and professional development. Included in the chapter are ideas for overcoming cultural barriers and biases that often interfere with the development of rewarding relationships with diverse people. It also identifies ways to learn effectively from people whose prior personal experiences and cultural backgrounds are different from your own. Simply stated, we learn more from people who differ from us than we do from people similar to us.

Chapter 7. Managing Money and Minimizing Debt

Research shows that accumulating high levels of debt while in college is associated with higher levels of stress, lower academic performance, and greater risk of withdrawing from college. The good news is that research also confirms that students who learn to use effective money-management strategies are able to minimize unnecessary spending, reduce accumulation of debt and stress, and improve the quality of their academic performance. This chapter identifies effective strategies and habits for tracking income and expenses, minimizing or avoiding debt, balancing time spent on school and work, and making wise decisions about spending, saving, and investing.

Chapter 8. Social and Emotional Intelligence

Communicating and relating effectively with others is an important life skill and an important type of human intelligence. Similarly, emotional intelligence—the ability to identify and manage your emotions when dealing with others and remain aware of how your emotions are influencing your thoughts and actions—has been found to an important life skill that influences personal success and academic performance. This chapter identifies effective ways to communicate, relate, and form meaningful relationships with others, as well as ways to understand and regulate emotions such as love, anger, stress, and depression. The information included in this chapter should not only improve not only the quality of your performance in college but the overall quality of your life as well.

Chapter 9. Health and Wellness

No one can reach our full potential and peak levels of performance without attending to our physical self. Sustaining health and attaining optimal levels of performance depend on how well you treat your *body*—what you put into it (healthy food), what you do with it (exercise), and how well you rejuvenate it (sleep quality). This chapter examines strategies for maintaining nutritional balance, promoting total fitness, and improving sleep quality.

THINK ABOUT IT	Journal Entry

What does being a "well-rounded" person and leading a "well-balanced" life mean to you?

_____

_____

_____

_____

_____

_____

Chapter 10. Educational Planning and Decision Making

Chapter 10 is designed to help you make wise choices about your college courses and your college major. Whether you're undecided about your educational goal or think you've reached a final decision, you need to be sure that you choose a path that's truly compatible with your personal interests, talents, and values. You should have a strategic plan in mind (and in hand) that enables you to strike a healthy balance between continuing to explore and making a final commitment. This chapter will help you to strike this balance and make educational decisions that put you in the best position to reach your long-term educational goal.

Chapter 11. Career Exploration, Planning, and Preparation

It may seem unusual or premature to find a chapter on career success in a book for beginning college students. However, career exploration and planning should begin in the first term of college because it gives you a practical, long-range goal to strive for and it enables you to appreciate how the skills that you're using and developing in college are strikingly similar the skills sought by employers and those that promote career success after college. Since career planning is really a form of *life* planning, the sooner you start this process, the sooner you start gaining control of your future and creating a future life, in which you find yourself doing what interests you, what you do well, and what matters most to you.

"It is hard to know how any student could truly understand whom [he or she] wants to be without thinking carefully about what career to pursue."

–Derek Bok, former president of Harvard University

Sequence of Chapter Topics

The chapters in this book have been arranged in an order that allows you to ask and answer the following sequence of questions:

1. Why am I here?
2. Where do I want to go?
3. What must I do to get there?
4. How do I know when I've arrived?

The beginning chapters are intended to help you get immediately situated and oriented to your new campus environment, reinforce your decision for being in college, and help you decide where you want college to take you. These initial chapters provide you a mental map for your trip through college, helping you to set your educational goals and become aware of the college environment that surrounds you that includes the array of campus resources available to you. Once you see why college is worth doing and where it will take you, you should gain enthusiasm and motivation to take action on the strategies suggested throughout the remainder of the book.

The middle chapters are devoted to helping you handle the more practical, day-to-day academic work responsibilities and realities and showing you how to get getting the job done. They focus on the core academic tasks of dealing with lectures, reading assignments, studying, and test taking.

The final chapters of shift to a focus on the future: planning for your major, your career, and your life beyond college.

Process and Style of Presentation

How information is delivered is as important as *what* information is delivered. When writing this text, we made an intentional attempt to deliver our message in a way that would

- Stimulate your motivation to learn;
- Increase the depth of your learning; and
- Strengthen your retention (memory) for what you've learned.

We attempted to do this by incorporating the following principles of motivation, learning, and memory throughout the text:

- We begin each chapter with a **Thought Starter** question that's designed to stimulate your thoughts and feelings about the upcoming topic. This prereading exercise is designed to "warm up" or "tune up" your brain, preparing it to relate the ideas you're about to encounter in the chapter with the ideas you already have in your head. It's an instructional strategy that implements one of the most powerful principles of human learning: we learn most effectively by connecting what we're about to learn to what we've already learned and stored in our brain.
- Within each chapter, we periodically interrupt your reading with a **Think About It** question and **Journal Entry** that asks you to stop, reflect, and think deeply about the material you've just read. These timely pauses keep you mentally alert and active throughout the reading process. The pauses interrupt and intercept "attention drift" that normally takes place when the brain continually takes in and processes information for an extended period, such as what happens while reading. The journal entries should also deepen your understanding of the material you read because you are *writing* in response to what you read. Writing encourages more thoughtful reflection and deeper thinking than simply underlining or highlighting sentences.
- **Exercises** are at the *end* of each chapter and ask you to reflect further on the knowledge you've acquired by reading the chapter and transform that knowledge into informed action. As discussed in Chapter 2, wisdom isn't achieved by acquiring knowledge, but by *applying* the knowledge that you've acquired—i.e., using your knowledge and by putting it into practice.

The strategic positioning of the Thought Starter at the beginning of each chapter, the Think About It questions interspersed during the chapter, and the application Exercises at the end of the chapter creates an effective learning sequence that keeps you actively involved in the reading process—from start to finish.

"One must learn by doing. For though you think you know, you have no certainty until you try."

–Sophocles, influential Ancient Greek author and playwright

- In each chapter, information is delivered through a variety of formats that include diagrams, pictures, cartoons, advice from current college students, words of wisdom from famous and successful people, and personal stories drawn from the authors' experiences. Using different delivery formats to communicate information allows it to pass through different multiple sensory modalities (input channels) and get stored in your brain in more than one place. This deepens learning by allowing it to form multiple connections and improves memory by forming multiple memory traces.

Here's a complete list of the book's instructional features.

Snapshot Summary Boxes

At different points in the text, you'll find boxes containing summaries of key concepts and strategies. These boxed summaries are designed to connect ideas related to the same concept by putting them in the same place (physically), which, in turn, should help you connect them (mentally).

"Remember" Cues

Periodically, you'll encounter a "Remember" statement. This is a cue indicating a high-priority recommendation that deserves special attention and retention.

!

> ### Remember
>
> This book is more than just a textbook for first-term students. It's a *college-* and *life-success* book containing principles and strategies that in addition to promoting your prospects for college success, promote your overall quality of life.

Quotes

Throughout the book, quotes from famous and influential people appear in the side margins that relate to and reinforce the ideas being discussed at that point in the chapter. You'll find quotes from accomplished individuals who've lived in different historical periods and who specialized in fields including politics, philosophy, religion, science, business, music, art, and athletics. The wide-ranging time frames, cultures, and fields of study represented by the people who've been quoted serve as testimony that the wisdom of their words is timeless and universal. You can learn a lot from the firsthand experiences and actual words of "real people." It's our hope that their words will inspire you to aspire to similar levels of achievement attained by these highly successful and respected individuals.

Student Perspectives

Throughout the book, you will find comments and advice from students at different stages of the college experience, including college graduates (alumni). Studies show that students can learn a great deal from other students—especially from students who've been there and experienced what you are about to experience. You can benefit from their experiences by hearing about their success stories and stumbling blocks.

Personal Stories

In each chapter, you'll find personal stories drawn from the authors' experiences. We've learned a lot from our own experiences as college students, our professional experiences working with students as instructors and advisors, and our life experiences. Studies show that sharing personal stories promotes understanding and memory for the concepts contained in the story. We share our personal stories with the intent of personalizing the book and with the hope that you'll learn from our experiences—even if it's learning not to make the same mistakes we made!

THINK ABOUT IT   Journal Entry

Have you received any tips or advice about from friends or family about what to do or what to avoid doing in college?

_____

_____

If yes, what was this advice? Do you think the advice is accurate and worth following?

_____

_____

_____

_____

_____

If no, why do you think you haven't received any advice or suggestions?

_____

_____

_____

_____

_____

_____

Concept Maps: Verbal–Visual Aids

The book contains many concept (idea) maps that visually organize ideas into diagrams or figures. By representing key concepts in a visual–spatial format, you're more likely to retain them because two memory tracks (traces) are recorded in your brain: verbal (words) and visual (images).

Cartoons: Emotional–Visual Aids

You'll find a sizable supply of cartoons sprinkled throughout the text. These intended attempts at humor are included to provide you with a little entertainment, but more importantly, they're intended to strengthen your retention of the concept depicted in the cartoon by reinforcing it with a visual image (drawing) and an emotional experience (humor). If the cartoon triggers at least a snicker, your body will release adrenalin—a hormone that facilitates memory formation. If the cartoon generates actual laughter, it's likely to stimulate release of endorphins—natural, morphine-like chemicals in the brain that lower stress and elevate your mood.

Learning More Through the World Wide Web

To find additional information relating to the chapter's major ideas, Web-based resources are included at the end of the chapter. One of the major goals of a college education is to prepare you to become an independent, self-directed learner. Our hope is that the material presented in each chapter will stimulate your interest and motivation to learn more about the topic. If it does, you can use the online resources cited at the end of the chapter to access additional information relating to the major ideas presented in the chapter.

THINK ABOUT IT	Journal Entry

What features of this book do you think will

1. Stimulate your interest in reading the book; and

_____

_____

_____

_____

_____

2. Promote learning from the book?

_____

_____

_____

_____

_____

_____

◆ Summary and Conclusion

It is our hope that the content of this book, and the manner in which the content is presented, will motivate and empower you to make the most of your college experience. Don't forget that the skills and strategies discussed in this book are relevant to life beyond college. Effective planning and decision making, learning deeply and remembering longer, thinking critically and creatively, speaking and writing persuasively, managing time and money responsibly, communicating and relating effectively with others, and maintaining health and wellness are more than just college skills; they are life skills.

Learning doesn't stop after college; it's a lifelong process. If you strive to apply the ideas in this book, you should thrive in college and beyond.

Sincerely,

Joe Cuseo, Aaron Thompson, Julie McLaughlin, and *Steady Moono*

Acknowledgments

I'd like to take this opportunity to thank several people who have played an important role in my life and whose positive influence made this book possible: My parents, Mildred (née Carmela) and Blase (née Biaggio) Cuseo, for the many sacrifices they made to support my education. My wife, Mary, and my son, Tony, for their kindness, courage, and love. Dr. Pam Brown Schachter, professor of sociology and transfer articulation director, for preparing me to help so many 2-year college students transfer successfully to 4-year colleges and universities across the country. Thank also to my students, who contributed to this book their insightful perspectives, poignant poems, and humorous cartoons.
—*Joe Cuseo*

I thank the people in my life who taught me how to think and those who helped me use that ability for myself and for others. Those who assisted me in recognizing when I didn't have a resource and those who taught me how to find and use needed resources. Those who taught me that education gives the opportunity to know how to get beyond where we are and not leave anyone behind. I thank my parents, Aaron and Margaret, who taught me to see education beyond their perspective and how I could use it to assist my children to live in their world and not in mine. I thank my brothers and sisters (Lawrence, Ruth, Marie, William, Priscilla, Naomi, and Perry), who allowed me to be the baby of the family, and my grandparents, Preacher Bill, Roy, and other spiritual advisors, who taught me how to respect (and sometimes be afraid) of authority while learning to question that authority. Thank you Ms. Ruby, Mr. Abner, Dr. Luhman, Dr. Wisenbaker, Dr. Savage, Dr. Garkovich, Ms. Mays, Dr. Wilkerson, Dr. Hougland, Dr. Enzie, Dr. Futrell, and many more fine educators for allowing me to take advantage of a little knowledge and turn it into a big gain. Thanks also to my many students, who have allowed me to show some insight while responding with a lot of learning. In addition, I thank all those who were on the front line in making this book possible (Joe, Rhonda, Julie, Steady, Paul, Lynn, and Deb). You guys are great. Thanks to my family (especially baby Olivia) for the willingness to give me time and freedom to be a part of this writing effort.
—*Aaron Thompson*

I thank my parents, OJ and Karen McLaughlin, for the unconditional love and support they have given me throughout the years. I would never be where I am today without their constant belief and encouragement. Thanks also to my entire FYE Advisory Committee (and especially my co-chair, Diane Stump) for input and encouragement throughout this project. Although there are too many to name, I thank all of those who have mentored me throughout my career. I give a special thank you to librarian Debbie Bogenschutz for always helping when I needed information. In addition, I thank Kendall Hunt for this incredible opportunity and my coauthors, who have been a joy to work with. Finally, and maybe most importantly, I thank my students who inspire me every day.
—*Julie McLaughlin*

My sincere thanks to several people who have been my vision supporters, who have played an important role in my life, and whose influence makes me dream: My wife, Kelly Moono, and my children, Micah Moono and Naomi Moono. Silas and Ethel Moono, my parents, for giving up the little they had to support my education. Karen Stout, Annette Conn, and James Linksz, my mentors, for their counsel and support. John Flynn, Susan Darrah, and Leonard Bass, my good friends, for being pillars of encouragement to me. Thanks to Kendall Hunt Publishing's director of the National Book Program, Paul Carty, and to Lynnette Rogers, senior editor of the National Book Program, for their wisdom and counsel throughout the writing and review process.
—*Steady Moono*

Joe Cuseo holds a Ph.D in educational psychology and assessment from the University of Iowa. Currently, he is professor emeritus of psychology at Marymount College in California, where for more than 25 years he directed the first-year seminar—taken by all new students. He is a columnist for a bi-monthly newsletter published by the National Resource Center for the First-Year Experience and Students in Transition and has received the resource center's Outstanding First-Year Advocate Award. He is also a 14-time recipient of the faculty Member of the Year Award on his home campus, a student-driven award based on effective teaching and academic advising. He has made more than 100 presentations at college campuses and conferences across the country and has authored articles, chapters, and books on the first-year experience, the transfer experience, the senior-year experience, and college success.

Aaron Thompson is the interim vice president of academic affairs at the Kentucky Council on Postsecondary Education and a professor of sociology in the Department of Educational Leadership and Policy Studies at Eastern Kentucky University. Thompson has a Ph.D in sociology in the areas of organizational behavior and race and gender relations. Thompson has researched, taught, and/or consulted in the areas of assessment, diversity, leadership, ethics, research methodology and social statistics, multicultural families, race and ethnic relations, student success, first-year students, retention, and organizational design. He is nationally recognized in the areas of educational attainment, academic success, and cultural competence. Thompson has worked in various capacities within 2- and 4-year academic institutions. He got his start in college teaching within a community college. His latest coauthored books are *Diversity and the College Experience, Thriving in College and Beyond: Research-Based Strategies for Academic Success and Personal Development, Focus on Success,* and *Black Men and Divorce.* His forthcoming books are *Infusing Diversity into Education: Research-Based Strategies for Appreciating and Learning Human Differences and Humanity, Diversity, & the Liberal Arts: The Foundation of a College Education.* His work has appeared in more than 30 publications, and he has given numerous research and peer-reviewed presentations. Thompson has traveled throughout the United States and has given more than 500 workshops, seminars, and invited lectures in the areas of race and gender diversity, living an unbiased life, overcoming obstacles to gain success, creating a school environment for academic success, cultural competence, workplace interaction, organizational goal setting, building relationships, the first-year seminar, and various other topics. He has been or is a consultant to educational institutions, corporations, nonprofit organizations, police departments, and other governmental agencies. In addition, Thompson's research has been cited in popular publications such as *Cosmopolitan, The Baltimore Sun, Orlando Sentinel,* and *The Tampa Tribune.*

Julie McLaughlin has an MA in college student personnel from Eastern Michigan University. She is an academic advisor and co-chair of the First-Year Experience (FYE) Advisory Committee at Cincinnati State Technical and Community College. She assisted in creating the three FYE courses that are offered at Cincinnati State and assists in training new FYE instructors each term. Julie is a three-time House-Bruckmann Faculty Excellence Award nominee. At Cincinnati State, she is also responsible for cocreating the Athletic Advising Program that has been recognized as an exemplary practice by the National Academic Advising Association (NACADA) and contributed to the NACADA monograph titled *Advising Student-Athletes: A Collaborative Approach to Success.*

Steady Moono, EdD, serves as vice president for student affairs at Montgomery County Community College and is an active NASPA (Student Affairs Administrators in Higher Education) board member for Region II. He was recently recognized as a 2008 Outstanding First-Year-Student Advocate by the National Resource Center for the First-Year Experience and Students in Transition. His research interests in institutional transformation, student retention, and student success in community colleges have led to several conference presentations.

Introduction

Congratulations and welcome! We applaud your decision to continue your education. You've made it to college, also known as "higher education"—where you'll be learning and thinking at a higher level than you did in high school and work situations. You're about to begin a new and exciting journey in your life, joining approximately 12 million students who are now enrolled at more than 1,000 community colleges in the United States today. America's community college system embodies the nation's ideal of equal educational opportunity for all people, regardless of their age, gender, race, ethnicity, prior educational history, family history, or family income. Community colleges in the United States represent the most diverse system of college education in the world. (See **Box I.1** for a snapshot summary of community college students in America today.)

It's probably safe to say that after your college experience you'll never again be a member of an organization or community with as many resources and services that are intentionally designed to promote your learning, development, and success. Your time in college has the potential to be the most enriching experience of your life. If you capitalize on the numerous resources available to you and use effective college-going strategies (such as those suggested in this book), you can create an experience that will transform your life.

Snapshot Summary   I.1

Student Diversity in America's Community Colleges

- There are 12 million students currently enrolled in approximately 1,200 community colleges in the United States; they account for almost half of all first-year college students in America today.
- More than 600,000 community college students will earn an associate degree this year, and more than 300,000 will earn a certificate.
- Most first-year community college students are employed either part or full time and attend college part time.
- The average age of the American community college student is 29.

- Almost 40 percent of all community college students are the first in their family to attend college.
- More than 35 percent of community college students are members of minority racial or ethnic groups.
- Close to 100,000 international students attend America's community colleges—accounting for almost 40 percent of all international students in the United States today.

Source: American Association of Community Colleges (2009).

There are two other groups of students that are growing in number and adding to the student diversity found in America's community colleges:

- Veterans returning from the war in the Middle East who have been afforded the opportunity to attend college with the help of generous financial aid provided by a GI Bill passed in 2009
- Displaced workers over the age of 20 who have lost full-time jobs due to job layoffs and company closings triggered by the current economic recession

---

Personal Story

There are some challenges us vets do face when we get out and go to college. There is that natural gap in maturity [between] the regular college student versus the veteran student. While some students come in late on a regular basis, veteran students are often early to class. Also some students talk during a lecture, while a veteran student gives the instructor the utmost attention. But these are things that are drilled into our heads being raised in the military. Things like loyalty, respect, and integrity.

—Veteran student

Student Perspective

"The scariest thing for me to have done was to get out [of the military] and not have a plan. I firmly believe that you have to plan for success. Success doesn't just happen; you have to work for it."

–First-year veteran student

Personal Story

Many of these new students [displaced workers] feel that going back to school was the best thing that they have ever done. They feel better about themselves because of the daily challenges, making contacts and developing new relationships with classmates, and the thrill of learning helps them to believe in themselves and feel successful. I hear these comments: "This is a wonderful opportunity for me." "I realized what was important to me." "I've wanted to go back to school for a long time."

—Community College Counselor

"

"I am very impressed by the displaced workers who are returning to school. While one would expect the workers to be down and depressed, most of them are viewing this as an opportunity to pursue an opportunity [and] a dream delayed."

–Community College Counselor

Student Perspective

Ready for take off,
On my adventure today,
As I take a seat in my chair
And clear the way.
Eager people around,
With destinations to go,
As a woman at the front says,
"Please find a seat in any row."
Some people are anxious,
Waiting to take flight,
To soar above the rest
With aspirations in sight
Our first day of college,
A chance to start anew,
To find out who we are,
And learn what is true.

—Waiting to Take Flight, a poem by Kimberly Castaneda, first-year student

Your previous enrollment in school was required; however, your decision to continue your education in college is entirely *your choice*. You have made a choice that will improve the quality of your life for the remainder of your life. (See **Box I.2** for a snapshot summary of the multiple, lifetime benefits of a college education and college degree.)

Why College Is Worth It: The Economic and Personal Benefits of a College Education

Less than 30 percent of Americans have earned a 4-year college degree (U.S. Census Bureau). When individuals who attend college are compared with people from similar social and economic backgrounds who did not continue their education beyond high school, research reveals that college is well worth the investment. College graduates experience multiple benefits, such as those summarized in the following list.

1. Career Benefits
- Security and stability. Lower rates of unemployment
- Versatility and mobility. More flexibility to move out of a position and into other positions
- Advancement. More opportunity to move up to higher professional positions
- Interest. More likely to find their work stimulating and challenging
- Autonomy. Greater independence and opportunity to be their own boss
- Satisfaction. More enjoyment of their work

and the feel that it allows them to use their special talents
- Prestige. Higher-status positions (i.e., careers that more socially desirable and respected)

2. Economic Advantages
- Make better consumer choices and decisions
- Make wiser long-term investments
- Receive greater pension benefits
- Earn higher income

The gap between the earnings of high school graduates and those of college graduates is *growing*. Individuals with a bachelor's (or baccalaureate) degree now earn an average annual salary of about $50,000 per year, which is 40 percent higher than high school graduates—whose average salary is less than $30,000 per year. When these differences are calculated over a lifetime, families headed by people with a bachelor's degree take in about $1.6 million more than families headed by people with a high school diploma.

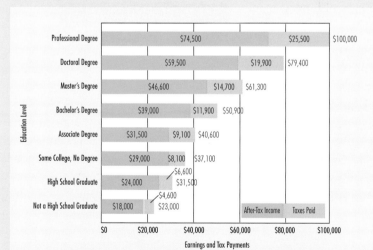

Note: Taxes paid include federal income, Social Security, and Medicare taxes, and state and local income, sales, and property taxes.
Sources: U.S. Census Bureau (2004), Internal Revenue Service (2004), College Board (2005).
The bars in this graph show median earnings at each education level. The lighter segments represent the average federal, state, and local taxes paid at these income levels. The darker segments show after-tax income.

Figure I.1 Median Earnings and Tax Payments of Full-Time Year-Round Workers Ages 25 and Older, by Education Level, 2005

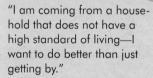

Student Perspective

"I am coming from a household that does not have a high standard of living—I want to do better than just getting by."

—First-year student, quoted in Franklin (2002)

"A bachelor's degree continues to be a primary vehicle of which one gains an advantaged socioeconomic position in American society."

—Ernest Pascarella and Patrick Terenzini,
How College Affects Students

"If you think education is expensive, try ignorance."

—Derek Bok, former president, Harvard University

3. Advanced Intellectual Skills

- Greater knowledge
- More effective problem-solving skills
- Better ability to deal with complex and ambiguous (uncertain) problems
- Greater openness to new ideas
- More advanced levels of moral reasoning
- Clearer sense of self-identity and greater awareness and knowledge of personal talents, interests, values, and needs
- Greater likelihood to continue learning throughout life

4. Better Physical Health

- Better health insurance—more comprehensive coverage and greater likelihood of being covered
- Better dietary habits
- More regular exercise
- Lower rates of obesity
- Longer and healthier life

5. Social Benefits

- Higher social self-confidence
- Better understanding and more effective communication with others
- Greater popularity
- More effective leadership skills
- Greater marital satisfaction

6. Emotional Benefits

- Lower levels of anxiety
- Higher levels of self-esteem
- Greater sense of self-efficacy and belief that they have more influence and control over their life

- Higher levels of psychological well-being
- Higher levels of personal happiness

7. Effective Citizenship

- Greater interest in national issues, both social and political
- Greater knowledge of current affairs
- Higher voting participation rates
- Higher rates of participation in civic affairs and community service

8. Higher Quality of Life for Their Children

- Less likelihood of smoking during pregnancy
- Better health care for their children
- More time spent with their children
- More likely to involve their children in educational activities that stimulate their mental development
- More likely to save money for their children to go to college
- More likely that their children will graduate from college
- More likely that their children will attain high-status and higher-paying careers

Sources: Astin (1993); Bowen (1977, 1997); College Board (2006); Dee (2004); Feldman & Newcomb (1969, 1994); Pascarella & Terenzini (1991, 2005); Tomasho (2009); U.S. Census Bureau (2008).

Student Perspectives

"My 3-month-old boy is very important to me, and it is important that I graduate from college so my son, as well as I, live a better life."

—First-year student responding to the question, "What is most important to you?"

"Being a first-generation college student, seeing how hard my parents worked these past 18 years to give all that they can to get me to where I am now, I feel I cannot let them down. It is my responsibility to succeed in school and life and to take care of them in their old age."

—First-year college student, quoted in Nunez (2005)

Student Perspective

"I noticed before when I wasn't going to college, they [my family] didn't look at me as highly as a person. But now since I have started college, everybody is lifting me up and saying how proud the [are] of me."

—First-year student, quoted in Franklin (2002)

Why have you decided to attend college?

_____

_____

_____

_____

_____

_____

Why are you are attending the college you're enrolled in now?

_____

_____

_____

_____

_____

_____

◆ The Importance of the First Year of College

Your movement into higher education represents an important life transition. Somewhat similar to an immigrant moving to a new country, you're moving into a new culture with different expectations, regulations, customs, and language (Chaskes, 1996). (See the Glossary and Dictionary of College Vocabulary at the end of this book for translations of the new language that is used in the college culture

The _first_ year of college is undoubtedly the most important year of the college experience because it's a stage of _transition_. During the first year of college, students report the most change, the most learning, and the most development (Flowers, 2001; Doyle, Edison, & Pascarella, 1998; Light, 2001). Other research suggests that the academic habits students establish in their first year of college are likely to persist throughout their remaining years of college (Schilling, 2001). When graduating seniors look back at their college experience, many of them say that the first year was the time of greatest change and the time during which they made the most significant improvements in their approach to learning. Here is how one senior put it during a personal interview (Chickering & Schlossberg, 1998, p. 47):

Interviewer: What have you learned about your approach to learning [in college]?

Student: I had to learn how to study. I got to the university and there was no structure. No one checked my homework. No one took attendance to make sure I was in class. No one told me I had to do something. There were no quizzes on the readings. I did not work well with this lack of structure. It took my first year and a half to learn to deal with it. But I had to teach myself to manage my time. I had to teach myself how to study. I had to teach myself how to learn in a different environment.

In many ways, the first-year experience in college is similar to surfing or downhill skiing: it can be filled with many exciting thrills, but there's also a risk of taking some dangerous spills. The first year is also the stage of the college experience during which students experience the most stress, the most academic difficulties, and the highest withdrawal rate (American College Testing, 2009; Bartlett, 2002; Sax, Bryant, & Gilmartin, 2004). The goal of surfing and downhill skiing is to experience the thrills, avoid the spills, and finish the run while you're still standing. The same is true for the first year of college; studies show that if you can complete your first-year experience in good standing, your chances for successfully completing college improve dramatically (American College Testing, 2009).

In a nutshell, your college success will depend on taking advantage of what your college does to help you and what you do to help yourself. You'll find that the research cited and the advice provided in this book point to one major conclusion: Success in college depends on *you*—you make it happen by what you do and how well you capitalize on ***resources*** available to you.

After reviewing 40 years of research on how college affects students, two distinguished researchers (Pascarella & Terenzini, 2005, p. 602) concluded the following:

> *The impact of college is largely determined by individual effort and involvement in the academic, interpersonal, and extracurricular [cocurricular] offerings on a campus. Students are not passive recipients of institutional efforts to "educate" or "change" them, but rather bear major responsibility for any gains they derive from their postsecondary [college] experience.*

Compared to your previous schooling, college will provide you with a broader range of courses, more resources to capitalize on, more freedom of choice, and more decision-making opportunities. Your own college experience will differ from that of any other college student because you have the freedom to actively shape or create it in a way that is uniquely your own. Don't let college happen *to* you; make it happen *for* you—take charge of your college experience and take advantage of the college resources that are at your command.

"What students do during college counts more than who they are or where they go to college."

–George Kuh *Student Success in College*

"Some people make things happen, while others watch things happen or wonder what has happened."

–Author unknown

THINK ABOUT IT   **Journal Entry**   **I.2**

To succeed in college, what do you think you'll have to do differently from what you've done in the past?

◆Importance of a Student Success Course (a.k.a. First-Year Experience Course)

If you're reading this book, you are already beginning to take charge of your college experience because you are probably enrolled in a course that's designed to promote your college success. Research strongly indicates that new students who participate in student-success courses (such as the one that's using this text) are more likely to stay in college, complete their degree, and achieve higher grades. These positive effects have been found for

- All types of students (underprepared and well prepared, minority and majority, residential and commuter, male and female);
- Students at all types of colleges (2- and 4-year, public and private);
- Students attending colleges of different sizes (small, midsized, and large); and
- Students attending colleges in different locations (urban, suburban, and rural).

Sources: Barefoot et al., (1998); Boudreau & Kromrey (1994); Cuseo & Barefoot (1996); Fidler & Godwin (1994); Glass & Garrett (1995); Grunder & Hellmich (1996); Hunter & Linder (2005); Porter & Swing (2006); Shanley & Witten (1990); Sidle & McReynolds (1999); Starke, Harth, & Sirianni (2001); Thomson (1998); Tobolowski (2005).

There has been more carefully conducted research on student- or college-success courses, and more evidence supporting their effectiveness for promoting success, than for any other course in the college curriculum. You're fortunate to be enrolled in this course, so give it your best effort and take full advantage of what it has to offer. If you do, you'll be taking an important first step toward thriving in college and beyond.

Enjoy the trip!

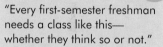

Student Perspective

"Every first-semester freshman needs a class like this—whether they think so or not."

–First-year student evaluating a first-year seminar (college success course)

"I am now one of the peer counselors on campus, and without this class my first semester, I don't think I could have done as well, and by participating in this class again (as a teaching assistant), it reinforced this belief."

–First-year student evaluating a first-year seminar (college success course)

Touching All the Bases

An Overview and Preview of the Most Powerful Principles of Community College Success

1. How do you think college will be different from high school?

_____

_____

_____

_____

_____

2. What do you think it will take to be successful in college? (What personal characteristics, qualities, or strategies do you feel are most important for college success?)

_____

_____

_____

_____

_____

_____

3. How well do you expect to do in your first term of college? Why?

_____

_____

_____

_____

_____

_____

◀LEARNING GOAL

To equip you with a set of powerful success strategies that you can use immediately to get off to a fast start in college and use continually throughout your college experience to achieve success.

◆ The Most Powerful Research-Based Principles of Community College Success

Research on human learning and student development indicates four powerful principles of college success:

1. Active involvement,
2. Use of campus resources,
3. Interpersonal interaction and collaboration, and
4. Personal reflection and self-awareness (Astin, 1993; Kuh, 2000; Light, 2001; Pascarella & Terenzini, 1991, 2005; Tinto, 1993).

These four principles represent the key bases of college success. They are introduced and examined carefully in this opening chapter for two reasons:

1. You can put them into practice to establish good habits for early success in college.
2. These principles represent the foundational bases for all success strategies recommended throughout this book.

The four bases of college success can be represented visually by a baseball diamond (See **Figure 1.1**).

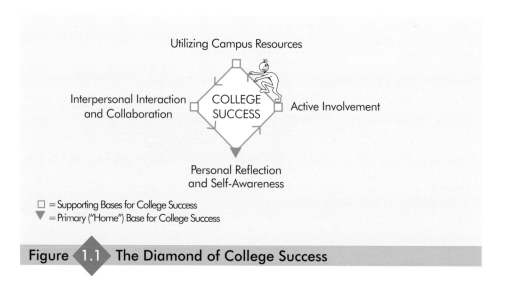

Figure ◀1.1▶ The Diamond of College Success

◆ Touching the First Base of Community College Success: Active Involvement

Research indicates that active involvement may be the most powerful principle of human learning and college success (Astin, 1993; Kuh, 2000). It could be considered the first base of college success because if it's not touched or covered you can't advance to any other base. This principle is the gateway to implementing all other principles of college success. The bottom line is this: To maximize your success in college, you cannot be a passive spectator; you need to be an active player in the learning process.

The principle of active involvement includes the following pair of processes:

- The amount of personal time you devote to learning in the college experience, and
- The degree of personal effort or energy (mental and physical) you put into the learning process.

Think of something you do with intensity, passion, and commitment. If you were to approach academic work in the same way, you would be faithfully implementing the principle of active involvement.

One way to ensure that you're actively involved in the learning process and putting forth high levels of energy or effort is to *act* on what you are learning. Engage in some physical action with respect to what you're learning. You can engage in any of the following actions to ensure that you are investing a high level of effort and energy:

Writing. Express what you're trying to learn in print.

Action: Write notes when reading rather than passively underlining sentences.

Speaking. Express what you're trying to learn orally.

Action: Explain a course concept to a study-group partner rather than just looking over it silently.

Organizing. Group or classify ideas you're learning into logical categories.

Action: Create an outline, diagram, or concept map (e.g., see **Figure 1.2**) to visually connect ideas.

The following section explains how you can apply both components of active involvement—spending time and expending energy—to the major learning challenges that you will encounter in college.

Time Spent in Class

Since the total amount of time you spend on learning is associated with how much you learn and how successful you learn, this association leads to a straightforward recommendation: Attend all class sessions in all your courses. It may be tempting to skip or cut classes because college professors are less likely to monitor your attendance or take roll than your teachers were in high school. However, don't let this new freedom fool you into thinking that missing classes will have no effect on your grades. Over the past 75 years, many research studies in many types of courses have shown a direct relationship between class attendance and course grades—as one goes up or down, so does the other (Anderson & Gates, 2002; Devadoss & Foltz, 1996; Grandpre, 2000; Launius, 1997; Moore, 2003, 2006; Moore, et al., 2003; Shimoff & Catania, 2001; Wiley, 1992; Wyatt, 1992). Figure 1.2 represents the results of a study conducted at the City Colleges of Chicago, which shows the relationship between students' class attendance during the first 5 weeks of the term and their final course grades.

Time Spent on Coursework Outside the Classroom

You will spend fewer hours per week sitting in class in college than you did in high school. However, you will be expected to spend more time on your own on academic work. Studies clearly show that when college students spend more time on academic work outside of class the result is better learning and higher grades. For example, one study of more than 25,000 college students found that the percentage of students receiving mostly A grades was almost

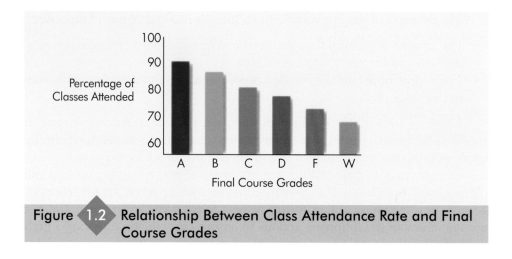

Figure 1.2 Relationship Between Class Attendance Rate and Final Course Grades

three times higher for students who spent 40 or more hours per week on academic work than it was for students who spent between 20 and 40 hours. Among students who spent 20 or fewer hours per week on academic work, the percentage receiving grades that were mostly Cs or below was almost twice as high as it was for students who spent 40 or more hours on academic work (Pace, 1990a, 1990b).

Unfortunately, more than 80 percent of beginning college students report having studied 10 or fewer hours per week during their final year in high school and just 3 percent report studying more than 20 hours per week (Sax et al., 2004). In addition, only 20 percent expect to spend more than 25 hours per week studying throughout college (National Survey of Student Engagement, 2005). This has to change if new college students are to earn good grades.

THINK ABOUT IT   **Journal Entry**   **1.2**

In high school, how many hours per week did you spend on schoolwork outside of class during your senior year?

_____

_____

_____

_____

_____

_____

If you need further motivation to achieve good grades, keep in mind that higher grades during college result in higher chances of career success after college. Research on college graduates indicates that the higher their college grades, the higher:

- The status (prestige) of their first job;
- Their job mobility (ability to change jobs or move into different positions); and
- Their total earnings (salary).

Thus, the more you learn, the more you'll earn. This relationship between college grades and career success exists for students at all types of colleges and universities regardless of the reputation or prestige of the institution that the students are attending (Pascarella & Terenzini, 1991, 2005). In other words, how well you do academically in college matters more to your career success than where you go to college and what institutional name appears on your diploma.

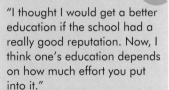

Student Perspective

"I thought I would get a better education if the school had a really good reputation. Now, I think one's education depends on how much effort you put into it."

–First-year college student (Bates, 1994)

Active Listening and Note Taking

You'll find that college professors rely heavily on the lecture method—they profess their knowledge by speaking for long stretches of time, and the students' job is to listen and take notes on the knowledge they dispense. This method of instruction places great demands on the ability to listen carefully and take notes that are both accurate and complete.

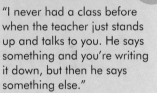

Student Perspective

"I never had a class before when the teacher just stands up and talks to you. He says something and you're writing it down, but then he says something else."

–First-year college student (Erickson & Strommer, 1991)

© Monkey Business Images, 2010. Under license from Shutterstock, Inc.

Taking notes during class is one way to become actively involved in the learning process.

! Remember

Research shows that, in all subject areas, most test questions on college exams come from the professor's lectures and that students who take better class notes get better course grades (Brown, 1988; Kiewra, 2000).

The best way to apply the principle of active involvement during a class lecture is to engage in the physical action of writing notes. Writing down what your instructor is saying in class "forces" you to pay closer attention to what is being said and reinforces your retention of what was said. By taking notes, you not only hear the information (auditory memory) but also see it on paper (visual memory) and feel it in the muscles of your hand as you write it (motor memory).

> **Remember**
>
> Your role in the college classroom is not to be a passive spectator or an absorbent sponge that sits back and simply soaks up information through osmosis. Instead, your role is more like an aggressive detective or investigative reporter who's on a search-and-record mission. You need to actively search for information by picking your instructor's brain, picking out your instructor's key points, and recording your "pickings" in your notebook.

See **Box 1.1** for top strategies on classroom listening and note taking, which you should put into practice immediately. Compared to high school, achieving academic success in college will require you to work harder (by investing more time and energy) and to work smarter (by using more effective learning strategies). Academic success will depend not only on the quantity of your work time but also on its quality; you need to work hard and you need to work smart—by using effective learning strategies and methods (such as those discussed in this text) that enable you to learn more efficiently and more deeply.

Take Action!

Top Strategies: Listening and Note Taking

One of the tasks that you will be expected to perform at the start of your first term in college is to take notes in class. Studies show that professors' lecture notes are the number one source of test questions (and test answers) on college exams. So, get off to a fast start by using the following strategies to improve the quality of your note taking.

1. **Get to every class.** Whether or not your instructors take roll, you're still responsible for all material covered in class. Remember that a full load of college courses (15 units) only requires that you be in class about 13 hours per week. If you consider your classwork to be a full-time job that only requires you to show up about 13 hours a week, that's a sweet deal, and it's a deal that allows more educational freedom than you had in high school. To miss a session when you're required to spend so little time in class per week is an abuse of your educational freedom. It's also an abuse of the money you pay, your family pays, or taxpaying American citizens pay to support your college education.

1.1

2. **Get to every class on time.** *The first few minutes* of a class session often contain valuable information, such as reminders, reviews, and previews.
3. **Get organized.** Arrive at class with the right equipment; get a separate notebook for each class, write your name on it, date each class session, and store all class handouts in it.
4. **Get in the right position.**
   - The ideal place to sit—front and center of the room, where you can hear and see most effectively
   - The ideal posture—upright and leaning forward, because your body influences your mind; if your body is in an alert and ready position, your mind is likely to follow
   - The ideal position socially—near people who will not distract your focus of attention or detract from the quality of your note taking

! Remember

These attention-focusing strategies are particularly important during the first year of college, when class sizes tend to be larger. In a large class, individuals tend to feel more anonymous, which can reduce their sense of personal responsibility and their drive to stay focused and actively involved. Thus, in large-class settings, it's especially important to use effective strategies that eliminate distractions (such as those described in Chapter 4) and attention drift.

5. **Get in the right frame of mind.** Get psyched up; come to class with attitude—an attitude that you're going to pick your instructor's brain, pick up answers to test questions, and pick up your grade.
6. **Get it down (in writing).** Actively look, listen, and record important points at all times in class. Pay special attention to whatever information instructors put in writing, whether it is on the board, on a slide, or in a handout.
7. **Don't let go of your pen.** When in doubt, write it out; it's better to have it and not need it than to need it and not have it.

! Remember

Most college professors do not write all important information on the board for you; instead, they expect you to listen carefully to what they're saying and write it down for yourself.

8. **Finish strong.** The *last few minutes* of class often contain valuable information, such as reminders, reviews, and previews.
9. **Stick around.** As soon as class ends, don't immediately bolt; instead, hang out for a few moments to briefly review your notes (by yourself or with a classmate). If you find any gaps, check them out with your instructor before he or she leaves the classroom. This quick end-of-class review will help your brain retain the information it just received.

Note: More detailed information on listening and note taking is provided in Chapter 4.

Finish class with a rush of attention, not a rush out the door!

THINK ABOUT IT   Journal Entry 1.3

When you enter a classroom, where do you usually sit?

_____

_____

_____

_____

_____

_____

_____

_____

Why do you think you sit there? Is it a conscious choice or more like an automatic habit?

_____

_____

_____

_____

_____

_____

_____

_____

Do you think that your usual seat places you in the best possible position for listening and learning in the classroom?

_____

_____

_____

_____

_____

_____

_____

Active Class Participation

You can become actively involved in the college classroom by arriving at class prepared (e.g., having done the assigned reading), by asking relevant questions, and by contributing thoughtful comments during class discussions. When you communicate orally, you elevate the level of active involvement you invest in the learning process because speaking requires you to exert both mental energy (thinking about what you are going to say) and physical energy (moving your lips to say it). Thus, class participation will increase your ability to stay alert and attentive in class. It also sends a clear message to the instructor that you are a motivated student who takes the course seriously and wants to learn. Since class participation accounts for a portion of your final grade in many courses, your attentiveness and involvement in class can have a direct, positive effect on your course grade.

Active Reading

Writing not only promotes active listening in class but also can promote active reading out of class. Taking notes on information that you're reading, or on information you've highlighted while reading, helps keep you actively involved in the reading process because it requires more mental and physical energy than merely reading the material or passively highlighting sentences with a highlighter. (See **Box 1.2** for top strategies for reading college textbooks that you should put into practice immediately.)

Top Strategies: Improving Textbook-Reading Comprehension and Retention

If you haven't already acquired textbooks for your courses, get them immediately and get ahead on your reading assignments. Information from reading assignments ranks right behind lecture notes as a source of test questions on college exams. Your professors are likely to deliver class lectures with the expectation that you have done the assigned reading and can build on that knowledge when they're lecturing. If you haven't done the reading, you'll have more difficulty following and taking notes on what your instructor is saying in class. Thus, by not doing the reading you pay a double penalty. College professors also expect you to relate or connect what they talk about in class to the reading they have assigned. Thus, it's important to start developing good reading habits now. You can do so by using the following strategies to improve your reading comprehension and retention.

Student Perspective

"I recommend that you read the first chapters right away because college professors get started promptly with assigning certain readings. Classes in college move very fast because unlike high school, you do not attend class five times a week but two or three times a week."

—Advice from a first-year student to new college students

1. Come fully equipped.
   - Writing tool and storage. Always bring a writing tool (pen, pencil, or keyboard) to record important information and a storage space (notebook or computer) in which you can save and later retrieve information acquired from your reading for use on tests and assignments.
   - Dictionary. Have a dictionary nearby to quickly find the meaning of unfamiliar words that may interfere with your ability to comprehend what you're reading. Looking up definitions of unfamiliar words does more than help you understand what you're reading; it's also an effective way to build your vocabulary. Building your vocabulary will improve your reading comprehension in all college courses, as well as your performance on standardized tests, such as those required for admission to graduate and professional schools.

   - Glossary of terms. Check the back of your textbook for a list of key terms included in the book. Each academic subject or discipline has its own special vocabulary, and knowing the meaning of these terms is often the key to understanding the concepts covered in the text. Don't ignore the glossary; it's more than an ancillary or afterthought to the textbook. Use it regularly to increase your comprehension of course concepts. Consider making a photocopy of the glossary of terms at the back of your textbook so that you can have a copy of it in front of you while you're reading, rather than having to repeatedly stop, hold your place, and go to the back of the text to find the glossary.

2. Get in the right position. Sit upright and have light coming from behind you, over the opposite side of your writing hand. This will reduce the distracting and fatiguing effects of glare and shadows.

3. Get a sneak preview. Approach the chapter by first reading its boldface headings and any chapter outline, summary, or end-of-chapter questions that may be provided. This will supply you with a mental map of the chapter's important ideas before you start your reading trip and provide an overview that will help you keep track of the chapter's major ideas (the "big picture"), thereby reducing the risk that you'll get lost among the smaller, more specific details you'll encounter along the way.

4. Use boldface headings and subheadings. These are cues for important information. Turn these headings into questions, and then read to find their answers. This will launch you on an answer-finding mission that will keep you mentally active while reading and enable you to read with a purpose. Turning headings into questions is also a good way to prepare for tests because you're practicing exactly what you'll be expected to do on tests—answer questions.

5. Pay special attention to the first and last sentences. Absorb those in sections of the text that lie beneath the chapter's major headings and subheadings. These sentences often contain an important introduction and conclusion to the material covered within that section of the text.

6. Finish each of your reading sessions with a short review. Recall what you have highlighted or noted as important information (rather

1.2

than trying to cover a few more pages). It's best to use the last few minutes of reading time to "lock in" the most important information you've just read because most forgetting takes place immediately after you stop processing (taking in) information and start doing something else (Underwood, 1983).

Remember

Your goal while reading should be to discover or uncover the most important information contained in what you're reading; and when you finish reading, your final step should be to reread (and lock in) the most important information you discovered while reading.

Note: More detailed information on reading comprehension and retention is provided in Chapter 4.

THINK ABOUT IT   Journal Entry   1.4

Think about all the resources or services available to you on your campus that are designed to support your success. List as many as you can, along with the kind of support you think they provide.

_____

_____

_____

_____

_____

_____

Student Perspective

"College teachers don't tell you what you're supposed to do. They just expect you to do it.

High school teachers tell you about five times what you're supposed to do."

–College sophomore (Appleby, 2008)

◆ Touching the Second Base of Community College Success: Use of Campus Resources

Your campus environment contains multiple resources designed to support your quest for educational and personal success. Studies show that students who use campus resources report higher levels of satisfaction with college and get more out of the college experience (Pascarella & Terenzini, 1991, 2005).

Remember

Involvement with campus services is not just valuable, it's free; the cost of these services has already been covered by your college tuition. By investing time and energy in campus resources, you not only increase your prospects for personal success but also maximize the return on your financial investment in college—that is, you get a bigger bang for your buck.

"Do not be a PCP (Parking Lot → Classroom → Parking Lot) student. The time you spend on campus will be a sound investment in your academic and professional success."

–Dr. Drew Appleby, professor of psychology

Your Key Campus Resources

Using your campus resources is an important, research-backed principle of college success, and it is a natural extension of the principle of active involvement. Successful students are active learners inside and outside the classroom, and this behavior extends to active use of campus resources. An essential first step toward putting this principle into practice is to become fully aware of all key support services that are available on campus. You can find this information in three major forms:

1. **In print.** Information published in written form. For in-print information on campus resources, consult your college catalog (also known as the college bulletin), and your student handbook. If you do not have a copy of the college catalog, you should be able to obtain one from the Office of Admissions or Center for Academic Advising. If you do not have a copy of the student handbook, you should be able to obtain one from the Office of Student Life or Student Affairs.

2. **Online.** Information posted electronically on the Internet. For online information on campus resources, check your college's Web site. Your college may have its entire catalog and student handbook available online.

3. **In person.** Information communicated directly to you by a knowledgeable person. For in-person information on campus resources, speak with professionals in different offices or centers on your campus, such as those listed here

   • **Academic Support Services (Tutoring/Writing Center).** Ask about the type of support the tutoring center provides for improving course learning and increasing academic success (e.g., study and test-taking strategies).

   • **College Library.** Ask about the type of support the library provides for finding information and completing research assignments (e.g., term papers and group projects). Librarians are professional educators who provide instruction outside the classroom. You can learn from them just as you can learn from faculty inside the classroom. Furthermore, the library is a place where you can acquire skills for locating, retrieving, and evaluating information that you may apply to any course you are taking or will ever take.

   • **Academic Advisement.** An academic advisor is a personal resource who can help guide you through the educational planning and decision-making process. Studies show that college students who have developed clear educational and career goals are more likely to continue their college education and complete their college degree (Willingham, 1985; Wyckoff, 1999). However, most beginning college students need help clarifying their educational goals, selecting an academic major, and exploring careers (Cuseo, 2005; Frost, 1991). As a first-year college student, being undecided or uncertain about your educational and career goals is nothing to be embarrassed about. However, you should start thinking about your future now. Connect early and often with an academic advisor to help you clarify your educational goals and choose a field that best complements your personal interests, talents, and values.

Your college library is your campus resource for developing research skills that let you access, retrieve, and evaluate information, which are key skills for achieving both educational and occupational success.

"WHEN DID THEY START USING A SEARCH ENGINE?"

- **Student Development Services (Student Affairs).** Ask about the type of support provided on issues relating to social and emotional adjustment, involvement in campus life outside the classroom, and leadership development.
- **Disability Services.** If you have a physical or learning disability that is interfering with your performance in college, or think you may have such a disability, Disability Services would be the resource on your campus to consult for assistance and support. Programs and services typically provided by this office include:
  - Assessment for learning disabilities;
  - Verification of eligibility for disability support services;
  - Authorization of academic accommodations for students with disabilities; and
  - Specialized counseling, advising, and tutoring.
- **Financial Aid.** If you have questions concerning how to obtain assistance in paying for college, the staff of your Financial Aid Office is there to guide you through the application process. Upon first glance, the materials that need to be submitted may seem confusing or overwhelming. Don't let this intimidate you from seeking assistance with this process from the knowledgeable staff in this office on your campus.
- **Counseling Center.** Counseling services can provide you with a valuable source of support in college, not only helping you cope with college stressors that may be interfering with your academic success but also helping you realize your full potential. Personal counseling can

promote your self-awareness and self-development in social and emotional areas of your life that are important for mental health, physical wellness, and personal growth.

THINK ABOUT IT   Journal Entry   1.5

Take a minute to look back at the major campus resources that have been mentioned in this section, and identify two or three of them that you think you should use immediately. Briefly explain why you have identified these resources as your top priorities at this time. Consider asking your course instructor or academic advisor for recommendations about what campus resources you should consult during your first term on campus.

_____

_____

_____

_____

_____

_____

Personal Story

There are two items that I have always told people it takes to be successful in high school, college, and even in life. The first one is being able to self-evaluate to the point of knowing when you don't have the resource(s) you need to accomplish your goal. The second item that assists your success is having the knowledge of where to find those resources. My mother and father always told me not to wait until someone leads you to water but to find a way to get there yourself. Since I was a first generation college student and did not have many friends to share their knowledge with me about succeeding in college, I quickly learned the art of finding my own path. I found successful students and watched what they did. I learned to ask questions of my professors with the knowledge that if they didn't know the answers, they would know where to find them. I found out where the library was located because I knew there would be books to guide me. I learned throughout my life that knowing where you want to go and asking for directions when needed is the fastest and most efficient way of reaching your destination.

—Aaron Thompson

◆Touching the Third Base of Community College Success: Interpersonal Interaction and Collaboration

Learning is strengthened when it takes place in a social context that involves interpersonal interaction. As some scholars put it, human knowledge is socially constructed, or built through interaction and dialogue with others. According to these scholars, your interpersonal conversations become mentally internalized (represented in your mind) and are shaped by the dialogue you've had with others (Bruffee, 1993). Thus, by having frequent, intelligent conversations with others, you broaden your knowledge and deepen your thinking.

Four particular forms of interpersonal interaction have been found to be strongly associated with student learning and motivation in college:

1. Student–faculty interaction
2. Student interaction with academic advisors
3. Student interaction with a mentor
4. Student–student (peer) interaction

Student–Faculty Interaction

Studies repeatedly show that college success is influenced heavily by the quality and quantity of student–faculty interaction *outside the classroom*. Such contact is positively associated with the following positive outcomes for college students:

- Improved academic performance,
- Increased critical thinking skills,
- Greater satisfaction with the college experience,
- Increased likelihood of completing a college degree, and
- Stronger desire to seek further education beyond college (Astin, 1993; Pascarella & Terenzini, 1991, 2005)

These positive results are so strong and widespread that we encourage you to seek interaction with college faculty outside of class time. Here are some of the most manageable ways to increase your out-of-class contact with college instructors during the first year of college.

1. Seek interaction with your instructors immediately after class.

This is when you may be interested in talking about something that was just discussed in class, and it may be when your instructor is interested in discussing it with you. Furthermore, interaction with your instructor immediately after class can help the professor get to know you as an individual, which should increase your confidence and willingness to seek subsequent contact.

2. Seek interaction with your course instructors during their office hours.

One of the most important pieces of information on the course syllabus is your instructor's office hours. Make specific note of these office hours, and make an earnest attempt to capitalize on them. College professors spend most of their

Student Perspective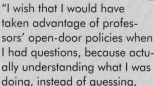

"I wish that I would have taken advantage of professors' open-door policies when I had questions, because actually understanding what I was doing, instead of guessing, would have saved me a lot of stress and re-doing what I did wrong the first time."

–Advice to new students from a college sophomore (Walsh, 2005)

professional time outside the classroom preparing for class, grading papers, conducting research, and serving on college committees. However, some of their out-of-class time is reserved specifically for office hours, during which they are expected to be available.

You can schedule an office visit with your instructor during the early stages of the course. You can use this time to discuss course assignments, term-paper topics, and career options in your instructor's field. Try to make at least one visit to the office of each of your instructors, preferably early in the term, when quality time is easier to find, rather than at midterm, when major exams and assignments begin to pile up.

Even if your early contact with instructors is only for a few minutes, it can serve as a valuable icebreaker that helps your instructors get to know you as a person and helps you feel more comfortable interacting with them in the future.

3. Seek interaction with your instructors through e-mail.

Electronic communication is another effective way to interact with an instructor, particularly if that professor's office hours conflict with your class schedule, work responsibilities, or family commitments. If you are a commuter student who does not live on campus, or if you are an adult student who is juggling family and work commitments along with your academic schedule, e-mail communication may be an especially effective and efficient mode of interaction for you. If you're shy or hesitant about "invading" your professor's office space, e-mail can provide a less threatening way to interact and may give you the self-confidence to seek face-to-face contact with an instructor.

Student–Advisor Interaction

An academic advisor can be an effective referral agent who can direct you to, and connect you with, campus support services that best meet your needs. An advisor can also help you understand college procedures and help you navigate the bureaucratic maze of college policies and politics.

! Remember

An academic advisor is not someone you see just once per term when you need to get a signature for class scheduling and course registration. An advisor is someone you should visit more regularly than your course instructors. Your instructors will change from term to term, but your academic advisor may be the one professional on campus with whom you have regular contact and a stable, ongoing relationship throughout your college experience.

Your academic advisor should be someone whom you feel comfortable speaking with, someone who knows your name, and someone who's familiar with your personal interests and abilities. Give your advisor the opportunity to get to know you personally, and seek your advisor's advice about courses, majors, and personal issues that may be affecting your academic performance.

THINK ABOUT IT   **Journal Entry**   **1.6**

Do you have a personally assigned advisor?

_____

If yes, do you know who this person is and where he or she can be found?

_____

If no, do you know where to go if you have questions about your class schedule
or academic plans?

_____

_____

If you have been assigned an advisor and you find that you cannot develop
a good relationship with this person, ask the director of advising or academic
dean if you could be assigned to someone else. Ask other students about their
advising experience and whether they know any advisors they can recommend
to you.

If your college does not assign you a personal advisor but offers advising
on a drop-by or drop-in basis, you may see a different advisor each time you
visit the center. If you are not satisfied with this system of multiple advisors,
find one advisor with whom you feel most comfortable and make that person
your personal advisor by scheduling your appointments in advance. This will
enable you to consistently connect with the same advisor and develop an ongoing relationship.

Interaction with a Mentor

A mentor may be described as an experienced guide who takes personal interest in you and the progress you're making toward your goals. (For example, in
the movie _Star Wars_, Yoda served as a mentor for Luke Skywalker.) Research in
higher education demonstrates that a mentor can make first-year students feel
significant and enable them to stay on track until they complete their college
degree (Campbell & Campbell, 1997; Knox, 2008). A mentor can assist you in
troubleshooting difficult or complicated issues that you may not be able to resolve on your own and is someone with whom you can share good news, such
as your success stories and personal accomplishments. Look for someone on
campus with whom you can develop this type of trusting relationship. Many
people on campus have the potential to be outstanding mentors, including the
following:

- Your instructor in a first-year seminar or experience course,
- Faculty in your intended major,
- Juniors, seniors, or graduate students in your intended field of study,
- Working professionals in careers that interest you,
- Academic support professionals (e.g., professional tutors in the Learning
  Center),
- Career counselors,

- Personal counselors,
- Learning assistance professionals (e.g., from the Learning Center),
- Student development professionals (e.g., the Director of Student Life or Residential Life),
- Campus minister or chaplain, and
- Financial aid counselors or advisors.

| THINK ABOUT IT | Journal Entry **1.7** |

Four categories of people have the potential to serve as mentors for you in college:

1. Experienced peers (to be discussed in the next section),
2. Faculty (instructors),
3. Administrators (e.g., office and program directors), and
4. Staff (e.g., student support professionals and administrative assistants).

Think about your first interactions with faculty, staff, and administrators on campus. Do you recall anyone who impressed you as being approachable, personable, or helpful? If you did, make a note of that person's name in case you would like to seek out the person again. (If you haven't met such a person yet, when you do, be sure you remember that person because he or she may be an effective mentor for you.)

_____

_____

_____

_____

_____

_____

Interaction with Peers (Student–Student Interaction)

Studies of college students repeatedly point to the power of the peer group as a source of social and academic support (Pascarella, 2005). One study of more than 25,000 college students revealed that when peers interact with one another while learning they achieve higher levels of academic performance and are more likely to persist to degree completion (Astin, 1993). In another study that involved in-depth interviews with more than 1,600 college students, it was discovered that almost all students who struggled academically had one particular study habit in common: They always studied alone (Light, 2001).

Peer interaction is especially important during the first term of college. At this stage of the college experience, new students have a strong need for belongingness and social acceptance because many of them have just left the lifelong security of family and hometown friends. As a new student, it may be useful to view your early stage of the college experience and academic perfor-

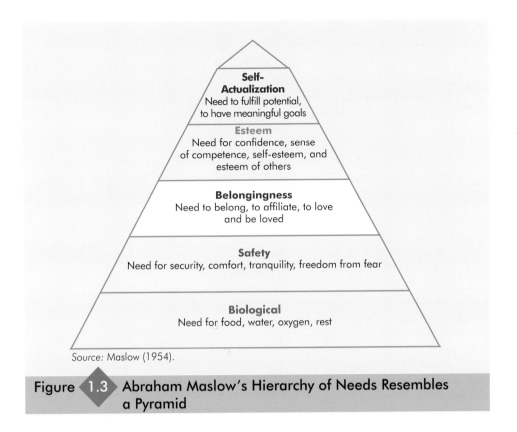

Source: Maslow (1954).

Figure 1.3 Abraham Maslow's Hierarchy of Needs Resembles a Pyramid

mance in terms of the classic hierarchy model of human needs, developed by American psychologist Abraham Maslow (See **Figure 1.3**).

According to Maslow's model, humans cannot reach their full potential and achieve peak performance until their more basic emotional and social needs have been met (e.g., their needs for personal safety, social acceptance, and self-esteem). Making early connections with your peers helps you meet these basic human needs, provides you with a base of social support to ease your integration into the college community, and prepares you to move up to higher levels of the need hierarchy (e.g., achieving educational excellence and fulfilling your potential).

Studies repeatedly show that students who become socially integrated or connected with other members of the college community are more likely to complete their first year of college and continue on to complete their college degree (Tinto, 1993). (For effective ways to make these interpersonal connections, see **Box 1.3**.)

1.3

Top Strategies: Making Connections with Key Members of Your College Community

Here is a list of 10 tips for making important interpersonal connections in college. Start making these connections now so that you can begin constructing a base of social support that will strengthen your performance during your first term and, perhaps, throughout your college experience.

1. Connect with a favorite peer or student development professional that you may have met during orientation.
2. Connect with peers who live near you or who commute to school from the same community in which you live. If your schedules are similar, consider carpooling together.
3. Join a college club, student organization, campus committee, intramural team, or volunteer-service group whose members may share the same personal or career interests as you.
4. Connect with a peer leader who has been trained to assist new students (e.g., peer tutor, peer mentor, or peer counselor) or with a peer who has more college experience than you (e.g., sophomore, junior, or senior).
5. Look for and connect with a motivated classmate in each of your classes and try working as a team to take notes, complete reading assignments, and study for exams. (Look especially to team up with a peer who may be in more than one class with you.)
6. Connect with faculty members in a field that you're considering as a major by visiting them during office hours, conversing briefly with them after class, or communicating with them via e-mail.
7. Connect with an academic support professional in your college's Learning Center for personalized academic assistance or tutoring related to any course in which you'd like to improve your performance.
8. Connect with an academic advisor to discuss and develop your educational plans.
9. Connect with a college librarian to get early assistance and a head start on any research project that you've been assigned.
10. Connect with a personal counselor or campus minister to discuss any college-adjustment or personal-life issues that you may be experiencing.

Getting involved with campus organizations or activities is one way to connect you with other students. Also, try to interact with students who have more college experience than you. Sophomores, juniors, and seniors can be valuable social resources for a new student. You're likely to find that they are willing to share their experiences with you because you have shown an interest in hearing what they have to say. You may even be the first person who has bothered to ask them what their experiences have been like on your campus. You can learn from their experiences by asking them which courses and instructors they would recommend or what advisors they found to be most well informed and personable.

! Remember

Your peers can be more than competitors or a source of negative peer pressure; they can also be collaborators, a source of positive social influence, and a resource for college success. Be on the lookout for classmates who are motivated to learn and willing to learn with you, and keep an eye out for advanced students who are willing to assist you. Start building your social-support network by surrounding yourself with success-seeking and success-achieving students. They can be a stimulating source of positive peer power that drives you to higher levels of academic performance and heightens your motivational drive to complete college.

Collaboration with Peers

Simply defined, collaboration is the process of two or more people working interdependently toward a common goal (as opposed to working independently or competitively). Collaboration involves true teamwork, in which teammates support one another's success and take equal responsibility for helping the team move toward its shared goal. Research on students from kindergarten through college shows that when students collaborate in teams their academic performance and interpersonal skills improve dramatically (Cuseo, 1996).

To maximize the power of collaboration, use the following guidelines to make wise choices about teammates who will contribute positively to the quality and productivity of your learning team.

1. Observe your classmates with an eye toward identifying potentially good teammates. Look for fellow students who are motivated and who should contribute to your team's success, rather than those who you suspect may just be hitchhikers looking for a free ride.

2. Don't team up exclusively with peers who are similar to you in terms of their personal characteristics, backgrounds, and experiences. Instead, include teammates who differ from you in age, gender, ethnic, racial, cultural or geographical background, learning style, and personality characteristics. Such variety brings different life experiences, styles of thinking, and learning strategies to your team, which enrich not only its diversity but its quality as well. If your team consists only of friends or classmates whose interests and lifestyles are similar to your own, this familiarity can interfere with your team's focus and performance because your common experiences can get you off track and on to topics that have nothing to do with the learning task (e.g., what you did last weekend or what you are planning to do next weekend).

"TEAM = **T**ogether **E**veryone **A**chieves **M**ore"

–Author unknown

"Surround yourself with only people who are going to lift you higher."

–Oprah Winfrey, actress and talk-show host

Research shows that when peers work collaboratively to reach a common goal, they learn more effectively and achieve "higher levels" of thinking.

> ! **Remember**
>
> Seek diversity; capitalize on the advantages of collaborating with peers with varied backgrounds and lifestyles. Simply stated, studies show that we learn more from people who are different from us than we do from people who are similar to us (Pascarella, 2001).

Keep in mind that learning teams are not simply study groups formed the night before an exam. Effective learning teams collaborate more regularly and work on a wider variety of academic tasks than late-night study groups. In the following series of important academic tasks and situations, learning teams may be formed to improve your performance.

Note-Taking Teams

Immediately after class sessions end, take a couple of minutes to compare and share notes with other students. Since listening and note taking are demanding tasks, one student often picks up an important point that the others overlooked, and vice versa. By teaming up immediately after class to review your notes, your team has the opportunity to consult with your instructor about any missing or confusing information before the instructor leaves the classroom.

> **Personal Story**
>
> During my first term in college, I was having difficulty taking complete notes in my biology course because the instructor spoke rapidly and with an unfamiliar accent. I noticed another student (Alex) sitting in the front row who was trying to take notes the best he could, but he was experiencing the same difficulty. Following one particularly fast and complex lecture, we both looked at each other and began to share our frustrations. We decided to do something about it by pairing up immediately after every class and comparing each other's notes to identify points we missed or found confusing. First, we helped each other by comparing and sharing our notes in case one of us got something that the other missed. If there were points that we both missed or couldn't figure out, we went up to the front of class together to consult with the instructor before he left the classroom. At the end of the course, Alex and I finished with the highest grades in the course.
>
> —Joe Cuseo

Reading Teams

After completing your reading assignments, you can compare your highlighting and margin notes with classmates. Consult with one another and share what you thought were the most important points in the reading that should be studied for upcoming exams.

Writing Teams

Teammates can provide one another with feedback that can be used to revise and improve the quality of their individual writing. You can form writing teams with peers at any or all of the following stages in the writing process:

- **Topic selection and refinement.** To help generate a list of potential topics and subtopics;

- **Prewriting.** To clarify your purpose and audience;
- **First draft.** To improve your general style and tone;
- **Final draft.** To proofread and correct mechanical errors before submitting your work.

Library Research Teams

Many first-year students are unfamiliar with the process of conducting library research, and some experience "library anxiety" and try to avoid even stepping into the library, particularly if it's large and intimidating (Malvasi, Rudowsky, & Valencia, 2009). Forming library research teams is an effective way for you to develop a social support group that can make trips to the library less intimidating and transform library research from a "flying solo" experience that's done on your own into a collaborative experience that's done as a team.

!

Remember

It is ethical and acceptable for you to team up with others to search for and share resources. This is not cheating or plagiarizing, as long as your final product is completed individually and what you turn in to your instructor represents your own work.

Team–Instructor Conferences

Visiting course instructors outside of class with other classmates is an effective way to get additional assistance in preparing for exams and completing assignments for several reasons:

- It enables you to feel more comfortable about seeing instructors on their turf if you are accompanied by peers, rather than entering this unfamiliar territory on your own. As the old expression goes, "There's safety in numbers."
- When you make an office visit as a team, the information shared by the instructor is heard by more than one person, so your teammates may pick up some useful information that you may have missed, misinterpreted, or forgotten and you may do the same for them.
- You save instructors time by allowing them to help multiple students at the same time rather than requiring them to engage in repeat "performances" for students who visit individually at different times.
- You send a message to instructors that you're serious about the course and are a motivated student because you've taken the time—ahead of time—to connect with your peers and prepare for the office visit.

> "Two heads are better than one, not because either is infallible, but because they are unlikely to go wrong in the same direction."
>
> –C. S. Lewis, English novelist and essayist

Study Teams

Research clearly demonstrates that college students learn from peers as much as, or more than, they do from instructors and textbooks (Astin, 1993; Pascarella, 2005). When seniors at Harvard University were interviewed, nearly everyone who had been part of a study group considered this experience to be crucial to their academic progress and success (Light, 1990, 1992).

Research shows that students who collaborate in teams improve their academic performance and their interpersonal skills.

Research on study groups also indicates that they are effective only if each member has done required coursework in advance of the team meeting, for example, if each group member has done the required reading and other course assignments (Light, 2001). Thus, to fully capitalize and maximize the power of study teams, each member should study individually *before* studying in a group. Each member should come prepared with specific information or answers to share with teammates, as well as specific questions or points of confusion about which they hope to receive help from the team. This ensures that all team members are individually accountable and equally responsible doing their own learning, as well as for contributing to the learning of their teammates.

Test Results–Review and Assignment-Review Teams

After you receive the results of your course exams and assignments, you can collaborate with peers to review your results as a team. By comparing answers, you can better identify the sources of your mistakes. By observing the answers of teammates who may have received maximum credit on particular questions, you can get a clearer picture of where you went wrong and what you need to do better next time.

Teaming up after tests and assignments given early in the term is especially effective, because it enables you to get a better idea of what the instructor expects from students throughout the remainder of the course. What you learn from your peers can be used as early feedback to diagnose your mistakes, improve your next performance, and raise your grade—while there's still plenty of time left in the course to do so.

Learning Communities

Your college may offer first-year students the opportunity to participate in a learning community program, whereby the same group of students takes the same block of courses together during the same academic term. If this opportunity is available to you, try to take advantage of it because research suggests that students who participate in learning community programs are more likely to:

- Become actively involved in classroom learning;
- Form their own learning groups outside the classroom;
- Report greater intellectual gains; and
- Continue their college education (Tinto, 1997, 2000).

If learning community programs are not offered on your campus, consider creating smaller, more informal learning communities by finding other first-year students who are likely to be taking the same courses as you (e.g., the same general education or premajor courses). Team up with these students before registration and plan to register for the same two to three courses together. This will allow you to reap the benefits of a learning community, even though your college does not offer a formal learning-community program.

THINK ABOUT IT   **Journal Entry**   **1.8**

Think about the students in your classes this term. Are there any students who might be good members to join with and form learning teams?

_____

_____

_____

_____

_____

_____

Do you have any classmates who are in more than one class with you and who might be good peer partners to work with on the courses you have in common?

_____

_____

_____

_____

_____

_____

_____

◆ Touching the Fourth (Home) Base of Community College Success: Personal Reflection and Self-Awareness

The final steps in the learning process, whether it be learning in the classroom or learning from experience, are to step back from the process, thoughtfully review it, and connect it to what you already know. Reflection may be defined as the flip side of active involvement; both processes are necessary for learning to be complete. Learning not only requires effortful action; it also requires thoughtful reflection. Active involvement gets and holds your focus of attention, which enables information to reach your brain, and personal reflection promotes consolidation, which "locks" that information into your brain's long-term memory (Bligh, 2000; Broadbent, 1970).

Brain research reveals that two different brain-wave patterns are associated with the mental states of involvement and reflection (Bradshaw, 1995; see **Figure 1.4**). The brain waves on the left reveal faster activity, indicating that the person is actively involved in the learning task and attending to it. The slower brain-wave pattern on the right indicates that the person is thinking deeply about information taken in, which will help consolidate or lock that information into long-term memory. Thus, effective learning combines active mental involvement (characterized by faster, shorter brain waves) with thoughtful reflection (characterized by slower, longer brain waves).

Personal reflection involves introspection—turning inward and inspecting yourself to gain deeper self-awareness of what you've done, what you're doing, or what you intend to do. Two forms of self-awareness are particularly important for success in college:

1. Self-assessment
2. Self-monitoring

Self-Assessment

Simply defined, self-assessment is the process of reflecting on and evaluating your personal characteristics, such as your personality traits, learning habits, and personal strengths or weaknesses. Self-assessment promotes self-awareness, which is the critical first step in the process of self-improvement, personal planning, and effective decision making. The following are important target areas for self-assessment and self-awareness because they reflect personal characteristics that play a pivotal role in promoting success in college and beyond:

• **Personal interests.** What you like to do or enjoy doing;

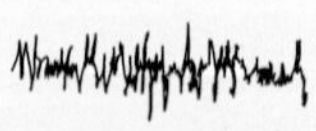

> "We learn to do neither by thinking nor by doing; we learn to do by thinking about what we are doing."
>
> –George Stoddard, former professor of psychology and education, University of Iowa

Faster Brain-Wave Pattern Associated with a Mental State of *Active Involvement*

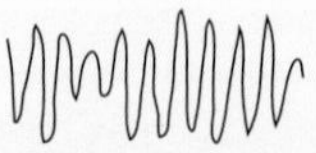

Slower Brain-Wave Pattern Associated with a Mental State of *Reflective Thinking*

Figure 1.4

- **Personal values.** What is important to you and what you care about doing;
- **Personal abilities or aptitudes.** What you do well or have the potential to do well;
- **Learning habits.** How you go about learning and the usual approaches, methods, or techniques you use to learn;
- **Learning styles.** How you prefer to learn; that is, the way you like to;
  - **Receive information.** Which learning format you prefer (e.g., reading, listening, or experiencing);
  - **Perceive information.** Which sensory modality you prefer (e.g., vision, sound, or touch);
  - **Process information.** How you mentally deal with information once you have taken it in (e.g., think about it on your own or discuss it with others);
- **Personality traits.** Your temperament, emotional characteristics, and social tendencies (e.g., whether you lean toward being outgoing or reserved);
- **Academic self-concept.** Your personal beliefs about what kind of student you think you are and how you perceive yourself as a learner (e.g., your level of self-confidence and whether you believe success is within your control or depends on factors beyond your control).

THINK ABOUT IT   **Journal Entry**   **1.9**

How would you rate your academic self-confidence at this point in your college experience? (Circle one)

Very Confident   Somewhat Confident   Somewhat Unconfident   Very Unconfident

Why did you make this choice?

_____

_____

_____

_____

_____

_____

Self-Monitoring

Research indicates that one key characteristic of successful learners is that they monitor or watch themselves and maintain self-awareness of the following:

- Whether they are using effective learning strategies. For example, they're aware of their level of attention or concentration in class.

- Whether they are comprehending what they are attempting to learn. For example, they're understanding it at a deep level or merely memorizing it at a surface level.
- How to self-regulate or self-adjust their learning strategies to meet the different demands of different tasks or subjects. For example, they read technical material in a science textbook more slowly and stop to test their understanding more frequently than when they're reading a novel (Pintrich, 1995; Weinstein, 1994; Weinstein & Meyer, 1991).

For instance, studies show that students who self-monitor their thought processes when solving math and science problems are more effective problem solvers than those who just go through the motions (Resnick, 1986). Effective problem solvers ask themselves such questions as "How did I go about solving this problem correctly?" and "What were the key steps I took to arrive at the correct solution?"

You can begin to establish good self-monitoring habits now by getting in the routine of periodically pausing to reflect on how you're going about learning and how you're "doing" college. For instance, consider these questions:

- Are you listening attentively to what your instructor is saying in class?
- Do you comprehend what you are reading outside of class?
- Are you effectively using campus resources that are designed to support your success?
- Are you interacting with campus professionals who can contribute to your current success and future development?
- Are you interacting and collaborating with peers who can contribute to your learning and increase your level of involvement in the college experience?
- Are you effectively implementing the key success strategies identified in this book?

◆ Summary and Conclusion

Research reviewed in this chapter points to the conclusion that successful students are

1. **Involved.** They invest time and effort in the college experience;
2. **Resourceful.** They capitalize on their surrounding resources;
3. **Interactive.** They interact and collaborate with others; and
4. **Reflective.** They are self-aware learners who assess and monitor their own performance.

Successful students are students who could honestly check almost every box in the following self-assessment checklist of success-promoting principles and practices.

A Checklist of Success-Promoting Principles and Practices

1. **Active Involvement**
    Inside the classroom:
    - ☑ **Get to class.** Treat it like a job; if you cut, your pay (grade) will be cut.
    - ☑ **Get involved in class.** Come prepared, listen actively, take notes, and participate.

    Outside the classroom:
    - ☑ **Read actively.** Take notes while you read to increase attention and retention.
    - ☑ **Double up.** Spend twice as much time on academic work outside the classroom than you spend in class—if you're a full-time student, that makes it a 40-hour academic workweek (with occasional "overtime").

2. **Use of Campus Resources**
    Capitalize on academic and student support services:
    - ☑ Learning Center
    - ☑ Writing Center
    - ☑ Disability Services
    - ☑ College Library
    - ☑ Academic Advisement
    - ☑ Career Development Center
    - ☑ Financial Aid Office
    - ☑ Counseling Center
    - ☑ Experiential Learning Resources

3. **Interpersonal Interaction and Collaboration**
    Interact with the following people:
    - ☑ **Peers.** Join student clubs and participating in campus organizations.
    - ☑ **Faculty members.** Connect with them immediately after class, in their offices, or via e-mail.
    - ☑ **Academic advisors.** See them for more than just a signature to register; find an advisor you can relate to and with whom you can develop an ongoing relationship.
    - ☑ **Mentors.** Try to find experienced people on campus who can serve as trusted guides and role models.

    Collaborate by doing the following:
    - ☑ **Form learning teams.** Join not only last-minute study groups but also teams that collaborate more regularly to work on such tasks as taking lecture notes, completing reading and writing assignments, conducting library research, and reviewing results of exams or course assignments.
    - ☑ **Participate in learning communities.** Enroll in two or more classes with the same students during the same term.

4. **Personal Reflection and Self-Awareness**
    - ☑ **Self-assessment.** Reflect on and evaluate your personal traits, habits, strengths and weaknesses.
    - ☑ **Self-monitoring.** Maintain self-awareness of how you're learning, what you're learning, and whether you're learning.

THINK ABOUT IT | **Journal Entry** | **1.10**

Before exiting this chapter, look back at the Checklist of Success-Promoting Principles and Practices and see how these ideas compare with those you recorded at the start of this chapter, when we asked you how you thought college would be different from high school and what it would take to be successful in college.

What ideas from your list and our checklist tend to match?

_____

_____

_____

_____

_____

Were there any ideas on your list that were not on ours, or vice versa?

_____

_____

_____

_____

_____

_____

Internet-Based Resources for Further Information on College Success

For additional information relating to the ideas discussed in this chapter, we recommend the following Web sites:

www.dartmouth.edu/~acskills/success/index.html

www.uni.edu/walsh/linda7.html

www.condor.depaul.edu/~plus/plus**tips**to**success**.html

1.1 Constructing a Master List of Campus Resources

1. Use each of the following sources to gain more in-depth knowledge about the specific support services available on your campus:

   - Information published in your college catalog and student handbook

   - Information posted on your college's Web site

   - Information gathered by speaking with a professional in different offices or centers on your campus

2. Using the preceding sources of information, construct a master list of all support services that are available to you on your campus. Your final product should be a list that includes the following:

   - The names of different support services your campus offers

   - The specific types of support each service provides

   - A short statement next to each specific support service listed, indicating whether you think you would benefit from this particular type of support

   - The name of a person whom you could contact for support from this service

Notes

- You can pair up with a classmate to work collaboratively on this assignment. Working together with a peer on any research task can reduce your anxiety, increase your energy, and generate synergy—which results in a final product that is superior to what could have been produced by one person working alone (independently).
- After you complete this assignment, save your master list of support services for future use. You might not have an immediate need for some of these services during your first term in college, but all of them are likely to be useful to you at some point in your college experience.

1.2 Support Services

Learning Center

Types of Support

Will I benefit?   Contact Person:

Will I benefit?   Contact Person:

Will I benefit?   Contact Person:

Writing Center

Types of Support

Will I benefit?   Contact Person:

Will I benefit?   Contact Person:

Will I benefit?   Contact Person:

Disability Services

Types of Services

Will I benefit?   Contact Person:

Will I benefit?   Contact Person:

Will I benefit?   Contact Person:

College Library

Types of Services

Will I benefit?   Contact Person:

Will I benefit?   Contact Person:

Will I benefit?   Contact Person:

Academic Advisement

Types of Services

_____

Will I benefit?   Contact Person:

_____

Will I benefit?   Contact Person:

_____

Will I benefit?   Contact Person:

Career Development Center

Types of Services

_____

Will I benefit?   Contact Person:

_____

Will I benefit?   Contact Person:

_____

Will I benefit?   Contact Person:

Financial Aid Office

Types of Services

_____

Will I benefit?   Contact Person:

_____

Will I benefit?   Contact Person:

_____

Will I benefit?   Contact Person:

Counseling Center

Types of Services

_____

Will I benefit?   Contact Person:

_____

Will I benefit?   Contact Person:

_____

Will I benefit?   Contact Person:

Experiential Learning Resources

Types of Services

Will I benefit?   Contact Person:

Will I benefit?   Contact Person:

Will I benefit?   Contact Person:

Other

Types of Services

Will I benefit?   Contact Person:

Will I benefit?   Contact Person:

Will I benefit?   Contact Person:

Alone and Disconnected: Feeling Like Calling It Quits

Josephine is a first-year student in her second week of college. She doesn't feel like she fits in with other students on her campus. She feels that by going to college she's taking time away from her family and longtime friends who are not in college, and she fears that her ties with them will be weakened or broken if she continues to spend so much time on school and schoolwork. Josephine is feeling so torn between college and her family and old friends that she's beginning to have second thoughts about whether she should have even begun college.

Reflection and Discussion Questions

1. What might you say to Josephine that might persuade her to stay in college?

2. Could the college have done more during her first two weeks on campus to make Josephine (and other students) feel more connected with college and less disconnected from family?

3. Do you see anything that Josephine could do now to minimize the conflict or balance the tension she's experiencing between her commitment to college and her ties to family and friends?

Goal Setting, Motivation, and Character

2

THOUGHT STARTER Journal Entry **2.1**

How would you define the word "successful"?

_____

_____

_____

_____

_____

_____

LEARNING GOAL

To develop meaningful goals to strive for, along with strategies for maintaining motivation and building character to achieve those goals.

◆ What Does "Being Successful" Mean to You?

The word "success" means to achieve a desired outcome; it derives from the Latin root *successus*, which means "to follow or come after" (as in the word "succession"). Thus, by definition, success involves an order or sequence of actions that lead to a desired outcome. The process starts with identifying an end (goal) and then finding a means (sequence of steps) to reach that goal (achieving success). Goal setting is the first step in the process of becoming successful because it gives you something specific to strive for and ensures that you start off in the right direction. Studies consistently show that setting specific goals is a more effective way to self-motivational strategy than to simply tell yourself that you should "try hard" or "do your best" (Boekaerts, Pintrich, & Zeidner, 2000; Locke & Latham, 1990).

By setting goals, you show initiative—you work to gain control of your future and take charge of your life. By taking initiative, you demonstrate what psychologists call an internal locus of control—you believe that the locus (location or source) of control for events in your life is *internal*, and thus within you and your control, rather than *external*, or outside of you and beyond your control (controlled by such factors as luck, chance, or fate; Rotter, 1966).

> "You've got to be careful if you don't know where you're going because you might not get there."
>
> —Yogi Berra, Hall of Fame baseball player

> "There is perhaps nothing worse than reaching the top of the ladder and discovering that you're on the wrong wall."
>
> —Joseph Campbell, American professor and writer

> "Success is getting what you want. Happiness is wanting what you get."
>
> —Dale Carnegie, author of the best-selling book *How to Win Friends and Influence People* (1936) and founder of The Dale Carnegie Course, a worldwide program for business based on his teachings

"The future is literally in our hands to mold as we like. But we cannot wait until tomorrow. Tomorrow is now."

–Eleanor Roosevelt, UN diplomat and humanitarian

"What lies behind us and what lies in front of us are small matters compared to what lies within us."

–Ralph Waldo Emerson, nineteenth-century American essayist and lecturer

"When we have begun to take charge of our lives, to own ourselves, there is no longer any need to ask permission of someone."

–George O'Neil, American poet and playwright

Research reveals that individuals with a strong internal locus of control display the following characteristics:

1. Greater independence and self-direction (Van Overwalle, Mervielde, & De Schuyer, 1995);
2. More accurate self-assessment (Hashaw, Hammond, & Rogers, 1990; Lefcourt, 1982);
3. Higher levels of learning and achievement (Wilhite, 1990);
4. Better physical health (Maddi, 2002; Seligman, 1991).

An internal locus of control also contributes to the development of another positive trait, which psychologists call self-efficacy—the belief that you have power to produce a positive effect on the outcomes of your life (Bandura, 1994). People with low self-efficacy tend to feel helpless, powerless, and passive; they think (and allow) things to happen *to* them rather than taking charge and making things happen *for* them. College students with a strong sense of self-efficacy believe they're in control of their educational success, regardless of their past or current circumstances.

If you have a strong sense of self-efficacy, you initiate action, put forth effort, and sustain that effort until you reach your goal. If you encounter setbacks or bad breaks along the way, you don't give up or give in; you persevere or push on (Bandura, 1986, 1997).

Students with a strong sense of academic self-efficacy have been found to:

1. Put great effort into their studies;
2. Use active-learning strategies;
3. Capitalize on campus resources; and
4. Persist in the face of obstacles (Multon, Brown, & Lent, 1991; Zimmerman, 1995).

THINK ABOUT IT   **Journal Entry**   **2.2**

You are not required by law or by others to attend college; you've made the decision to continue your education. Do you believe you are in charge of your educational destiny?

Why or why not?

_____

_____

_____

_____

_____

_____

Students with self-efficacy also possess a strong sense of personal responsibility. As the breakdown of the word "responsible" implies, they are "response" "able"—i.e., they believe they are able to respond effectively to personal challenges, including educational challenges.

Students with self-efficacy do not have a false sense of entitlement. They don't feel they're entitled to, or owed, anything; they believe that success is earned and is theirs for the taking. For example, studies show that students who convert their college degree into a successful career have two common characteristics: personal initiative and a positive attitude (Pope, 1990). They don't take a passive approach and assume a good position will fall into their lap; nor do they believe they are owed a position simply because they have a college degree or credential. Instead, they become actively involved in the job-hunting process and use various job-search strategies (Brown & Krane, 2000).

"The price of greatness is responsibility."

–Winston Churchill, British prime minister during World War II and Nobel Prize winner in literature

"Man who stand on hill with mouth open will wait long time for roast duck to drop in."

–Confucius, Chinese philosopher who emphasized sincerity and social justice

THINK ABOUT IT   Journal Entry   2.3

In what area or areas of your life do you feel that you've been able to exert the most control and achieve the most positive results?

_____

_____

_____

_____

_____

In what area or areas of your life do you wish you had more control and were achieving better results?

_____

_____

_____

_____

What have you done in the area or areas of your life for which you've taken charge and gained control that might be transferred or applied to the area or areas in which you need to gain more control?

_____

_____

_____

_____

_____

◆ Strategies for Effective Goal Setting

Goals may be classified into three general categories: long range, mid-range, and short range, depending on the length of time it takes to reach them and the order in which they are to be achieved. Short-range goals need to be completed before a mid-range goal can be reached, and mid-range goals must be reached before a long-range goal can be achieved. For example, if your long-range goal is a successful career, you must complete the courses required for a degree or credential that will allow you entry into a career (mid-range goal); to reach your mid-range goal of a college degree, you need to successfully complete the courses you're taking this term (short-range goal).

Setting Long-Range Goals

Setting effective long-range goals involves two processes: (a) self-awareness, or insight into who you are now, and (b) self-projection, or a vision of what you want to become in the future. When you engage in both of these processes, you're able to see a connection between your short- and your long-range goals.

Long-range goal setting enables you to take an approach to your future that is proactive—acting beforehand to anticipate and control your future life rather than putting it off and being forced to react to it without a plan. Research shows that people who neglect to set goals for themselves are more likely to experience boredom with life (Bargdill, 2000). Setting long-range goals and planning ahead also help reduce feelings of anxiety about the future because you've given it forethought, which gives you greater power to control it (i.e., it gives you a stronger sense of self-efficacy). As the old saying goes, "To be forewarned is to be forearmed."

Remember that setting long-range goals and developing long-range plans doesn't mean you can't adjust or modify them. Your goals can undergo change as you change, develop new skills, acquire new knowledge, and discover new interests or talents. Finding yourself and your path in life is one of the primary purposes of a college education. Don't think that the process of setting long-range goals means you will be locked into a premature plan and reduced options. Instead, it will give you something to reach for and some momentum to get you moving in the right direction.

"To fail to plan is to plan to fail."

–Robert Wubbolding, internationally known author, psychologist, and teacher

You have brains in your head. You have feet in your shoes. You can steer yourself any direction you choose.

–Theodore Seuss Giesel, a.k.a. Dr. Seuss, famous author of children's books including *Oh the Places You'll Go*

◆ Steps in the Goal-Setting Process

Effective goal setting involves a four-step sequence:

1. **Awareness of yourself.** Your personal interests, abilities and talents, and values

    ↓

2. **Awareness of your options.** The choices available to you

    ↓

3. **Awareness of the options that best fit you.** The goals most compatible with your personal abilities, interests, values, and needs

    ↓

4. **Awareness of the process.** The specific steps that you need to take to reach your chosen goal

Discussed in the next sections are strategies for taking each of these steps in the goal-setting process.

Step 1. Gaining Self-Awareness

The goals you choose to pursue say a lot about who you are and what you want from life. Thus, self-awareness is a critical first step in the process of goal setting. You must know yourself before you can choose the goals you want to achieve. While this may seem obvious, self-awareness and self-discovery are often overlooked aspects of the goal-setting process. Deepening your self-awareness puts you in a better position to select and choose goals and to pursue a personal path that's true to who you are and what you want to become.

> *"Know thyself, and to thine own self be true."*
>
> –Plato, ancient Greek philosopher

!

Remember
Self-awareness is the first, most important step in the process of making any important life choice or decision.

No one is in a better position to know who you are, and what you want to be, than *you*. One effective way to get to know yourself more deeply is through self-questioning. You can begin to deepen your self-awareness by asking yourself questions that can stimulate your thinking about your inner qualities and priorities. Effective self-questioning can launch you on an inward quest or journey to self-discovery and self-insight, which is the critical first step to effective goal setting. For example, if your long-range goal is career success, you can launch your voyage toward achieving this goal by asking yourself thought-provoking questions relating to your personal

- **Interests.** What you like to do;
- **Abilities.** What you're good at doing; and
- **Values.** What you believe is worth doing.

> *"In order to succeed, you must know what you are doing, like what you are doing, and believe in what you are doing."*
>
> –Will Rogers, Native American humorist and actor

Self-awareness is the first and most important step in the process of making effective choices and/or decisions.

Know Thyself

The following questions are designed to sharpen your self-awareness with respect to your interests, abilities, and values. As you read each question, briefly note what thought or thoughts come to mind about yourself.

Your Personal Interests

1. What tends to grab your attention and hold it for long periods?

2. What sorts of things are you naturally curious about or tend to intrigue you?

3. What do you enjoy and do as often as you possibly can?

4. What do you look forward to or get excited about?

5. What are your favorite hobbies or pastimes?

6. When you're with your friends, what do you like to talk about or spend time doing together?

7. What has been your most stimulating or enjoyable learning experience?

8. If you've had previous work or volunteer experience, what jobs or tasks did you find most enjoyable or stimulating?

9. When time seems to "fly by" for you, what are you usually doing?

10. What do you like to read about?

11. When you open a newspaper or log on to the Internet, what do you tend to read first?

12. When you find yourself daydreaming or fantasizing about your future life, what do you most find yourself doing?

THINK ABOUT IT   **Journal Entry**   **2.4**

From your responses to the preceding questions, identify a long-range goal you could pursue that's compatible with your personal interests. In the space that follows, note the goal and the interests that are compatible with it.

_____

_____

_____

_____

_____

_____

Your Personal Abilities and Talents

1. What seems to come easily or naturally to you?

2. What would you say is your greatest talent or personal gift?

3. What do you excel at when you apply yourself and put forth your best effort?

4. What are your most advanced or well-developed skills?

5. What would you say has been the greatest accomplishment or achievement in your life thus far?

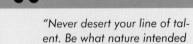

"Never desert your line of talent. Be what nature intended you for and you will succeed."

–Sydney Smith, eighteenth-century English writer and defender of the oppressed

6. What about yourself are you most proud of or do you take the most pride in doing?

7. When others come to you for advice or assistance, what is it usually for?

8. What would your best friend or friends say is your best quality, trait, or characteristic?

9. When you had a strong feeling of being successful after you had done something, what was it that you did?

10. If you've received awards or other forms of recognition, what have you received them for?

11. On what types of learning tasks or activities have you experienced the most success?

12. In what types of courses do you tend to earn the highest grades?

THINK ABOUT IT   **Journal Entry**   **2.5**

From your responses to the preceding questions, identify a long-range goal you could pursue that's compatible with your personal abilities. In the space that follows, note the goal and the abilities that are compatible with it.

_____

_____

_____

_____

_____

_____

Your Personal Values

1. What matters most to you?

2. If you were to single out one thing you stand for or believe in, what would it be?

3. What would you say are your highest priorities in life?

4. What makes you feel good about what you're doing when you're doing it?

5. If there were one thing in the world you could change, improve, or make a difference in, what would it be?

> "Do what you value; value what you do."
>
> –Sidney Simon, *Values Clarification* and *In Search of Values*

6. When you have extra spending money, what do you usually spend it on?

7. When you have free time, what do you usually find yourself doing?

8. What does living a "good life" mean to you?

9. How would you define success? (What would it take for you to feel that you were successful?)

10. How do you define happiness? (What would it take for you to feel happy?)

11. Do you have any heroes or anyone you admire, look up to, or feel has set an example worth following? If yes, who and why?

12. Would you rather be thought of as:

   - Smart,   _____

   - Wealthy,   _____

   - Creative, or _____

   - Caring?   _____

   (Rank from 1 to 4, with 1 being the highest.)

THINK ABOUT IT   **Journal Entry**   **2.6**

From your responses to the preceding questions, identify a long-range goal you could pursue that's compatible with your personal values. In the space that follows, note the goal and the values that are compatible with it.

_____

_____

_____

_____

_____

Step 2. Gaining Awareness of Your Options

The second critical step in the goal-setting process is to become aware of your long-range goal choices. For example, to effectively choose a career goal, you need to be aware of what career options are available to you and have a realistic understanding of the type of work done in these careers. To gain this knowledge, you'll need to capitalize on available resources, such as the following:

1. Reading books about different careers;
2. Taking career development courses;
3. Interviewing people in different career fields;
4. Observing (shadowing) people working in different careers.

One characteristic of effective goal setting is to create goals that are realistic. In the case of careers, getting firsthand experience in actual work settings (e.g., shadowing, internships, volunteer services, and part-time work) would allow you to get a realistic view of what work is like in certain careers—as opposed to the idealized or fantasized way careers are portrayed on TV and in the movies.

Step 3. Gaining Awareness of the Options That Best Fit You

In college, you'll have many educational options and career goals from which to choose. To deepen your awareness of what fields may be a good fit for you, take a course in that field to test out how well it matches your interests, values, talents, and learning style. Ideally, you want to select a field that most closely taps into, or builds on, your strongest skills and special talents. Choosing a field that's compatible with your strongest abilities should enable you to master the skills required by that field more deeply and efficiently. You're more likely to succeed or excel in a field that taps your talents, and the success you experience will, in turn, strengthen your self-esteem, self-confidence, and drive to continue with it. You've probably heard of the old proverb "If there's a will, there's a way" (i.e., when you're motivated, you're more likely to succeed). However, it's also true that "If there's a way, there's a will" (i.e., when you know the way to do something well, you're more motivated to do it).

> "Students [may be] pushed into careers by their families, while others have picked one just to relieve their anxiety about not having a career choice. Still others may have picked popular or lucrative careers, knowing nothing of what they're really like or what it takes to prepare for them."
>
> –Lee Upcraft, Joni Finney, and Peter Garland, Student Development Specialists

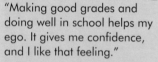

Student Perspective

> "Making good grades and doing well in school helps my ego. It gives me confidence, and I like that feeling."
>
> –First-year student (Franklin, 2002)

THINK ABOUT IT   **Journal Entry**   **2.7**

Think about a career you're considering and answer the following questions:

1. Why are you considering this career? (What led or caused you to become interested in this choice?)

_____

_____

_____

_____

_____

2. Would you say that your interest in this career is motivated primarily by intrinsic factors (i.e., factors "inside" of you, such as your personal abilities, interests, needs, and values)? Or, would you say that your interest in the career is motivated more heavily by extrinsic factors (i.e., factors "outside" of you, such as starting salary, pleasing parents, meeting family expectations or societal expectations for your gender or ethnicity)?

_____

_____

_____

_____

_____

_____

Step 4. Gaining Awareness of the Process

The fourth and final step in an effective goal-setting process is becoming aware of the steps needed to reach your goal. For example, if you've set the goal of achieving a college degree in a particular major, you need to be aware of the course requirements that need to be completed for you to graduate in that major. Similarly, to set a career goal, you need to know what major or majors lead to that career, because some careers require a specific major but other careers may be entered through various majors.

! Remember

The four-step process for effective goal setting applies to more than just educational goals. It's a strategic process that could and should be applied to any goal you set for yourself in life, at any stage of your life.

◆ Motivation: Moving Toward Your Long-Range Goals

The word "motivation" derives from the Latin *movere*, meaning "to move." Success comes to those who exert effort to move toward their goal. Knowledge of all kinds of success-promoting strategies, such as those discussed in this text, provides only the potential for success; turning this potential into reality requires motivation, which converts knowledge into action. If you have all the knowledge, strategies, and skills for being successful but don't have the will to succeed, there's no way you will succeed. Studies show that without a strong personal commitment to attain a goal it will not be reached, no matter how well designed the goal and the plan to reach it are (Locke & Latham, 1990).

"Mere knowledge is not power; it is only possibility. Action is power; and its highest manifestation is when it is directed by knowledge."

–Francis Bacon, English philosopher, lawyer, and champion of modern science

"You can lead a horse to water, but you can't make him drink."

–Proverb

Motivation consists of three elements that may be summarized as the "three Ds" of motivation:

1. **D**rive
2. **D**iscipline
3. **D**etermination

Drive

Drive is the force within you that supplies you with the energy needed to overcome inertia and initiate action. Much like shifting into the drive gear is necessary to move your car forward, it takes personal drive to move forward and toward your goals.

People with drive aren't just dreamers: They're dreamers and doers. They take action to convert their dreams into reality, and they hustle—they go all out and give it their all, all of the time to achieve their goals. College students with drive approach college with passion and enthusiasm. They don't hold back and work halfheartedly; they give 100 percent and put their whole heart and soul into the experience.

"Education is not the filling of a pail, but the lighting of a fire."

–William Butler Yeats, Irish poet and playwright

"Success comes to those who hustle."

–Abraham Lincoln, 16th American president and author of the *Emancipation Proclamation,* which set the stage for the abolition of slavery in the United States

---

THINK ABOUT IT   **Journal Entry**   **2.8**

Think about something that you do with drive, effort, and intensity. What thoughts, attitudes, and behaviors do you display when you do it?

_____

_____

_____

_____

_____

Do you see ways in which you could apply the same approach to your college experience?

_____

_____

_____

_____

_____

_____

_____

Discipline

Discipline includes such positive qualities as commitment, devotion, and dedication. These personal qualities enable you to keep going over an extended period. Successful people think big, but start small—they take all the small steps and diligently do all the little things that need to be done, which in the long run, add up to a big accomplishment: the achievement of their long-range goal.

People who are self-disciplined accept the day-to-day sweat, toil, and perspiration needed to attain their long-term aspirations. They're willing to tolerate short-term strain or pain for long-term gain. They have the self-control and self-restraint needed to resist the impulse for instant gratification or the temptation to do what they feel like doing instead of what they need to do. They're willing to sacrifice their immediate needs and desires in the short run to do what is necessary to put them where they want to be in the long run.

> ### Remember
>
> Sacrifices that are made for a short time can bring benefits that last a lifetime.

The ability to delay short-term (and short-sighted) gratification is a distinctively human characteristic that differentiates people from other animals. As you can see in **Figure 2.1**, the upper front part of the human brain that's responsible for long-range planning and controlling the emotions and impulses is much larger in humans than even one of the most intelligent and human-like animals, the chimpanzee.

Student Perspectives

"Why is it so hard when I *have* to do something and so easy when I *want* to do something?"

–First-year student

"Self-discipline is the ability to make yourself do the thing you have to do, when it ought to be done, whether you like it or not."

–Thomas Henry Huxley, nineteenth-century English biologist

The part of the brain responsible for long-range planning and controlling emotions and impulses is much larger in humans than other animals, including the highly intelligent chimpanzee.

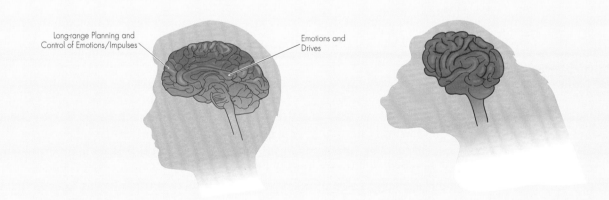

Long-range Planning and Control of Emotions/Impulses

Emotions and Drives

Figure 2.1   **Where Emotions, Impulses, and Drives Are Experienced in the Brain**

! Remember

Sometimes you've got to do what you have to do in order to get to do what you want to do.

Postponing immediate or impulsive satisfaction of material desires is a key element of effective college financing and long-term financial success.

Studies show that individuals with dedication—who are deeply committed to what they do—are more likely to report that they are healthy and happy (Maddi, 2002; Myers, 1993).

Personal Story   When I entered college in the mid-1970s, I was a first-generation student from an extremely impoverished background. Not only did I have to work to pay for part of my education, but I also needed to assist my family financially. I stocked grocery store shelves at night during the week and waited tables at a local country club on the weekends. Managing my life, time, school, and work required full-time effort. However, I always understood that my purpose was to graduate from college and all of my other efforts supported that goal. Thus, I went to class and arrived on time even when I did not feel like going to class. One of my greatest successes in life was to keep my mind and body focused on the ultimate prize of getting a college education. That success has paid off many times over.

—Aaron Thompson

Determination

People who are determined pursue their goals with a relentless tenacity. They have the fortitude to persist in the face of frustration and the resiliency to bounce back after setbacks. When the going gets tough, they keep going. If they encounter something on the road to their goal that's hard to do, they work harder and longer to do it. They don't give up or give in; they dig deeper and give more.

People with determination are also more likely to seek out challenges. Research indicates that people who continue to pursue opportunities for personal growth and self-development throughout life are more likely to report feeling happy and healthy (Maddi, 2002; Myers, 1993). Rather than remaining stagnant and simply doing what's safe, secure, or easy, they stay hungry and display an ongoing commitment to personal growth and development; they keep striving and driving to be the best they can possibly be in all aspects of life.

"If you are going through hell, keep going."

–Winston Churchill, British prime minister during World War II and Nobel Prize winner in literature

"Success is peace of mind which is a direct result of self-satisfaction in knowing you made the effort to become the best that you are capable of becoming."

–John Wooden, college basketball coach and author of the *Pyramid of Success*

!

Remember

On the highway to success, you can't be a passive passenger; you're the driver and at the wheel. Your goal setting will direct you there, and your motivation will drive you there.

Strategies for Maintaining Motivation and Progress Toward Your Goals

Reaching your goals requires will and energy; it also requires skill and strategy. Listed here are strategies for maintaining your motivation and commitment to reaching your goals.

1. Visualize reaching your long-range goals.

Imagine vivid images of being successful, including not only what success looks like but also what it feels like. For example, if your goal is to achieve a college degree, imagine a crowd of cheering family, friends, and faculty at your graduation. Visualize how you'll be able to cherish and carry this proud memory with you for the rest of your life and how the benefits of a college degree will last a lifetime. Imagine yourself in the career that college enabled you to enter and your typical workday going something like this: You wake up in the morning and hop out of bed enthusiastically, looking forward to your day at work. When you're at work, time flies by, and before you know it, the day's over. When you return to bed that night and look back on your day, you feel good about what you did and how well you did it.

You can also use negative imagery to motivate yourself by imagining the worst case scenario: failing to reach your goal and paying the consequences. For example, vividly imagine yourself without any alternative other than to work in a poor-paying, back-breaking job that you have to do to survive and that you need to do for the rest your working life.

My father, who spent 50 years working in the coal mines of eastern Kentucky, always had a simple motivating statement for me to gain more education than he had. He would always say, "Son, I did not have the chance to go to school so I have to write my name with an X and work in the coal mines. You have the opportunity to get an education and you do not have to break your back in those mines." What my father was telling me was that education would give me options in life that he did not have and that I should take advantage of those options by going to college. My dad's lack of education supplied me with drive and dedication to pursue education. My experience suggests that when you are developing your goals and motivating yourself to achieve them it may be as important to know what you don't want as it is to know what you do want.

—Aaron Thompson

2. Put your goals in writing.

When you put your goals in writing, they become visible and memorable. Doing so can provide you with a sense of direction, a source of motivation for putting your plan into action, or a written contract with yourself that makes you more accountable to following through on your commitment.

3. Create a visual map of your goals.

Lay out your goals in the form of a flowchart to show the flow of steps you'll be taking from your short- through mid- to long-range goals. Visual diagrams can help you "see" where you want to go, enabling you to connect where you are now and where you want to be. Diagramming can be energizing because it gives you a sneak preview of the finish line and a maplike overview of how to get you there. (See Chapter 10, p. 343, for a visual map of the college experience, from start to finish.)

4. Keep a record of your progress.

Research indicates that the act of monitoring and recording progress toward goals can increase motivation to continue pursuing them (Matsui, Okada, & Inoshita, 1983). The act of keeping records of your progress probably increases your motivation by giving you frequent feedback on your progress and positive reinforcement for staying on track and moving toward your target (long-range goal) (Bandura & Cervone, 1983; Schunk, 1995). For example, you can keep a journal of the goals you've reached. Your entries can keep you motivated by supplying you with concrete evidence of your progress and commitment. You can also chart or graph your progress, which can sometimes provide a powerful visual display of your upward trends and patterns. Place it where you see it regularly to keep your goals in your sight and on your mind.

5. Develop a "skeletal résumé" of your goals.

Include your goals as separate sections or categories that will be progressively fleshed out as you complete them. Your to-be-completed résumé can provide a framework or blueprint for organizing, building, and tracking progress toward your goals. It can also serve as a visual reminder of the things you plan to accomplish and eventually showcase to potential employers. Furthermore, every time you look at your growing résumé, you're reminded of your past accomplishments, which can energize and motivate you to reach your future goals. As you fill in and build up your résumé, you can literally see how much you've achieved, which boosts your self-confidence and motivation to continue achieving. (See Chapter 11, p. 400, for a sample skeletal résumé.)

6. Reward yourself for making steady progress toward your long-range goals.

Reward is already built into reaching your long-range goal because it represents the end of your trip, which lands you at your desired destination (e.g., in a successful career). However, short- and mid-range goals may not be desirable ends in themselves but rather the means to a desirable end (your long-range goal). Consequently, you need to intentionally reward yourself for landing on these smaller stepping stones on the way to your long-range goal. When you complete these short- and mid-range goals, record and reward your accomplishment (e.g., celebrate your successful completion of midterms or finals by treating yourself to something you enjoy).

A habit of perseverance and persistence through all intermediate steps needed to reach a long-range goal, like any other habit, is more likely to continue if it's followed by a reward (positive reinforcement). Setting small goals, moving steadily toward them, and rewarding yourself for reaching them are components of a simple but powerful strategy. This strategy will help you maintain motivation over the extended period needed to reach a long-range goal.

"Life isn't a matter of milestones but of moments."

–Rose Fitzgerald Kennedy, philanthropist and mother of John F. and Robert F. Kennedy

7. Capitalize on available campus resources that can help you stay on track and move toward your goal.

Research indicates that college success results from a combination of what students do for themselves (personal responsibility) and what they do to capitalize on resources that are available to them (resourcefulness) (Pascarella & Terenzini, 1991, 2005). Successful college students are resourceful students; they seek out and take advantage of college resources to help them reach their goals.

For example, a resourceful student who's having trouble deciding what field of study to pursue for a degree or credential will seek assistance from an academic advisor on campus. A resourceful student who's interested in a particular career but is unclear about the best educational path to take toward that career will use the Career Development Center as a resource.

"Willpower is the personal strength and discipline, rooted in strong motivation, to carry out your plans. 'Waypower' is the exertion of will power that helps you find resources and support."

–Jerry Pattengale, historian, author, and advocate for first-year student success

8. Use your social resources.

The power of social support groups for helping people achieve personal goals is well documented by research in various fields (Ewell, 1997; Moeller, 1999). You can use the power of people by surrounding yourself with peers who are committed to successfully achieving their educational goals and by avoiding "toxic" people who are likely to poison your plans or dampen your dreams.

For example, find a supportive and motivating friend and make a mutual pact to help each other reach your respective goals. This step could be taken to a more formal level by drawing up a "social contract" whereby you and your partner are "cowitnesses" or designated social-support agents whose role is to help each other stay on track and move toward long-range goals. Studies show

"Develop an inner circle of close associations in which the mutual attraction is not sharing problems or needs. The mutual attraction should be values and goals."

–Denis Waitley, former mental trainer for U.S. Olympic athletes and author of *Seeds of Greatness* (1983)

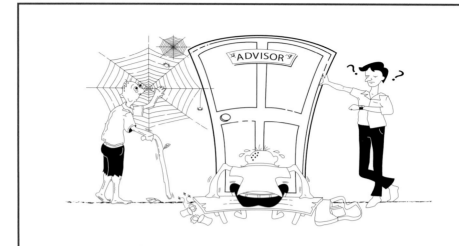

Don't only see your advisor during the "mad rush" of registration for the short-range purpose of scheduling next term's class; schedule advisor appointments at less hectic times to discuss your long-range educational goals.

> "I make progress by having people around who are smarter than I am."
>
> –Henry Kaiser, successful industrialist, known as the father of American shipbuilding

that making a public commitment to a goal increases your commitment to it, probably because it becomes a matter of personal pride and integrity that's seen not only through your own eyes but also through the eyes of others (Hollenbeck, Williams, & Klein, 1989).

THINK ABOUT IT   Journal Entry   2.9

What would you say is the biggest setback or obstacle you've overcome in your life thus far?

_____

_____

_____

_____

_____

_____

How did you overcome it? (What enabled you to get past it or prevented you from being blocked by it?)

_____

_____

_____

_____

_____

_____

_____

9. Convert setbacks into comebacks.

The type of thoughts you have after experiencing a setback can affect your emotional reaction to it and the action you take in response. For instance, what you think about a poor performance (e.g., a poor test grade) can affect your emotional reaction to that grade and what action, or lack of action, you take in response to it. You can react to the poor grade by knocking yourself down with self-putdowns ("I'm a loser") or by building yourself back up with positive pep talk ("I'm going to learn from my mistakes on this test and rebound with a stronger performance on the next one").

If a poor past performance is seen not as a personal failure but as a learning opportunity, the setback may be turned into a comeback. Here are some notable people who turned early setbacks into successful comebacks:

- Louis Pasteur, famous bacteriologist, who failed his admission test to the University of Paris
- Albert Einstein, Nobel Prize–winning physicist, who failed math in elementary school
- Thomas Edison, prolific inventor, who was once expelled from school as "uneducable"
- Johnny Unitas, Hall-of-Fame football player, who was cut twice from professional football teams early in his career

In response to their early setbacks, these successful people didn't get bitter; they got better. Getting mad or sad about a setback will likely make you stressed or depressed and leave you focused on a past event that you can no longer control. Reacting rationally to a poor performance by focusing on how the results can be used as feedback to improve your future performance allows you to gain control of it and gives you the opportunity to convert the setback into a comeback.

This can be a challenging task because when you have an experience, your response to it passes through emotional areas of the brain before it reaches areas of the brain involved in rational thinking and reasoning (LeDoux, 1998). (See **Figure 2.2.**)

"We are what we think."

–Hindu Prince Siddhartha Gautama, a.k.a. Buddha, founder of the philosophy and religion of Buddhism

"What happens is not as important as how you react to what happens."

–Thaddeus Golas, *Lazy Man's Guide to Enlightenment*

"When written in Chinese, the word 'crisis' is composed of two characters. One represents danger, and the other represents opportunity."

–John F. Kennedy, 35th U.S. President

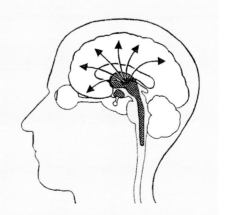

Information first passes through the emotional center of the brain (lower, shaded area) before reaching the centers responsible for rational thinking (upper area). Thus, we need to counteract our tendency to respond emotionally and irrationally to personal setbacks by making a conscious attempt to respond rationally and reflectively.

Figure 2.2 The Human Brain's Attention System

Thus, your brain reacts to events emotionally before it does rationally. If the experience triggers intense emotions (e.g., anger, anxiety, or sadness after receiving a bad test grade), your emotional reaction has the potential to "short-circuit" or wipe out rational thinking. Thus, if you find yourself beginning to feel overwhelmed by negative emotions following a setback, you need to consciously and quickly block them by rational thoughts (e.g., thinking or saying to yourself, "Before I get carried away emotionally, let me think this through rationally"). This involves more than simply saying, "I have to think positively." Instead, you should develop a set of specific, counterthinking strategies ready to use as soon as you begin to think negatively. Described here are thinking strategies that you can use to maintain motivation and minimize negative thinking in reaction to setbacks.

- **Develop self-awareness of your thinking patterns and habits.** Becoming aware of the nature of your thoughts is the first step to controlling them. Thinking often involves silent self-talk (i.e., talking silently to yourself). Thus, negative thinking often involves negative self-talk (e.g., "I'm a loser," "What's happening to me is just horrible," or "There's absolutely nothing I can do"). One of the best ways to become more aware of your self-talk, particularly negative self-talk, is to periodically write down your thoughts in a "thought journal" and reviewing it with an eye for patterns of negative self-talk that you tend to use in certain situations (e.g., setbacks).
- **Substitute positive thoughts for negative thoughts.** Once you've become aware of your negative thoughts and the situations in which they occur, replace them with positive alternative thoughts. Let's say that one situation in which you experience negative thinking is during exams, especially when you see students turning in their tests well before you're finished. You think, "I must be doing terribly on this exam because others are getting through it so quickly. They must be smarter and better prepared than I am." You can stop this negative thinking by immediately substituting the following thought: "They're getting up and getting out because the test was difficult for them and they're giving up." Or, you can think to yourself, "They're rushing out because they're not taking the time to review their test carefully before turning it in." The key to this thought-substitution strategy is to have specific, positive self-talk statements ready to use in situations in which you tend to think negatively. Practice them so well that you think of them automatically and immediately. If those situations include personal setbacks or disappointing performances, your positive self-talk statements could include expressions such as "This isn't the end of the world," "Tomorrow's another day," or "I'll turn this setback into a comeback." By choosing and repeatedly using these positive self-talk statements, you train your mind to develop the habit of thinking in ways that are self-motivating rather than self-defeating.

Whatever you do, don't let setbacks make you mad or sad, particularly at early stages in your college experience, because you're just beginning to learn what it takes to be successful in college. Look at mistakes in terms of what they can do *for* you, not *to* you. A bad performance can be turned into a good learning experience by using the results as an error detector for identifying sources or causes of your mistakes and as feedback for improving your future performance.

"The greatest weapon against stress is our ability to choose one thought over another."

–William James, philosopher and one of the founders of American psychology

> ! **Remember**
>
> Don't let past mistakes bring you down emotionally or motivationally; however, don't ignore or neglect them either. Instead, inspect them, reflect on them, and correct them so that they don't happen again.

10. Maintain positive expectations.

Just as your thoughts in reaction to something that's already taken place can affect your motivation, so can thoughts about what you *expect* to happen next. Your expectations of things to come can be either positive or negative. For example, before a test you could think, "I'm poised, confident, and ready to do it." Or you could think, "I know I'm going to fail this test; I just know it."

Expectations can lead to what sociologists and psychologists have called a self-fulfilling prophecy—a positive or negative expectation that leads you to act in ways that are consistent with your expectation, which, in turn, make your expectation come true. For instance, if you expect you're going to fail an exam, you're less likely to put forth as much effort into studying for the test. ("What's the use? I'm going to fail anyway.") During the test, your negative expectation is likely to reduce your test confidence and elevate your test anxiety; for example, if you experience difficulty with the first item on a test, you get anxious and begin to think you're going to have difficulty with all remaining items and flunk the entire exam. All of this negative thinking is likely to increase the probability that your expectation of doing poorly on the exam will become a reality.

In contrast, positive expectations can lead to a positive self-fulfilling prophecy: If you expect to do well on an exam, you're more likely to demonstrate higher levels of effort, confidence, and concentration, all of which combine to increase the likelihood that you'll earn a higher test grade. Research shows that learning and practicing positive self-talk increase a sense of hope—a belief in the ability to reach goals and the ability to actually reach them (Snyder, 1994).

> **"**
> *"Whether you think you can or you can't, you're right."*
>
> –Henry Ford, founder of Ford Motor Co. and one of the richest people of his generation

---

THINK ABOUT IT   **Journal Entry** **2.10**

Would you consider yourself to be an optimist or a pessimist?

_____

_____

_____

_____

_____

_____

In what situations are you more likely to think optimistically and pessimistically?

_____

_____

_____

_____

_____

_____

"A pessimist sees the difficulty in every opportunity; an optimist sees the opportunity in every difficulty."

—Winston Churchill, British prime minister during World War II and Nobel Prize winner in literature

Why?

_____

_____

_____

_____

_____

_____

"Many people take no care of their money till they come nearly to the end of it, and others do just the same with their time."

—Johann Wolfgang von Goethe, German poet, dramatist, and author of the epic Faust

Student Perspective

"I want to make it big in life."

—College sophomore

"Whoever wants to reach a distant goal must take many small steps."

—Helmut Schmidt, former chancellor of West Germany

11. Keep your eye on the prize.

Don't lose sight of the long-term consequences of your short-term choices and decisions. Long-range thinking is the key to reaching long-range goals. Unfortunately, however, humans are often more motivated by short-range thinking because it produces quicker results and more immediate gratification. It's more convenient and tempting to think in the short term ("I like it; I want it; I want it now.") Studies show that the later consequences occur, the less likely people are to consider those consequences when they make their decisions (Ainslie, 1975; Elster & Lowenstein, 1992; Lewin, 1935). For example, choosing to do what you feel like doing instead of working to meet a future deadline and choosing to buy something with a credit card instead of saving money for future use cause people to suffer the negative long-term consequences of procrastination and credit-card debt, respectively.

To be successful in the long run, you need to keep your focus on the big picture—your long-range goals and dreams that provide your motivation. At the same time, you need to focus on the details—the due dates, to-do lists, and day-to-day duties that require your perspiration.

Thus, setting an important life goal and steadily progressing toward that long-range goal requires two focus points. One is a narrow-focus lens that allows you to view the details immediately in front of you. The other is a wide-focus lens that gives you a big-picture view of what's farther ahead of you (your long-range goal). Success involves seeing the connection between the small, short-term chores and challenges (e.g., completing an assignment that's due next week) and the large, long-range picture (e.g., college graduation and a successful future). Thus, you need to periodically shift from a wide-focus lens that gives you a vision of the bigger, more distant picture to a narrow-focus lens that shifts your attention to completing the smaller tasks immediately ahead of you and keeping you on the path to your long-range goal: future success.

Personal Story

When I was an assistant coach for a youth soccer team, I noticed that many of the less successful players tended to make either one of two mistakes when they were trying to move with the ball. Some spent too much time looking down, focusing on the ball at their feet, trying to be sure that they did not lose control of it. By not lifting their head and looking ahead periodically, they often missed open territory, open teammates, or an open goal. Other unsuccessful players made the opposite mistake: They spent too much time with their heads up, trying to see saw where they were headed. By not looking down at the ball immediately in front of them, they often lost control of the ball, moved ahead without it, or sometimes stumbled over it and fell flat on their face. Successful soccer players were in the habit of shifting their focus between looking down to maintain control of the ball immediately in front of them and lifting their head to see where they were headed.

The more I thought about how successful players alternate between handling the ball in front of them and viewing the goal farther ahead, it struck me that this was a metaphor for success in life. Successful people alternate between both of these perspectives so that they don't lose sight of how completing the short-range tasks in front of them connect with the long-range goal ahead of them.

—Joe Cuseo

!

Remember

Keep your future dreams and current tasks in clear focus. Integrating these two perspectives will produce an image that can provide you with the inspiration to complete your college education and the determination to complete your day-to-day tasks.

◆ Personal Character

Reaching your goals depends on acquiring and using effective strategies, but it takes something more. Ultimately, success emerges from the inside out; it flows from positive qualities or attributes found within you, which, collectively, form your personal character.

We become successful and effective humans when our actions and deeds become a natural extension of who we are and how we live. At first, developing the habits associated with achieving success and leading a productive life may require effort and intense concentration because these behaviors may be new to you. However, if your effortful actions occur frequently enough, they are transformed into regular and natural habits.

When you engage in effective habits consistently, they become virtues. A virtue may be defined as a characteristic or trait that is valued as good or admirable, and someone who possesses a collection of important virtues is said to be a person of character (Peterson & Seligman, 2004).

Three virtues in particular are important for success in college and beyond:

1. Wisdom
2. Integrity
3. Civility

"If you do not find it within yourself, where will you go to get it?"

–Zen saying (Zen is a branch of Buddhism that emphasizes seeing deeply into the nature of things and ongoing self-awareness)

"We are what we repeatedly do. Excellence, then, is not an act, but a habit."

–Aristotle, ancient Greek philosopher

"Sow an act and you reap a habit; sow a habit and you reap a character; sow a character and you reap a destiny."

–Frances E. Willard, nineteenth-century American educator and woman's rights activist

Wisdom

When you use the knowledge you acquire to guide your behavior toward doing what is effective or good, you demonstrate wisdom (Staudinger & Baltes, 1994). For example, if you apply your knowledge of the four research-based principles found in this book (i.e., involvement, resourcefulness, collaboration, and reflection) to guide your behavior in college, you would be exhibiting wisdom.

"As gold which he cannot spend will make no man rich, so knowledge which he cannot apply will make no man wise."

–Dr. Samuel Johnson, famous English literary figure and original author of the *Dictionary of the English Language* (1747)

THINK ABOUT IT   **Journal Entry** **2.11**

Thus far in your college experience, which of the following four principles of success have you put into practice most effectively?

1. Active involvement
2. Collaboration
3. Resourcefulness
4. Reflection

Which of the four principles do you think will be the most difficult for you to put into practice?

_____

_____

_____

_____

_____

_____

Why?

_____

_____

_____

_____

_____

_____

Integrity

The word "integrity" comes from the same word root as "integrate," which captures a key characteristic of people with integrity: their outer self is integrated or in harmony with their inner self. For example, "outer-directed" people decide on their personal standards of conduct by looking outward to see what others are doing (Riesman, Glazer, & Denney, 2001). In contrast, individuals with integrity are "inner directed"—their actions reflect their inner qualities and are guided by their conscience.

People with character are not only wise but also ethical. Besides doing what is effective, they do what is good or right. They don't pursue success at any ethical cost. They have a strong set of personal values that guide them in the right moral direction.

For example, college students with integrity don't cheat and then rationalize that their cheating is acceptable because "others are doing it." They don't look to other people to determine their own values, and they don't conform to the norm if the norm is wrong; instead, they look inward and let their conscience be their guide.

Students with academic integrity also don't steal the ideas of others; they give credit where credit is due. For example, when writing papers and reports, students with academic integrity are sure to cite their sources and reference the ideas they've borrowed from others. (See **Box 2.1** for a summary of the various forms of plagiarism, which represent violations of academic integrity.)

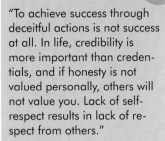

"There is no pillow as soft as a clear conscience."

–French proverb

"Our character is what we do when we think no one is looking."

–Henry David Thoreau, American philosopher and lifelong abolitionist who championed the human spirit over materialism and conformity

THINK ABOUT IT   **Journal Entry**   **2.12**

Have you observed an example of personal integrity that you thought was exceptionally admirable or particularly despicable?

_____

_____

_____

_____

_____

What was the situation, and what was done that demonstrated integrity or an integrity violation?

_____

_____

_____

_____

_____

_____

Take Action!

Plagiarism: A Violation of Academic Integrity

What Is Plagiarism?

Plagiarism is the deliberate or unintentional use of someone else's work without acknowledging it, giving the reader the impression it's your own work.

Various Forms of Plagiarism

1. Submitting an entire paper, or portion thereof, that was written by someone else
2. Copying sections of someone else's work and inserting it into your own work
3. Cutting paragraphs from separate sources and pasting them into the body of your own paper
4. Paraphrasing (rewording) someone else's words or ideas without citing that person as a source

For examples of acceptable paraphrasing versus plagiarism, go to www.princeton.edu/pr/pub/integrity/pages/plagiarism. html.

5. Not placing quotation marks around someone else's exact words that appear in the body of your paper.
6. Failing to cite the source of factual information included in your paper that's not common knowledge.

Note: If the source for information included in your paper is listed at the end of your paper in your reference (works cited) section but is not cited in the body of your paper, this still qualifies as plagiarism.

Sources: Academic Integrity at Princeton (2003); Pennsylvania State University (2005); Purdue University Online Writing Lab (1995–2004).

Student Perspective   2.1

"My intent was not to plagiarize. I realize I was unclear [about] the policy and am actually thankful for now knowing exactly what I can and cannot do on assignments and how to prevent academic dishonesty in the future."

–First-year student's reflection on a plagiarism violation

Student Perspective

"When a student violates an academic integrity policy no one wins, even if the person gets away with it. It isn't right to cheat and it is an insult to everyone who put the effort in and did the work, and it cheapens the school for everyone. I learned my lesson and have no intention of ever cheating again."

–First-year student's reflection on an academic integrity violation

---

THINK ABOUT IT   **Journal Entry** **2.13**

Look back at the definition and forms of plagiarism described in **Box 2.1**. List any form of plagiarism contained in that box that you were not aware of, or didn't already know.

_____

_____

_____

_____

_____

_____

People with integrity have the courage to admit when they're wrong and when they haven't done what they should have done. They don't play the role of victim and look for something or someone else to blame; they're willing to accept the blame and "take the heat" when they're wrong and to take responsibility for making it right. They feel remorse or guilt when they haven't lived up to their own ethical standards, and they use this guilt productively to motivate them to do what's right in the future.

Civility

People of character are personally and socially responsible. They model what it means to live in a civilized community by demonstrating civility—they respect the rights of other members of their community, including members of their college community. In exercising their own rights and freedoms, they don't step (or stomp) on the rights and freedoms of others. People with civic character not only behave civilly but also treat other members of their community in a sensitive and courteous manner and are willing to confront others who violate the rights of their fellow citizens. They are model citizens whose actions visibly demonstrate to others that they oppose any attempt to disrespect or interfere with the rights of fellow members of their community.

Insensitive Use of Personal Technology in the Classroom: A Violation of Civility

Behavior that interferes with the rights of others to learn or teach in the college classroom represents a violation of civility. Listed below are behaviors illustrating classroom incivility that involve student use of personal technology. These behaviors are increasing in college, as is the anger of college instructors who witness them; so be careful not to engage in them.

Using Cell Phones

Keeping a cell phone on in class is a clear example of classroom incivility because if it rings it will interfere with the right of others to learn. In a study of college students who were exposed to a cell phone ringing during a class session and were later tested for their recall of information presented in class, they scored approximately 25 percent worse when attempting to recall information that was presented at the time a cell phone rang. This attention loss occurred even though the material was covered by the professor before the cell phone ringing and was projected on a slide during the call. This study also showed that students were further distracted when classmates frantically searched through handbag or pockets to find and silence a ringing (or vibrating) phone (Shelton, Elliot, Eaves, & Exner, 2009). These findings clearly suggest that the civil thing to do is turn your cell phone off before entering the classroom or keep it out of the classroom altogether.

Sending and Receiving Text Messages

Just as answering a cell phone during class represents violations of civility because it interferes with the learning of other members of the classroom community, so too does text messaging. Although messaging is often viewed as a quick and soundless way to communicate, it can momentarily disrupt learning

Emollit mores nec sinit esse feros ("*Learning humanizes character and does not permit it to be cruel.*")

—Motto of the University of South Carolina

"*The right to do something does not mean that doing it is right.*"

—William Safire, American author, journalist, and presidential speech writer if it takes place when the instructor is covering critical or complex information. Text messaging while driving a car can take your eyes and mind off the road, thereby putting yourself and others in danger. Similarly, messaging in the classroom takes your eyes and mind off the instructor and any visual aids being displayed at the time. It's also discourteous or disrespectful to instructors when you put your head down and turn your attention from them while they're speaking to the class. Finally, it can be distracting or disturbing to classmates who see you messaging instead of listening and learning.

Snapshot Summary   2.1

Guidelines for Civil and Responsible Use of Personal Technology in the College Classroom

- Turn your cell phone completely off or leave it out of the classroom. In the rare case of an emergency when you think you need to leave it on, inform you instructor.
- Don't check your cell phone during the class period by turning it off and on.
- Don't text message during class.
- Don't surf the Web during class.
- Don't touch your cell phone during any exam because this may be viewed by the instructor as a form of cheating.

◆ Summary and Conclusion

Goal setting only becomes meaningful if you have motivation to reach the goals you set. Motivation may be said to consist of three Ds: drive, dedication, and determination. Drive is the internal force that gives you the energy to overcome inertia and initiate action. Discipline consists of positive, personal qualities such as commitment, devotion, and dedication that enable you to sustain your effort over time. Determination enables you to relentlessly pursue your goals, persist in the face of frustration, and bounce back after any setback.

Reaching your goals requires all three Ds; it also involves the use of effective self-motivational strategies, such as:

- Visualizing reaching your long-range goals;
- Putting goals in writing;
- Creating a visual map of your goals;
- Keeping a record of your progress;
- Developing a skeletal résumé;
- Rewarding yourself for progress toward long-range goals;
- Capitalizing on available campus and social resources;
- Converting setbacks into comebacks by using positive self-talk, maintaining positive expectations, and avoiding negative self-fulfilling prophecies; and
- Keeping your eye on the long-term consequences of your short-term choices and decisions.

To reach your goals you must acquire and use effective strategies, but you also need character. Three character traits or virtues are particularly important for college and life success:

- **Wisdom.** Using knowledge to guide your behavior toward effective or good actions.
- **Integrity.** Doing what is ethical. Plagiarism, or giving readers the impression (intentionally or not) that someone else's work is your own, is a violation of academic integrity.
- **Civility.** Respecting the rights of other members of your college and larger communities. Violations of civility include insensitive use of personal technology in the classroom (e.g., using cell phones and text messaging).

Studies of highly successful people, whether they be scientists, musicians, writers, chess masters, or basketball stars, consistently show that achieving high levels of skill and success requires practice (Levitin, 2006). This is true even of people whose success is thought to be due to natural gifts or talents. For example, during the Beatles' first four years as a band and before they burst into musical stardom, they performed live an estimated 1,200 times, and many of these performances lasted five or more hours a night. They performed (practiced) for more hours during those first four years than most bands perform during their entire career. Similarly, before Bill Gates became a computer software giant and creator of Microsoft, he logged almost 1,600 hours of computer time during one 7-month period alone, averaging eight hours a day, seven days a week (Gladwell, 2008).

What these extraordinary success stories show is that it takes time and practice for effective skills to take hold and take effect. Reaching long-range goals means making small steps; they aren't achieved in one quick, quantum leap. If you are patient and persistent and consistently practice effective strategies, their positive effects will accumulate gradually and eventually have a significant impact on your success in college and beyond.

!

Remember

Success isn't a short-range goal; it's not a sprint but a long-distance run that takes patience and perseverance to complete. What matters most is not how fast you start but where you finish.

Internet-Based Resources for Further Information on Goal Setting

For additional information related to the ideas discussed in this chapter, we recommend the following Web sites:

www.siue.edu/SPIN/activity.html

www.selfmotivationstrategies.com/

www.academicintegrity.org/useful_links/index.php

Chapter 2 Exercises

2.1 Prioritizing Important Life Goals

Consider the following life goals. Rank them in order of their priority for you (1 = highest, 5 = lowest).

___ Emotional well-being

___ Spiritual growth

___ Physical health

___ Social relationships

___ Rewarding career

Self-Assessment Questions

1. What was the primary reason behind your first- and last-ranked choices?

2. Have you established any short- or mid-range goals for reaching your highest-ranked choice? If yes, what are they? If not, what could they be?

2.2 Setting Goals for Reducing the Gap Between the Ideal Scenario and the Current Reality

Think of an aspect of your life with a gap between what you hoped it would be (the ideal) and what it is (the reality). On the lines that follow, identify goals you could pursue that would reduce this gap:

Long-range goal: _____

Mid-range goal: _____

Short-range goal: _____

(For information on long-, mid-, and short-range goals, see p. 42.) Use the form below to identify more strategies for reaching each of these three goals. Consider the following areas for each goal:

- Actions to be taken
- Available resources
- Possible roadblocks
- Potential solutions to roadblocks

Long-range goal: _____

Actions to be taken:

Available resources:

Possible roadblocks:

Potential solutions to roadblocks:

Mid-range goal: _____

Actions to be taken:

Available resources:

Possible roadblocks:

Potential solutions to roadblocks:

Short-range goal: _____

Actions to be taken:

Available resources:

Possible roadblocks:

Potential solutions to roadblocks:

2.3 Converting Setbacks into Comebacks: Transforming Pessimism into Optimism

In *Hamlet,* Shakespeare wrote: "There is nothing good or bad, but thinking makes it so." His point was that experiences have the potential to be positive or negative, depending on how people interpret them and react to them.

Listed here is a series of statements representing negative interpretations and reactions to a situation or experience:

1. "I'm just not good at this."

2. "There's nothing I can do about it."

3. "Things will never be the same."

4. "Nothing is going to change."

5. "This always happens to me."

6. "This is unbearable."

7. "Everybody is going to think I'm a loser."

8. "I'm trapped, and there's no way out."

For each of the preceding statements, replace the negative statement with a statement that represents a more positive interpretation or reaction.

Is It or Is It Not Plagiarism?

The following are four incidents that were brought to a judicial review board to determine whether plagiarism had occurred and, if so, what the penalty should be. After you read each case, answer the questions that follow it.

Case 1

A student turned in an essay that included substantial material copied from a published source. The student admitted that he didn't cite the sources properly but argued that it was because he misunderstood the directions, not because he was attempting to steal someone else's ideas.

Reflection and Discussion Questions

1. Is this plagiarism?

2. How severe is it? (Rate it on the following scale: 1 = lowest, 10 = highest.)

3. What should the consequence or penalty be for the student?

4. How could the suspicion of plagiarism have been avoided in this case?

Case 2

A student turned in a paper that was identical to a paper submitted by another student for a different course.

Reflection and Discussion Questions

1. Is this plagiarism?

2. How severe is it? (Rate it on the following scale: 1 = lowest, 10 = highest.)

3. What should the consequence or penalty be for the student?

4. How could the suspicion of plagiarism have been avoided in this case?

Case 3

A student submitted a paper he wrote in a previous course as an extra-credit paper for a course.

Reflection and Discussion Questions

1. Is this plagiarism?

2. How severe is it? (Rate it on the following scale: 1 = lowest, 10 = highest.)

3. What should the consequence or penalty be for the student?

4. How could the suspicion of plagiarism have been avoided in this case?

Case 4

A student submits a paper in an art history course that contains some ideas from art critics that she read about and whose ideas she agrees with. The student claimed that not citing these critics' ideas wasn't plagiarism because their ideas were merely their subjective judgments or opinions, not facts or findings; furthermore, they were opinions that she agreed with.

Reflection and Discussion Questions

1. Is this plagiarism?

2. How severe is it? (Rate it on the following scale: 1 = lowest, 10 = highest.)

3. What should the consequence or penalty be for the student?

4. How could the suspicion of plagiarism have been avoided in this case?

Looking back at these four cases, which of them do you think represents the most severe and least severe violation of academic integrity? Why?

Managing Time and Preventing Procrastination

3

LEARNING GOAL

To help you appreciate the significance of managing time and supply you with a powerful set of time-management strategies that can be used to promote your success in college and beyond.

◆ The Importance of Time Management

For many first-year students, the beginning of college means the beginning of more independent living and self-management. Even if you've lived on your own for some time, managing time is an important skill to possess because you're likely juggling multiple responsibilities, including school, family, and work. Studies show that most first-year community college students are attending classes while working either part time or full time (American Association of Community Colleges, 2009).

In college, the academic calendar and your class schedule will differ radically from those during high school. You will have less "seat time" in class each week and more "free time" outside of class, which you will have the freedom to self-manage; it will not be closely monitored by school authorities or family members, and you will be expected to do more academic work on your own outside of class. Personal time-management skills grow in importance when a person's time is less structured or controlled by others, leaving the

Student Perspective

"The major difference [between high school and college] is time. You have so much free time on your hands that you don't know what to do for most of the time."

–First-year college student (Erickson & Strommer, 1991)

Student Perspective

"I cannot stress enough that you need to intelligently budget your time."

–Words written by a first-year student in a letter of advice to students who are about to begin college

individual with more decision-making power about how personal time will be spent. Thus, it is no surprise that research shows the ability to manage time effectively as playing a crucial role in college success (Erickson, Peters, & Strommer, 2006).

Simply stated, college students who have difficulty managing their time have difficulty managing college. In one study, sophomores who had an outstanding first year in college (both academically and socially) were compared with another group of sophomores who struggled during their freshman year. Interviews conducted with these students revealed one key difference between the two groups: The sophomores who experienced a successful first year repeatedly brought up the topic of time during the interviews. The successful students said they had to think carefully about how they spent their time and that they needed to budget their time because it was a scarce resource. In contrast, the sophomores who experienced difficulty in their first year of college hardly talked about the topic of time during their interviews, even when they were specifically asked about it (Light, 2001).

Studies also indicate that managing time plays a pivotal role in the lives of working adults. Setting priorities and balancing multiple responsibilities (work, family, and school) that compete for limited time and energy can be a juggling act and a source of stress for people of all ages (Harriott & Ferrari, 1996).

For these reasons, time management should be viewed not only as a college-success strategy but also as a life-management and life-success skill. Studies show that people who manage their time well report they are more in control of their life and are happier (Myers, 1993). In short, when you gain greater control of your time, you become more satisfied with your life.

Personal Story

I started the process of earning my doctorate a little later in life than other students. I was a married father with a preschool daughter (Sara). Since my wife left for work early in the morning, it was always my duty to get up and get my daughter's day going in the right direction. In addition, I had to do the same for me—which was often harder than doing it for my daughter. Three days of my week were spent on campus in class or in the library. (We did not have quick access to research on computers then as you do now.) The other two days of the workweek and the weekend were spent on household chores, family time, and studying. I knew that if I was going to have any chance of finishing my Ph.D in a reasonable amount of time and have a decent family life, I had to adopt an effective schedule for managing my time. Each day of the week I held to a very strict routine. I got up in the morning, drank coffee while reading the paper, took a shower, got my daughter ready for school, and took her to school. Once I returned home, I put a load of laundry in the washer, studied, wrote, and spent time concentrating on what I needed to do to be successful from 8:30 a.m. to 12:00 p.m. every day. At lunch, I had a pastrami and cheese sandwich and a soft drink while rewarding myself by watching *Perry Mason* reruns until 1:00 p.m. I then continued to study until it was time to pick up my daughter from school. Each night I spent time with my wife and daughter and prepared for the next day. I lived a life that had a preset schedule. By following this schedule, I was able to successfully complete my doctorate in a decent amount of time while giving my family the time they needed. (By the way, I still watch *Perry Mason* reruns.)

—*Aaron Thompson*

Strategies for Managing Time

1. Analyze. Break down your time and become more aware about how it's spent.

Have you ever asked yourself "Where did all the time go?" or told yourself "I just can't seem to find the time." One way to find out where your time went is by taking a time inventory (Webber, 1991). To do this, you conduct a time analysis by breaking down and tracking your time, recording what you do and when you do it. By mapping out how you spend time, you become more aware of how much total time you have available to you and how its component parts are used up, including patches of wasted time in which you get little or nothing accomplished. You don't have to do this time analysis for more than a week or two. This should be long enough to give you some sense of where your time is going and allow you to start developing strategies for using your time more effectively and efficiently.

THINK ABOUT IT   Journal Entry   **3.2**

What is your greatest time waster?

_____

_____

_____

_____

_____

Is there anything you can do right now to stop or eliminate it?

_____

_____

_____

_____

_____

_____

> "Doesn't thou love life? Then do not squander time, for that is the stuff life is made of."
>
> —Benjamin Franklin, eighteenth-century inventor, newspaper writer, and cosigner of the *Declaration of Independence*

2. Itemize. Identify which specific tasks you need to accomplish and when you need to accomplish them.

We make lists to be sure we don't forget items we need from the grocery store or people we want to be sure are invited to a party. We can use the same list-making strategy for work tasks so that we don't forget to do them or forget to do them on time. Studies of effective people show that they are list makers and they write out lists not only for grocery items and wedding invitations but also for things they want to accomplish each day (Covey, 1990).

You can itemize your tasks by listing them in either of the following time-management tools:

- **Small, portable planner.** List all your major assignments and exams for the term, along with their due dates. By pulling all work tasks from different courses in one place, it is easier to keep track of what you have to do and when you have to do it.
- **Large, stable calendar.** Record in the calendar's date boxes your major assignments for the academic term and when they are due. Place the calendar in a position or location where it's in full view and you can't help but see it every day (e.g., on your bedroom or refrigerator door). If you regularly and literally "look" at the things you have to do, you're less likely to "overlook" them, forget about them, or subconsciously push them out of your mind.

THINK ABOUT IT   Journal Entry **3.3**

Do you have a calendar for the current academic term that you carry with you?

_____

If yes, why? If no, why not?

_____

_____

_____

_____

_____

If you carry neither a calendar nor a work list, why do you think you don't?

_____

_____

_____

_____

_____

Personal Story

My mom was the person who ensured I got up for school on time. Once I got to school the bell would ring to let me know to move on to the next class. When I returned home I had to do my homework and chores. My daily and weekly schedules were dictated by someone else.

When I entered college, I quickly realized that I needed to develop my own system for being organized, focused, and productive without the assistance of my mother. Since I came from a modest background, I had to work my way through college. Juggling schedules became an art and science for me. I knew the things that I could not miss, such as work and school, and the things I could miss—TV and girls. (OK, TV, but not girls.)

After college, I spent 10 years in business—a world where I was measured by being on time and a productive "bottom line." It was during this time that I discovered a scheduling book. When I became a professor, I had other mechanisms to make sure I did what I needed to do when I needed to do it. This was largely based on when my classes were offered. Other time was dedicated to working out and spending time with my family. Now, as an administrator, I have an assistant who keeps my schedule for me. She tells me where I am going, how long I should be there, and what I need to accomplish while I am there. Unless you take your parents with you or have the luxury of a personal assistant, it's important to determine which activities are required and to allow time in your schedule for fun. Use a planner!

—*Aaron Thompson*

3. Prioritize. Rank your tasks in order of their importance.

Once you've itemized your work by listing all tasks you need to do, prioritize them—determine the order in which you will do them. Prioritizing basically involves ranking your tasks in terms of their importance, with the highest-ranked tasks appearing at the top of your list to ensure that they are tackled first. How do you determine which tasks are most important and should be ranked highest? Two key criteria or standards of judgment can be used to help determine which tasks should be your priorities:

1. **Urgency.** Tasks that are closest to their deadline or due date should receive high priority. For example, finishing an assignment that's due tomorrow should receive higher priority than starting an assignment that's due next month.
2. **Gravity.** Tasks that carry the heaviest weight (count the most) should receive highest priority. For example, if an assignment worth 100 points and another worth 10 points are due at the same time, working on the 100-point task should receive higher priority. You want to be sure you invest your work time on work tasks that matter most. Just like investing money, you want to invest your time on tasks that yield the greatest dividends or payoff.

One strategy for prioritizing your tasks is to divide them into A, B, and C lists (Lakein, 1973). The A list is for *essential* tasks—what you *must* do now. The B list is for *important* tasks—what you *should* do soon. Finally, the C list is for *optional* tasks—what you *could* or *might* do later if there is time remaining after you've completed the tasks on the A and B lists. Organizing your tasks in this fashion can help you decide how to divide your labor in a way that ensures you put first things first. What you don't want to do is waste time doing unimportant things and deceive yourself into thinking that you're keeping busy and getting things done when actually you're doing things that just take your time (and mind) away from the more important things that should be done.

At first glance, itemizing and prioritizing may appear to be rather boring chores. However, if you look at these mental tasks carefully, they require many higher-level thinking skills, such as

1. **Analysis.** Breaking down time into its component elements or segments and breaking down work into specific tasks;
2. **Evaluation.** Critically evaluating the relative importance or value of tasks; and
3. **Synthesis.** Organizing individual tasks into classes or categories based on their level of priority.

Thus, developing self-awareness about how you spend time is more than a menial, clerical task; when done with thoughtful reflection, it's an exercise in higher-level thinking. It's also a good exercise in values clarification because what people choose to spend their time on is a more accurate indicator of what they truly value than what they say they value.

Develop a Time-Management Plan

Humans are creatures of habit. Regular routines help us organize and gain control of our lives. Doing things by design, rather than leaving them to chance or accident, is the first step toward making things happen for us rather than allowing them to happen to us—by chance or accident. By developing an intentional plan for how you're going to spend your time, you're developing a plan to gain greater control of your life.

Don't buy into the myth that you don't have time to plan because it takes too much time that could be spent on getting started and getting things done. Time-management experts estimate that the amount of time you spend planning your work reduces your total work time by a factor of three (Lakein, 1973). In other words, for every one unit of time you spend planning, you save three units of work time. Thus, 5 minutes of planning time will typically save you 15 minutes of total work time, and 10 minutes of planning time will save you 30 minutes of work time. This saving of work time probably occurs because you develop a clearer game plan or plan of attack for identifying what needs to be done and the best order in which to get it done. A clearer sense of direction reduces the number of mistakes you may make due to false starts—starting the work but then having to restart it because you started off in the wrong direction. If you have no plan of attack, you're more likely to go off track and in the wrong direction; when you discover this at some point after you've started, you're then forced to retreat and start over.

As the old proverb goes, "A stitch in time saves nine." Planning your time represents the "stitch" (in time) that saves you nine additional stitches (units of time). Similar to successful chess players, successful time managers plan ahead and anticipate their next moves.

Elements of a Comprehensive Time-Management Plan

Once you've accepted the notion that taking the time to plan your time saves you time in the long run, you're ready to design a time-management plan. The following are the key elements of a comprehensive, well-designed plan for managing time.

"Time = Life. Therefore waste your time and waste your life, or master your time and master your life."

–Alan Lakein, international expert on time management and author of the best-selling book, *How to Get Control of Your Time and Your Life* (1973)

"Failing to plan is planning to fail."

–Alan Lakein, author, *How to Get Control of Your Time and Your Life* (1973)

1. A good time-management plan should have several time frames.

Your academic time-management plan should include:

- A *long-range* plan for the entire academic term that identifies deadline dates for reports and papers that are due toward the end of the term;
- A *mid-range* plan for the upcoming month and week; and
- A *short-range* plan for the following day.

The preceding time frames may be integrated into a total time-management plan for the term by taking the following steps:

- Identify deadline dates of all assignments, or the time when each of them must be completed (your long-range plan).
- Work backward from these final deadlines to identify dates when you plan to begin taking action on these assignments (your short-range plan).
- Identify intermediate dates when you plan to finish particular parts or pieces of the total assignment (your mid-range plan).

This three-stage plan should help you make steady progress throughout the term on college assignments that are due later in the term. At the same time, it will reduce your risk of procrastinating and running out of time.

Here's how you can put this three-stage plan into action this term.

a. **Develop a long-range plan for the academic term.**
   - Review the *course syllabus* (*course outline*) for each class you are enrolled in this term, and highlight all major exams, tests, quizzes, assignments, and papers and the dates on which they are due.

! Remember

College professors are more likely than high school teachers to expect you to rely on your course syllabus to keep track of what you have to do and when you have to do it.

- Obtain a large calendar for the academic term (available at your campus bookstore or Learning Center) and record all your exams, assignments, and so on, for all your courses in the calendar boxes that represent their due dates. To fit this information within the calendar boxes, use creative abbreviations to represent different tasks, such as E for exam and TP for term paper (not toilet paper). When you're done, you'll have a centralized chart or map of deadline dates and a potential master plan for the entire term.
b. **Plan your week.**
   - Make a map of your *weekly schedule* that includes times during the week when you are in class, when you typically eat and sleep, and if you are employed, when you work.
   - If you are a full-time college student, find *at least 25 total hours per week* when you can do academic work outside the classroom. (These 25 hours can be pieced together in any way you like, including time between daytime classes and work commitments, evening time, and weekend time.) When adding these 25 hours to the time you spend in class each week, you will end up with a 40-hour workweek, similar to any full-time job. If you are a part-time student, you should plan on spending at least 2 hours on academic work outside of class for every 1 hour that you're in class.

Student Perspective

"The amount of free time you have in college is much more than in high school. Always have a weekly study schedule to go by. Otherwise, time slips away and you will not be able to account for it."

–First-year college student (Rhoads, 2005)

- Make good use of your *free time between classes* by working on assignments and studying in advance for upcoming exams. See **Box 3.1** for a snapshot summary of how you can make good use of your out-of-class time to improve your academic performance and course grades.
c. **Plan your day.**
  - Make a *daily to-do list*.

> **Remember**
>
> If you write it out, you're less likely to block it out and forget about it.

- Attack daily tasks in *priority order*.

> **Remember**
>
> "First things first." Plan your work by placing the most important and most urgent tasks at the top of your list, and work your plan by attacking tasks in the order in which you have listed them.

- Carry a *small calendar, planner, or appointment book* with you at all times. This will enable you to record appointments that you may make on the run during the day and will allow you to jot down creative ideas or memories of things you need to do—which sometimes pop into your mind at the most unexpected times.
- Carry *portable work* with you during the day—that is, work you can take with you and do in any place at any time. This will enable you to take advantage of "dead time" during the day. For example, carry material with you that you can read while sitting and waiting for appointments or transportation, allowing you to resurrect this dead time and convert it to "live" work time.
- Wear a *watch* or carry a cell phone that can accurately and instantly tell you what time it is and what date it is. You can't even begin to manage time if you don't know what time it is, and you can't plan a schedule if you don't know what date it is. Set the time on your watch or cell phone slightly ahead of the actual time; this will help ensure that you arrive to class, work, or meetings on time.

THINK ABOUT IT   Journal Entry   **3.4**

Do you make a to-do list of things you need to get done each day?

NEVER   SELDOM   OFTEN   ALMOST ALWAYS

If you selected "never" or "seldom," why don't you?

_____

_____

_____

_____

_____

3.1

Top Strategies: Making Productive Use of Free Time Outside the Classroom

Unlike high school, homework in college often does not involve turning things in to your instructor daily or weekly. The academic work you do outside the classroom may not even be collected and graded. Instead, it is done for your own benefit as you prepare yourself for upcoming exams and major assignments (e.g., term papers or research reports). Rather than formally assigning work to you as homework, your professors expect that you will do this work on your own and without supervision. Listed here are strategies for working independently and in advance of college exams and assignments, which will increase the quality of your preparation and performance.

Independent Work in Advance of Exams

- Complete reading assignments in advance of lectures that relate to the same topic as the reading. This will make lectures easier to understand and will prepare you to ask intelligent questions and make relevant comments in class.
- Review your class notes between class periods so that you can construct a mental bridge from one class to the next and make each upcoming lecture easier to follow. When reviewing your notes before the next class, rewrite any class notes that may be sloppily written. If you find notes relating to the same point all over the place, reorganize them by combining them into one set of notes. Lastly, if you find any information gaps or confusing points in your notes, seek out the course instructor or a trusted classmate to clear them up before the next class takes place.
- Review information that you have highlighted in your reading assignments to improve your memory of the information. If certain points are confusing to you, discuss them with your course instructor or a fellow classmate.

- Integrate key ideas in your class notes with information that you have highlighted in your assigned reading and that is related to the same major point or general category. In other words, put related information from your lecture notes and your reading in the same place.
- Use a part-to-whole study method whereby you study key material from your class notes and reading in small parts during short, separate study sessions that take place well in advance of the exam (the parts). Then, make your last study session before the exam a longer review session during which you restudy all the small parts together (the whole).

The belief that studying in advance is a waste of time because you will forget it all anyway is a myth. As you will see in Chapter 4, information studied in advance of an exam remains in your brain and is still there when you later review it. Even if you cannot recall the previously studied information when you first start reviewing it, you will relearn it faster than you did the first time, thus proving that some memory of it was retained.

Independent Work in Advance of Term Papers or Research Reports

Work on these large, long-term assignments by breaking them into the following smaller, short-term tasks:

- Search for and select a topic.
- Locate sources of information on the topic.
- Organize the information obtained from these sources into categories.
- Develop an outline of the report's major points and the order or sequence in which you plan to discuss them.
- Construct a first draft of the paper (and, if necessary, a second draft).
- Write a final draft of the paper.
- Proofread the final draft of your paper for minor mechanical mistakes, such as spelling and grammatical errors, before submitting it to your instructor.

2. A good time-management plan should include reserve time to take care of the unexpected.

You should always hope for the best but should always be prepared for the worst. Your time-management plan should include a buffer zone or safety net, building in extra time that you can use to accommodate unforeseen developments or unexpected emergencies. Just as you should plan to save money in your bank for unexpected extra costs (e.g., emergency medical expenses), you should plan to save time in your schedule for unexpected events that cost you time (e.g., dealing with unscheduled tasks or taking longer than expected to complete already-planned tasks).

3. A good time-management plan should capitalize on your biological rhythms.

When you plan your daily schedule, be aware of your natural peak periods and down times. Studies show that individuals differ in terms of the time of day when their body naturally tires and prefers to sleep or becomes energized and prefers to wake up. Some people are "early birds" who prefer to go to sleep early and wake up early; others are "night owls" who prefer to stay up late at night and get up late in the morning (Natale & Ciogna, 1996). (Teenagers are more likely to fall into the category of night owls.) Individuals also vary with respect to the times of day when they are at their highest and lowest levels of energy. Naturally, early birds are more likely to be morning people whose peak energy period occurs before noon; night owls are likely to be more productive in the late afternoon and evening. Also, most people experience a postlunch dip in energy in the early afternoon (Monk, 2005).

Be aware of your most productive hours of the day and schedule your highest-priority work and most challenging tasks for when you tend to work at peak performance levels. For example, schedule out-of-class academic work so that you're tackling academic tasks that require intense thinking (e.g., technical writing or complex problem solving) when you are most productive; schedule lighter work (e.g., light reading or routine tasks) at the times your energy level tends to be lower. Also, keep your natural peak and down times in mind when you schedule your courses. Try to arrange your class schedule in such a way that you experience your most challenging courses at times of the day your body (brain) is most ready and able to accept that challenge.

4. A good time-management plan should include a balance of work and recreation.

Don't only plan work time; plan time to relax, refuel, and recharge. Your overall plan shouldn't turn you into an obsessive-compulsive workaholic. Instead, it should represent a balanced blend of work and play, which includes activities that promote your mental and physical wellness—such as relaxation, recreation, and reflection. You could also arrange your schedule of work and play as a self-motivation strategy by using your play time to reward your work time.

A good time-management plan includes a balanced blend of time planned for both work and recreation.

! Remember

A good time-management plan should help you stress less, learn more, and earn higher grades while leaving you time for other important aspects of your life. A good plan not only enables you to get your work done on time but also enables you to attain and maintain balance in your life.

THINK ABOUT IT   Journal Entry   3.5

What activities do you engage in for fun or recreation?

_____

_____

_____

_____

_____

_____

What do you do to relax or relieve stress?

_____

_____

_____

_____

_____

_____

_____

Do you intentionally plan to engage in these activities?

_____

_____

_____

_____

_____

_____

"Some people regard discipline as a chore. For me, it is a kind of order that sets me free to fly."

–Julie Andrews, Academy award–winning English actress who starred in the Broadway musicals *Mary Poppins* and *The Sound of Music*

5. A good time-management plan should have some flexibility.

Some people are immediately turned off by the idea of developing a schedule and planning their time because they feel it overstructures their lives and limits their freedom. It's only natural for you to prize your personal freedom and resist anything that appears to restrict your freedom in any way. A good plan preserves your freedom by helping you get done what must be done, reserving free time for you to do what you want and like to do.

A good time-management plan shouldn't enslave you to a rigid work schedule. It should be flexible enough to allow you to occasionally bend it without having to break it. Just as work commitments and family responsibilities can crop up unexpectedly, so, too, can opportunities for fun and enjoyable activities. Your plan should allow you the freedom to modify your schedule so that you can take advantage of these enjoyable opportunities and experiences. However, you should plan to make up the work time you lost. In other words, you can borrow or trade work time for play time, but don't "steal" it; you should plan to pay back the work time you borrowed by substituting it for a play period that existed in your original schedule.

!

Remember

When you create a personal time-management plan, remember that it is *your* plan—you own it and you run it. It shouldn't run you.

Converting Your Time-Management Plan into an Action Plan

Once you've planned the work, the next step is to work the plan. A good action plan is one that gives you a preview of what you intend to accomplish and an opportunity to review what you actually accomplished. You can begin to implement an action plan by constructing a daily to-do list, bringing that list with you as the day begins, and checking off items on the list as you get them done. At the end of the day, review your list and identify what was completed and what still needs to be done. The uncompleted tasks should become high priorities for the next day.

At the end of the day, if you find yourself with many unchecked items still remaining on your daily to-do list, this could mean that you are spreading yourself too thin by trying to do too many things in a day. You may need to be more realistic about the number of things you can reasonably expect to accomplish per day by shortening your daily to-do list.

Being unable to complete many of your intended daily tasks may also mean that you need to modify your time-management plan by adding work time or subtracting activities that are drawing time and attention away from your work (e.g., taking cell-phone calls during your planned work times).

| THINK ABOUT IT | Journal Entry | **3.6** |

By the end of a typical day, how often do you find that you accomplished most of the important tasks you hoped to accomplish?

NEVER   SELDOM   OFTEN   ALMOST ALWAYS

Why?

_____

_____

_____

_____

_____

_____

◆ Dealing with Procrastination

Procrastination Defined

The word "procrastination" derives from two roots: *pro* (meaning "forward") plus *crastinus* (meaning "tomorrow.") As these roots suggest, procrastinators don't abide by the proverb "Why put off to tomorrow what can be done today?" Their philosophy is just the opposite: "Why do today what can be put off until tomorrow?" Adopting this philosophy promotes a perpetual pattern of postponing what needs to be done until the last possible moment, which results in rushing frantically to get it done (and compromising its quality), getting it only partially done, or not finishing it.

Research shows that 75 percent of college students label themselves as procrastinators (Potts, 1987), more than 80 percent procrastinate at least occasionally (Ellis & Knaus, 1977), and almost 50 percent procrastinate consistently (Onwuegbuzie, 2000). Furthermore, the percentage of people reporting that they procrastinate is on the rise (Kachgal, Hansen, & Nutter, 2001).

Procrastination is such a serious issue for college students that some colleges and universities have opened "procrastination centers" to provide help exclusively for students who are experiencing problems with procrastination (Burka & Yuen, 1983).

Student Perspective

"I believe the most important aspect of college life is time management. DO NOT procrastinate because, although this is the easy thing to do at first, it will catch up with you and make your life miserable."

–Advice from a first-year student to new college students

A procrastinator's idea of planning ahead and working in advance often boils down to this scenario.

List of Things To Do Today
1. Write Paper
2. Study for Math Test
3. Prepare Speech

List of Things Due Today
1. Turn in Paper
2. Take Math Test
3. Deliver Speech

Next time I'll start sooner!

Personal Story

During my early years in college, I was quite a procrastinator. During my sophomore year, I waited to do a major history paper until the night before it was due. Back then, I had a word processor that was little more than a typewriter; it allowed you save your work to a floppy disk before printing. I finished writing my paper around 3:00 a.m. and hit "print," but about halfway through the printing I ran out of paper. I woke up my roommate to ask if she had paper, but she didn't. So, at 3:00 a.m. I was forced to get out of my pajamas, get into my street clothes, get into my car and drive around town to find someplace open at three in the morning that sold typing paper. By the time I found a place, got back home, printed the paper, and washed up, it was time to go to class. I could barely stay wake in any of my classes that day, and when I got my history paper back, it wasn't exactly the grade I was hoping for. I never forgot that incident. My procrastination on that paper caused me to lose sleep the night before it was due, lose attention in all my other classes on the day it was due, and lose points on the paper that I managed to do. Thereafter, I was determined not to let procrastination get the best of me.

—*Julie McLaughlin*

Procrastination is by no means limited to college students. It is a widespread problem that afflicts people of all ages and occupations (Harriott & Ferrari, 1996). This is why you'll find many books on the subject of time management in the self-help section of any popular bookstore. It's also why you see so many people at the post office on April 15 every year, mailing their tax returns at the last possible moment ("Haven't Filed Yet," 2003).

Myths That Promote Procrastination

Before there can be any hope of putting a stop to procrastination, procrastinators need to let go of two popular myths (misconceptions) about time and performance.

Myth 1. "I work better under pressure" (e.g., on the day or night before something is due).

Procrastinators often confuse desperation with motivation. Their belief that they work better under pressure is often just a rationalization to justify or deny the truth, which is that they *only* work when they're under pressure—that is, when they're running out of time and are under the gun to get it done just before the deadline.

© JupiterImages Corporation.

> Although you may work quicker under pressure, you are probably not working better.

It's true that some people will only start to work and will work really fast when they're under pressure, but that does not mean they're working more *effectively* and producing work of better *quality*. Because they're playing "beat the clock," procrastinators' focus is no longer on doing the job *well* but is on doing the job *fast* so that it gets done before they run out of time. This typically results in a product that turns out to be incomplete or inferior to what could have been produced if the work process began earlier.

Confusing rapidity with quality is a sin. It's an indisputable fact that it takes more time to do higher-quality work, particularly if that job requires higher-level thinking skills such as thinking critically and creatively (Ericsson & Charnes, 1994). Academic work in college often requires deep learning and complex thinking, which require time for reflection. Deep thoughts and creative ideas take time to formulate, incubate, and eventually "hatch," which is not likely to happen under time pressure (Amabile, Hadley, & Kramer, 2002). Working under pressure on tasks that require higher-level thinking would be similar to trying to complete a long, challenging test within a short time frame. What happens is people have less time to think, to attend to fine details, to double-check their work, and to fine-tune their final product. Research indicates that most procrastinators admit that the work they produce is of poorer quality because they procrastinate (Steel, Brothen, & Wambach, 2001; Wesley, 1994) and that they experience considerable anxiety and guilt about their procrastination habit (Tice & Baumeister, 1997).

"Haste makes waste."

–Benjamin Franklin, eighteenth-century inventor, newspaper writer, and cosigner of the *Declaration of Independence*

"I wasted time, and now time doth waste me."

–William Shakespeare's *The Tragedy of King Richard II*, Act V (1595)

Myth 2. "Studying in advance is a waste of time because you will forget it all by test time."

This misconception is commonly used to justify procrastinating with respect to preparing for upcoming exams. As will be discussed in Chapter 4, studying that is distributed (spread out) over time is more effective than massed (crammed) studying. Furthermore, last-minute studying that takes place the night before exams often results in lost sleep time due to the need to pull late-nighters or all-nighters. This fly-by-night strategy interferes with retention of information that has been studied and elevates test anxiety because of lost dream (a.k.a. rapid eye movement, or REM) sleep, which enables the brain to store memories and cope with stress (Hobson, 1988; Voelker, 2004). Research indicates that procrastinators experience higher rates of stress-related physical disorders, such as insomnia, stomach problems, colds, and flu (McCance & Pychyl, 2003).

Working under time pressure adds to performance pressure because procrastinators are left with no margin of error to correct mistakes, no time to seek help on their work, and no chance to handle random catastrophes that may arise at the last minute (e.g., an attack of the flu or a family emergency).

THINK ABOUT IT   **Journal Entry**   **3.7**

Do you tend to put off work for so long that getting it done turns into an emergency or panic situation?

_____

_____

_____

_____

_____

_____

If your answer is yes, why do you think you find yourself in this position? If your answer is no, what is it that prevents this from happening to you?

_____

_____

_____

_____

_____

_____

Psychological Causes of Procrastination

Sometimes, procrastination has deeper psychological roots. People may procrastinate for reasons related not directly to poor time-management habits but more to emotional issues involving self-esteem or self-image. For instance, studies show that procrastination is sometimes used as a psychological strategy to protect one's self-esteem, which is referred to as self-handicapping. This strategy may be used by some procrastinators (consciously or unconsciously) to give themselves a "handicap" or disadvantage. Thus, if their performance turns out to be less than spectacular, they can conclude (rationalize) that it was because they were performing under a handicap—lack of time (Smith, Snyder, & Handelsman, 1982).

For example, if the grade they receive on a test or paper turns out to be low, they can still "save face" (self-esteem) by concluding that it was because they waited until the last minute and didn't put much time or effort into it. In other words, they had the ability or intelligence to earn a good grade; they just didn't try very hard. Better yet, if they happened to luck out and get a good grade—despite doing it at the last minute—then the grade just shows how intelligent they are! Thus, self-handicapping creates a fail-safe scenario that's guaranteed to protect the procrastinators' self-image: If the work performance or product is less than excellent, it can be blamed on external factors (e.g., lack of time); if it happens to earn them a high grade, then they can attribute the result to themselves—their extraordinary ability, which enabled them to do so well, despite doing it all at the last minute.

In addition to self-handicapping, other psychological factors have been found to contribute to procrastination, including the following:

- **Fear of failure.** Feeling that it's better to postpone the job, or not do it, than to fail at it (Burka & Yuen, 1983; Soloman & Rothblum, 1984);
- **Perfectionism.** Having unrealistically high personal standards or expectations, which leads to the belief that it's better to postpone work or not do it than to risk doing it less than perfectly (Flett, Blankstein, Hewitt, & Koledin, 1992; Kachgal et al., 2001);
- **Fear of success.** Fearing that doing well will show others that the procrastinator has the ability to achieve success and will allow others to expect the procrastinator to maintain those high standards by doing "repeat performances" (Beck, Koons, & Milgram, 2000; Ellis & Kraun, 1977);
- **Indecisiveness.** Having difficulty making decisions, including decisions about what to do or how to begin doing it (Anderson, 2003; Steel, 2003);
- **Thrill seeking.** Enjoying the adrenaline rush triggered by rushing to get things done just before a deadline (Szalavitz, 2003).

If these or any other issues are involved, their underlying psychological causes must be dealt with before procrastination can be overcome. Because they have deeper roots, it may take some time and professional assistance to uproot them. A good place to get such assistance is the Personal Counseling Office. Personal counselors on college campuses are professional psychologists who are trained to deal with psychological issues that can contribute to procrastination.

"We didn't lose the game; we just ran out of time."

–Vince Lombardi, legendary football coach

"Procrastinators would rather be seen as lacking in effort than lacking in ability."

–Joseph Ferrari, professor of psychology and procrastination researcher

"Striving for excellence motivates you; striving for perfection is demoralizing."

–Harriet Braiker, psychologist and best-selling author

THINK ABOUT IT   Journal Entry **3.8**

How often do you procrastinate?

RARELY   OCCASIONALLY   FREQUENTLY   CONSISTENTLY

When you do procrastinate, what is the usual reason?

_____

_____

_____

_____

_____

_____

Self-Help Strategies for Beating the Procrastination Habit

Once inaccurate beliefs or emotional issues underlying procrastination have been identified and dealt with, the next step is to move from gaining self-insight to taking direct action on the procrastination habit itself. Listed here are our top strategies for minimizing or eliminating the procrastination habit.

1. Continually practice effective time-management strategies.

If effective time-management practices, such as those previously cited in this chapter, are implemented consistently, they can turn into a habit. Studies show that when people repeatedly practice effective time-management strategies they gradually become part of their routine and develop into habits. For example, when procrastinators repeatedly practice effective time-management strategies with respect to tasks that they procrastinate on, their procrastination tendencies begin to fade and are gradually replaced by good time-management habits (Ainslie, 1992; Baumeister, Heatherton, & Tice, 1994).

2. Make the start of work as inviting or appealing as possible.

Getting started can be a key stumbling block for many procrastinators. They experience what's called "start-up stress" when they're about to begin a task they expect will be unpleasant, difficult, or boring (Burka & Yuen, 1983). If you have trouble starting your work, one way to give yourself a jump start is to arrange your work tasks in an order that allows you to start on tasks that you're likely to find most interesting or are most likely to experience success with. Once you've overcome the initial inertia and get going, you can ride the momentum you've created to attack the tasks that you find less appealing and more daunting.

You're also likely to discover that the dreaded work wasn't as difficult, boring, or time consuming as it appeared to be. When you sense that you're mak-

> "Just do it!"
>
> —Commercial slogan of a popular athletic equipment company, named after the Greek goddess of victory: Nike

ing some progress toward getting work done, your anxiety begins to decline. Like many experiences in life that are dreaded and avoided, the anticipation of the event turns out to be worse than the event itself. Research on students who hadn't started a project until it was about to be due indicates that these students experience anxiety and guilt about delaying their work but that once they begin working these negative emotions decline and are replaced by more positive feelings (McCance & Pychyl, 2003).

For many procrastinators, getting *started* is often their biggest obstacle.

© Elnur, 2010. Under license from Shutterstock, Inc.

3. Make the work manageable.

Work becomes less overwhelming and less stressful when it's handled in small chunks or pieces. You can conquer procrastination for large tasks by using a "divide and conquer" strategy: Divide the large task into smaller, more manageable units, and then attack and complete them one at a time.

Don't underestimate the power of short work sessions. They can be more effective than longer sessions because it's easier to maintain momentum and concentration for shorter periods. If you're working on a large project or preparing for a major exam, dividing your work into short sessions will enable you to take quick jabs and poke small holes in it, reducing its overall size with each successive punch. This approach will also give you the sense of satisfaction that comes with knowing that you're making steady progress toward completing a big task—continually chipping away at it in short strokes and gradually taking away the pressure associated with having to go for a big knockout punch right before the final bell (deadline).

The two biggest projects I've had to complete in my life were writing my doctoral thesis and writing this textbook! The strategy that enabled me to keep going until I completed both of these large tasks was to make up short-term deadlines for myself (e.g., complete 5–10 pages each week). I psyched myself into thinking that these were real "drop-dead" deadlines and that if I didn't meet them, and complete these small, shorter-term tasks, I was going to drop the ball and fail to get the whole job done. I think these self-imposed deadlines worked for me because it gave me short, more manageable tasks to work on that allowed me to make steady progress toward my larger, long-term task. It was as if I took a huge, hard-to-digest meal and broke it up into small, bite-sized pieces that I could easily swallow and gradually digest over time—as opposed to trying to consume a large, late-night meal right before bedtime (the final deadline).

—Joe Cuseo

4. Understand that organization matters.

Research indicates that disorganization is a factor that contributes to procrastination (Steel, 2003). How well we organize our workplace and manage our work materials can reduce our risk of procrastination. Having the right materials in the right place at the right time can make it easier to get to our work and get going on our work. Once we've made a decision to get the job done, we don't want to waste time looking for the tools we need to begin doing it. For procrastinators, this time delay may be just the amount of time they need to change their mind and not start their work.

One simple yet effective way to organize your college work materials is by developing your own file system. You can begin to create an effective file system by filing (storing) materials from different courses in different colored folders or notebooks. This will allow you to keep all materials related to the same course in the same place and give you direct and immediate access to the materials you need as soon as you need them. Such a system helps you get organized, reduces stress associated with having things all over the place, and reduces the risk of procrastination by reducing the time it takes for you to start working.

5. Recognize that location matters.

Where you work can influence when or whether you work. Research demonstrates that distraction is a factor that can contribute to procrastination (Steel, 2003). Thus, it may be possible for you to minimize procrastination by working in an environment whose location and arrangement prevents distraction and promotes concentration.

Distractions tend to come in two major forms: social distractions (e.g., people nearby who are not working) and media distractions (e.g., cell phones, e-mails, text messages, CDs, and TV). Research indicates that the number of hours per week that college students spend watching TV is *negatively* associated with academic success, including lower college grade point average, less likelihood of graduating college with honors, and lower levels of personal development (Astin, 1993).

Remember

Select a workplace and arrange your workspace to minimize distraction from people and media. Try to remove everything from your work site that's not directly relevant to your work.

THINK ABOUT IT   **Journal Entry**   **3.9**

List your two most common sources of distraction while working, and
next to each distracter, identify a strategy that you might use to reduce
or eliminate it.

Source of Distraction   Strategy for Reducing This Source of Distraction

_____   _____

_____   _____

_____   _____

_____   _____

_____   _____

_____   _____

Lastly, keep in mind that you can arrange your work environment in a
way that not only disables distraction but also enables concentration. You can
enable or empower your concentration by working in an environment that
allows you easy access to work-support materials (e.g., class notes, textbooks,
and a dictionary) and easy access to social support (e.g., working with a group
of motivated students who will encourage you to get focused, stay on task, and
keep on track to complete you work tasks).

Student Perspective

"To reduce distractions, work
at a computer on campus
rather than using one in your
room or home."

–Suggestion for avoiding work
distractions from a college student
in a first-year seminar class

6. Arrange the order or sequence of your work tasks to intercept procrastination when you're most likely to experience it.

While procrastination often involves difficulty starting work, it can also involve difficulty continuing and completing work (Lay & Silverman, 1996). As
previously mentioned, if you have trouble starting work, it might be best to
first do tasks that you find most interesting or easiest. However, if you have
difficulty maintaining or sustaining your work until it's finished, you might try
to schedule work tasks that you find easier and more interesting _in the middle
or toward the end_ of your planned work time. If you're performing tasks of
greater interest and ease at a point in your work when you typically lose interest or energy, you may be able to sustain your interest and energy long enough
to continue working until you complete them, which means that you'll have
completed your entire list of tasks. Also, doing your most enjoyable and easiest
tasks later can provide an incentive or reward for completing your less enjoyable tasks first.

Student Perspective

"I'm very good at starting
things but often have trouble
keeping a sustained effort."

–First-year college student

7. Learn that momentum matters.

It's often harder to restart a task than it is to finish a task that you've already
started; this occurs because you've overcome the initial inertia associated with
getting started and can ride the momentum that you've already created. Furthermore, finishing a task can give you a sense of closure—the feeling of per-

sonal accomplishment and self-satisfaction that comes from knowing that you "closed the deal." Placing a checkmark next to a completed task and seeing that it's one less thing you have to do can motivate you to continue working on the remaining tasks on your list.

◆ Summary and Conclusion

Mastering the skill of managing time is critical for success in college and in life beyond college. Time is a valuable personal resource; the better you use it, the greater control you have over your life. On the other hand, if you ignore or abuse this resource, you run the risk of reducing the quality of your work and the quality of your life. Once you let go of the pervasive and pernicious procrastination-promoting myth that you work better under pressure (e.g., on the day or night before something is due), you can begin planning how to manage your time and control your future.

Managing time involves three key processes:

1. Analysis of how we spend time, which will allow us to become more consciously aware of our time-spending habits and enable us to know where all our time actually goes
2. Development of a plan that connects our short-range, mid-range, and long-range tasks (i.e., for the next day, the next week, and the end of the term)
3. Evaluation of our priorities to ensure that we put most of our time into what's most important or matters the most

These are the three keys to effective time management; they are also likely to be the keys to managing any personal resource, such as your money or your relationships.

Internet-Based Resources for Further Information on Time Management

For additional information related to the ideas discussed in this chapter, we recommend the following Web sites:

www.time-management-guide.com/procrastination.html

www.studygs.net/timman.htm

www.essortment.com/lifestyle/timemanagement_sjmu.htm (This site includes time-management strategies designed specifically for adult or non-traditional-age students.)

3.1 Who's in Charge?

You have a paper due tomorrow for your 10:00 a.m. class. You stay up late writing the paper, and then your friends call and ask you to go out. The paper is finished, and you decide you can print it off when you get to school tomorrow. You have a great time with your friends and oversleep, waking at 9:45 a.m. You go straight to the computer lab and experience difficulties printing off your paper. You find a lab technician to help you, but it takes him 40 minutes to retrieve the paper. You run into class (45 minutes late) and give the paper to your instructor who informs you she will take the paper for late credit because the class policy states that any papers handed in after the beginning of class are considered late.

1. Who is primarily responsible for this paper being late? Why?

2. How could the situation have been avoided or handled differently?

3.2 Term at a Glance

Review the syllabus (course outline) for all classes you're enrolled in this term, and complete the following information for each course.

Term_____, Year _____

Course ↓	Professor ↓	Exams ↓	Projects & Papers ↓	Other Assignments ↓	Attendance Policy ↓	Late & Make-up Assignment Policy ↓

1. Is the overall workload what you expected? Are your surprised by the amount of work required in any particular course or courses?

2. At this point in the term, what do you see as your most challenging or demanding course or courses? Why?

3. Do you think you can handle the total workload required by the full set of courses you're enrolled in this term?

4. What adjustments or changes could you make to your personal schedule that would make it easier to accommodate your academic workload this term?

3.3 Your Week at a Glance

On the blank grid that follows, map out your typical week for this term. Start by recording what you usually do on these days, including when you have class, when you work, and when you relax or recreate. You can use abbreviations or write tasks out in full if you have enough room in the box (J = job, R&R = rest/relaxation, etc.). List the abbreviations you created at the bottom of the page so that your instructor can follow them.

If you're a *full-time* student, find *25 hours* in your week that you could devote to homework (HW). These 25 hours could be found between classes, during the day, in the evenings, or on the weekends. If you can find 25 hours per week for homework, in addition to your class schedule, you'll have a 40-hour schoolwork week, which research has shown to result in good grades and success in college.

If you're a *part-time* student, find *2 hours* you could devote to homework *for every hour* that you're in class (e.g., if you're in class 9 hours per week, find 18 hours of homework time).

	Sunday	Monday	Tuesday	Wednesday	Thursday	Friday	Saturday
7:00 a.m.							
8:00 a.m.							
9:00 a.m.							
10:00 a.m.							
11:00 a.m.							
12:00 p.m.							
1:00 p.m.							
2:00 p.m.							
3:00 p.m.							
4:00 p.m.							
5:00 p.m.							
6:00 p.m.							
7:00 p.m.							
8:00 p.m.							
9:00 p.m.							
10:00 p.m.							
11:00 p.m.							

3.4 Personal Time Inventory

1. Go to the following Web site:
   www.ulc.psu.edu/studyskills/time_management.html#monitoring_your_time

2. Complete the time management exercise at this site. The exercise asks you to estimate the hours per day or week that you spend doing various activities (e.g., sleeping, employment, and commuting). As you enter the amount of time you engage in these activities, the total number of remaining hours available in the week for academic work will be automatically computed.

3. After completing your entries, answer the following questions:

   • How many hours per week do you have available for academic work?

   • Do you have 2 hours available for academic work outside of class for each hour you spend in class?

   • What time wasters do you detect that might be easily eliminated or reduced to create more time for academic work outside of class?

Procrastination: The Vicious Cycle

Delilah has a major paper due at the end of the term. It's now past midterm, and she still hasn't started to work on her paper. She tells herself, "I should have started sooner."

However, Delilah continues to postpone starting her work on the paper and begins to feel anxious and guilty about it. To relieve her growing anxiety and guilt, she starts doing other tasks instead, such as cleaning her room and returning e-mails. This makes Delilah feel a little better because these tasks keep her busy, take her mind off the term paper, and give her the feeling that at least she's getting something accomplished. Time continues to pass, and the deadline for the paper is growing dangerously close. Delilah now finds herself in the position of having lots of work to do and little time in which to do it.

Source: Based on the procrastination research and the procrastination-counseling experiences of Jane Burka and Lenora Yuen, as reported in *Procrastination: Why You Do It, What to Do About It* (1983).

Reflection and Discussion Questions

1. What do you predict Delilah will do at this point?

2. Why did you make this prediction?

3. What grade do you think Delilah will receive on her paper?

4. What do you think Delilah will do on the next term paper she's assigned?

5. Other than starting sooner, what recommendations would you have for Delilah (and other procrastinators like her) to break this cycle of procrastination and prevent it from happening repeatedly?

Strategies for Deep Learning and High-Level Thinking

4

What do you think is the difference between learning and memorizing?

_____

_____

_____

_____

_____

_____

LEARNING GOAL

To develop a set of effective strategies that will enable you to learn deeply and think at a higher level—critically and creatively.

◆ Stages in the Learning and Memory Process

Learning deeply, and remembering what you've learned, is a process that involves three stages:

1. **Sensory input (perception).** Taking information into the brain;
2. **Memory storage.** Saving that information in the brain;
3. **Memory retrieval.** Recalling it when it's needed.

You can consider these stages of the learning and memory process to be similar to the way information is processed by a computer: (a) information is typed onto the screen (input), (b) the information is saved in a file (memory storage), and (c) the saved information is recalled and used when it's needed (memory retrieval).

These three stages in the learning–memory process are summarized visually in **Figure 4.1**.

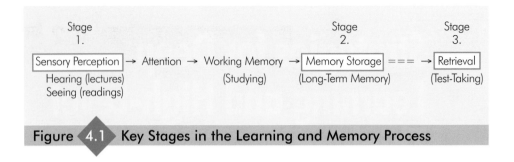

Figure 4.1 Key Stages in the Learning and Memory Process

The process of learning and remembering can be used to create a systematic set of practical strategies you can use to improve your performance on each of the two major routes through which learning takes place in college:

1. Learning by listening to lectures and taking notes
2. Learning by reading textbooks

◆ Learning Strategically from Listening to Lectures and Taking Notes

The importance of effective listening and note taking for college success is highlighted by a study conducted with an entire class of more than 400 first-year students who were given a listening test at the start of their first term in college. At the end of their first year, 49 percent of those students who scored low on the listening test were on academic probation at the end of their first year, compared to only 4.4 percent of students who scored high on the listening test. On the other hand, 68.5 percent of students who scored high on the listening test were eligible for the Honors program at the end of their first year, compared to only 4.17 percent of those students who had low listening-test scores (Conaway, 1982).

Contrary to the popular belief that writing interferes with listening, students report that taking notes actually increases their attention and concentration in class (Hartley, 1998; Hartley & Marshall, 1974). Studies also show that when students write down information that is presented to them rather than just listening to it, they are more likely to remember the most important aspects of that information when they are later given a memory test (Bligh, 2000; Kiewra et al., 1991). For instance, one study discovered that successful students (with grade point averages, or GPAs, of 2.53 or higher) record more information in their notes and retain a larger percentage of the most important information than students with GPAs less than 2.53 (Einstein, Morris, & Smith, 1985). These findings are not surprising when you consider that *hearing* lecture information, *writing* it, and *seeing* it while you write it provide three memory traces in the brain that can combine to improve memory for that information. Furthermore, students with a good set of notes have a written record of that information, which can be reread, reflected on, and studied later.

THINK ABOUT IT | **Journal Entry** | **4.2**

Do you think writing notes in class helps or hinders your ability to pay attention and learn from your instructors' lectures?

_____

_____

_____

_____

_____

_____

Why?

_____

_____

_____

_____

_____

_____

Studies show that information delivered during lectures is the number one source of test questions (and answers) on college exams (Brown, 1988; Kuhn, 1988). When lecture information appears on a test and has not been recorded in students' notes, it has only a 5 percent chance of being recalled (Kiewra et al., 2000). When you write down information presented in lectures, rather than just listen to it, you are more likely to remember that information. For example, students who write notes during lectures achieve higher course grades than students who just listen to lectures (Kiewra, 1985), and students with a more complete set of notes are more likely to demonstrate higher levels of overall academic achievement (Johnstone & Su, 1994; Kiewra & Fletcher, 1984).

What this research suggests is that you should view each lecture as if it were a test-review session during which your instructor is giving out test answers and you have the opportunity to write all those answers in your notes. Come to class with the attitude that your instructors are dispensing answers to test questions as they speak; your purpose for being there is to pick out and pick up these answers.

!

Remember

If important points your professors make in class make it into your notes, they can become points learned, and these learned points will turn into earned points on your exams (and higher grades in your courses).

The next sections give specific strategies for making the most of lectures and maximizing your course grades.

Prelecture Strategies

1. Before individual class sessions, check your syllabus to see where you are in the course and determine how the upcoming class fits into the total course picture.

This strategy will strengthen your learning by allowing you to see how each part (individual class session) relates to the whole (the entire course). It also capitalizes on the human brain's natural tendency to seek larger patterns; rather than seeing things in separate parts, the brain is naturally inclined to perceive parts as interconnected and forming a meaningful whole (Caine & Caine, 1991).

2. If possible, get to class ahead of time so that you can look over your notes from the previous class session and from any reading assignment relating to the day's lecture topic.

Research indicates that when students preview information related to an upcoming lecture topic it improves their ability to take more accurate and complete lecture notes (Ladas, 1980). Thus, a good strategy to help you learn from lectures is to review your notes from the previous class session and read textbook information relating to an upcoming lecture topic *before* hearing the lecture. This strategy will help you better understand the lecture and take more detailed notes on the lecture. Reviewing previously learned information activates your previous knowledge, enabling you to build a mental bridge from one class session to the next and connect new information to what you already know—which is the key to deep learning (Piaget, 1978; Vygotsky, 1978). Acquiring knowledge isn't a matter of simply pouring information into the brain, as if it were an empty jar. It's a matter of attaching or connecting new ideas to ideas that are already stored in the brain. When you learn deeply, you actually make a biological connection between nerve cells in the brain (Alkon, 1992), as illustrated in **Figure 4.2.**

When something is learned, it's stored in the brain as a link in an interconnected network of brain cells. Thus, deep learning involves making connections between what you're trying to learn and what you already know.

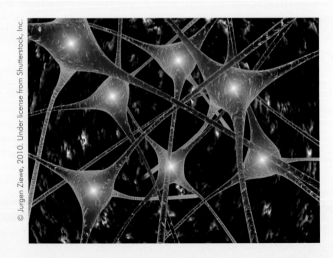

© Jurgen Ziewe, 2010. Under license from Shutterstock, Inc.

Figure 4.2 **Brain Cells**

3. Adopt a seating location that maximizes your focus of attention and minimizes sources of distraction.

Studies show that students who sit in the front and center of class tend to earn higher exam scores (Rennels & Chaudhair, 1988.) These results are found even when students are assigned seats by their instructor, so it's not just a matter of more motivated and studious students tending to sit in the front of the classroom; instead, the academic performance of students sitting front and center is likely higher because a learning advantage is provided by this seating location. Front-and-center seating probably aids academic performance by improving vision of the board and hearing of the instructor's words—as well as allowing eye contact with the instructor, which increases students' attention and heightens their sense of personal responsibility in the classroom. There's another advantage to sitting up front: It increases your comfort level about speaking in class because if you ask a question or contribute a comment, you will not have numerous classmates sitting in front of you who turn around to look at you when you speak.

When you enter the classroom, get in the habit of heading for a seat in the front and center of class. In large classes, it is particularly important that you get "up close and personal" with your instructors. This not only will improve your attention, note taking, and participation in class but also should improve your instructors' ability to remember who you are and how well you performed in class, which will work to your advantage when you ask for letters of recommendation.

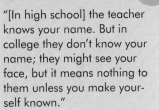

Student Perspective

"I tend to sit at the very front of my classrooms. It helps me focus and take notes better. It also eliminates distractions."

—First-year student

Student Perspective

"[In high school] the teacher knows your name. But in college they don't know your name; they might see your face, but it means nothing to them unless you make yourself known."

—First-year student (Nunez, 2005)

4. Be aware of how your social seating position affects your academic performance in the classroom.

Intentionally sit near classmates who will not distract you or interfere with the quality of your note taking. Attention comes in degrees or amounts; you can give all of it or part of it to whatever task you're performing. Trying to grasp complex information in class is a task that demands your undivided attention.

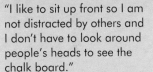

Student Perspective

"I like to sit up front so I am not distracted by others and I don't have to look around people's heads to see the chalk board."

—First-year student

!

Remember

When you enter a class, you have a choice about where you're going to sit. Choose wisely by selecting a location that will maximize your attentiveness to the instructor and the aggressiveness of your note taking.

5. Adopt a seating posture that screams attention.

Sitting upright and leaning forward is more likely to increase your attention because these signals of bodily alertness will reach your brain and increase mental alertness. If your body is in an alert and ready position, your mind tends to pick up these bodily cues and follows your body's lead by also becoming alert and ready to learn. Just as baseball players assume a ready position in the field before a pitch is delivered to put their body in position to catch batted balls, learners who assume a ready position in the classroom put themselves in a better position to "catch" ideas batted around in the classroom. Studies show that when humans are ready and expecting to capture an idea, greater amounts of the brain chemical C-kinase are released at the connection points between different brain cells, which increases the likelihood that a learning connection is formed between them (Howard, 2000).

There is another advantage from being attentive in class: You send a clear message to your instructor that you're a motivated, conscientious, and courteous student. This can influence your instructor's perception and evaluation of your academic performance, which can earn you the benefit of the doubt at the end of the term if you're on the border between a higher and a lower course grade.

During Lectures

1. Take your own notes in class.

Don't rely on someone else to take notes for you. Taking your own notes in your own words ensures they make sense and have personal meaning to you. You can collaborate with classmates to compare one another's notes for completeness and accuracy or to get notes if you happen to miss class. However, do not routinely rely on others to take notes for you. Studies show that students who record and review their own notes earn higher scores on memory tests for that information than students who review the notes of others (Fisher, Harris, & Harris, 1973). These findings point to the importance of taking and studying your own notes because they will be most meaningful to you.

2. Focus your attention on important information.

Attention is the critical first step to successful learning and memory. Since the human attention span is limited, it's impossible to attend to and make note of every piece of given information, including information that's delivered in the college classroom. Thus, you need to use your attention selectively to focus on and choose the most important information. Here are some strategies for attending to and recording the most important information delivered by professors in the college classroom:

- Pay attention to information your instructors put in writing—on the board, on a slide, or in a handout. If your instructor takes the time and energy to write it out, that's usually a good clue the information is important and you're likely to see it again—on an exam.
- Pay attention to information presented during the first and last few minutes of class. Instructors are more likely to provide valuable reminders, reviews, and previews at the start and end of class.
- Use your instructor's verbal and nonverbal cues to detect important information. Don't just tune in when the instructor is writing something down and tune out at other times. It's been found that students record almost 90 percent of information that is written on the board (Locke, 1977) but less than 50 percent of important ideas that professors state but don't write on the board (Johnstone & Su, 1994). Don't fall into the reflex-like routine of just writing something in your notes when you see your instructor writing on the board. You also have to listen actively to record important ideas in your notes that you hear your instructor saying. In **Box 4.1**, you'll find specific strategies for detecting important information that professors deliver orally during lectures.

Take Action!

4.1

Detecting When Instructors Are Delivering Important Information During Class Lectures

1. Verbal cues
   - Phrases signal important information (e.g., "The point here is . . ." or "What's most significant about this is . . .").
   - Information is repeated or rephrased in a different way (e.g., "In other words, . . .").
   - Stated information is followed with a question to check understanding (e.g., "Is that clear?" "Do you follow that?" "Does that make sense?" or "Are you with me?").

2. Vocal (tone of voice) cues
   - Information is delivered in a louder tone or at a higher pitch than usual, which may indicate excitement or emphasis.

- Information is delivered at a slower rate or with more pauses than usual, which may be your instructor's way of giving you more time to write down these important ideas.

3. Nonverbal cues
   - Information is delivered by the instructor with more than the usual:
     a. facial expressiveness (e.g., raised or furrowed eyebrows);
     b. body movement (e.g., more gesturing and animation); or
     c. eye contact (e.g., looking more directly and intently at the faces of students to see whether they are following or understanding what's being said).
   - The instructor moves closer to the students (e.g., moving away from the podium or blackboard).
   - The instructor's body is oriented directly toward the class (i.e., both shoulders directly or squarely face the class).

3. Take organized notes.

Keep taking notes in the same paragraph if the instructor is continuing on the same point or idea. When the instructor shifts to a new idea, skip a few lines and shift to a new paragraph. Be alert to phrases that your instructor may use to signal a shift to a new or different idea (e.g., "Let's turn to . . . " or "In addition to . . . "). Use these phrases as cues for taking notes in paragraph form. By using paragraphs, you improve the organizational quality of your notes, which will improve your comprehension and retention of them. Leave an extra space between successive paragraphs (ideas) to give yourself room to add information that you may have missed or to translate the professor's words into your own words, making them more meaningful to you.

Another strategy for taking organized notes, called the Cornell Note-Taking System, is summarized in **Box 4.2**.

The Cornell Note-Taking System

1. On the page you're taking notes, draw a horizontal line about 2 inches from the bottom edge of the page.
2. If there's no vertical line on the left side of the page, draw one line about 2½ inches from the left edge of the page (as shown in the scaled-down illustration here).

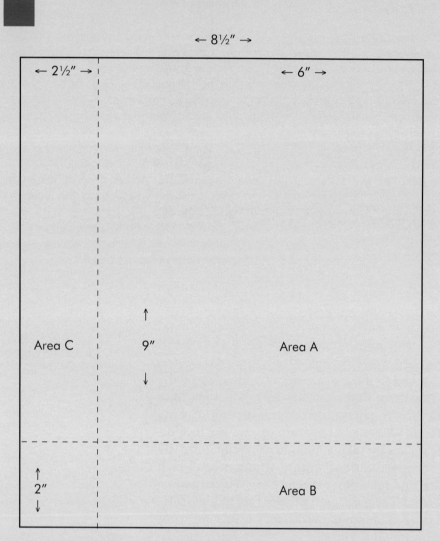

3. When your instructor is lecturing, use the large space to the right of the vertical line (area A) to record your notes.
4. After lectures, use the space at the bottom of the page (area B) to summarize the main points you recorded on that page.
5. Use the column of space on the left side of the page (area C) to write questions that are answered in the notes on the right.
6. Quiz yourself by looking at the questions listed in the left margin while covering the answers to them found in the class notes on the right.

Note: You can use this note-taking and note-review method on your own, or you could team up with two or more students and do it collaboratively.

4. If you don't immediately understand what your instructor is saying, don't stop taking notes.

Keep taking notes, even if you are temporarily confused, because this will at least leave you with a record of the information that you can review later—when you have more time to think about it and grasp it. If you still don't understand it after taking time to review it, check it out in your textbook, with your instructor, or with a classmate.

!

> ### Remember
>
> Your primary goal during lectures is to get important information into your brain long enough to note it mentally and then make note of it physically—by recording it in your notes. Making sense of that information often has to come later, when you have time to reflect on the notes you took in class.

THINK ABOUT IT   Journal Entry   4.3

What do you tend to do immediately after a class session ends?

_____

_____

_____

_____

_____

Why?

_____

_____

_____

_____

_____

After Lectures

1. As soon as class ends, quickly check your notes for missing information or incomplete thoughts.

We recommend a quick check immediately after class because the information is likely to be fresh in your mind and more easily locked into your memory before forgetting takes place. This quick review can be done alone or, better yet, with a motivated classmate. If you both have gaps in your notes, check them out with your instructor before he or she leaves the classroom. Even though it may be weeks before you will be tested on the material, the quicker you address missed points and clear up sources of confusion, the better, because you'll be able to use your knowledge to help you understand and learn upcoming material. Catching confusion early in the game also enables you to avoid the last-minute, mad rush of students seeking help from the instructor just before test time. You want to reserve the critical time just before exams for studying a set of notes that you know are complete and accurate, rather than rushing around and trying to find missing information and getting fast-food help on concepts that were presented weeks ago.

2. Before the next class session meets, reflect on and review your notes to make sense of them.

Your professors will often lecture on information that you may have little prior knowledge about, so it is unrealistic to expect that you will understand everything that's being said the first time you hear it. Instead, you'll need to set aside time for making notes on your own notes (i.e., rewriting them in your own words so that they make sense to you).

During this reflect-and-rewrite process, we recommend that you take notes on your notes by:

- Translating technical information into your own words to make them more meaningful to you; and
- Reorganizing your notes to get ideas relating to the same point in the same place.

Studies show that when students organize lecture information into meaningful categories they show greater recall on a delayed memory test for that information than students who simply review their notes (Howe, 1970).

!

Remember

Look at note taking as a two-stage process: Stage 1 is aggressively taking notes in class (active involvement), and stage 2 occurs later—when you think about those notes more deeply (personal reflection).

Personal Story

My first year in college was mainly spent trying to manipulate my schedule to find some free time. I took all of my classes in a row without a break to save some time at the end of the day for relaxation and hanging out with friends before I went to work. Seldom did I look over my notes and read the material that I was assigned on the day I took the lecture notes and received the assignment. Thus, on the day before the test I was in a panic trying to cram the lecture notes into my head for the upcoming test. Needless to say, I did not perform well on many of these tests. Finally, I had a professor who told me that if I spent time each day after a couple of my classes catching up on the reading and rewriting my notes I would retain the material longer, increase my grades, and decrease my stress at test time. I employed this system, and it worked wonderfully.

—Aaron Thompson

THINK ABOUT IT   **Journal Entry**   **4.4**

Rate yourself in terms of how frequently you use these note-taking strategies according to the following scale:

4 = ALWAYS, 3 = SOMETIMES, 2 = RARELY, 1 = NEVER

1. I take notes aggressively in class.   4 3 2 1

2. I sit near the front of the room in my classes.   4 3 2 1

3. I sit upright and lean forward while in class.   4 3 2 1

4. I take notes on what my instructors say, not just what they write on the board.   4 3 2 1

5. I pay special attention to information presented at the start and end of class.   4 3 2 1

6. I take notes in paragraph form.   4 3 2 1

7. I review my notes immediately after class to check that they are complete and accurate.   4 3 2 1

◆ Reading Strategically to Comprehend and Retain Textbook Information

Second only to information from lecture notes is information from reading assignments as a source of test questions on college exams (Brown, 1988). You're likely to find exam questions that your professors haven't talked about directly, or even mentioned, in class but that were drawn from your assigned reading. College professors often expect you to relate or connect what they are lecturing about in class with material that you've been assigned to read. Furthermore, they often deliver class lectures with the assumption that you have done the assigned reading, so if you haven't done it, you're likely to have more difficulty following what your instructor is talking about in class.

!

Remember

Do the assigned reading and do it according to the schedule your instructor has established. It will help you better understand class lectures, improve the quality of your participation in class, and raise your overall grade in the course.

Also, when completing your reading assignments, use effective reading strategies that are based on sound principles of human learning and memory, such as those listed here.

| **THINK ABOUT IT** | **Journal Entry** | **4.5** |

When you open a textbook to read a chapter, how do you start the reading process? That is, what's the first thing you do?

_____

_____

_____

_____

_____

_____

Prereading Strategies

1. Before jumping into your reading, step back and look at how the assigned reading fits into the overall organizational structure of the book and course.

You can do this efficiently by taking a quick look at the book's table of contents to see where the chapter you're about to read is placed in the overall sequence of chapters, particularly in relation to chapters that immediately precede and follow the assigned chapter. This will give you a sense of how the particular part you're focusing on connects with the bigger picture. Research shows that if learners have advance knowledge of how the information they're about to learn is organized—if they see how the parts relate to the whole *before* they attempt to start learning the specifics—they're better able to comprehend and retain the material (Ausubel, 1978; Kintsch, 1994). Thus, the first step toward improving reading comprehension and retention of a textbook chapter is to see how its parts relate to the whole—before you begin to examine the chapter part by part.

© Photoroller, 2010. Under license from Shutterstock, Inc.

2. Preview a chapter by reading its boldface headings and any chapter outline, objectives, summary, or end-of-chapter questions.

Get in the habit of previewing what's in a chapter to gain an overall sense of its organization before jumping right into the content. If you dive into details too quickly, you lose sight of how the smaller details relate to the larger picture. The brain's natural tendency is to perceive and comprehend whole patterns rather than isolated bits of information. Start by seeing how the different parts of the chapter are integrated into the whole. This will enable you to better connect the separate pieces of information you encounter while you read, much like seeing the whole picture of a completed jigsaw puzzle helps you connect its separate pieces while assembling the puzzle.

3. Take a moment to think about what you already know that relates to the material in the chapter.

By thinking about knowledge you possess about the topic you're about to read, you activate areas of your brain where that knowledge is stored, thereby preparing it to make meaningful connections with the material you're about to read.

Strategies to Use While Reading

1. Read selectively to find important information.

You can use the following three strategies to help you determine what information in your reading should be noted or highlighted while you read:

a. **Use boldface or dark-print headings and subheadings as cues for identifying important information.** These headings organize the chapter's major points; thus, you can use them as "traffic signs" to direct you to the most important information in the chapter. Better yet, turn the headings into questions and then read to find answers to these questions. This question-and-answer strategy will ensure that you read actively and with a purpose. (You can do this when you preview the chapter by placing a question mark after each heading contained in the chapter.) Creating and answering questions while you read also keeps you motivated, because the questions help stimulate your curiosity and finding answers as you read rewards you for reading (Walter, Knudsbig, & Smith, 2003). Lastly, this strategy is an effective way to prepare for tests because you are practicing exactly what you'll be expected to do on exams—answer questions. You can quickly write the heading questions on separate index cards and use them as flash cards to review for exams. Use the question on the flash card to "flashback" and attempt to recall the information from the text that answers the question.

b. **Pay special attention to words that are *italicized*, <u>underlined,</u> or appear in boldface print.** These usually represent building-block terms whose specific meaning must be understood before you can grasp the meaning of higher-level ideas and more general concepts covered in the reading. Don't simply highlight these words because their special appearance suggests they are important. Read these terms carefully and be sure you understand their meaning before you continue reading.

c. **Pay special attention to the first and last sentences in each paragraph.** These sentences contain an important introduction and conclusion to the ideas covered in that passage. In fact, when reading sequential or cumulative material that requires understanding of what was previously covered to understand what will be covered next, it's a good idea to reread the first and last sentences of each paragraph before you move on to the next paragraph.

d. **Reread the chapter after you've heard your instructor lecture on the material contained in the chapter.** You can use your lecture notes as a guide to help you focus on what information in the chapter your instructor feels is most important. If you adopt this strategy, your reading before lectures will help you understand the lecture and take better class notes and your reading after lectures will help you locate and learn the most important information contained in your textbook.

! Remember

Your goal when reading is not merely to "cover" the assigned pages but to "uncover" the most important information and ideas contained in those pages.

---

2. Adjust your reading speed to the type of subject matter you are reading.

"The art of reading is the art of adopting the pace the author has set. Some books are fast and some are slow, but no book can be understood if it is taken at the wrong speed."

–Mark Van Doren, Pulitzer Prize–winning poet and former professor of English at Columbia University

Academic reading is more technical and mentally challenging than popular reading (e.g., magazines or newspapers), so don't attempt to read college texts at the same speed you would use for general reading. Furthermore, certain academic subjects place greater demands on your memory than others, so you cannot expect to read all types of academic material at the same rate. For instance, material in the natural and social sciences is likely to have more technical terminology that will need to be read at a slower rate than a novel or short story. For more technical subjects, don't expect to understand the material when you first read it; you'll likely need to reread what you've read to get a deeper understanding of it.

3. Look up the meaning of unfamiliar words you encounter while reading.

Knowing the meaning of specific terms is important in any college course, but it's critical in courses whose subject matter builds on knowledge of previously covered information, such as math and science. If you don't learn the meaning of key terms as you read them, you can't build on your prior knowledge to learn concepts covered later.

First, try to figure out the meaning of a word from the context of the sentence in which it's used. If you can't, look it up in a dictionary (in print or online). Always have a dictionary at hand while you read. If the textbook you're reading has a glossary, use it regularly. As recommended in Chapter 1, you may want to make a photocopy of the textbook's glossary (typically located at the end of the text). Having a copy of it will save you the hassle of repeatedly holding your place in the chapter with one hand while using the other to find the meaning of unfamiliar terms at the back of the textbook. The more effort it takes to look up words you don't know, the less likely you are to do it, so make your access to a glossary and dictionary as convenient as possible.

4. Take written notes on what you're reading.

Just as you write notes in response to your instructor's lectures in class, take notes in response to the author's words in the text. For example, write short answers to the boldface heading questions in a reading notebook or in the text itself by using its side, top, and bottom margins. Writing requires more active thinking than highlighting because you're creating words of your own rather than passively highlighting words written by someone else. Don't get into the habit of using your textbook as a coloring book in which the artistic process of highlighting what you're reading with spectacular kaleidoscopic colors distracts you from the more important process of learning actively and thinking deeply.

"I would advise you to read with a pen in your hand, and enter in a little book of short hints of what you find that is curious, or that might be useful; for this will be the best method of imprinting such particulars in your memory, where they will be ready."

–Benjamin Franklin, eighteenth-century inventor, newspaper writer, and cosigner of the *Declaration of Independence*

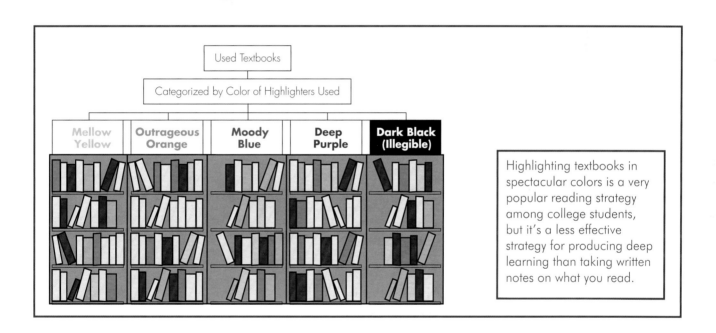

Highlighting textbooks in spectacular colors is a very popular reading strategy among college students, but it's a less effective strategy for producing deep learning than taking written notes on what you read.

Don't be afraid to write in your textbook because you own it. Even if you intend to sell the book back at the end of the term, you can still write in it with a pencil or highlight with a pencil by bracketing or underlining key sentences. If you eventually decide to sell your book back, you can erase the pencil markings and probably end up with a book that will have higher resale value than one you've painted with brightly colored highlighters. Pencils are more versatile reading tools than highlighters because they can be used more easily to do various things, such as recording written notes, drawing figures or symbols, and making changes to your notes by erasing and rewriting.

5. Pause periodically to summarize and paraphrase what you're reading in your own words.

If you can express the words that someone else has written in words that make sense to you, this means that you understand what you're reading and can relate it to what you already know—a telltale sign of deep learning (Demmert & Towner, 2003). A good time to pause and paraphrase is when you encounter a boldface heading that indicates you're about to be introduced to a new concept. This may be the ideal place to stop and summarize what you read in the section you just completed.

> **!**
>
> ### Remember
>
> Effective reading isn't a passive or mechanical process in which you just follow printed words on a page. Instead, it's a reflective process in which you actively search for and find meaning in the words you read.

Your goal when reading is not just to read but to think about what you're reading. You know you're reading effectively when you periodically stop reading and your eyes move from looking down at the page to looking up and to the side. These lateral eye movements are an indication that you're thinking deeply about what you're reading (Glenberg, Schroeder, & Robertson, 1998), rather than reading at a shallow or surface level.

THINK ABOUT IT   Journal Entry   4.6

When reading a textbook, do you usually have the following tools on hand?

Highlighter:	yes	no
Pen or pencil:	yes	no
Notebook:	yes	no
Class notes:	yes	no
Dictionary:	yes	no
Glossary:	yes	no

6. Use the visual aids included in your textbook.

Don't fall into the trap of thinking that visual aids can or should be skipped because they're merely add-ons that are secondary to the written words of the text. Visual aids, such as charts, graphs, diagrams, and concept maps, are powerful learning and memory tools for a couple of reasons:

a. They enable you to "see" the information in addition to reading (hearing) it.

b. They organize separate pieces of information into an integrated "whole picture."

Furthermore, visuals allow you to periodically experience a different mode of information input than repeatedly reading words. This occasional change of pace brings variety to the reading process, which can recharge your attention and motivation to read.

Postreading Strategies

1. End a reading session with a short review of the information you've noted or highlighted.

Most forgetting that takes place after you receive and process information occurs immediately after you stop focusing on the information and turn your attention to another task (Underwood, 1983). Taking a few minutes at the end of your reading time to review the most important information you've read locks that information into your memory before you turn your attention to something else and forget it.

2. Collaborate with peers to review your reading notes and highlights.

The same benefits of participating in small-group discussions and study groups, which we explained in Chapter 1, may be experienced by participating in reading groups. After completing your reading assignments individually, you can team up with classmates to compare your highlighting and margin notes. Help one another identify major points and information in the reading should be studied for upcoming exams.

3. Seek outside help from informed sources.

If you find that a concept explained in your text is difficult to understand even after you've reread and reviewed it, try the following strategies:

- **Look at how another textbook explains it.** Not all textbooks are created equally; some do a better job of explaining certain concepts than others. Check to see whether your library has other texts in the same subject as your course, or check your campus bookstore for textbooks in the same subject area as the course you're taking. A different text may be able to explain a hard-to-understand concept much better than the textbook you purchased for the course.
- **Seek help from your instructor.** If you have done the reading and made every effort to understand a particular concept but still can't grasp it, your instructor should be willing to assist you.

In addition to the reading strategies that we recommended in this section, another way to organize strategies that you can use to improve reading comprehension and retention is a method known as SQ3R. See **Box 4.3** for a summary of steps involved in this reading method.

Take Action!

4.3

The SQ3R Method

SQ3R is an acronym representing five sequential steps that can be taken to increase textbook-reading comprehension and retention, particularly when reading highly technical or complex material. The steps involved in this method are as follows:

1. Survey
2. Question
3. Read
4. Recite
5. Review

S = **S**urvey: *Get a preview and overview of what you're about to read before you begin reading.*

1. Read the title to activate your thoughts about the subject and prepare your mind to receive information related to it.
2. Read the introduction, chapter objectives, and chapter summary to become familiar with the author's purpose, goals, and most important points.
3. Note the boldface headings and subheadings to get a sense of the chapter's organization before you begin to read. It will help you understand or create a mental structure for the information to come.
4. Notice any graphics, such as charts, maps, and diagrams. They provide valuable visual support and reinforcement for the material you're reading, so don't ignore them.
5. Pay special attention to reading aids (e.g., italics and boldface print) that you can use to identify, understand, and remember key concepts.

Q = **Q**uestion: *Stay active and curious.*
As you read, use the boldface headings to formulate questions you think will be answered in that particular section. When your mind is actively searching for answers to questions, it becomes more engaged in the learning process. As you continue to read, add any questions that you have about the reading.

R = **R**ead: *Find the answer to the question or questions.*
Read one section at a time, with your questions in mind, and search for answers to these questions. Also, keep an eye out for new questions that need to be asked.

R = **R**ecite: *Rehearse your answers.*
After you read each section, recall the questions you asked and see whether you can answer them from memory. If not, look at the questions again and practice your answers to them until you can recall them without looking. Don't move onto the next section until you're able to answer all questions in the section you've just completed.

R = **R**eview: *Look back and get a second view of the whole picture.*
Once you've finished the chapter, review all the questions you've created for different parts or sections of the chapter. See whether you can still answer them all without looking. If not, go back and refresh your memory.

THINK ABOUT IT . **Journal Entry** **4.7**

Rate yourself in terms of how frequently you use these reading strategies according to the following scale:

4 = ALWAYS, 3 = SOMETIMES, 2 = RARELY, 1 = NEVER

1. I read the chapter outlines and summaries before I start reading a chapter.   4 3 2 1

2. I preview a chapter's boldface headings and subheadings before I begin to read the chapter.   4 3 2 1

3. I adjust my reading speed to the type of subject I am reading.   4 3 2 1

4. I look up the meaning of unfamiliar words and unknown
   terms that I come across before I continue reading.   4 3 2 1

5. I take written notes on information I read.   4 3 2 1

6. I use the visual aids included in my textbooks.   4 3 2 1

7. I finish my reading sessions with a review of important
   information that I noted or highlighted.   4 3 2 1

◆ Thinking at a Higher Level: Critically and Creatively

| **THINK ABOUT IT** | **Journal Entry** | **4.8** |

To me, thinking is . . . .

_____

_____

_____

_____

_____

_____

The term "higher-level thinking" refers to thinking that involves a more advanced level of thought than the thinking used for basic learning. For instance, reviewing information in your textbook that you've taken notes on or highlighted involves thinking and will help you learn that information. However, higher-level thinking occurs when you reflect on that information and perform a more advanced mental act, such as evaluating its usefulness or integrating it with your class notes to create a larger, more comprehensive product.

Contestants performing on TV quiz shows such as *Jeopardy* or *Who Wants to Be a Millionaire?* are responding with factual knowledge to questions that ask for information about who, what, when, and where. If these contestants were to be tested for higher-level thinking, they would be answering more challenging questions about why, how, and what if.

As its name implies, higher-level thinking involves setting the bar higher and "jacking up" your thinking to levels that go beyond merely remembering, reproducing, or regurgitating factual information. In college, simply remembering information may get you a C grade, demonstrating comprehension of that information level may give you a B, and going beyond comprehension to demonstrate higher-level thinking should earn you an A. Simply stated,

Student Perspective

"To me, thinking at a higher level means deep thought. It is when you have to put your time and effort into whatever you are thinking or writing."

–First-year college student

> "What is the hardest task in the world? To think."
>
> –Ralph Waldo Emerson, nineteenth-century American essayist and lecturer

Student Perspectives

"To me, thinking at a higher level means to think and analyze something beyond the obvious and find the deeper meaning."

–First-year college student

"To me, thinking at a higher level means going beyond understanding something on a superficial and general level; it requires a deep and profound thought process."

–First-year college student

The *Thinker* by Auguste Rodin, 19th-century French sculptor.

college professors are more concerned about teaching you *how* to think than teaching you *what* to think (e.g., what facts to remember).

> ! **Remember**
>
> Your college professors will often expect you to do more than just retain or reproduce information; they'll ask you to demonstrate higher levels of thinking with respect to what you've learned, such as analyze it, evaluate it, apply it, or connect it with other concepts you've learned.

This is not to say that basic knowledge and comprehension are unimportant. Rather, they provide the foundational steps necessary for you to climb to higher levels of thinking, as illustrated in **Figure 4.3**.

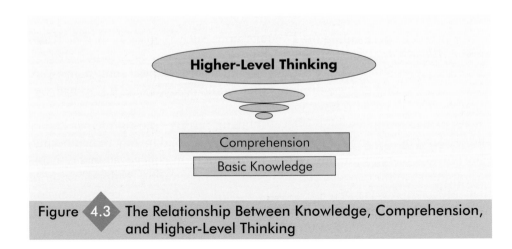

Higher-Level Thinking

Comprehension

Basic Knowledge

Figure 4.3 The Relationship Between Knowledge, Comprehension, and Higher-Level Thinking

Critical Thinking

Critical thinking is a form of higher-level thinking that involves evaluation or judgment. This evaluation can be either positive or negative; for example, a movie critic can give a good ("thumbs up") or bad ("thumbs down") review of a film.

THINK ABOUT IT   Journal Entry   **4.9**

Flash back to the journal entry on **p. 127** of this chapter and look at your response to the incomplete sentence. How does it match up with the definition of critical thinking we just provided?

_____

_____

_____

_____

_____

_____

_____

If you wrote that critical thinking means "being critical" or negatively criticizing something or somebody, don't feel bad. Many students think that critical thinking has this negative meaning or connotation.

Critical thinking is used to evaluate many things besides films, art, or music; it's also used to judge the quality of ideas, beliefs, choices, and decisions—whether they be your own or those of others. (See **Snapshot Summary 4.1** for common errors in logic and reasoning that may be detected through critical thinking.)

In a national survey of 40,000 college professors who taught freshman-through senior-level courses in various fields, 97 percent of them reported that the most important goal of a college education is to develop students' ability to think critically (Milton, 1982). Similarly, college professors who teach introductory courses to freshmen and sophomores indicate that the primary educational purpose of their courses is to develop students' critical thinking skills (Stark et al., 1990).

Since thinking skills are valued by professors who are teaching students at all stages of the college experience and in all subjects in the curriculum, developing these skills should be time well spent and should improve your academic performance significantly.

Snapshot Summary

Logical Fallacies and Errors of Reasoning

Critical thinking is a higher-level thinking skill that allows you to evaluate and detect errors in your own reasoning and in the reasoning of others. Some of the more common reasoning errors are summarized here. As you read the following list of logical errors, make a brief note in the margin of any example of these errors that you have observed or experienced.

- **Dogmatism.** Stubbornly clinging to a personally held viewpoint that's unsupported by evidence and remaining closed minded (nonreceptive) to other viewpoints that are better supported by evidence (e.g., believing that America's version of capitalism is the only economic system that can work in a successful democracy and refusing to acknowledge that other successful countries do not have a capitalistic economy).

- **Selective perception.** The tendency to focus on and perceive instances that support one's position or belief while overlooking those that contradict it (e.g., believing in astrology and only noticing and talking about people whose personalities fit their astrological sign).

- **Double standard.** Having two sets of standards for judgment: a higher standard for judging others and a lower standard for judging oneself. This is the classic "do as I say, not as I do" hypocrisy (e.g., critically evaluating and challenging the opinions of others but not your own).

- **Wishful thinking.** Thinking that something is true not because logic or evidence indicates

> "Belief can be produced in practically unlimited quantity and intensity, without observation or reasoning, and even in defiance of both by the simple desire to believe."
>
> –George Bernard Shaw, Irish playwright and 1925 Nobel Prize winner for literature

that it's true but because the person *wants* it to be true (e.g., a teenage girl not wanting to become pregnant and believing that she will not even though she and her boyfriend always have sex without using a contraceptive).

- **Hasty generalization.** Reaching a general conclusion based on a limited number of specific instances or experiences (e.g., concluding that people belonging to a group are all or nearly all "that way" on the basis of one or two personal experiences).

- **Jumping to a conclusion.** Making a leap of logic to reach a conclusion that's based on only one reason or factor while ignoring other possible reasons or contributing factors (e.g., concluding, after being rejected for a date or a job, that "I must be a real loser").

- **Glittering generality.** Making a positive general statement without supplying specific details or evidence to back it up (e.g., writing a letter of recommendation describing someone as a "wonderful human" with a "great personality" but not providing any specific reasons or evidence for these claims).

- **Straw man argument.** Distorting an opponent's argument position and then attacking it (e.g., attacking an opposing political candidate for supporting censorship and restricting civil liberties when the opponent supported only a ban on violent pornography).

- ***Ad hominem* argument.** Aiming an argument at the person rather than the person's argument (e.g., telling a younger person, "You're too young and inexperienced to know what you're talking about" or telling an older person, "You're too old-fashioned to understand this issue"). Literally translated, the term *ad hominem* means "to the man."

- **Red herring.** Bringing up an irrelevant issue that disguises or distracts attention from the real issue being discussed or debated (e.g., responding to criticism of former President Richard Nixon's involvement in the Watergate scandal by arguing, "He was a good president who accomplished many good things while he was in office"). The term "red herring" derives from an old practice of dragging a herring—a strong-smelling fish—across a trail to distract the scent of pursuing dogs. In the example, Nixon's effectiveness as a president is an irrelevant issue or a red herring; the real issue being discussed is Nixon's behavior in the Watergate scandal.

- **Smoke screen.** Intentionally disguising or covering up one's true reasons or motives with reasons that are designed to confuse or mislead others (e.g., opposing gun control legislation by arguing that it is a violation of the constitutional right to bear arms without revealing that the opponent is receiving financial support from gun manufacturing companies).

- **Slippery slope.** Using a fear tactic and arguing that not accepting a position will result in a "domino effect," whereby a negative event will inevitably lead to another negative event, and so on, like a series of falling dominoes (e.g., saying, "If someone experiments with marijuana, it will automatically lead to harder drugs, loss of motivation, withdrawal from college, and a ruined life").

- **Rhetorical deception.** Using deceptive language to conclude that something is true without providing reasons or evidence (e.g., confidently making such statements as "*Clearly* this is . . ." "It is *obvious* that . . ." or "Any *reasonable* person can see . . ." without explaining why it's so clear, obvious, or reasonable).

- **Circular reasoning (a.k.a. "begging the question").** Drawing a conclusion that is merely a rewording or restatement of the premise, which leaves the original question unanswered or the original problem unsolved (e.g., concluding that "Cursing is immoral because it's a sin").

- **Appealing to authority or prestige.** Thinking that if someone with authority or prestige says it's true then it must be true or should be done (e.g., thinking, "I should buy product X because this famous and prestigious actor or athlete uses it" or "My superior told me to do it, so I should—whether it's right or wrong").

- **Appealing to the traditional or the familiar.** Concluding that if something has been thought true or done the same way for a long time then it must be valid or the best method (e.g., stating that "This is the way it's always been done, so it's the way it should be done."

- **Appealing to popularity or the majority (a.k.a. "jumping on the bandwagon").** Concluding that if a belief is popular or is held by the majority then it must be true (e.g., arguing "So many people believe in psychics, it has to be true; they can't all be wrong").

- **Appealing to emotion.** Reaching a conclusion based on the intensity of feelings experienced or expressed, rather than the quality of reasoning used to reach the conclusion (e.g., believing that "If I feel strongly about something, it must be true"). The expressions, "always trust your feelings" and "just listen to your heart" may not always lead to the most accurate conclusions and the best decisions because they are based on emotion rather than reason.

Creative Thinking

To think creatively is to generate something new or different, whether it's a product, an idea, or a strategy. Critical thinking leads you to ask the question "Why?" (e.g., "Why am I doing it this way?"); creative thinking leads you to ask the question "Why not?" (e.g., "Why not try doing it a different way?"). When you think critically, you look "inside the box" and evaluate the quality of its content; when you think creatively, you look "outside the box" to imagine other packages containing different content. Your previous experiences in school or at work may have trained you to answer questions asked by others. However, in college, you're creating questions that stimulate new or original ways of thinking.

Although creative and critical thinking are two different forms of higher-level thinking, they go hand in hand. You use creative thinking to ask new questions and generate ideas, and you use critical thinking to evaluate the ideas

"Creativity is allowing oneself to make mistakes; art is knowing which ones to keep."

–Scott Adams, creator of the Dilbert comic strip and author of *The Dilbert Principle*

"Imagination should give wings to our thoughts, but imagination must be checked and documented by the factual results of the experiment."

–Louis Pasteur, French microbiologist, chemist, and founder of "pasteurization" (a method for preventing milk and wine from going sour)

you create (Paul & Elder, 2004). A creative idea must not only be different or original; it must also be effective (Sternberg, 2001; Runco, 2004). If critical thinking reveals that the quality of what you've created is poor, then shift back to creative thinking to generate something new and improved. Alternatively, you can start by using critical thinking to evaluate an old idea or approach and come to the judgment that it's not accurate or effective. This unfavorable evaluation naturally leads to and turns on the creative thinking process, which tries to come up with a new idea or different approach that is better than the old one.

The problem-solving process of brainstorming is a classic example of how creative and critical thinking work together. See **Box 4.4** for the steps or stages involved in the process of brainstorming.

As the brainstorming process suggests, creativity doesn't just happen suddenly or effortlessly, like the so-called stroke of genius; instead, it takes considerable mental effort (Paul & Elder, 2004; Torrance, 1963). Although creative thinking may include some sudden breakthroughs or intuitive leaps, it also involves carefully reflecting on those leaps and critically evaluating whether any of them landed you on a good idea.

Using Self-Questioning Strategies to Promote Your Critical and Creative Thinking

As we mentioned in Chapter 1, effective learners are effective self-monitors—they watch themselves while learning and monitor whether they are really understanding what they're attempting to learn (Weinstein & Underwood,

Take Action!

The Process of Brainstorming

4.4

1. List as many ideas as you can, generating them rapidly without stopping to evaluate their validity or practicality. Studies show that worrying about whether an idea is correct often blocks creativity (Basadur, Runco, & Vega, 2000). So, at this stage of the process, let your imagination run wild; don't worry about whether the idea you generate is impractical, unrealistic, or outrageous.

2. Use the ideas on your list as a springboard to trigger additional ideas, or combine them to create new ideas.

3. After you run out of ideas, review and evaluate the list of ideas you've generated and eliminate those that you think are least effective.

4. From the remaining list of ideas, choose the best idea or best combination of ideas.

"The principle mark of genius is not perfection but originality, the opening of new frontiers."

–Arthur Koestler, Hungarian novelist and philosopher

Note that the first two steps in the brainstorming process involve creative thinking that goes off in different directions to generate multiple ideas. In contrast, the last two steps in the process involve critical thinking that narrows in on the ideas that have been created to evaluate them and identify the best one.

Personal Story   Several years ago, I was working with a friend to come up with ideas for a grant proposal that he was going to write. We started out by sitting at his kitchen table, sipping coffee, and then we both got up and began to pace back and forth, walking all around the room while throwing out different ideas and bouncing ideas off each other. Whenever a new idea was thrown out, one of us would jot it down (whoever was pacing closer to the kitchen table at the moment).

After we ran out of ideas, we shifted gears, slowed down, and sat down at the table to carefully review each of the ideas we just generated during our "binge-thinking" episode. After some debate, we finally settled on an idea that we judged to be the best one of all the ideas we produced, and he made it his grant proposal.

Although I was not fully aware of it at the time, the stimulating thought process we were using was called brainstorming, which involved creative thinking (our fast-paced walking and idea-production stage) followed by critical thinking (our slower-paced sitting and idea-evaluation stage).

—Joe Cuseo

1985). Similarly, effective thinkers engage in a slightly different form of self-monitoring known as metacognition—they think about how they are thinking (Flavell, 1985).

One simple but powerful way to think about your thinking is through self-questioning. Since thinking often involves talking silently to yourself, if you remain consciously aware of the types of questions you ask yourself, you become more aware of your thinking and better able to stimulate your mind to think at a higher level. High-quality questions are those that trigger higher-level thinking to answer them. It could be said that a good question is one that ignites your mind and launches your thinking to higher levels in a quest to answer it.

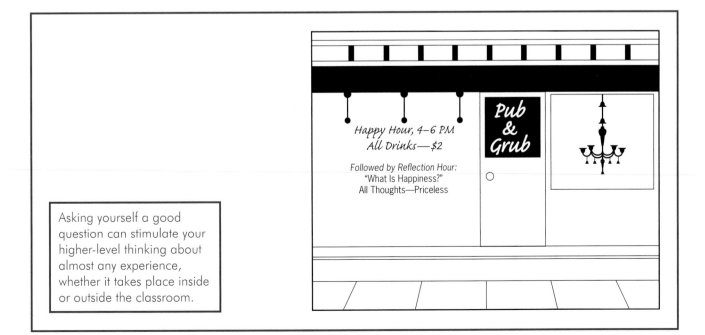

Asking yourself a good question can stimulate your higher-level thinking about almost any experience, whether it takes place inside or outside the classroom.

| **THINK ABOUT IT** | **Journal Entry** | **4.10** |

Critically evaluate the common practice of bars selling alcoholic drinks at reduced prices that's depicted in the preceding cartoon by answering the following questions:

What are the assumptions or implications of calling this practice "happy hour?"

_____

_____

_____

_____

_____

_____

What are arguments for and against this practice?

_____

_____

_____

_____

_____

_____

_____

Since questions have the power to activate and elevate your thinking, you can capitalize on their power by intentionally asking yourself good questions. The higher the level of thinking called for by the questions you regularly ask yourself, the higher the level of thinking you will display in class discussions, on exams, and in the papers you write. In **Box 4.5**, the questions have been intentionally designed to promote critical and creative thinking. The questions are constructed in a way that will allow you to easily fill in the blank and apply that type of thinking to any idea or issue under discussion or on your mind. Considerable research indicates that students can learn to use questions effectively to stimulate higher-level thinking in many subject areas (King, 1990, 1995).

We recommend that you save a copy of these higher-level thinking questions so that you can use them while completing academic tasks required by your courses (e.g., preparing for exams, writing papers or reports, and participating in class discussions or study-group sessions).

4.5

Questions for Stimulating Creative and Critical Thinking

Creative thinking. Generating new or different ideas, products, methods, or strategies.

Trigger questions:

- What could be invented to _____ ?

- What would happen if _____ ?

- What might be a different way to _____ ?

- How would this change if _____ ?

- What would be an original idea for _____ ?

Critical thinking. Making well-informed evaluations or judgments.

Trigger questions for thinking critically about *validity* (*truth*):

- Is _____ true or accurate?

- Is there sufficient evidence to support the conclusion that _____ ?

- Is the reasoning behind _____ strong or weak?

Trigger questions for thinking critically about *morality* (*ethics*):

- Is _____ fair?

- Is _____ just?

- Is this action consistent with the professed or stated values of _____ ?

Trigger questions for thinking critically about *beauty* (*aesthetics*):

- What is the artistic merit of _____ ?

- Does _____ have any aesthetic value?

- Does _____ contribute to the beauty of

  _____ ?

Trigger questions for thinking critically about *practicality* (*usefulness*):

- Will _____ work?

- How can _____ be put to good use?

- What benefit would result from _____ ?

Trigger questions for thinking critically about *priority* (*order of importance or quality*):

- Which one of these _____ is the most effective?

- Is this _____ the best option or choice available?

- How should these _____ be ranked from first to last (best to worst) in terms of their quality?

THINK ABOUT IT   **Journal Entry**   **4.11**

Look back at the forms of thinking described in **Box 4.5.** Take one question listed under each set of triggers and fill in the blank with a concept or issue you're learning about in a course you're taking this term.

◆ Summary and Conclusion

Information delivered during lectures is most likely to form questions and answers on college tests. At exam time, students who did not record lectures in notes have a slim chance of recalling the information presented. Thus, effective note taking is critical to successful academic performance in college.

Information from reading assignments is the next most common source of test questions on college exams. Professors often won't discuss these assignments in detail in class and sometimes don't even bring up the information from this reading. Thus, the assigned reading, and doing it in a way that's most effective for promoting comprehension and retention, plays an important role in your academic success.

Surveys show that college professors believe that developing students' critical think skills is the most important goal at all stages of the college experience. These higher-level thinking skills are highly valued by professors for a good reason: they will likely result in higher levels of academic performance.

The most effective strategies for promoting effective classroom listening, textbook reading, and higher-level thinking are those that reflect three of the college-success principles discussed in the first chapter of this text: (1) active involvement, (2) interpersonal interaction and collaboration, and (3) personal reflection and self-awareness.

Active involvement is critical for learning from lectures (e.g., actively taking notes while listening to lectures) and learning from reading (e.g., actively taking notes while reading). While active involvement is necessary for learning because it engages your attention and thus enables information to reach your brain, personal reflection is necessary for deep learning because it promotes consolidation, retaining information in your brain by locking it into long-term memory. Reflection also encourages deep learning by promoting self-awareness. By periodically pausing to reflect on whether you are truly attending to and understanding the words you're hearing in lectures and the words you're seeing while reading, you become a more self-aware learner and a more effective learner.

Lastly, learning from note taking, reading, and higher-level thinking can all be magnified if they're done collaboratively. You can collaborate with peers to take better notes in class, to identify what's most important in your assigned reading, and to ask questions of one another that promote higher-level thinking.

Internet-Based Resources for Further Information on Higher-Level Thinking

For additional information related to the ideas discussed in this chapter, we recommend the following Web sites:

Note Taking and Reading

www.utexas.edu/student/utlc

www.dartmouth.edu/~acskills/success/index.html

www.muskingum.edu/~cal/database/general/

Critical Thinking

www.criticalthinking.org

Creative Thinking

www.amcreativityassoc.org

Chapter 4 Exercises

4.1 Self-Assessment of Note Taking and Reading Habits

Look back at the ratings you gave yourself for effective note-taking strategies (**p. 119** and reading strategies (**pp. 126–127**). Add up your total score for each of these sets of learning strategies (the maximum score for each set is 14):

Note Taking = _____

Reading = _____

Total Learning Strategy Score = _____

Self-Assessment Questions

1. In which learning strategy area did you score lowest?

2. Do you think that the strategy area in which you scored lowest has anything to do with your lowest course grade at this point in the term?

3. Of the seven specific strategies listed within the area in which you scored lowest, which ones could you immediately put into practice to improve your lowest course grade this term?

4. What is the likelihood that you will put the preceding strategies into practice this term?

4.2 Self-Assessment of Higher-Level Thinking Characteristics

Listed here are four general characteristics of higher-level thinkers, along with a set of specific traits relating to each characteristic. When you read the list, place a checkmark next to any specific trait that you think is true of you.

Characteristics of a Higher-Level Thinker

1. **Inquisitive and Open Minded**

   - Is eager to continue learning different things from different people and different experiences

   - Has an "inquiring mind" that's curious, inquisitive, and ready to explore new ideas

   - Finds differences of opinion or opposing viewpoints interesting and stimulating

   - Attempts to understand why people hold different viewpoints and tries to find common ground among them

2. **Reflective and Tentative**

   - Suspends judgment until all evidence is in rather than making snap judgments before knowing the whole story

   - Acknowledges the complexity, ambiguity, or uncertainty of some issues and may say things like "I need to give this more thought" or "I need more evidence before I can draw a conclusion"

   - Takes time to think things through before drawing conclusions, making choices, and reaching decisions

   - Periodically reexamines personal viewpoints to see whether they should be maintained or changed as a result of new experiences and evidence

3. **Tolerant and Accepting**

   - Keeps emotions under control when someone criticizes one's viewpoint

   - Does not tune out ideas that conflict with one's own

   - Feels comfortable with disagreement

   - Is receptive to hearing different points of view

4. **Honest and Courageous**

   - Gives fair consideration to ideas that other people may instantly disapprove of or find distasteful

   - Expresses personal viewpoints that may not conform with those of the majority

   - Changes old opinions or beliefs when they are contradicted by new evidence

   - Acknowledges the limitations or weaknesses of one's own attitudes and beliefs

Look back at the list and count the number of checkmarks you placed underneath each of the four general areas.

1. Inquisitive and open minded   _____

2. Reflective and tentative   _____

3. Tolerant and accepting   _____

4. Honest and courageous   _____

- Under which characteristic did you have the most checkmarks?
- Under which did you have the fewest checkmarks?
- How would you interpret the meaning of this difference?
- Why do you think this difference occurred?

Too Fast, Too Frustrating: A Note-Taking Nightmare

Joanna Scribe is a first-year student who is majoring in journalism, and she's enrolled in an introductory course that is required for her major (Introduction to Mass Media). Her instructor for this course lectures at a rapid rate and uses vocabulary words that go right over her head. Since she cannot get all the instructor's words down on paper and cannot understand half the words she does manage to write down, she becomes frustrated and stops taking notes. She wants to do well in this course because it's the first course in her major, but she's afraid she will fail it because her class notes are so pitiful.

Reflection and Discussion Questions

1. Can you relate to this case personally, or do you know any students who are in the same boat as Joanna?

2. What would you recommend that Joanna do at this point?

3. Why did you make the preceding recommendation?

Strategic Studying and Test Taking

Are learning and remembering the same thing? Can one take place without the other?

_____

_____

_____

_____

_____

_____

◆LEARNING GOAL

To develop study strategies that you can use to learn deeply, remember longer, and improve your performance on college exams.

◆ Strategies for Learning Deeply and Remembering Longer

Learning gets information into your brain; the next step is to save that information in your brain (memory storage) and bring it back to mind at test time (memory retrieval). Described here is a series of effective study strategies for acquiring knowledge (learning) and keeping that knowledge in your brain (memory).

Give Studying Your "Undivided" Attention

Attention comes in a fixed amount. You only have so much of it available to you at any point in time, and you can give all of it or part of it to whatever task you're working on. If study time is spent on multiple tasks that provide other sources of external stimulation (e.g., listening to music, watching TV, or text-messaging friends), the total attention time available for studying is subtracted and divided among the other tasks. In other words, studying doesn't receive your "undivided attention."

Studies show that when people multitask they don't pay equal attention to different tasks at the same time. Instead, what they do is divide their attention by shifting it back and forth between tasks (Howard, 2000), and performance on the task that demands the most concentration or deepest thinking suffers the most (Crawford & Strapp, 1994). Furthermore, research shows that multitasking can increase boredom with tasks that involve concentration. One study found that with even a low level of distraction, such as a TV turned on a low volume in the next room, students were more likely to describe the mental task they were concentrating on as "boring" (Damrad-Frye & Laird, 1989).

The reality is that when performing tasks that cannot be done automatically (mindlessly), including complex mental tasks, other tasks and sources of external stimulation interfere with the quiet, internal reflection needed for permanent connections to form between brain cells (Jensen, 1998)—which is what has to happen biologically for deep, long-lasting learning to take place.

> Studies show that doing challenging academic work while multi-tasking divides up attention and drives down comprehension and retention.

"The extent to which we remember a new experience has more to do with how it relates to existing memories than with how many times or how recently we have experienced it."

—Morton Hunt, *The Universe Within: A New Science Explores the Human Mind* (1982)

Make What You're Learning Meaningful to You

Relating what you're trying to learn to something you already know is a powerful learning strategy because learning is all about making connections in the brain. The first and most effective way to learn something deeply and remember it longer is to find *meaning* in what you're learning. Before starting to repeatedly pound what you're learning into your head like a hammer against a nail, first look for a hook to hang it on—by relating it to something you already know that's stored in your brain. It may take a little while to discover the right hook, but once you've found it, the information will store in your brain quickly and remain there a long time.

For example, consider a meaningful way to learn and remember how to correctly spell one of the most frequently misspelled words in the English language: "separate" (not "seperate"). By remembering that "to par" means to divide, as in the words *par*ts or *par*tition, it makes sense that the word "separate" should be spelled se*par*ate because its meaning is "to divide into parts."

!

Remember

The more meaningful you make what you're learning, the deeper you learn it and the longer you remember it.

THINK ABOUT IT   Journal Entry   **5.2**

Can you think of information you're learning in a course this term that you could form a meaningful association to remember?

_____

_____

_____

_____

_____

_____

What is the information you're attempting to learn?

_____

_____

_____

_____

_____

_____

What is the meaningful association you could use to help you remember it?

_____

_____

_____

_____

_____

_____

_____

Find (or Make) Meaning Out of Unfamiliar Terms

Each academic field has specialized vocabulary that can sound like a foreign language to someone who has no experience with the subject area. Before you start to brutally beat these terms into your brain through sheer repetition, try to find some meaning in them. You can make a term more meaningful to you by looking up its word root in the dictionary or by identifying its prefix or suffix, which may give away the term's meaning. For instance, suppose you were studying the autonomic nervous system in biology, which is the part of the nervous system that operates without your conscious awareness or voluntary control (e.g., your heart beating and lungs breathing). The meaning of the phrase is given away by the prefix "auto," which means self-controlling—as in the word "automatic" (e.g., automatic transmission).

If the term's root, prefix, or suffix doesn't give away its meaning, then see whether you can make it more meaningful to you in some other way. For instance, suppose you looked up the root of the term "artery" and nothing about the origins of this term suggested its meaning or purpose. You could then create your own meaning for this term by taking its first letter (a), and have it stand for "*a*way"—to help you remember that arteries carry blood *away* from the heart. Thus, you've taken a biological term and made it personally meaningful (and memorable).

Compare and Contrast

When you're studying something new, get in the habit of asking yourself the following questions:

1. Is this idea similar or comparable to something that I've already learned? **(Compare)**
2. How does this idea differ from what I already know? **(Contrast)**

Research indicates that this simple strategy is one of the most powerful ways to promote learning of academic information (Marzano, Pickering, & Pollock, 2001). The power of the compare-and-contrast strategy probably stems from asking the question "How is this similar to and different than concepts that I already know?" By working to answer this question, you make learning more personally meaningful to you by relating what you're trying to learn to what you already know.

Integrate and Organize

Pull together or integrate information from your class notes and assigned reading relating to the same major concept or category. For example, get them in the same place by recording them on the same index card under the same category heading. Index cards are a good tool for such purposes; you can use each card as a miniature file cabinet for a separate category of information. The category heading on each card functions like the hub of a wheel, around which individual pieces of related information are attached like spokes. Integrating information related to the same topic in the same place and studying it at the same time helps divide the total material you need to learn into more identifiable and manageable parts. In contrast, when ideas pertaining to the same point or concept are spread all over the place, they're more likely to take that form in your mind—leaving them mentally disconnected and leaving you confused (as well as feeling stressed and overwhelmed).

THINK ABOUT IT   **Journal Entry**   **5.3**

Are you more likely to study in advance of exams or cram just before exams?

_____

_____

_____

_____

_____

Why?

_____

_____

_____

_____

_____

Divide and Conquer

Effective learning depends not only on *how* you learn (your study method); it also depends on *when* you learn (your study timing). Although cramming just before exams is better than not studying, it is far less effective than studying that's spread out across time. Rather than cramming all your studying into one long session, use the distributed practice method, which spreads study time over several shorter sessions. Research consistently shows that short, periodic practice sessions are more effective than a single marathon session.

Distributing your study time into several shorter sessions improves your learning and memory by:

- Reducing loss of attention due to fatigue or boredom; and
- Reducing mental interference—giving the brain some downtime to cool down and lock in information that it's received without being interrupted by the need to deal with additional information (Murname & Shiffrin, 1991).

If the brain's downtime is interfered with by the arrival of additional information, it gets overloaded and its capacity for handling information becomes impaired. This is what cramming does—it overloads the brain with lots of information in a limited period. In contrast, distributed study does just the opposite—it uses shorter sessions with downtime between sessions, thereby giving the brain the time and opportunity to save (retain) the information that it's processing (studying).

Student Perspective

"When I have to retain knowledge, I do not procrastinate; I can usually slowly remember everything. The knowledge is in [my] long-term memory, so I usually have no problems retaining it."

–First-year student's response to the question: "When you need to remember information, what strategy works best for you?"

Another major advantage of distributed study is that it's less stressful and more motivating than cramming. Shorter sessions can be an incentive to study because you know that you're not going to be doing it for a long stretch of time or lose any sleep over it. It's easier to maintain your interest and motivation for any task that's done for a shorter rather than a longer period. Furthermore, you should feel more relaxed because if you run into difficulty understanding anything you know there's still time to get help with it before you're tested and graded on it.

Consuming large doses of caffeine or other stimulants to stay awake for all-night cram sessions is likely to maximize anxiety and minimize memory.

Use the Part-to-Whole Study Method

Student Perspective

"Do not cram. If you start to prepare for a test about 3–5 days before, then you will only need to do a quick review the night before."

–Advice to freshmen from an experienced student (Walsh, 2005)

The part-to-whole method of studying is a natural extension of the distributed practice method of studying just discussed. With the part-to-whole method, you break the material you need to study into separate parts and study those parts in separate sessions in advance of the exam. You then use your last study session just before the exam to review (restudy) all the parts that you previously studied in separate sessions. Thus, your last study session is actually a review session, rather than a study session, because you're not trying to learn information for the first time.

Don't buy into the myth that studying ahead of time is a waste of time because you'll forget it all by test time. This is the myth that procrastinators use to put off studying until the last moment and then cram for their exams. Do not underestimate the power of breaking material to be learned into smaller parts and studying those parts in advance of a major exam. Even if you cannot recall what you previously studied, when you first start reviewing it, you'll find that you will relearn it much faster than when you studied it the first time. This proves that studying in advance is not a waste of time, because it takes less time to relearn the material the second time. This indicates that memory of it remained in your brain from the time you studied it earlier (Kintsch, 1994).

Begin Study Sessions by Reviewing

For sequential or cumulative subjects that build on understanding of previously covered material to learn new concepts (e.g., math), it's especially important to begin each study session with a quick review of what you learned in your previous study session.

Research shows that students of all ability levels learn material in college courses more effectively when it's studied in small units and when progression to the next unit takes place only after the previous unit has been mastered or understood (Pascarella & Terenzini, 1991, 2005). This strategy has two key advantages: (1) it reinforces your memory for what you previously learned and (2) it builds on what you already learned to help you learn new material. This is particularly important in cumulative subjects that require memory for problem-solving procedures or steps, such as math and science. By repeatedly practicing these procedures, they become more automatic, so you're able to retrieve them quicker (e.g., on a timed test) and use them efficiently without having to expend a lot of mental effort and energy on them (Newell & Rosenbloom, 1981). This frees up your working memory for more important tasks, such as critical thinking and creative problem solving (Schneider & Chein, 2003).

Bring Variety to the Study Process

Periodically vary the type of academic work you do while studying. Changing the nature of your work activities or the type of mental tasks you're performing while studying increases your level of alertness and concentration by reducing habituation—a psychological term referring to the attention loss that occurs after repeated engagement in the same type of mental task (McGuiness & Pribram, 1980). To combat attention loss due to habituation, occasionally vary the type of study task you're performing. For instance, shift periodically among tasks that involve reading, writing, studying (e.g., rehearsing or reciting), and practicing skills (e.g., solving problems).

Study different subjects in different places. Studying in different locations provides different environmental contexts for learning, which reduces the amount of interference that normally builds up when all information is studied in the same place (Anderson & Bower, 1974). Thus, it may be a good idea to spread out your studying not only at different times but also in different places. The great public speakers in ancient Greece and Rome used this method of changing places to remember long speeches; they walked through different rooms while rehearsing their speech, learning each major part of their speech in a different room (Higbee, 1998).

Changing the nature of the learning task and the learning environment provides changes of pace that infuse variety into the learning process, which stimulates attention. Although it's useful to have a set time and place to study for getting you into a regular work routine, this doesn't mean that learning occurs best by habitually performing all types of academic tasks in the same place. Instead, research suggests that you should periodically change the learning tasks you perform and the environment in which you perform them to maximize attention and minimize interference (Druckman & Bjork, 1991).

!

Remember

Change of pace and place while studying can stimulate your attention to, and your interest in, what you're studying.

THINK ABOUT IT   **Journal Entry**   **5.4**

Would you say that you're more of a visual learner or verbal learner?

_____

_____

_____

_____

_____

_____

How do you think most people would answer this question?

_____

_____

_____

_____

_____

Use All of Your Senses

When studying, try to use as many different sensory channels as possible. Research shows that information that's perceived through multiple sensory modalities or channels is remembered better (Bjork, 1994; Schacter, 1992) because it forms more interconnections in long-term memory areas of the brain (Zull, 2002). When a memory is formed in the brain, different sensory aspects of it are stored in different areas. For example, when your brain receives visual, auditory (hearing), and motor (movement) stimulation that accompany with what you're learning, each of these associations is stored in a different part of the brain. See **Figure 5.1** for a map of the surface of the human brain; you can see how different parts of the brain are specialized to receive input from different sensory modalities. When you use all of these sensory modalities while learning, multiple "memory traces" of what you're studying are recorded in different parts of your brain, which leads to deeper learning and stronger memory (Education Commission of the States, 1996).

Listed here are some major channels through which learning occurs and memories are stored, along with specific strategies for using each of these channels while studying.

Visual Learning

The human brain consists of two hemispheres (half rounds): the left and the right hemispheres (See **Figure 5.2**).

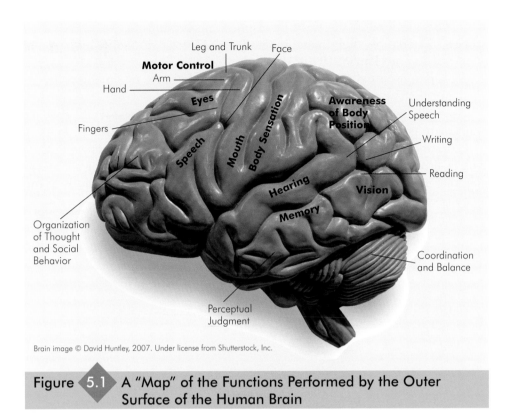

Brain image © David Huntley, 2007. Under license from Shutterstock, Inc.

Figure 5.1 A "Map" of the Functions Performed by the Outer Surface of the Human Brain

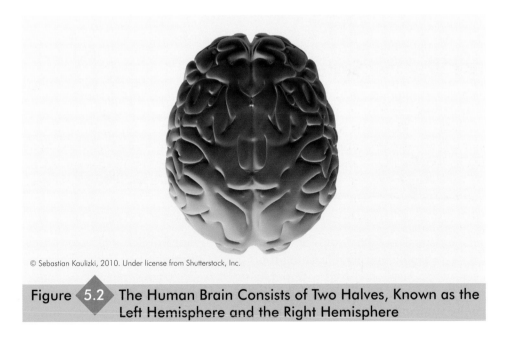

© Sebastian Kaulizki, 2010. Under license from Shutterstock, Inc.

Figure 5.2 The Human Brain Consists of Two Halves, Known as the Left Hemisphere and the Right Hemisphere

Each hemisphere of the brain specializes in different types of learning. In most people, the left hemisphere specializes in verbal learning, dealing primarily with words. In contrast, the right hemisphere specializes in visual–spatial learning, dealing primarily with images and objects that occupy physical space. If you use both hemispheres while studying, you lay down two different memory traces (tracks) in your brain: one in the left hemisphere, where words are stored, and one in the right hemisphere, where images are stored. This process of laying down a double memory trace (verbal and visual) is referred to as dual coding (Paivio, 1990). When this happens, memory for what you're learning is substantially strengthened, primarily because two memory traces are better than one.

To capitalize on the advantage of dual coding, use any visual aids that are available to you. Use the visual aids provided in your textbook and by your instructor, or create your own by drawing pictures, symbols, and concept maps, such as flowcharts or branching tree diagrams. See **Figure 5.3** for a concept map that could be used to help you remember the parts and functions of the human nervous system.

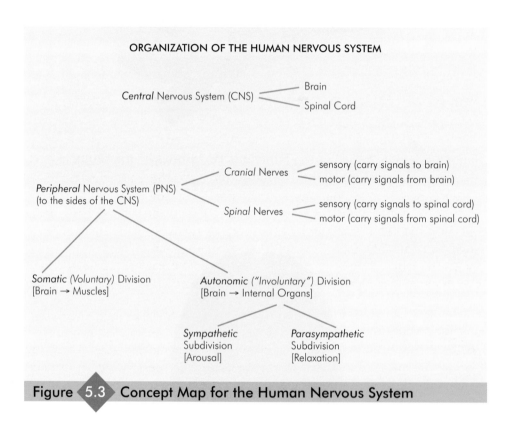

ORGANIZATION OF THE HUMAN NERVOUS SYSTEM

Central Nervous System (CNS) ⎯ Brain
⎯ Spinal Cord

Peripheral Nervous System (PNS)
(to the sides of the CNS)

Cranial Nerves ⎯ sensory (carry signals to brain)
⎯ motor (carry signals from brain)

Spinal Nerves ⎯ sensory (carry signals to spinal cord)
⎯ motor (carry signals from spinal cord)

Somatic (Voluntary) Division
[Brain → Muscles]

Autonomic ("Involuntary") Division
[Brain → Internal Organs]

Sympathetic
Subdivision
[Arousal]

Parasympathetic
Subdivision
[Relaxation]

Figure 5.3 Concept Map for the Human Nervous System

Drawing and other forms of visual illustration are not just artistic exercises; they also can be powerful learning tools (i.e., you can draw to learn). Drawing keeps you actively involved with the material you're trying to learn. By representing the material in visual form, you're able to dual-code the information you're studying, thus doubling its number of memory traces in your brain. As the old saying goes, "A picture is worth a thousand words."

| **THINK ABOUT IT** | **Journal Entry** | **5.5** |

Think of a course you're taking this term in which you're learning related pieces of information that could be joined together to form a concept map. In the space that follows, make a rough sketch of this map that includes the information you need to remember.

_____

_____

_____

_____

_____

_____

Motor Learning (a.k.a. Muscle Memory)

In addition to hearing and seeing, movement is a sensory channel. When you move, your brain receives kinesthetic stimulation—the sensations generated by your muscles when your body moves. Research shows that memory traces for movement are commonly stored in an area of your brain that plays a major role for all types of learning (Middleton & Strick, 1994). Thus, associating movement with what you're learning can improve your ability to retain it because you record an additional "muscle memory" trace of it to another area of your brain.

| **Personal Story** |

I was talking about memory in class one day and mentioned that when I temporarily forget how to spell a word, once I start to write it, its correct spelling comes back to me. One of my students raised her hand and said the same thing happens to her when she forgets a phone number—it comes back to her when she starts dialing it. In both of these cases, motor memory brought information back to mind that was temporarily forgotten, which points to the power of movement for promoting learning and memory.

—Joe Cuseo

You can use movement to help you learn and retain academic information by using your body to act out what you're studying or to symbolize it with your hands (Kagan & Kagan, 1998). For example, if you're trying to remember five points about something (e.g., five key consequences of the Civil War), when you're studying these points, count them out on your fingers as you try to recall each of them. Also, remember that talking involves muscle movement of your lips and tongue. Thus, by speaking aloud when you're studying, either to a friend or to yourself, your memory of what you're studying may be improved by adding kinesthetic stimulation to your brain (in addition to the auditory or sound stimulation your brain receives from hearing what you're saying).

Learning with Emotion

Information reaches the brain through your senses and can be stored in the brain as a memory trace. The same is true of emotions. Numerous connections occur between brain cells in the emotional and memory centers of the human brain (Zull, 1998). For instance, when you're experiencing emotional excitement about what you are learning, adrenaline is released and is carried through the bloodstream to your brain. Once adrenaline reaches the brain, it increases blood flow and glucose production, which can stimulate learning and strengthen memory (LeDoux, 1998; Rosenfield, 1988). If you have an emotionally intense experience, such a substantial amount of adrenaline is released in your body that it can lead to immediate, long-term storage of that memory, which you'll remember for the rest of your life. For instance, most people remember exactly what they were doing at the time they experienced such emotionally intense events as the September 11 terrorist attack on the United States, their first kiss, or their favorite team winning a world championship.

What does this emotion–memory link have to do with helping you remember academic information that you're studying? Research indicates that emotional intensity, excitement, and enthusiasm affects memory of academic information just as it does memory for life events and personal experiences. If you get psyched up about what you're learning, you have a much better chance of learning and remembering it. Even telling yourself that it's important to remember what you're learning can increase your memory of it (Howard, 2000; Minninger, 1984).

> **Remember**
>
> You will learn most effectively when you actively involve all your senses (including bodily movement), and when you learn with passion and enthusiasm. In other words, learning grows deeper and lasts longer when you put your "whole self" into it—your heart, your mind, and your body.

Learn Collaboratively: Form Study Groups

"We are born for cooperation, as are the feet, the hands, the eyelids, and the upper and lower jaws."

–Marcus Aurelius, Roman Emperor, A.D. 161–180

Group learning is a natural, brain-compatible form of learning. The human brain is biologically wired to communicate and collaborate because these skills are critical to survival of the human species (Jensen, 1998). Brain-imaging studies reveal that more activity occurs in thinking parts of the brain when people learn through social interaction than when they learn individually or in isolation (Carter, 1998). One way to put the power of group learning into practice is by forming study groups. Research indicates that college students who work regularly in small groups of four to six become more actively involved in the learning process and actually learn more (Light, 2001).

To maximize the power of study groups, each member should study individually *before* studying in a group and should come prepared with specific information or answers to share with teammates, as well as specific questions or points of confusion for which they'd like help from the team.

Personal Story

When I was in my senior year of college, I had to take a theory course by independent study because the course would not be offered again until after I planned to graduate. Another senior found himself in the same situation. The instructor allowed both of us to take this course together and agreed to meet with us every 2 weeks. My fellow classmate and I studied independently for the first 2 weeks. I prepared for the biweekly meetings by reading thoroughly, yet I had little understanding of what I had read. After our first meeting, I left with a strong desire to drop the course but decided to stick with it. Over the next 2 weeks, I spent many sleepless nights trying to prepare for our next meeting and was feeling pretty low about not being the brightest student in my class of two. During the next meeting with the instructor, I found out that the other student was also having difficulty. Not only did I notice, so did the instructor. After that meeting, the instructor gave us study questions and asked us to read separately and then get together to discuss the questions. During the next 2 weeks, my classmate and I met several times to discuss what we were learning (or attempting to learn). By being able to communicate with each other about the issues we were studying, we both ended up gaining greater understanding. Our instructor was delighted to see that he was able to suggest a learning strategy that worked for both of us.

—Aaron Thompson

THINK ABOUT IT   **Journal Entry**   **5.6**

Rate yourself in terms of how frequently you use these study strategies according to the following scale:

4 = ALWAYS,   3 = SOMETIMES,   2 = RARELY,   1 = NEVER

1. I block out all distracting sources of outside stimulation when I study.   4 3 2 1
2. I try to find meaning in technical terms by looking at their prefix or suffix or by looking up their word root in the dictionary.   4 3 2 1
3. I compare and contrast what I'm currently studying with what I've already learned.   4 3 2 1
4. I organize the information I'm studying into categories or classes.   4 3 2 1
5. I integrate or pull together information from my class notes and readings that relate to the same concept or general category.   4 3 2 1
6. I distribute or spread out my study time over several short sessions in advance of the exam, and I use my last study session before the test to review the information I previously studied.   4 3 2 1
7. I participate in study groups with my classmates.   4 3 2 1

Self-Monitor: Check to See How Effectively You're Learning

Successful learners reflect and check on themselves to see whether they really understand what they're attempting to learn. They monitor their comprehension as they go along by asking themselves questions such as "Am I following this?" and "Do I really understand it?"

How do you know if you really know it? Probably the best answer to this question is "I find *meaning* in it—that is, I can relate to it personally or put it in terms that make sense to me" (Ramsden, 2003). When you really understand a concept, you learn it at a deeper level than by merely memorizing it; and when you comprehend it, you're more likely to remember it because your learning is deeper and more durable—you remember it longer (Kintsch, 1970).

Discussed here are some specific strategies for checking whether you truly understand what you're trying to learn. These strategies can be used as indicators or checkpoints for determining whether you've moved beyond memorization to deep learning.

- **Can you paraphrase what you're learning? Can you restate or translate it into your own words?** When you can paraphrase what you're learning, you're able to complete the following sentence: "In other words, . . . " If you can complete that sentence in your own words, this is a good indication that you've moved beyond memorization to comprehension because you've transformed what you're learning into words that are meaningful to you. Thus, you learn deeply not by simply stating what your instructor or textbook states but by restating in words that are your own.

- **Can you explain what you're learning to someone else who is unfamiliar with it?** If you can explain to a friend what you've learned, this is a good sign that you've moved beyond memorization to comprehension because you are able to translate it into less technical language that someone hearing it for the first time can understand. Often, we don't realize how well we know or don't know something until we have to explain it to someone else who's never heard of it before (just ask any teacher). Simply put: If you can't explain it to someone else, you don't really understand it yourself. Studies show that students gain deeper levels of understanding for what they're learning when they are asked to explain it to someone else (Chi, de Leeuw, Chiu, & LaVancher, 1994). If you cannot find someone else to explain it to, then explain it aloud as if you were talking to an imaginary friend.

- **Can you think of an example of what you've learned?** If you can come up with a specific example or instance of what you're learning that is *your own* example—not one given by your instructor or textbook—this is a good sign that you truly comprehend it. It shows you're able to take a general, abstract concept and apply it to a specific, real-life experience (Bligh, 2000). Furthermore, a personal example is a powerful memory tool. Studies show that when we retrieve a concept from memory we first recall an example of it, which then serves as a memory-retrieval cue to trigger our memory of other details about the concept, such as its definition and relationship to other concepts (Norman, 1982; Park, 1984).

- **Can you represent or describe what you've learned in terms of an analogy or metaphor that compares it to something else with similar meaning or that works in a similar way?** Analogies and metaphors are basically ways of learning something new by understanding it in terms of its similarity to something you already understand. For instance, the computer can be used as a metaphor for the human brain to get a better understanding of learning and memory as a three-stage process in which (1) information is perceived or received (through lectures and readings), (2) stored or saved (through studying), and (3) retrieved (recalled at test time). If you can use an analogy or metaphor to represent what you're learning, this is a good sign that you're grasping it at a deep level because you're able to build a mental bridge that connects it to what you already know (Cameron, 2003).

- **Can you apply what you're learning to solve a new problem that you haven't previously seen?** The ability to use your knowledge is a good sign of deep learning (Erickson & Strommer, 2005). Learning specialists refer to this mental process as decontextualization—taking what you learned in one particular context (situation) and applying it to another (Bransford, Brown, & Cocking, 1999). For instance, you know that you've really learned a mathematical concept when you can use that concept to solve math problems that are different from the ones initially used by your instructor or textbook to help you learn it. This is why your math instructors rarely include on exams the exact problems solved in class or in your textbook. They're not trying to "trick you" at test time; they're trying to test your comprehension to determine whether you've learned the concept or principle deeply or just memorized it at a superficial level.

"Each problem that I solved became a rule which served afterwards to solve other problems."

–Rene Descartes, seventeenth-century French philosopher and mathematician

◆ Test-Taking Strategies

The first stage of the college learning process involves acquiring information from lectures and readings; the second stage involves studying that information and storing it in your brain; and the third stage involves remembering it on exams. Described here is a series of test-taking strategies for improving your ability to remember information at test time, which in turn, will improve your test performance and course grades.

Pretest Strategies

1. Come to tests prepared. Good test performance begins with good test preparation.

Naturally, the best strategy for improving your test performance is to be ready for the test by putting in study time and studying wisely by using effective study strategies—such as those discussed in this chapter. Studies show that college students who are well prepared for exams achieve higher test scores and experience lower test anxiety (Zohar, 1998). Research indicates that the most effective strategy for reducing test anxiety is to use effective learning strategies to prepare for exams (Benjamin, McKeachie, Lin, & Holinger, 1981; Jones & Petruzzi, 1995; Zeidner, 1995).

| **THINK ABOUT IT** | **Journal Entry** | **5.7** |

Do you change or modify your study strategies depending on the
type of test you're taking (e.g., multiple-choice or essay test), or do you tend to
study for all tests in the same way?

_____

_____

_____

_____

_____

_____

2. Adjust your study strategy to the type of test you will be taking.

You're ability to remember what you've studied will depend not only on how
much and how well you studied but also on how your memory will be tested
(Stein, 1978). You may be able to remember what you've studied if you are
tested in one format (e.g., multiple-choice questions) but not as well if the test
is in a different format (e.g., essay questions). You need to be aware of the type
of test you'll be taking and adjust your study strategy accordingly.

College test questions fall into two major categories: (1) recognition questions and (2) recall questions. Each of these types of questions requires a different type of memory and a different study strategy.

Recognition test questions. These questions ask you to select or choose
the correct answer from answers that are provided for you. Falling into this
category are multiple-choice, true–false, and matching questions. These test
questions don't require you to supply or produce the correct answer on your
own; instead, you're asked to recognize or pick out the correct answer—similar to picking out the "correct" criminal from a lineup of potential suspects.

Multiple-choice questions require
recognition memory similar to that used
to identify the correct criminal from a
line-up of possible suspects.

"IT'S NUMBER THREE, MR. HUGO, OUR SEVENTH GRADE TEACHER--THE ONE WHOSE
EXAMS CONTAINED QUESTIONS NOT COVERED IN THE ASSIGNED READING."

Recall test questions. These test questions require you to retrieve information you've stored in your brain and reproduce it on your own at test time. As the word "recall" implies, you have to recall or "call back" to mind the information you need and supply it yourself, rather than select or pick it out from information that's supplied for you. Recall test questions include essay and short-answer questions, which require a written response.

Since recognition test questions ask you to recognize or identify the correct answer from among answers that are provided for you, repeatedly reading over your class and textbook notes to identify important concepts may be an effective study strategy for multiple-choice and true–false test questions. Doing so matches the type of mental activity you'll be asked to perform on the exam—read over and identify correct answers.

On the other hand, recall test questions, such as essay questions, require you to retrieve information and generate correct answers on your own. Studying for essay tests by looking over your class notes and highlighted reading will not prepare you to retrieve and recall information on your own because it does not simulate what you'll be doing on the test itself. However, if you prepare for essay tests by writing out answers on your own, you ensure that your practice (study) sessions match your performance (test) situation because you'll be rehearsing what you'll be expected to do on the test—write essays.

Two strategies that are particularly effective for practicing the type of memory retrieval you will need to perform on recall tests are reciting and creating retrieval cues.

3. Reciting.

Recitation involves saying the information you need to recall—without looking at it. Research studies indicate that memory for information is significantly strengthened when students study by trying to generate that information on their own, rather than reviewing or rereading it (Graf, 1982). Reciting strengthens recall memory in three key ways:

- Reciting forces you to actively retrieve information, which is what you will have to do on the test, rather than passively reviewing information that's in front of you and in full view, which is not what you will do on the test.
- Reciting gives you clear feedback on whether you can recall the information you're studying. If you cannot retrieve and recite it without looking at it, you know for sure that you will not be able to recall it at test time and that you need to study it further. One way to provide yourself with this feedback is to put the question on one side of an index card and the answer on the flip side. If you find yourself flipping over the index card to look at the answer in order to state it, you clearly cannot retrieve the information on your own and need to study it further.
- Reciting encourages you to use your own words; this gives you feedback on whether you can paraphrase it. If you can paraphrase it (rephrase it in your own words), it's a good indication you really understand it; and if you really understand it, you're more likely to recall it at test time.

Reciting can be done silently, by speaking aloud, or by writing what you are saying. We recommend speaking or writing out what you're reciting because these strategies involve physical action, which keeps you more actively involved when you're studying.

4. Creating retrieval cues.

Suppose you're trying to remember the name of a person you know but just cannot recall it. If a friend gives you a clue (e.g., the first letter of the person's name or a name that rhymes with it), then it may suddenly trigger your memory of the person's entire name. What your friend did was provide you with a retrieval cue. A retrieval cue is a type of memory reminder (like a string tied around your finger), which brings back to your mind what you've temporarily forgotten. Human memories are stored as parts in an interconnected network (Pribram, 1991). If you're able to recall one key piece or segment of an interconnected network (the retrieval cue), it can trigger recall of the other pieces of information linked to it in the same organizational network (Collins & Loftus, 1975).

Studies show that students who are unable to remember previously studied information are better able to recall that information if they are given a retrieval cue. For instance, suppose students have studied a list of items that includes different animals (e.g., giraffe, coyote, and turkey) but they're unable to recall all these animals on a later memory test. If a retrieval cue is provided at the time of the recall test (e.g., if the word "animals" is written on top of the answer sheet), the students often are then able to recall many animals they couldn't name before the retrieval cue was provided (Kintsch, 1968). These research findings suggest that category names can serve as powerful retrieval cues. By taking information that you'll need to recall on an essay test and organizing it into categories, you can then use the category names as retrieval cues at the time of the test.

THINK ABOUT IT   **Journal Entry**   **5.8**

Think of material in a course you're taking this term that could be easily grouped into categories to help you remember that material.

What is the course?

_____

_____

_____

_____

_____

What categories could you use to organize information that's been covered in the course?

_____

_____

_____

_____

_____

_____

Another strategy for creating retrieval cues is to create catchwords or catchphrases that you can use as a net to "catch" related ideas that you need to recall. For example, an acronym can serve as a catchword, with each letter acting as a retrieval cue for a set of related ideas. Suppose you're studying for a test in abnormal psychology that is likely to include essay questions that will test your knowledge about types of mental illness. You could create the acronym "SCOT" to serve as a retrieval cue to help you remember to include each of the following key elements of mental illness in your answers: symptoms (S), causes (C), outcomes (O), and therapies (T).

!

Remember

Unlike multiple-choice questions on which you choose from answers given to you, on essay questions your mind can "go blank" because you're facing a blank sheet of paper that requires you to provide answers. To avoid drawing blanks on essay questions, you need to study differently—you need to recite (rehearse) your answers while studying and bring retrieval cues with you to the test.

Students can go "completely blank" on essay tests because they face a blank sheet that requires them to provide information on their own—as opposed to multiple-choice tests, which ask students to recognize or pick-out a correct answer from information that is provided them.

"When I looked at the first essay question, my whole life flashed before my eyes, then my whole mind went totally blank!"

Strategies to Use Before Starting the Test

1. Come to the test room fully equipped with all the test-taking tools you'll need.

In addition to the required supplies (e.g., No. 2 pencil, pen, blue book, Scantron, calculator, etc.), bring backup equipment in case you experience equipment failure (e.g., an extra pen in case your first one runs out of ink, or extra pencils in case your original one breaks).

2. Try to get to the test a few minutes early.

Arriving at the test ahead of time will give you time to review any terms, formulas, and equations you may have struggled to remember and any recall shortcuts you may have created (e.g., acronyms). You want to be sure that you have this key information in your working memory when you receive the exam so that you can get it down on paper—before you forget it. Arriving early will also allow you to take a few minutes to get into a relaxed pretest state of mind by thinking positive thoughts; taking slow, deep breaths; and stretch your muscles. Try to avoid discussing the test with other students immediately before the test begins because their last-minute questions, confusion, and anxiety may "rub off" on you. (Anxiety can be contagious.)

3. Sit in the same seat that you normally occupy in class.

Research indicates that memory is improved when information is recalled in the same place where it was originally received or reviewed (Sprenger, 1999). Thus, taking the test in the same seat you normally occupy during lectures, which is the place where you originally heard much of the information appearing on the test, may improve your test performance.

Strategies to Use During the Test

1. As soon as you receive a copy of the test, write down key information.

Writing down any hard-to-remember terms, formulas, and equations and any memory-improvement shortcuts you may have created as soon as you start the exam will ensure that you don't forget this information once you get involved with answering specific test questions.

2. Answer the easier test questions first.

As soon as you receive the test, before launching into the first question, take a moment to check out the layout of the test. Note the questions that are worth the most points and the questions that you know well. One way to implement this recommendation is to first survey the test and put a checkmark by difficult questions and come back to them later—after you've answered the easier ones. This practice is effective for several reasons:

- It prevents you from devoting so much time trying to answer difficult questions that you end up running out of time before getting to questions you know well and for which you would receive full credit.

- Once you've answered all the questions you know well, you'll have a good number of points under your belt; this will help you feel more relaxed and confident when you tackle the more difficult items. Studies show that when students answer easier questions at the start of a test they tend to perform better on more difficult questions encountered later in the test (Savitz, 1985) and achieve higher overall test scores (Roos, Wise, Yoes, & Rocklin, 1996). Research also shows that the ability to solve difficult problems and think creatively improves when anxiety levels aren't high (Teigen, 1994).

- It allows you to put the difficult questions out of your mind for a while before coming back to them. Sometimes answers or solutions suddenly pop into your mind after you get away from the problem (Csikszentmihalyi, 1996).

- By skipping difficult questions and proceeding to the more manageable ones, you may find information in the easier questions that relates to the more difficult ones and may help you answer them.

THINK ABOUT IT   **Journal Entry**   **5.9**

During tests, if I experience memory block, I usually . . .

_____

_____

_____

_____

_____

I am most likely to experience memory block in the following subject areas:

_____

_____

_____

_____

_____

---

3. Prevent memory block from setting in.

If you experience memory block for information that you know you've studied and have stored in your brain, use the following strategies:

- Mentally put yourself back in the environment or situation in which you studied the information. Recreate the steps in which you learned the information that you've temporarily forgotten by mentally picturing the place where you first heard or saw it and where you studied it, including the sights, sounds, smells, and time of day. This memory-improvement strategy is referred to as guided retrieval, and research supports its effectiveness for recalling information, including information recalled by eyewitnesses to a crime (Glenberg, Bradley, Kraus, & Renzaglia, 1983).

- Think of any idea or piece of information that may be related to the information you cannot remember. Studies show that when students experience temporary forgetting they're more likely to suddenly recall that information if they first recall partial information that relates to it in some way (Reed, 1996). This related piece of information may trigger your memory for the forgotten information because related pieces of information are likely to be stored as memory traces within the same network of brain cells.

- Take your mind off the question and turn to another question. This allows your subconscious to work on the problem, which may trigger your memory of the information you've forgotten. Also, by turning to other test questions, you may find some information included in those questions that can trigger memory for the information you forgot.

4. Use strategies to minimize test anxiety.

The following strategies can be applied before and during a test to ensure you don't become overly anxious:

- **Avoid cramming for exams.** Cramming increases test anxiety by creating higher levels of pretest tension stemming from the frantic rush to obtain and retain information in a short period. Evidence shows that college students who procrastinate experience higher levels of test anxiety (Rothblum, Solomon, & Murakami, 1986). High levels of pretest tension associated with rushing and late-night cramming are likely to carry over to the day of the test itself. Further aggravating matters is the loss of sleep the night before an exam because of cramming. Dream (rapid eye movement) sleep reduces your levels of anxiety (Voelker, 2004), so losing dream sleep the night before a test is likely to result in higher anxiety on the day of the test.

- **Focus all of your attention on the here and now.** Concentrate fully on the process of answering the test question that you're currently working on. Don't spend test time thinking about the future (e.g., what your test grade will turn out to be).

- **Focus your vision on the test in front of you, not the students around you.** Don't spend valuable test time looking at what others are doing and wondering whether they are doing better than you are. If you came to the test well prepared and are still finding the test difficult, it's likely that other students are finding it difficult too.

- **Don't spend time focusing on the amount of time remaining to complete the exam.** Repeatedly checking the clock during the test can distract your thought process and increase your stress level. Only check the time remaining periodically, and do your checking after you've completed a test question, rather than interrupting your work and losing your train of thought. Also, consider taking off your wristwatch and laying it on your desk during the test so that you can check the time without taking your eyes off the test and looking around to find the clock in the classroom.

- **Control your thoughts.** Focus on thinking positively and showing what you know, rather than worrying about what answers you don't know and how many points you have lost. Your thoughts can influence your emotions (Ellis, 1995). Positive emotions—such as feeling optimistic and confident—can improve your mental performance by improving your brain's ability to retrieve information that it's stored or saved (Rosenfield, 1988). In contrast, negative thinking can trigger feelings of anxiety, which is an emotion that interferes with memory retrieval (O'Keefe & Nadel, 1985).
- **Keep the test in perspective.** The exam isn't measuring your overall intelligence, your general academic ability, or your personal worth and character. A low test grade may not reflect lack of effort or ability on your part; rather, it may reflect the complexity of the course material or the complexity of the test itself. College exams are going to be more difficult than high school tests, so it's less likely that college students will get close to 100 percent of the total points on any given exam. Remember that you can achieve a good grade on a college exam without achieving a near-perfect test score.

"The perfect is the enemy of the good."

–Voltaire, eighteenth-century French author and philosopher

Snapshot Summary

5.1

Identifying Test Anxiety

If your stress level gets too high during exams, you may begin to experience test anxiety—a negative emotional state that weakens test performance by interfering with attention (Jacobs and Nadel, 1985), retention (O'Keefe & Nadel, 1985), and the ability to think at higher levels (Caine & Caine, 1991). If you experience the following symptoms during tests, your stress level may be high enough to be accurately called test anxiety (Tobias, 1985).

1. Feeling physical symptoms of tension during the test, such as pounding heartbeat, rapid pulse, muscle tension, sweating, or an upset stomach.
2. Being so distracted by feelings of nervousness that it becomes difficult to concentrate on the test.
3. Having negative or pessimistic thoughts during the test (e.g., "I know I'm going to fail this test" or "I always mess up on exams").
4. Rushing through the test just to get it over with (and get rid of the feeling of being nervous).

5. Going blank on the exam and forgetting what was studied but then remembering everything after leaving the test room.

Student Perspective

"Taking tests are for the most part a constant battle for me, as I tend to get anxious during a test or exam. The anxiety issue causes me to then forget the information retained prior to the test."

–First-year student's response to the question: "Do you consider yourself to be a good test taker?"

Note: If you experience these symptoms (signs) of test anxiety, and continue to experience them even after implementing the self-help strategies suggested on **pp. 162–165**, seek assistance from a professional in your Learning (Academic Support) Center or Counseling Center.

| **THINK ABOUT IT** | **Journal Entry** | **5.10** |

How would you rate your general level of test anxiety during most exams?

High   Moderate   Low

What types of tests or subjects tend to produce the most test stress or test anxiety for you?

_____

_____

_____

_____

_____

Why?

_____

_____

_____

_____

_____

Strategies for Answering Multiple-Choice Questions

Multiple-choice questions are commonly used on college tests, on exams to be admitted to graduate school (e.g., for master and doctoral degree programs) or professional school (e.g., law school and medical school), and on certification or licensing exams to practice in particular professions (e.g., nursing and teaching). Since multiple-choice tests are so common in college and beyond, this section of the text is devoted to a detailed discussion of strategies for answering such test questions.

1. Read all choices listed and use a process-of-elimination approach.

You can find an answer by eliminating choices that are clearly wrong and continuing doing so until you're left with one answer that seems to be the most accurate option. Keep in mind that the correct answer is often the one that has the highest probability or likelihood of being true; it doesn't have to be absolutely true—just "more true" than the other choices listed.

A *process-of-elimination* approach is an effective test-taking strategy to use when answering difficult multiple-choice questions.

2. Use test-wise strategies when you don't know the correct answer.

Your first strategy on any multiple-choice question should be to choose an answer based on your knowledge of the material, not to try to outsmart the test or the test maker by guessing the correct answer based on how the question is worded. However, if you've relied on your knowledge and used the process-of-elimination strategy to eliminate clearly wrong choices but you're still left with two or more answers that appear to be correct, then you should turn to being "test wise," which refers your ability to use the characteristics of the test question itself (such as its wording or format) to increase your chances of selecting the correct answer (Millman, Bishop, & Ebel, 1965). Listed here are three key, test-wise strategies for making a choice for multiple-choice questions whose answer you don't know or can't remember:

- **Pick an answer that contains qualifying words.** Look for words such as "usually," "probably," "likely," "sometimes," "perhaps," or "may." Truth often doesn't come neatly wrapped in the form of an absolute or definitive statement, so choices that are stated as broad generalizations or absolute truths are more likely to be false. For example, answers containing words such as "always," "never," "only," "must," and "completely" are more likely to be false than true.
- **Pick the longest answer.** True statements often require more words to make them true.
- **Pick a middle answer rather than the first or last answer.** For example, on a question with four choices, select answer "b" or "c" rather than "a" or "d." Studies show that many instructors have a tendency to place correct answers as middle choices rather than as the first or last choice (Linn & Gronlund, 1995)—perhaps because they think the correct answer will be too obvious or stand out if it's listed as the beginning or end.
- **Check that your answers are in line.** When looking over your test before turning it in, search carefully for questions you may have skipped and intended to go back to later. Sometimes you may skip a test question on a multiple-choice test and forget to skip the number of that question on the

answer form, which will throw off your answers to all the other answers by one space or line. On a computer-scored test, this means that you may get multiple items marked wrong because your answers to them on the answer form are off by one space or line. This can produce a domino effect of wrong answers that will severely damage your test score and test grade. As a damage-prevention measure, check all of your answers to be sure no blank lines or spaces on your answer sheet could set off this damaging domino effect.

- **Don't feel locked into your answers.** When checking your answers on multiple-choice or true–false tests, don't be afraid to change an answer after you've given it more thought. There have been numerous studies on the topic of changing answers on multiple-choice and true–false tests dating back to 1928 (Kuhn, 1988). These studies consistently show that most changed test answers go from being incorrect to correct, resulting in improved test scores (Benjamin, Cavell, & Shallenberger, 1984; Shatz & Best, 1987). In one study of more than 1,500 students' midterm exams in an introductory psychology course, it was found that when students changed their answers they went from right to wrong only 25 percent of the time (Kruger, Wirtz, & Miller, 2005). These findings probably reflect that students may catch a mistake they made when they read the question the first time or discover some information later in the test that causes them to reconsider their first answer. So, don't buy into the common belief that your first answer is always your best answer. If you have good reason to think a change should be made, don't be afraid to make it. However, if you find yourself changing many of your original answers, this may indicate that you were not well prepared for the exam and are just doing a lot of guessing (and second guessing).

THINK ABOUT IT   Journal Entry **5.11**

On exams, do you ever change your original answers?

_____

_____

_____

_____

If you do change answers, what's the usual reason you make changes?

_____

_____

_____

_____

Strategies for Answering Essay Questions

Along with multiple-choice questions, essay questions are among the most commonly used test questions on college exams. Listed here are strategies that will help you reach peak levels of performance on essay questions.

1. Focus on the main ideas.

Make a brief outline or list of bullet points to represent the main ideas you will include in your answers before you begin to write them. This strategy is effective for several reasons:

- An outline will help you remember the major points you intend to make and the order in which you intend to make them. This should help prevent you from forgetting the "big picture" and the most important concepts when you become wrapped up in the details of constructing sentences and choosing words for your answers.
- An outline improves your answer's organization, which is one factor that instructors will consider when determining its grade. (You can make your answer's organization clearer by underlining your major sections or numbering your major points.)

Exhibit 1

Identical twins
Adoption
Parents/family tree

$\dfrac{6}{6}$

1. There are several different studies that scientists conduct, but one study that they conduct is to find out how genetics can influence human behavior in <u>identical twins</u>. Since they are identical, they will most likely end up very similar in behavior because of their identical genetic make up. Although environment has some impact, genetics are still a huge factor and they will, more likely than not, behave similarly. Another type of study is with <u>parents and their family trees</u>. Looking at a subject's family tree will alleviate why a certain person is bi-polar or depressed. It is most likely a cause of a gene in the family tree, even if it was last seen decades ago. Lastly, another study is with <u>adopted children</u>. If an <u>adopted child</u> acts a certain way that is unique to that child, and researchers find the parents' family tree, they will most likely see similar behavior in the parents and siblings as well.

No freewill
No afterlife

$\dfrac{6}{6}$

2. The monistic view of the mind-brain relationship is so strongly opposed and criticized because there is a belief or assumption that <u>freewill</u> is taken away from people. For example, if a person commits a horrendous crime, it can be argued "monastically" that the chemicals in the brain were the reason, and that a person cannot think for themselves to act otherwise. This view limits responsibility.
Another reason that this view is opposed is because it has been said that <u>there is no afterlife</u>. If the mind and brain are one and the same, and there is NO difference, then once the brain is dead and is no longer functioning, so is the mind. Thus, it cannot continue to live beyond what we know today as life. <u>And</u> this goes against many religions, which is why this reason, in particular, is heavily opposed.

> Written answers to two short essay questions given by a college sophomore, which demonstrate effective use of bulleted lists or short outlines to ensure recall of most important points.

- Having an advanced idea of what you will write can reduce your test anxiety. The outline will take care of the answer's organization in advance so that you don't have the added stress of organizing your answer and explaining it while you're writing it.
- If you run out of test time, your instructor will be able to see your outline for any questions that you didn't have time to complete. Even if you didn't have the opportunity to convert it into sentence form, your outline should earn you points because it demonstrates your knowledge of the major ideas called for by the question. In contrast, if you skip an outline and just start writing answers to test questions one at a time, you run the risk of not getting to questions you know well before your time is up; you'll then have nothing written on your test to show what you know about those unfinished questions.

2. Get directly to the point on each essay question.

Avoid elaborate introductions that take up your test time (and your instructor's grading time) but don't earn you any points. For example, an answer that begins with the statement "This is a very interesting question that we had a great discussion on in class . . ." is pointless because it will not add points to your test score. The time available to you on essay tests is often limited, so you can't afford flowery introductions that are pointless—both in their content and in what they would add to your score.

One effective way to focus your response is to include part of the question in the first sentence of your answer. For example, suppose the test says, "Argue for or against capital punishment by explaining how it will or will not reduce the nation's murder rate." Your first sentence could read, "Capital punishment will not reduce the murder rate for the following reasons . . ." Thus, your first sentence becomes your thesis statement, which points you directly to the major points you're going to make in your essay and to earning points for your essay.

3. Answer all essay questions as precisely and completely as possible.

Don't assume that your instructor already knows what you're talking about or will be bored by details. Instead, take the approach that you're writing to someone who knows little or nothing about the subject—as if you're an expert teacher and the reader is a clueless student.

! | **Remember**

As a rule, it's better to overexplain than underexplain your answers to essay questions.

4. Avoid making broad statements or offering personal opinions that lack specific, supporting details.

Always try to reinforce or support your points with specific evidence—facts, statistics, quotes, or examples.

When taking essay tests, take on the role of a criminal lawyer who makes a case by presenting concrete evidence (exhibit A, exhibit B, etc.). Keep in mind that the time allotted for essay tests may not allow you to supply lots of details. Be selective and prioritize: Cite your most powerful or persuasive evidence first. You could always return to add more evidence later if you have time—and space. (See the next suggestion for reserving space.)

5. Leave extra space between your answers to each essay question.

This strategy will enable you to easily add information to your original answer that you may recall at a later point in the test.

6. Edit your work.

When checking your answers to essay questions before turning in your test, proofread what you have written and correct any spelling or grammatical errors you find. Eliminating them is likely to improve your test score. Even if your instructor doesn't explicitly state that grammar and spelling will be counted in determining your grade, these mechanical mistakes may still subconsciously influence your professor's overall evaluation of your written work.

7. Remember that neatness counts.

Research indicates that neatly written essays tend to be scored higher than sloppy ones, even if the answers are essentially the same (Klein & Hart, 1968). This is understandable when you consider that grading essay answers is a time-consuming task that requires your weary instructor to plod through multiple styles of handwriting whose readability may range from crystal clear to cryptic code. Thus, make a point of writing as clearly as possible, and if you finish the test with time to spare, clean up your answers by rewriting any sloppily written words or sentences.

8. Before turning in your test, carefully review and double-check your answers.

This is the critical last step in the process of effective test taking. Sometimes the rush and anxiety of taking a test can cause test takers to overlook details, misread instructions, skip questions unintentionally, or make absentminded mistakes. When taking essay tests that require writing, you may get tired of writing toward the end of the test and get into the mindset that the instant you're done you're going to turn it in and get the whole thing over with. Avoid the temptation to immediately cut out because you're tired or to take off on an ego trip by trying to be among the first and fastest students in class to finish their test. Instead, when you're done, take a little time to step back and look over your answers to be sure you didn't make any mindless mistakes. If you take into account the amount of time and effort you put into preparing for the exam, it's foolish not to take just a few more minutes to be sure you got maximum mileage out of the time and effort you've put into the test.

| THINK ABOUT IT | Journal Entry | **5.12** |

Rate yourself in terms of how frequently you use these test-taking strategies according to this scale:

4 = ALWAYS, 3 = SOMETIMES, 2 = RARELY, 1 = NEVER

1. I take tests in the same seat that I usually sit in to take class notes.   4 3 2 1

2. I answer easier test questions first.   4 3 2 1

3. I use a process-of-elimination approach on multiple-choice tests to eliminate choices until I find one that is correct or appears to be the most accurate option.   4 3 2 1

4. For essay test questions, I outline or map out my ideas before I begin to write the answer.   4 3 2 1

5. I look for information included on the test that may help me answer difficult questions or that may help me remember information I've forgotten.   4 3 2 1

6. I leave extra space between my answers to essay questions in case I want to come back and add more information later.   4 3 2 1

7. I carefully review my work, double-checking for errors and skipped questions before turning in my tests.   4 3 2 1

Posttest Strategies

1. Use your test results as feedback to improve your future performance.

Your test results are not just an end result; they may also be used as a means to an end—to improve your future test performances and your final course grade. Examine your tests carefully when you get them back, being sure to note any written comments your instructor may have made.

If your test results are disappointing, don't become mad or sad; instead, get even by using the results as feedback to assess where you went wrong so that you can avoid making the same mistake again. If your test results were positive, use them to see where you went right so that you can do it the same way again.

2. Ask for additional feedback.

In addition to using your own test results as a source of feedback, actively seek feedback from people whose judgment you trust and value. Three key social resources you can use to obtain feedback on how to improve your performance are your instructors, professionals in your Learning or Academic Support Center, and your peers.

You can make an appointment with your instructors to visit them during office hours and get their feedback on how you might be able to improve your

"People can't learn without feedback. It's not teaching that causes learning. Attempts by the learner to perform cause learning, dependent upon the quality of the feedback and opportunities to use it."

–Grant Wiggins, *Feedback: How Learning Occurs* (1997)

performance. You'll likely find it easier to see your instructors after a test than before it, because most students don't realize that it's just as valuable to seek feedback from their instructors following an exam as it is to try and get last-minute help before it.

Tutors and other learning support professionals on your campus can also be excellent sources of feedback about what adjustments to make in your study habits or test-taking strategies to improve your future performance.

Also, be alert and open to receiving feedback from trusted peers. While feedback from experienced professionals is valuable, don't overlook your peers as another source of feedback on how to improve your performance. You can review your test with another student in class, particularly with students who did exceptionally well. Their tests can provide you with a model of what type of work your instructor expects on exams. Also, ask successful students what they did to be successful—for example, what they did to prepare for the test that enabled them to perform so well.

THINK ABOUT IT   **Journal Entry** **5.13**

Have you ever received feedback from others that you used to improve yourself, your behavior, or your performance?

_____

_____

_____

_____

_____

_____

If yes, what type of feedback did you receive, and what improvement did you make?

_____

_____

_____

_____

_____

_____

Whatever you do, don't let a bad test grade get you mad, sad, or down, particularly if it occurs early in the course when you're still learning the rules of the game. Look at mistakes in terms of what they can do for you, rather than to you. A poor test performance can be turned into a valuable learning experience by using test results as feedback or an error detector to locate the specific source of your mistakes.

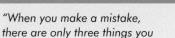

"When you make a mistake, there are only three things you should do about it: admit it; learn from it; and don't repeat it."

–Paul "Bear" Bryant, legendary college football coach

> **!** **Remember**
>
> Your past mistakes shouldn't be ignored or neglected; instead, they should be inspected, detected, and corrected so that you don't replay them on future tests.

Strategies for Pinpointing the Reason for Lost Points on Exams

On test questions where you lost points, identify the stage in the learning process at which the breakdown occurred by asking yourself the following questions.

1. Did you have the information you needed to answer the question correctly?

If you didn't have the information, what was the source of the missing information? Was it information presented in class that didn't get into your notes? If so, take a look at the strategies for improving listening and note-taking habits (**pp. 110–119**). If the missing information was contained in your assigned reading, check whether you're using effective reading strategies (**pp. 120–126**).

2. Did you have the information but not study it because you didn't think it was important?

If this occurred, then you might want to review the study strategies for finding and focusing on the most important information in class lectures and reading assignments (**see Chapter 4**).

3. Did you know the information but not retain it?

This may mean one of three things:

    a. You didn't store the information adequately in your brain, so your memory trace wasn't strong enough for you to recall it at the time you took the test. This suggests that more study time needs to be spent on recitation or rehearsal (**p. 159**).

    b. You may have tried to cram in too much information in too little time just before the exam and didn't give your brain time enough to digest it and store it in long-term memory. The solution here would be to distribute your study time more evenly in advance of the next exam and take advantage of the effective part-to-whole study method (**p. 148**).

    c. You put in enough study time and didn't cram, but you didn't study effectively or strategically. For example, you may have studied for essay questions by just reading over your class and reading notes rather than by writing and rehearsing them. The solution would be to adjust your study strategy so that it better matches or aligns with the type of test you'll be taking (**pp. 158–159**).

4. Did you study the material but not really understand it or learn it deeply?

If so, you may need to self-monitor your comprehension more carefully while studying to monitor or track whether you truly understand the material at a deeper level (**pp. 156–157**).

5. Did you know the information but were not able to retrieve it during the exam?

If you had the information on the "tip of your tongue" during the exam, this indicates that you did retain it and it was stored (saved) in your brain but you couldn't get at it and get it out (retrieve it) when you needed. This error may be corrected by making better use of memory-retrieval cues (**pp. 160–161**).

6. Did you know the answer but just make a careless test-taking mistake?

If so, the solution may be simply to take more time to review your test once you've completed it and check for absentminded errors before turning it in.

◆ Summary and Conclusion

This chapter focused on strategies designed to help you learn deeply, remember longer, and retrieve knowledge from your memory at test time. To improve the effectiveness of studying and retrieving information stored (saved) in your brain, the following strategies were recommended:

- **Give studying your undivided attention.** Don't multitask while studying.
- **Make what you're learning meaningful to you.** Relate what you're learning to something you already know.
- **Compare and contrast.** When you're studying something new, get in the habit of asking yourself, "Is this idea similar to or different from something I've learned already?"
- **Integrate and organize.** Pull together or integrate information from your class notes and assigned reading relating to the same major concept or category, and get them in the same place.
- **Divide and conquer.** Use the distributed practice method of study, which spreads your study time over several shorter sessions rather than cramming it into a single marathon session.
- **Use the part-to-whole study method.** Study the material you need to learn in separate sessions—in advance of the exam. Then just before the exam, restudy the parts at the same time in a final review session.
- **Begin study sessions by reviewing what you learned in your previous session.** This is especially important for sequential or cumulative subjects that build on understanding of previously covered material to learn new concepts (e.g., math).
- **Bring variety to the study process.** Periodically vary the type of academic work you do while studying and the place where you study to combat attention loss and increase interest.

- **Use all of your senses.** Use as many sensory channels as possible, including hearing, seeing, touching, and moving.
- **Study collaboratively.** Form study groups.
- **Self-monitor.** Check on how effectively you're learning while you're learning.
- **Adjust your study strategy to the type of test you will be taking.** Multiple-choice tests require you to recognize correct answers that are presented to you, and essay tests require you to recall and generate the correct answers yourself. For multiple-choice questions, you can prepare by reading over your notes and identifying correct answers. For essay tests, you'll need to rehearse by reciting your answers and creating retrieval cues to help you recall the information at test time.
- **Use your test results as feedback to improve your future performance.** Pinpoint the source or reason for lost points so that you don't make the same mistake again, and identify what you did right to gain points so that you can do it next time.

All specific study and test-taking strategies identified in this chapter are effective because they involve one or more of the following five qualities:

1. Undivided attention and engagement (active involvement);
2. Multiplicity and variety of sensory input;
3. Division of learning into multiple, short learning sessions;
4. Integration and organization of related pieces of information into conceptual categories;
5. Personal reflection that relates what is being learned to what is already known and uses performance results as feedback for improving future performance.

Internet-Based Resources for Further Information on Strategic Studying and Test Taking

For additional information related to the ideas discussed in this chapter, we recommend the following Web sites:

www.academictips.org/acad/index.html

www.dartmouth.edu/~acskills/success/index.html

www.studygs.net/tsttak1.htm

www.campuslife.byu.edu/learning/strategy.php

5.1 Self-Assessment of Learning Strategies and Habits

Look back at the ratings you gave yourself for effective study strategies (**p. 155**) and test-taking strategies (**p. 172**). Add up your score for each of these sets of learning strategies (the maximum score for each set is 7):

Studying = _____

Test Taking = _____

Total Learning Strategy Score = _____

Self-Assessment Questions

1. In which learning strategy area did you score lowest?

2. Do you think that the strategy area in which you scored lowest has anything to do with your lowest course grade at this point in the term?

3. Of the seven specific strategies listed within the area in which you scored lowest, which ones could you immediately put into practice to improve your lowest course grade this term?

4. What is the likelihood that you will put the preceding strategies into practice this term?

5.2 Midterm Self-Evaluation

Since you are near the midpoint of this text book, you may be near the midpoint of your first term in college. At this point in the term you are likely to experience the midterm crunch—a wave of midterm exams and due dates for certain papers and projects. This may be a good time for you to step back and assess your academic progress thus far.

Use the form that follows to list the courses you're taking this term and the grades you are currently receiving in each of these courses. If you do not know what your grade is, take a few minutes to check your syllabus for your instructor's grading policy and add up your scores on completed tests and assignments; this should give you at least a rough idea of where you stand in your courses. If you're having difficulty determining your grade in any course, even after checking your course syllabus and returned tests or assignments, then ask your instructor how you could estimate your current grade.

Course No.	Course Title	Instructor	Grade
1.			
2.			
3.			
4.			
5.			

Self-Assessment Questions

1. Were these the grades you were hoping for? Are you pleased or disappointed with them?

2. Were these the grades you expected to get? (Or were they better or worse than expected?)

3. Do you see any patterns in your performance that suggest specific things you are doing well or things that you need to improve?

4. If you had to pinpoint one action step you could immediately take to improve your lowest course grades, what would it be?

5.3 Calculating Your Midterm Grade Point Average

Use the information in **Snapshot Summary 5.2** to calculate what your grade point average (GPA) would be if these grades turn out to be your final course grades for the term.

1. What is your overall GPA at this point in the term?

2. When this term began, what GPA were you hoping to attain?

3. Do you think your actual GPA at the end of the term will be higher or lower than it is now? Why?

Bad Feedback: Shocking Midterm Grades

Joe Frosh has really enjoyed his first weeks on campus. He has met lots of interesting people and feels that he really fits in socially. He also likes that his college schedule does not require him to be in class for 5 to 6 hours per day, like it did in high school. This is the good news. The bad news is that unlike high school, where his grades were all As and Bs, his first midterm grades in college are three Cs, one D, and one F. He was stunned and a bit depressed by his midterm grades because he thought he was doing well. Since he never received grades this low in high school, he's beginning to think that he is not college material and may flunk out.

Reflection and Discussion Questions

1. What factors may have caused or contributed to Joe's bad start?

2. What are Joe's options at this point?

3. What do you recommend Joe do now to get his grades up and avoid being placed on academic probation?

4. What might Joe do in the future to prevent this midterm setback from happening again?

Diversity and the College Experience

Appreciating the Value of Human Differences for Promoting Learning and Personal Development

Complete the following sentence:

When I hear the word "diversity," the first thoughts that come to my mind are . . .

_____

_____

_____

_____

_____

_____

_____

_____

LEARNING GOAL

To appreciate the value of human differences and acquire skills for making the most of diversity in college and beyond.

◆ The Spectrum of Diversity

The word "diversity" derives from the Latin root *diversus*, meaning "various." Thus, human diversity refers to the variety of differences that exist among the people that comprise humanity (the human species). In this chapter, we use "diversity" to refer primarily to differences among the major groups of people who, collectively, comprise humankind or humanity. The relationship between diversity and humanity is represented visually in the **Figure 6.1**.

SPECTRUM OF DIVERSITY*

HUMANITY→

Gender (male-female)
Age (stage of life)
Race (e.g., White, Black, Asian)
Ethnicity (cultural background)
Socioeconomic status (educational level/income level)
National *citizenship* (citizen of U.S. or another country)
Native (first-learned) **language**
National *origin* (nation of birth)
National *region* (e.g., raised in north/south)
Generation (historical period when people are born and live)
Political ideology (e.g., liberal/conservative)
Religious and *Spiritual* beliefs (e.g., Christian/Buddhist/Muslim)
Family status (e.g., single-parent/two-parent family)
Marital status (single/married)
Parental status (with/without children)
Sexual orientation (heterosexual/gay/lesbian/bisexual/transgender)
Body type (e.g., underweight, overweight, obese)
Physical ability/disability (e.g., able to hear/hearing impaired)
Mental ability/disability (e.g., mentally able/challenged)
Learning ability/disability (e.g., absence/presence of dyslexia)
Learning styles (e.g., visual, auditory, kinesthetic)
Mental health/illness (e.g., absence/presence of depression)

*This list represents some of the major dimensions of human diversity; it does not represent a complete list of all possible forms of human diversity. Also, disagreement exists about certain dimensions of diversity (e.g., whether certain groups should be considered races or ethnic groups).

Figure 6.1 Humanity and Diversity

"We are all brothers and sisters. Each face in the rainbow of color that populates our world is precious and special. Each adds to the rich treasure of humanity."

–Morris Dees, civil rights leader and cofounder of the Southern Poverty Law Center

The relationship between humanity and human diversity is similar to the relationship between sunlight and the spectrum of colors. Just as the sunlight passing through a prism is dispersed into all groups of colors that make up the visual spectrum, the human species that's spread across the planet is dispersed into all groups of people that make up the human spectrum (humanity).

As you can see in Figure 6.1, groups of people differ from one another in numerous ways, including physical features, religious beliefs, mental and physical abilities, national origins, social backgrounds, gender, sexual orientation, and other personal dimensions.

THINK ABOUT IT   Journal Entry   **6.2**

Look at the diversity spectrum in Figure 6.1 and look over the list
of groups that make up the spectrum. Do you notice any groups that are missing from the list that should be added, either because they have distinctive backgrounds or because they have been targets of prejudice and discrimination?

_____

_____

_____

_____

_____

_____

Since diversity has been interpreted (and misinterpreted) in different ways
by different people, we begin by defining some key terms related to diversity
that should lead to a clearer understanding of its true meaning and value.

What Is Race?

A racial group (race) refers to a group of people who share some distinctive
physical traits, such as skin color or other facial characteristics. The U.S. Census Bureau (2000) identifies three races: White, Black, and Asian. However,
as Anderson and Fienberg (2000) caution, racial categories are social–political
constructs (concepts) that are not scientifically based but socially determined.
There continues to be disagreement among scholars about what groups of
people constitute a human "race" or whether distinctive races exist (Wheelright, 2005). No specific genes differentiate one race from another. In other
words, you couldn't do a blood test or any type of internal genetic test to
determine a person's race. Humans have simply decided to categorize people
into races on the basis of certain external differences in physical appearance,
particularly the color of their outer layer of skin. The U.S. Census Bureau
could just as easily have divided people into categories based on such physical

Personal Story   My mother was from Alabama and was dark in skin color, with high cheek
bones and long curly black hair. My father stood approximately 6 feet and had
light brown straight hair. His skin color was that of a Western European with a slight suntan. If you did not
know that my father was of African American descent, you would not have thought of him as Black. All of my
life I have thought of myself as African American, and all of the people who are familiar with me thought of
me as African American. I have lived half of a century with that as my racial description. Several years ago,
after carefully looking through records available on births and deaths in my family history, I discovered that
fewer than 50 percent of my ancestors were of African lineage. Biologically, I am no longer Black. Socially
and emotionally, I still am. Clearly, race is more of a social concept than a biological fact.

—Aaron Thompson

characteristics as eye color (blue, brown, and green) or hair texture (straight, wavy, curly, and frizzy).

The differences in skin color that now occur among humans are likely due to biological adaptations that evolved over long periods among groups of humans who lived in regions of the world with different climatic conditions. For instance, darker skin tones developed among humans who inhabited and reproduced in hotter regions nearer the equator (e.g., Africans), where darker skin enabled them to adapt and survive by providing their bodies with better protection from the potentially damaging effects of the sun (Bridgeman, 2003) and allowing their bodies to better use the vitamin D supplied by sunlight (Jablonski & Chaplin, 2002). In contrast, lighter skin tones developed over time among humans inhabiting colder climates that were farther from the equator (e.g., Scandinavia) to enable their bodies to absorb greater amounts of sunlight, which was in shorter supply in their region of the world.

While humans may display diversity in skin color or tone, the biological reality is that all members of the human species are remarkably similar. More than 98 percent of the genes that make up humans from different racial groups are the same (Bridgeman, 2003; Molnar, 1991). This large amount of genetic overlap among humans accounts for the many similarities that exist, regardless of what differences in color appear at the surface of the skin. For example, all humans have similar external features that give them a "human" appearance and clearly distinguish people from other animal species, all humans have internal organs that are similar in structure and function, and no matter what the color of the outer layer of skin, when it's cut, all humans bleed in the same color.

Personal Story

I was proofreading this chapter while sitting in a coffee shop in the Chicago O'Hare airport. I looked up from my work for a second and saw what appeared to be a white girl about 18 years old. As I lowered my head to return to my work, I did a double-take to look at her again because something about her seemed different or unusual. When I looked at her more closely the second time, I noticed that although she had white skin, the features of her face and hair appeared to be those of an African American. After a couple of seconds of puzzlement, I figured it out: she was an *albino* African American. That satisfied me for the moment, but then I began to wonder: Would it still be accurate to say that she was "Black" even though her skin was white? Would her hair and facial features be sufficient for her to be considered or classified as Black? If yes, then what about someone who had a black skin tone but did not have the typical hair and facial features characteristic of Black people? Is skin color the defining feature of being African American, or are other features equally important? I was unable to answer these questions, but I found it amusing that these thoughts were taking place while I was working on a book dealing with diversity. Later, on the plane ride home, I thought again about that albino African American girl and realized that she was a perfect example of how classifying people into races is based not on objective, scientifically determined evidence but on subjective, socially constructed categories.

—Joe Cuseo

THINK ABOUT IT | **Journal Entry** | **6.3**

What race do you consider yourself to be? Would you say you identify strongly with your race, or are you rarely conscious of it?

_____

_____

_____

_____

What Is Culture?

Culture may be defined as a distinctive pattern of beliefs and values learned by a group of people who share the same social heritage and traditions. In short, culture is the whole way in which a group of people has learned to live (Peoples & Bailey, 1998); it includes style of speaking (language), fashion, food, art, music, values, and beliefs.

Cultural differences can exist within the same society (multicultural society), within a single nation (domestic diversity), or across different nations (international diversity).

A major advantage of culture is that it helps bind its members together into a supportive, tight-knit community; however, it can also blind them from other cultural perspectives. Since culture shapes the way people think, it can cause groups of people to view the world solely through their own cultural lens or frame of reference (Colombo, Cullen, & Lisle, 1995). Optical illusions are a good illustration of how cultural perspectives can blind people, or lead them to inaccurate perceptions. For instance, compare the lengths of the two lines in **Figure 6.2.**

If you perceive the line on the right to be longer than the line on the left, welcome to the club. Virtually all Americans and people from Western cultures perceive the line on the right to be longer. Actually, both lines are

© Jupiterimages Corporation.

Culture is a distinctive pattern of beliefs and values that develop among a group of people who share the same social heritage and traditions.

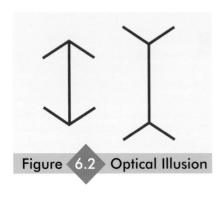

Figure 6.2 Optical Illusion

equal in length. (If you don't believe it, take out a ruler and check it out.) Interestingly, this perceptual error is not made by people from non-Western cultures that live in environments populated with circular structures rather than structures with linear patterns and angled corners, like Westerners use (Segall, Campbell, & Herskovits, 1966).

The key point underlying this optical illusion is that cultural experiences shape and sometimes distort perceptions of reality. We think we are seeing things objectively or "as they really are," but we are often seeing things subjectively from our limited cultural vantage point. Being open to the viewpoints of diverse people who perceive the world from different cultural vantage points widens our range of perception and helps us overcome our "cultural blind spots." As a result, we tend to perceive the world around us with greater clarity and accuracy.

What Is an Ethnic Group?

An ethnic group (ethnicity) is a group of people who share the same culture. Thus, culture refers to *what* an ethnic group has in common and an ethnic group refers to a group of people *who* share the same culture. Unlike a racial group, whose members share physical characteristics that they are born with and that have been passed on biologically, an ethnic group's shared characteristics that have been passed on through socialization—that is, their common characteristics that have been *learned* or acquired through shared social experiences.

Major ethnic groups in the United States include:

- Native Americans (American Indians)
  - Cherokee, Navaho, Hopi, Alaskan natives, Blackfoot, etc.
- African Americans (Blacks)
  - People who have cultural roots in the continent of Africa, Caribbean Islands, etc.
- Hispanic Americans (Latinos)
  - People who have cultural roots in Mexico, Puerto Rico, Central America, South America, etc.
- Asian Americans
  - Cultural descendents from Japan, China, Korea, Vietnam, etc.
- European Americans (Whites)
  - Descendents from Scandinavia, England, Ireland, Germany, Italy, etc.

Currently, European Americans are the majority ethnic group in the United States because they account for more than 50 percent of the American population. Native Americans, African Americans, Hispanic Americans, and Asian Americans are considered to be ethnic minority groups because each of these groups represents less than 50 percent of the American population.

| **THINK ABOUT IT** | **Journal Entry** | **6.4** |

Which ethnic group or groups do you belong to or identify with? What are the most common cultural values shared by your ethnic group or groups?

_____

_____

_____

_____

_____

_____

Student Perspective

"I'm the only person from my 'race' in class."

–Hispanic student commenting on why he felt uncomfortable in his Race, Ethnicity, & Gender class

As with the concept of race, whether a particular group of people is defined as an ethnic group can be arbitrary, subjective, and interpreted differently by different groups of people. Currently, the only races recognized by the U.S. Census Bureau are White, Black, and Asian; Hispanic is not defined as a race but is classified as an ethnic group. However, among those who checked "some other race" in the 2000 Census, 97 percent were Hispanic. This fact has been viewed by Hispanic advocates as a desire for their "ethnic" group to be reclassified as a racial group (Cianciotto, 2005).

This disagreement illustrates how difficult it is to conveniently categorize groups of people into particular racial or ethnic groups. The United States will continue to struggle with this issue because the ethnic and racial diversity of its population is growing and members of different ethnic and racial groups are forming cross-ethnic and interracial families. Thus, it is becoming progressively more difficult to place people into distinct categories based on their race or ethnicity. For example, by 2050, the number of people who will identify themselves as being of two or more races is projected to more than triple, growing from 5.2 million to 16.2 million (U.S. Census Bureau, 2008).

| **Personal Story** | As the child of a Black man and a White woman, someone who was born in the racial melting pot of Hawaii, with a sister who's half Indonesian but who's usually mistaken for Mexican or Puerto Rican, and a brother-in-law and niece of Chinese descent, with some blood relatives who resemble Margaret Thatcher and others who could pass for Bernie Mac, family get-togethers over Christmas take on the appearance of a UN General Assembly meeting. I've never had the option of restricting my loyalties on the basis of race, or measuring my worth on the basis of tribe.

—Barack Obama (2006)

What Is Humanity?

It is important to realize that human *variety* and human *similarity* exist side by side and complement each other. Diversity is a "value that is shown in mutual respect and appreciation of similarities and differences" (Public Service Enterprise Group, 2009). Experiencing diversity not only enhances our appreciation of the unique features of different cultures but also provides us with a larger perspective on the universal aspects of the human experience that are common to all humans, no matter what their particular cultural background may be. For example, despite our racial and cultural differences, all of us express the same emotions with the same facial expressions (See **Figure 6.3**).

Humans all over the world display the same facial expressions when experiencing certain emotions. See if you can detect the emotions being expressed in the following faces. (To find the answers, turn your book upside down.)

Answers: The emotions shown. Top, left to right: anger, fear, and sadness. Bottom, left to right: disgust, happiness, and surprise.

All images © JupiterImages Corporation.

Figure ◆ **6.3**

THINK ABOUT IT   **Journal Entry**   **6.5**

List three human experiences that you think are universal—that is, they are experienced by all humans in all cultures:

1. _____

2. _____

3. _____

Other human characteristics that anthropologists have found to be shared across all groups of people in every corner of the world include storytelling, poetry, adornment of the body, dance, music, decoration of artifacts, families, socialization of children by elders, a sense of right and wrong, supernatural beliefs, explanations of diseases and death, and mourning of the dead (Pinker, 1994). Although different ethnic groups may express these shared experiences in different ways, these universal experiences are common to all humans.

!

Remember

Diversity represents variations on the common theme of humanity. Although people have different cultural backgrounds, they are still cultivated from the same soil—they are all grounded in the common experience of being human.

Thus, different cultures associated with different ethnic groups may be viewed simply as variations on the same theme: being human. You may have heard the question "We're all human, aren't we?" The answer to this important question is "yes and no." Yes, we are all the same, but not in the same way.

A good metaphor for understanding this apparent contradiction is to visualize humanity as a quilt in which we are all joined together by the common thread of humanity—by the common bond of being human. Yet the different patches that make up the quilt represent diversity—the distinctive or unique cultures that comprise our common humanity. The quilt metaphor acknowledges the identity and beauty of all cultures. It differs from the old American melting pot metaphor, which viewed differences as something that should be melted down or eliminated, or the salad bowl metaphor, which suggested that America is a hodgepodge or mishmash of different cultures thrown together without any common connection. In contrast, the quilt metaphor suggests that the cultures of different ethnic groups should be recognized and celebrated. Nevertheless, our differences can be woven together to create a unified whole—as in the Latin expression *E pluribus Unum* ("Out of many, one")—the motto of the United States, which you will find printed on all U.S. coins.

To appreciate diversity and its relationship to humanity is to capitalize on the power of our differences (diversity) while still preserving our collective strength through unity (humanity).

"We are all the same, and we are all unique."

–Georgia Dunston, African American biologist and research specialist in human genetics

"We have become not a melting pot but a beautiful mosaic."

–Jimmy Carter, 39th president of the United States and winner of the Nobel Peace Prize

> **Remember**
>
> By learning about diversity (our differences), we simultaneously learn more about our commonality (our shared humanity).

Personal Story

Student Perspective

When you see me, do not look at me with disgrace.

Know that I am an African-American

Birthed by a woman of style and grace.

Be proud
   To stand by my side.

Hold your head high Like me.

Be proud.
   To say you know me.

Just as I stand by you, proud to be me.

–A poem by Brittany Beard, first-year student

When I was 12 years old and living in New York City, I returned from school one Friday afternoon and my mother asked me if anything interesting happened at school that day. I mentioned to her that the teacher went around the room, asking students what we had eaten for dinner the night before. At that moment, my mother began to become a bit agitated and nervously asked me, "What did you tell the teacher?" I said, "I told her and the rest of the class that I had pasta last night because my family always eats pasta on Thursdays and Sundays." My mother exploded and fired back at me, "Why couldn't you tell her that we had steak or roast beef!" For a moment, I was stunned and couldn't figure out what I had done wrong or why I should have lied about eating pasta. Then it suddenly dawned on me: My mother was embarrassed about being an Italian American. She wanted me to hide our family's ethnic background and make it sound like we were very "American." After this became clear to me, a few moments later, it also became clear to me why her maiden name was changed from the Italian-sounding DeVigilio to the more American-sounding Vigilis and why her first name was changed from Carmella to Mildred. Her family wanted to minimize discrimination and maximize their acculturation (absorption) into American culture.

I never forgot this incident because it was such an emotionally intense experience. For the first time in my life, I became aware that my mother was ashamed of being a member of the same group to which every other member of my family belonged, including me. After her outburst, I felt a combined rush of astonishment and embarrassment. However, these feelings eventually faded and my mother's reaction ended up having the opposite effect on me. Instead of making me feel inferior or ashamed about being Italian American, her reaction that day caused me to become more aware of, and take more pride in, my Italian heritage.

As I grew older, I also grew to understand why my mother felt the way she did. She grew up in America's "melting pot" era—a time when different American ethnic groups were expected to melt down and melt away their ethnicity. They were not to celebrate diversity; they were to eliminate it.

—Joe Cuseo

What Is Individuality?

It's important to keep in mind that *individual* differences within the same racial or ethnic group are greater than the *average* differences between two different groups. For example, although you live in a world that is conscious of differences among races, differences in physical attributes (e.g., height and weight) and behavior patterns (e.g., personality characteristics) among individuals within the same racial group are greater than the average differences among various racial groups (Caplan & Caplan, 1994).

As you proceed through this chapter, keep in mind the following distinctions among humanity, diversity, and individuality:

- **Diversity.** We are all members of *different groups* (e.g., different gender and ethnic groups).
- **Humanity.** We are all members of the *same group* (the human species).
- **Individuality.** Each of us is a *unique person* who is different from any person in any group to which we may belong.

> "Every human is, at the same time, like all other humans, like some humans, and like no other human."
>
> –Clyde Kluckholn, American anthropologist

◆ Major Forms or Types of Diversity

International Diversity

Moving beyond our particular country of citizenship, we are also members of an international world that includes multiple nations. Global interdependence and international collaboration are needed to solve current international problems, such as global warming and terrorism. Communication and interaction across nations are now greater than at any other time in world history, largely because of rapid advances in electronic technology (Dryden & Vos, 1999; Smith, 1994). Economic boundaries between nations are also breaking down due to increasing international travel, international trading, and development of multinational corporations. Today's world really is a "small world after all," and success in it requires an international perspective. By learning from and about different nations, you become more than a citizen of your own country; you become cosmopolitan—a citizen of the world.

Taking an international perspective allows you to appreciate the diversity of humankind. If it were possible to reduce the world's population to a village of precisely 100 people, with all existing human ratios remaining the same, the demographics of this "world village" would look something like this:

> 60 Asians, 14 Africans, 12 Europeans, 8 Latin Americans, 5 from the United States and Canada, and 1 from the South Pacific.
> 51 males, 49 females
> 82 non-Whites, 18 Whites
> 67 non-Christians, 33 Christians
> 80 living in substandard housing
> 67 unable to read
> 50 malnourished and 1 dying of starvation
> 33 without access to a safe water supply
> 39 who lack access to improved sanitation
> 24 without any electricity (and of the 76 who do have electricity, most would only use it for light at night)
> 7 with access to the Internet
> 1 with a college education
> 1 with HIV
> 2 near birth; 1 near death
> 5 who control 32 percent of the entire world's wealth; all 5 wold be citizens of the United States
> 33 who receive and attempt to live on just 3 percent of the village's income

Source: Family Care Foundation (2005).

Ethnic and Racial Diversity

America is rapidly becoming a more racially and ethnically diverse nation. In 2008, the minority population in the United States reached an all-time high of 34 percent of the total population. The population of ethnic minorities is now growing at a much faster rate than the White majority. This trend is expected to continue, and by the middle of the twenty-first century, the minority population will have grown from one-third of the U.S. population to more than one-half (54 percent), with more than 60 percent of the nation's children expected to be members of minority groups (U.S. Census Bureau, 2008).

By 2050, the U.S. population is projected to be more than 30 percent Hispanic (up from 15 percent in 2008), 15 percent Black (up from 13 percent), 9.6 percent Asian (up from 5.3 percent), and 2 percent Native Americans (up from 1.6 percent). The Native Hawaiian and Pacific Islander population is expected to more than double between 2008 and 2050. In the same time frame, the percentage of Americans who are White will drop from 66 percent (2008) to 46 percent (2050). As a result of these population trends, ethnic and racial minorities will become the "new majority" because they will constitute the majority of Americans by the middle of the twenty-first century. (See **Figure 6.4.**)

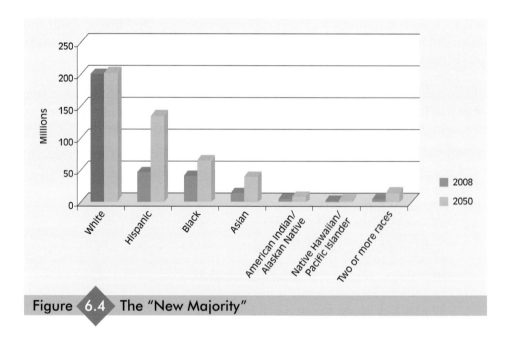

Figure **6.4** The "New Majority"

◆ Diversity and the College Experience

There are more than 3,000 public and private colleges in the United States. They vary in size (small to large) and location (urban, suburban, and rural), as well as their purpose or mission (research universities, comprehensive state universities, liberal arts colleges, and community colleges). This variety makes the American higher-education system the most diverse and accessible in the world. The diversity of educational opportunities in American colleges and universities reflects the freedom of opportunity in the United States as a democratic nation (American Council on Education, 2008).

The U.S. system of higher education is also becoming more diverse with respect to the people enrolled in the system. (See the **Snapshot Summary 6.1** below for recent statistics related to diversity in U.S. community colleges.) The ethnic and racial diversity of students in American colleges and universities is rapidly rising. In 1960, Whites made up almost 95 percent of the total college population; in 2005, that percentage had decreased to 69 percent. At the same time, there was increase in the percentage of Asian, Hispanic, Black, and Native American students attending college (*Chronicle of Higher Education*, 2003).

The rise in ethnic and racial diversity on American campuses is particularly noteworthy when viewed in light of the historical treatment of minority groups in the United States. In the early nineteenth century, education was not a right but a privilege available only to those who could afford to attend private schools. Members of certain minority groups were left out of the educational process altogether or were forced to be educated in racially segregated settings. For example, Americans of color were once taught in separate, segregated schools that were typically inferior in terms of educational facilities. This continued until the groundbreaking U.S. Supreme Court ruling in *Brown v. Board of Education* in 1954, which changed the face of education for people of color by ruling that "separate educational facilities are inherently unequal." The decision made it illegal for Kansas and 20 other states to deliver education in segregated classrooms.

"Of all the civil rights for which the world has struggled and fought for 5,000 years, the right to learn is undoubtedly the most fundamental."

—W. E. B. Du Bois, African-American sociologist, historian, and civil rights activist

Snapshot Summary

6.1

Diversity in America's Community Colleges

- 58% of community college students are women
- 53% are 22 years of age or older
- Among full-time students, 50% are employed part time and 27% are employed full time
- Among part-time students, 50% are employed full time and 33% are employed part time
- 39% are the first in their family to attend college
- 36% are members of a minority ethnic or racial group
- 17% are single parents

Source: American Association of Community Colleges (2009).

THINK ABOUT IT   Journal Entry   **6.6**

Are you the first in your family to attend college?

_____

_____

Whether yes or no, how does that make you feel?

_____

_____

_____

_____

_____

_____

_____

_____

Personal Story

My mother was a direct descendent of slaves and moved with her parents from the Deep South at the age of 17. My father lived in an all-Black coal mining camp, into which my mother and her family moved in 1938. My father remained illiterate because he was not allowed to attend public schools in eastern Kentucky.

In the early 1960s my brother, my sister, and I were integrated into the White public schools. Physical violence and constant verbal harassment caused many other Blacks to forgo their education and opt for jobs in the coal mines at an early age. But my father remained constant in his advice to me: "It doesn't matter if they call you n_____; but don't you ever let them beat you by walking out on your education." He would say to me, "Son, you will have opportunities that I never had. Just remember, when you do get that education, you'll never have to go in those coal mines and have them break your back. You can choose what you want to do, and then you can be a free man."

My parents, who could never provide me with monetary wealth, truly made me proud of them by giving me the gift of insight and an aspiration for achievement.

—*Aaron Thompson*

THINK ABOUT IT   **Journal Entry**   **6.7**

1. What diverse groups do you see represented on your campus?

_____

_____

_____

_____

2. Are there groups on your campus that you did not expect to see or to see in such large numbers?

_____

_____

_____

_____

3. Are there groups on your campus that you expected to see but do not see or see in smaller numbers than you expected?

_____

_____

_____

_____

◆ The Benefits of Experiencing Diversity

Diversity Promotes Self-Awareness

Learning from people with diverse backgrounds and experiences sharpens your self-knowledge and self-insight by allowing you to compare and contrast your life experiences with others whose life experiences differ sharply from your own. This comparative perspective gives you a reference point for viewing your own life, which places you in a better position to see more clearly how your unique cultural background has influenced the development of your personal beliefs, values, and lifestyle. By viewing your life in relation to the lives of others, you see more clearly what is distinctive about yourself and how you may be uniquely advantaged or disadvantaged.

When students around the country were interviewed about their diversity experiences in college, they reported that these experiences often helped them learn more about themselves and that their interactions with students from different races and ethnic groups produced "unexpected" or "jarring" self-insights (Light, 2001).

!

Remember

The more opportunities you create to learn from others who are different from yourself, the more opportunities you create to learn about yourself.

Diversity Stimulates Social Development

Interacting with people from various groups widens your social circle. By widening the pool of people with whom you have contact, you increase your capability and confidence in relating to people with varied life experiences, as well as your ability to converse with people on a wider range of topics. Just as seeking variety in what you eat provides greater stimulation to your taste buds, seeking variety in the people with whom you interact stimulates your social life and social skills. Research indicates that students who have more diversity experiences in college report higher levels of satisfaction with their college experience (Astin, 1993).

Student Perspective

"I remember that my self-image was being influenced by the media. I got the impression that women had to look a certain way. I dyed my hair, wore different clothes, more makeup . . . all because magazines, TV, [and] music videos 'said' that was beautiful. Luckily, when I was 15, I went to Brazil and saw a different, more natural beauty and came back to America more as myself. I let go of the hold the media image had on me."

–First-year college student

"Variety is the spice of life."

–American proverb

Viva la difference! ("Long live difference!")

–Famous French saying

"Variety is the spice of life, O'Toole; but at this firm conformity is the meat and potatoes."

Diversity Enriches a College Education

Diversity magnifies the power of a college education because it helps liberate you from the tunnel vision of ethnocentric (culture-centered) and egocentric (self-centered) thinking, enabling you to get beyond yourself and your own culture to see yourself in relation to the world around you. Just as the various subjects you take in the college curriculum open your mind to multiple perspectives, so does your experience with people from varied backgrounds; it equips you with a wide-focus lens that allows you to take a multicultural perspective. A multicultural perspective helps you become aware of cultural "blind spots" and avoid the dangers of group think—the tendency for tight, like-minded groups of people to think so much alike that they overlook flaws in their own thinking that can lead to poor choices and faulty decisions (Janis, 1982).

Diversity Strengthens Learning and Critical Thinking

Research consistently shows that we learn more from people who are different from us more than we do from people who are similar to us (Pascarella, 2001; Pascarella & Terenzini, 2005). When your brain encounters something that is unfamiliar or different than you're accustomed to, you must stretch beyond your mental comfort zone and work harder to understand it because doing so forces you to compare and contrast it to what you already know (Acredolo & O'Connor, 1991; Nagda, Gurin, & Johnson, 2005). This mental "stretch" requires the use of extra psychological effort and energy, which strengthens and deepens learning.

A good example of how "group think" can lead to ethnocentric decisions that are ineffective (and unjust).

Diversity Promotes Creative Thinking

Experiences with diversity supply you with a broader base of knowledge and a wider range of thinking styles that better enable you to think outside your own cultural box or boundaries. In contrast, limiting your number of cultural vantage points is akin to limiting the variety of mental tools you can use to solve new problems, thereby limiting your creativity.

Drawing on different ideas from people with diverse backgrounds and bouncing your ideas off them is a great way to generate energy, synergy, and serendipity—unanticipated discoveries and creative solutions.

"When the only tool you have is a hammer, you tend to see every problem as a nail."

–Abraham Maslow, humanistic psychologist, best known for his self-actualization theory of achieving human potential

Diversity Enhances Career Preparation and Success

Learning about and from diversity has a practical benefit: It better prepares you for the world of work. Whatever career you may choose to pursue, you are likely to find yourself working with employers, employees, co-workers, customers, and clients from diverse cultural backgrounds. America's workforce is now more diverse than at any other time in the nation's history, and it will grow ever more diverse. For example, the percentage of America's working-age population that represents members of minority groups is expected to grow from 34 percent in 2008 to 55 percent in 2050 (U.S. Bureau of Labor Statistics, 2008).

In addition to increasing diversity in America, today's work world is characterized by a global economy. Greater economic interdependence among nations, more international trading (imports and exports), more multinational corporations, and almost-instantaneous worldwide communication increasingly occur—thanks to advances in the World Wide Web (Dryden & Vos, 1999; Smith, 1994). Because of these trends, employers of college graduates now seek job candidates with the following skills and attributes: sensitivity to human differences, the ability to understand and relate to people from different cultural backgrounds, international knowledge, and foreign language skills (Fixman, 1990; National Association of Colleges & Employers, 2003; Office of Research, 1994; Smith, 1997). In one national survey, policymakers, business leaders, and employers all agreed that college graduates should be more than just "aware" or "tolerant" of diversity; they should have *experience* with diversity (Education Commission of the States, 1995).

The wealth of diversity on college campuses today represents an unprecedented educational opportunity. You may never again be a member of a community that includes so many people from such a rich variety of backgrounds. Seize this opportunity! You're now in the right place at the right time to experience the people and programs that can infuse and enrich the quality of your college education with diversity.

> "Empirical evidence shows that the actual effects on student development of emphasizing diversity and of student participation in diversity activities are overwhelmingly positive."
>
> –Alexander Astin, *What Matters in College* (1993)

◆ Stumbling Blocks and Barriers to Experiencing Diversity: Stereotypes, Prejudice, and Discrimination

Stereotypes

The word "stereotype" derives from a combination of two roots: "stereo" (to look at in a fixed way) and "type" (to categorize or group together, as in the word "typical"). Thus, stereotyping is viewing individuals of the same type (group) in the same (fixed) way. In effect, stereotyping ignores or disregards a person's individuality; instead, all people who share a similar group characteristic (e.g., race or gender) are viewed as having the same personal characteristics—as in the expression, "You know what they are like; they're all the same." Stereotypes involve bias, which literally means "slant." A bias can be either positive or negative. Positive bias results in a favorable stereotype (e.g., "Italians are great lovers"); negative bias produces an unfavorable stereotype (e.g., "Italians are in the Mafia"). **Snapshot Summary 6.2** lists some common stereotypes.

Snapshot Summary

6.2

Examples of Common Stereotypes

- Muslims are terrorists
- Whites can't jump (or dance)
- Blacks are lazy
- Asians are brilliant in math
- Irish are alcoholics
- Gay men are feminine; lesbian women are masculine
- Jews are cheap
- Hispanic men are abusive to women
- Men are strong
- Women are weak

THINK ABOUT IT | **Journal Entry** | **6.8**

1. Have you ever been stereotyped, such as based on your appearance or group membership? If so, how did it make you feel and how did you react?

_____

_____

_____

_____

_____

_____

2. Have you ever unintentionally perceived or treated someone in terms of this group stereotype rather than as an individual? What assumptions did you make about that person? Was that person aware of, or affected by, your stereotyping?

_____

_____

_____

_____

_____

_____

Personal Story   When I was 6 years old, I was told by another 6-year-old from a different racial group that all people of my race could not swim. Since I could not swim at that time and she could, I assumed she was correct. I asked a boy, who happened to be of the same racial group as that little girl, if that statement were true; he responded: "Yes, it is true." Since I was from an area where few other African Americans were around to counteract this belief about Blacks, I bought into this stereotype for a long time until I finally took swimming lessons as an adult. I am now a lousy swimmer after many lessons because I did not even attempt to swim until I was an adult. The moral of this story is that group stereotypes can limit the confidence and potential of individuals who are members of the stereotyped group.

—Aaron Thompson

Whether you are male or female, don't let gender stereotypes limit your career options.

"Let us all hope that the dark clouds of racial prejudice will soon pass away and the deep fog of misunderstanding will be lifted from our fear-drenched communities, and in some not too distant tomorrow the radiant stars of love and brotherhood will shine over our great nation."

–Martin Luther King, Jr., civil rights activist and clergyman

Prejudice

If virtually all members of a stereotyped group are judged or evaluated in a negative way, the result is prejudice. (The word "prejudice" literally means to "pre-judge.") Technically, prejudice may be either positive or negative; however, the term is most often associated with a negative prejudgment or stigmatizing—associating inferior or unfavorable traits with people who belong to the same group. Thus, prejudice may be defined as a negative judgment, attitude, or belief about another person or group of people, which is formed before the facts are known. Stereotyping and prejudice often go hand in hand because individuals who are placed in a negatively stereotyped group are commonly prejudged in a negative way.

Someone with a prejudice toward a group typically avoids contact with individuals from that group. This enables the prejudice to continue unchallenged because there is little or no chance for the prejudiced person to have positive experiences with a member of the stigmatized group that could contradict or disprove the prejudice. Thus, a vicious cycle is established in which the prejudiced person continues to avoid contact with individuals from the stigmatized group, which, in turn, continues to maintain and reinforce the prejudice.

Discrimination

Literally translated, the term "discrimination" means "division" or "separa-tion." Whereas prejudice involves a belief or opinion, discrimination involves an *action* taken toward others. Technically, discrimination can be either negative or positive—for example, a discriminating eater may be careful about eating only healthy foods. However, the term is most often associated with a negative action that results in a prejudiced person treating another person, or group of people, in an unfair way. Thus, it could be said that discrimination is prejudice put into action. Hate crimes are examples of extreme discrimination because they are acts motivated solely by prejudice against members of a stigmatized group. Victims of hate crimes may have their personal property damaged or they may be physically assaulted, sometimes referred to as "gay bashing" if the victim is a homosexual. Other forms of discrimination are more subtle and may take place without people being fully aware that they are discriminating. For example, evidence shows that some White, male college professors tend to treat female students and students from ethnic or racial minority groups dif-ferently than they do males and nonminority students. In particular, females and minority students in classes taught by White, male instructors tend to:

- Receive less eye contact from the instructor,
- Be called on less frequently in class,
- Be given less time to respond to questions asked by the instructor in class, and
- Have less contact with the instructor outside of class (Hall & Sandler, 1982, 1984; Sedlacek, 1987; Wright, 1987).

In most of these cases, the discriminatory treatment received by these fe-male and minority students was subtle and not done consciously or deliber-ately by the instructors (Green, 1989). Nevertheless, these unintended actions are still discriminatory, and they may send a message to minority and female students that their ideas are not worth hearing or that they are not as capable as other students (Sadker & Sadker, 1994).

> "See that man over there?
> 'Yes.'
> 'Well, I hate him.'
> 'But you don't know him.'
> "That's why I hate him.'"
>
> –Gordon Allport, *The Nature of Prejudice* (1954)

Student Perspective

> "A lot of us never asked ques-tions in class before—it just wasn't done, especially by a woman or a girl, so we need to realize that and get into the habit of asking questions and challenging if we want to—regardless of the reactions of the profs and other students."
>
> –Adult female college student (Wilkie & Thompson, 1993)

> "The best way to beat prejudice is to show them. On a midterm, I got 40 points above the average. They all looked at me differently after that."
>
> –Mexican American student (Nemko, 1988)

THINK ABOUT IT   Journal Entry   6.9

Prejudice and discrimination can be subtle and only begin to surface when the social or emotional distance among members of different groups grows closer. Rate your level of comfort (high, moderate, or low) with the following situations. Someone from another racial group:

1. Going to your school;	high	moderate	low
2. Working in your place of employment;	high	moderate	low
3. Living on your street as a neighbor;	high	moderate	low
4. Living with you as a roommate;	high	moderate	low
5. Socializing with you as a personal friend;	high	moderate	low
6. Being your most intimate friend or romantic partner; or	high	moderate	low
7. Being your partner in marriage.	high	moderate	low

For any item you rated "low," what do you think was responsible for the low rating?

_____

_____

_____

_____

_____

Snapshot Summary

 6.3

Stereotypes and Prejudiced Belief Systems about Group Inferiority

Ethnocentrism. Considering one's own culture or ethnic group to be "central" or "normal," and viewing different cultures as "deficient" or "inferior." For example, people who are ethnocentric might claim that another culture is "weird" or "abnormal" for eating certain animals that they consider unethical to eat, even though they eat certain animals that the other culture would consider unethical to eat.

Racism. Prejudice or discrimination based on skin color. For example, Cecil Rhodes (Englishman and empire builder of British South Africa), once claimed, "We [the British] are the finest race in the world and the more of the world we inhabit the better it is for the human race." Currently, racism is exemplified by the Klu Klux Klan, a domestic terrorist group that believes in the supremacy of the White race and considers all other races to be inferior.

"The Constitution of the United States knows no distinction between citizens on account of color."

–Frederick Douglass, abolitionist, author, advocate for equal rights for all people, and former slave

Classism. Prejudice or discrimination based on social class, particularly toward people of low socioeconomic status. For example, a classist

might focus only on the contributions made by politicians and wealthy industrialists to America, ignoring the contributions of poor immigrants, farmers, slaves, and pioneer women.

Nationalism. Excessive interest and belief in the strengths of one's own nation without acknowledging its mistakes or weaknesses, the needs of other nations, or the common interests of all nations. For example, "blind patriotism" blinds people to the shortcomings of their own nation, causing patriots to view any questioning or criticism of their nation as disloyalty or being "unpatriotic" (as in the slogans, "America: right or wrong" and "America: love it or leave it!")

Regionalism. Prejudice or discrimination based on the geographical region of a nation in which an individual has been born and raised. For example, a Northerner thinking that all Southerners are racists.

Student Perspective

"I would like to change the entire world, so that we wouldn't be segregated by continents and territories."

–College sophomore

Religious Bigotry. Denying the fundamental human right of other people to hold religious beliefs or to hold religious beliefs that differ from one's own. For example, an atheist might force nonreligious (secular) beliefs on others, or a member of a religious group may believe that people who hold different religious beliefs are immoral or sinners.

Xenophobia. Extreme fear or hatred of foreigners, outsiders, or strangers. For example, someone might believe that all immigrants should be kept out of the country because they will increase the crime rate.

Anti-semitism. Prejudice or discrimination toward Jews or people who practice the religion of Judaism. For example, someone could claim to hate Jews because they're the ones who "killed Christ."

Genocide. Mass murdering of one group by another group. An example is the Holocaust during World War II in which millions of Jews were murdered. Other examples include the murdering of Cambodians under the Khmer Rouge, the murdering of Bosnian Muslims in the former country of Yugoslavia, and the slaughter of the Tutsi minority by the Hutu majority in Rwanda.

Terrorism. Intentional acts of violence against civilians that are motivated by political or religious prejudice. An example would be the September 11, 2001, attacks on the United States.

Ageism. Prejudice or discrimination based on age, particularly toward the elderly. For example, an agiest might believe that all "old" people are bad drivers with bad memories.

Ableism. Prejudice or discrimination toward people who are disabled or handicapped—physically, mentally, or emotionally. For example, someone shows ableism by avoiding interaction with handicapped people because of anxiety about not knowing what to say or how to act around them.

Sexism. Prejudice or discrimination based on sex or gender. For example, a sexist might believe that no one should vote for a female president because she would be too "emotional."

Heterosexism. Belief that heterosexuality is the only acceptable sexual orientation. For example, using the slang "fag" or "queer" as an insult or put down; or believing that gays should not have the same legal rights and opportunities as heterosexuals shows heterosexism.

Homophobia. Extreme fear or hatred of homosexuals. For example, people who engage in gay bashing (acts of violence toward gays) or who create and contribute to antigay Web sites show homophobia.

THINK ABOUT IT   Journal Entry   **6.10**

Have you ever held a prejudice against a particular group of people?

_____

If you have, what was the group, and how do you think your prejudice developed?

_____

_____

_____

_____

The following practices and strategies may be used to accept and appreciate individuals from other groups toward whom tou may hold prejudices, stereotypes, or subtle biases that bubble beneath the surface of your conscious awareness.

1. Consciously avoid preoccupation with physical appearances.

Go deeper and get beneath the superficial surface of appearances to judge people not in terms of how they look but in terms of who they are and how they act. Remember the old proverb "It's what's inside that counts." Judge others by the quality of their personal character, not by the familiarity of their physical characteristics.

2. Perceive each person with whom you interact as having a unique personal identity.

Make a conscious effort to see each person with whom you interact not merely as a member of a same group but as a unique individual. Form your impressions of each person case by case rather than by using some rule of thumb.

This may seem like an obvious and easy thing to do, but research shows that humans have a natural tendency to perceive and conceive of individuals who are members of unfamiliar groups as being more alike (or all alike) than members of their own group (Taylor, Peplau, & Sears, 2006). Thus, you may have to consciously resist this tendency to overgeneralize and "lump together" individuals into homogenous groups and make an intentional attempt to focus on treating each person you interact with as a unique human.

"The common eye sees only the outside of things, and judges by that. But the seeing eye pierces through and reads the heart and the soul, finding there capacities which the outside didn't indicate or promise."

–Samuel Clemens, a.k.a. Mark Twain; writer, lecturer, and humorist

"Stop judging by mere appearances, and make a right judgment."

–Bible, John 7:24

"You can't judge a book by the cover."

–Hit record, 1962, by Elias Bates, a.k.a. Bo Diddley (Note: a bo diddley is a one-stringed African guitar)

> ! **Remember**
>
> While it is valuable to learn about different cultures and the common characteristics shared by members of the same culture, differences exist among individuals who share the same culture. Don't assume that all individuals from the same cultural background share the same personal characteristics.

Interacting and Collaborating with Members of Diverse Groups

Once you overcome your biases and begin to perceive members of diverse groups as unique individuals, you are positioned to take the next step of interacting, collaborating, and forming friendships with them. Interpersonal contact between diverse people takes you beyond multicultural awareness and moves you up to a higher level of diversity appreciation that involves intercultural interaction. When you take this step to cross cultural boundaries, you transform diversity appreciation from a value or belief system into an observable action and way of living.

Your initial comfort level with interacting with people from diverse groups is likely to depend on how much experience you have had with diversity before college. If you have had little or no prior experience interacting with members of diverse groups, it may be more challenging for you to initiate interactions with diverse students on campus.

Student Perspective

"I am very happy with the diversity here, but it also frightens me. I have never been in a situation where I have met people who are Jewish, Muslim, atheist, born-again, and many more."

–First-year student (Erickson, Peters, & Strommer, 2006)

However, if you have had little or no previous experience with diversity, the good news is that you have the most to gain from experiencing diversity. Research consistently shows that when humans experience social interaction that differs radically from their prior experiences they gain the most in terms of learning and cognitive development (Piaget, 1985; Acredolo & O'Connor, 1991).

| **THINK ABOUT IT** | **Journal Entry** | **6.11** |

Rate the amount or variety of diversity you have experienced in the following settings:

1. The high school you attended	high	moderate	low
2. The college or university you now attend	high	moderate	low
3. The neighborhood in which you grew up	high	moderate	low
4. Places where you have worked or been employed	high	moderate	low

Which setting had the most and least diversity? What do you think accounts for this difference?

_____

_____

_____

_____

_____

_____

What follows is a series of strategies for meeting and interacting with people from diverse backgrounds.

1. Intentionally create opportunities for interaction and conversation with individuals from diverse groups.

Consciously resist the natural tendency to associate only with people who are similar to you. One way to do this is by intentionally placing yourself in situations where individuals from diverse groups are nearby and potential interaction can take place. Research indicates that meaningful interactions and friendships are more likely to form among people who are in physical proximity to one another (Latané, Liu, Nowak, Bonevento, & Zheng, 1993). Studies show that stereotyping and prejudice can be sharply reduced if contact between members of different racial or ethnic groups is frequent enough to allow time for the development of friendships (Pettigrew, 1998). You can create this condition in the college classroom by sitting near students from different ethnic or racial groups or by joining them if you are given the choice to select whom you will work with in class discussion groups and group projects.

2. Take advantage of the Internet to "chat" with students from diverse groups on your campus or with students in different countries.

Electronic communication can be a more convenient and more comfortable way to initially interact with members of diverse groups with whom you have had little prior experience. After you've communicated successfully *online*, you may then feel more comfortable about interacting with them *in person*. Online and in-person interaction with students from other cultures and nations can give you a better understanding of your own culture and country, as well as increase awareness of its customs and values that you may have taken for granted (Bok, 2006).

3. Seek out the views and opinions of classmates from diverse backgrounds.

For example, during or after class discussions, ask students from different backgrounds if there was any point made or position taken in class that they would strongly question or challenge. Seeking out divergent (diverse) viewpoints has been found to be one of the best ways to develop critical thinking skills (Kurfiss, 1988).

4. Join or form discussion groups with students from diverse backgrounds.

You can gain exposure to diverse perspectives by joining or forming groups of students who differ from you in terms of such characteristics as gender, age, race, or ethnicity. You might begin by forming discussion groups composed of students who differ in one way but are similar in another way. For instance, form a learning group of students who have the same major as you do but who differ with respect to race, ethnicity, or age. This strategy gives the diverse members of your group some common ground for discussion (your major) and can raise your group's awareness that although you may be members of different groups you can, at the same time, be similar with respect to your educational goals and life plans.

> **! Remember**
>
> Including diversity in your discussion groups not only provides social variety, but also promotes the quality of the group's thinking by allowing its members to gain access to the diverse perspectives and life experiences of people from different backgrounds.

5. Form collaborative learning teams.

A learning team is more than a discussion group or a study group. It moves beyond discussion to collaborative learning—in other words, members of a learning team "colabor" (work together) as part of a joint and mutually supportive effort to reach the same goal. Studies show that when individuals from different ethnic and racial groups work collaboratively toward the attainment of a common goal, it reduces racial prejudice and promotes interracial friendships (Allport, 1954; Amir, 1976). These positive findings may be explained as follows: If individuals from diverse groups work together on the same team, no one is a member of an "out" group (them); instead, all are members of the same "in" group: us (Pratto et al., 2000; Sidanius et al., 2000).

◆ Summary and Conclusion

Diversity refers to differences among groups of people who, together, comprise humanity. Experiencing diversity enhances our appreciation of the unique features of different cultures, and it provides us with a larger perspective on those aspects of the human experience that are common to all people, no matter what their particular cultural background happens to be.

Culture is a distinctive pattern of beliefs and values learned by a group of people who share the same social heritage and traditions. A major advantage of culture is that it helps bind groups of people into supportive, tight-knit communities. However, it can also lead its members to view the world solely through their own cultural lens, known as ethnocentrism, which can blind them from seeing the world and from taking on other cultural perspectives. Ethnocentrism can contribute to stereotyping—viewing individual members of the same group in the same way and thinking they all have similar personal characteristics.

If members of a stereotyped group are judged or evaluated in a negative way, the result is prejudice—a negative prejudgment about another person or group of people, which is formed before the facts are known. Stereotyping and prejudice often go hand in hand because if the stereotype is negative, individual members of the stereotyped group are then prejudged in a negative way. Discrimination takes prejudice one step further by converting the negative prejudgment into action that results in unfair treatment of others. Thus, discrimination is prejudice put into action.

If stereotyping and prejudice are overcome, you are then positioned to experience diversity and reap its multiple benefits, which include sharpened self-awareness, social stimulation, broadened personal perspectives, deeper learning and higher-level thinking, and career success.

College campuses today have such diversity that the educational opportunities available are unprecedented. This may be the only time in your life when you are the member of an organization or community that includes so many diverse members. Seize this unique opportunity to experience the diversity of people and programs available to you and profit from the power of diversity.

Internet-Based Resources for Further Information on Diversity

For additional information related to the ideas discussed in this chapter, we recommend the following Web sites:

www.tolerance.org

www.amnesty.org

www.amnesty.org/en/universal-declaration-human-rights-anniversary/decision-text

Name _____   Date _____

6.1 Multi-Group Self-Awareness

You can be members of multiple groups at the same time, and your membership in these groups can influence your personal development and self-identity. In the figure that follows consider the shaded center circle to be yourself and the six nonshaded circles to be six groups you belong to that you think have influenced your personal development or personal identity.

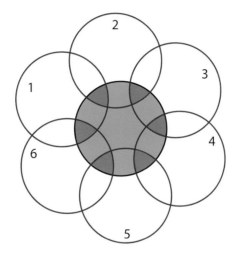

Fill in the nonshaded circles with the names of groups to which you belong that have had the most influence on your personal development. You can use the diversity spectrum that appears on the first page of this chapter to help you identify different groups. Do not feel you have to come up with six groups and fill all six circles. What is more important is to identify those groups that have had a significant influence on your personal development or identity.

Self-Assessment Questions

1. Which one of your groups has had the greatest influence on your personal identity, and why?

2. Have you ever felt limited or disadvantaged by being a member of any group or groups?

3. Have you ever felt that you experienced advantages or privileges because of your membership in any group or groups?

6.2 Switching Group Identity

Imagine you were to be born again as a member of a different racial or ethnic group.

1. What group would you want it to be? Why?

2. With your new group identity, what things would change in your personal life?

3. What things would remain the same in your life even though your group identity has changed?

Source: Adapted from University of New Hampshire (2001).

6.3 Intercultural Interview

Find a student, faculty member, or administrator on campus whose cultural background is different than yours, and ask if you could interview that person about his or her culture. Use the following questions in your interview:

1. How is "family" defined in your culture, and what are the traditional roles and responsibilities of different family members?

2. What are the traditional gender (male vs. female) roles associated with your culture? Are they changing?

3. What is your culture's approach to time (e.g., Is there an emphasis on punctuality? Is doing things fast valued or frowned upon?)

4. What are your culture's staple foods or favorite foods?

5. What cultural traditions or rituals are highly valued and commonly practiced?

6. What special holidays are celebrated?

6.4 Hidden Bias Test

Go to www.tolerance.org/activity/test-yourself-hidden-bias and take one or more of the hidden bias tests on the Web site. These tests assess subtle bias with respect to gender, age, Native Americans, African Americans, Asian Americans, religious denominations, sexual orientations, disabilities, and body weight. You can assess whether you have a bias toward any of these groups.

Self-Assessment Questions

1. Did the results reveal any bias that you were unaware of?

2. Did you think the assessment results were accurate or valid?

3. What do you think best accounts for or explains your results?

4. If your parents and best friends took the test, how do you think their results would compare with yours?

Hate Crime: A Racially Motivated Murder

Jasper County, Texas, has a population of approximately 31,000 people. In this county, 80 percent of the people are White, 18 percent are Black, and 2 percent are of other races. The county's poverty rate is considerably higher than the national average, and its average household income is significantly lower. In 1998, the mayor, president of the Chamber of Commerce, and two councilmen were Black. From the outside, Jasper appeared to be a town with racial harmony, and its Black and White leaders were quick to state there was racial harmony in Jasper.

However, on June 7, 1998, James Byrd, Jr., a 49-year-old African American male, was walking home along a road one evening and was offered a ride by three White males. Rather than taking Byrd home, Lawrence Brewer (31), John King (23), and Shawn Berry (23), three individuals linked to White-supremacist groups, took Byrd to an isolated area and began beating him. They then dropped his pants to his ankles, painted his face black, chained Byrd to their truck, and dragged him for approximately 3 miles. The truck was driven in a zigzag fashion to inflict maximum pain on the victim. Byrd was decapitated after his body collided with a culvert in a ditch alongside the road. His skin, arms, genitalia, and other body parts were strewn along the road, while his torso was found dumped in front of a Black cemetery. Medical examiners testified that Byrd was alive for much of the dragging incident.

While in prison awaiting trial, Brewer wrote letters to King and other inmates. In one letter, Brewer wrote: "Well, I did it and am no longer a virgin. It was a rush and I'm still licking my lips for more." Once the trials were completed, Brewer and King were sentenced to death. Both Brewer and King, whose bodies were covered with racist tattoos, had been on parole before the incident, and they had previously been cellmates. King had spent an extensive amount of time in prison, where he began to associate with White males in an environment in which each race was pitted against the other.

As a result of the murder, Byrd's family created the James Byrd Foundation for Racial Healing in 1998. On January 20, 1999, a wrought iron fence that separated Black and White graves for more than 150 years in Jasper Cemetery was removed in a special unity service. Members of the racist Ku Klux Klan have since visited the gravesite of Byrd several times, leaving racist stickers and other marks that have angered the Jasper community and Byrd's family.

Sources: San Antonio Express News (September 17, 1999), *Louisiana Weekly* (February 3, 2003), *Houston Chronicle* (June 14, 1998).

Reflection and Discussion Questions

1. What factors do you think were responsible for causing this incident to take place?

2. Could this incident have been prevented? If yes, how? If not, why not?

3. What do you think will be the long-term effects of this incident on the town?

4. How likely do you think it is that an incident like this could take place in your hometown or near your college campus?

5. If this event took place in your hometown, how would you and members of your family and community react?

Managing Money and Minimizing Debt

7

Balancing Saving, Spending, Learning, and Earning

Complete the following sentence with the first thought that comes to your mind:

For me, money is . . . .

_____

_____

_____

_____

_____

LEARNING GOAL

To become more self-aware, knowledgeable, and strategic with respect to managing your money and financing your college education.

In addition to managing time, a personal resource you need to manage to be successful in college (and life) is money. Managing time and managing money have a lot in common. Both require self-awareness of how these resources are spent; both can be saved, or else you could run out of either one of them. Poor time management can also cost people money. For example, a report from H&R Block® indicates that procrastinating on filing tax returns costs Americans an average of $400 a year due to errors resulting from last-minute rushing to meet the deadline (Kasper, 2004). How you spend your time and money often represents the true test of what really matters to you and what you truly value.

Beginning college often means the beginning of greater personal independence and greater demands for economic self-sufficiency, critical thinking about consumerism, and effective management of personal finances. The importance of money management for college students is growing for two major reasons. One is the rising cost of a college education, which is causing more students to work while in college and to work more hours per week (Levine

& Cureton, 1998). The rising cost of a college education is also requiring students to make more complex decisions about what options (or combination of options) they will use to meet their college expenses. Unfortunately, research indicates that many students today are not choosing financial strategies that contribute most effectively to their educational success in college and their long-term financial success after college (King, 2005).

A second reason money management is growing in importance for college students is the availability and convenience of credit cards. For students today, credit cards are easy to get, easy to use, and easy to abuse. College students can do everything right, such as getting solid grades, getting involved on campus, and getting work experience before graduating, but a poor credit history due to irresponsible use of credit cards in college can reduce students' chances of obtaining credit after college and their chances of being hired after graduation. Credit reporting agencies or bureaus collect information about how well you make credit-card payments and report your credit score to credit-card companies and banks. Potential employers will check your credit score as an indicator or predictor of how responsible you will be as an employee because of a statistical relationship between using credit cards responsibly and being a responsible employee. Thus, being irresponsible with credit while you're in college can affect your ability to land a job after (or during) college. Your credit score report will also affect your likelihood of qualifying for car loans and home loans, as well as your ability to rent an apartment (Pratt, 2008).

Furthermore, research indicates that accumulating high levels of debt while in college is associated with higher levels of stress (Kiecolt et al., 1986), lower academic performance (Susswein, 1995), and greater risk of withdrawing from college (Ring, 1997). On the positive side of the ledger, studies show that when students learn to use effective money-management strategies, they can decrease unnecessary spending, prevent accumulation of significant debt, and reduce personal stress (Health & Soll, 1996; Walker, 1996).

> "If we command our wealth, we shall be rich and free; if our wealth commands us, we are poor indeed."
>
> –Edmund Burke, eighteenth-century author, political philosopher, and supporter of the American Revolution

◆ Strategies for Managing Money Effectively

Developing Financial Self-Awareness

Developing any good habit begins with the critical first step of self-awareness. Developing the habit of effective money management begins with awareness of your cash flow—the amount of money you have flowing in and flowing out. As illustrated in **Figure 7.1**, cash flow can be tracked by:

- Watching how much money you have coming in (income) versus going out (expenses or expenditures); and
- Watching how much money you have accumulated but not spent (savings) versus how much money you've borrowed but not paid back (debt).

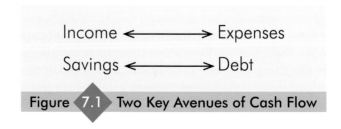

Income ⟷ Expenses

Savings ⟷ Debt

Figure 7.1 Two Key Avenues of Cash Flow

Income for college students typically comes from one or more of the following sources:

- Scholarships or grants, which don't have to be paid back,
- Loans, which must be repaid,
- Salary earned from part-time or full-time work,
- Personal savings,
- Gifts or other forms of monetary support from parents and other family members.

Your sources of expenses or expenditures may be classified into three categories:

1. **Basic needs or essential necessities**—expenses that tend to be fixed because you cannot do without them (e.g., expenses for food, housing, tuition, textbooks, phone, transportation to and from school, and health-related costs).
2. **Incidentals or extras**—expenses that tend to be flexible because spending money on them is optional or discretionary (i.e., you choose to spend at your own discretion or judgment); these expenses typically include:
   - Money spent on entertainment, enjoyment, or pleasure (e.g., music, movies, and spring-break vacations); and
   - Money spent primarily for reasons of promoting personal status or self-image (e.g., buying expensive, brand name products; fashionable clothes; jewelry; and other personal accessories).
3. **Emergency expenses**—unpredicted, unforeseen, or unexpected costs (e.g., money paid for doctor visits and medicine resulting from illnesses or accidents).

THINK ABOUT IT   Journal Entry   **7.2**

What do you estimate to be your two or three most expensive incidentals (optional purchases)?

_____

_____

_____

_____

_____

Do you think you should reduce these expenses or eliminate them altogether?

_____

_____

_____

_____

_____

Developing a Money-Management Plan

Once you're aware of the amount of money you have coming in (and from what sources) and the amount of money you're spending (and for what reasons), the next step is to develop a plan for managing your cash flow. The bottom line is to ensure that the money coming in (income) is equal to or greater than the money going out (expenses). If the amount of money you're spending exceeds the amount you have coming in, you're "in the red" or have negative cash flow.

Strategic Selection and Use of Financial Tools for Tracking Cash Flow

Several financial tools or instruments can be used to track your cash flow and manage your money. These cash-flow instruments include:

- Checking accounts;
- Credit cards;
- Charge cards; and
- Debit cards.

Checking Account

Long before credit cards were created, a checking account was the method most people used to keep track of their money. Many people still use checking accounts in addition to (or instead of) credit cards.

A checking account may be obtained from a bank or credit union; its typical costs include a deposit ($20–$25) to open the account, a monthly service fee (e.g., $10), and small fees for checks. Some banks charge customers a service fee based on the number of checks written, which is a good option if you don't plan to write many checks each month. If you maintain a high enough balance of money deposited in your account, the bank may not charge any extra fees, and if you're able to maintain an even higher balance, the bank may also pay you interest—known as an interest-bearing checking account.

Along with your checking account, banks usually provide you with an automatic teller machine (ATM) card that you can use to get cash. Look for a checking account that does not charge you fees for ATM transactions but provides this as a free service with your account. Also, look for a checking account that doesn't charge you if your balance drops below a certain minimum figure.

Strategies for Using Checking Accounts Effectively

- Whenever you write a check or make an ATM withdrawal, immediately subtract its amount from your balance—i.e., amount of money remaining in your account to determine your new balance.
- Keep a running balance in your checkbook; it will ensure that you know exactly how much money you have in your account at all times. This will reduce the risk that you'll write a check that "bounces," i.e., a check that you don't have enough money in the bank to cover. If you do bounce a check, you'll probably have to pay a charge to the bank and possibly to the business that attempted to cash your bounced check.

- Double-check your checkbook balance with each monthly statement you receive from the bank. Be sure to include the service charges your bank makes to your account that appear on your monthly statement. This practice will make it easier to track errors—on either your part or the bank's part. (Banks can and do make mistakes occasionally.)

Advantages of a Checking Account

A checking account has several advantages:

- You can carry checks instead of cash.
- You have access to cash at almost any time through an ATM machine.
- It allows you to keep a visible track record of income and expenses in your checkbook.
- A properly managed checking account can serve as a good credit reference for future loans and purchases.

Credit Card (e.g., MasterCard®, Visa®, or Discover®)

A credit card is basically money loaned to you by the credit-card company that issues you the card, which you pay back to the company monthly. You can pay the whole bill or a portion of the bill each month—as long as some minimum payment is made. However, for any remaining (unpaid) portion of your bill, you are charged a high interest rate, which is usually about 18 percent.

Strategies for Selecting a Credit Card

If you decide to use a credit card, pay attention to its annual percentage rate (APR). This is the interest rate you pay for previously unpaid monthly balances, and it can vary depending on the credit-card company. Credit-card companies also vary in terms of their annual service fee. You will likely find companies that charge higher interest rates tend to charge lower annual fees, and vice versa. As a general rule, if you expect to pay the full balance every month, you're probably better off choosing a credit card that does not charge you an annual service fee. On the other hand, if you think you'll need more time to make the full monthly payments, you may be better off with a credit-card company that offers a low interest rate.

Another feature that differentiates one credit-card company from another is whether or not you're allowed a "grace period"—i.e., a certain period of time after you receive your monthly statement during which you can pay back the company without paying added interest fees. Some companies may allow you a grace period of a full month, while others may provide none and begin charging interest immediately after you fail to pay on the bill's due date.

Credit cards may also differ in terms of their credit limit (a.k.a. a credit line or line of credit), which refers to the maximum amount of money the credit-card company will make available to you. If you are a new customer, most companies will set a credit limit beyond which you will not be granted any additional credit.

Advantages of a Credit Card

If a credit card is used responsibly, it has some key advantages as a money-management tool. Its features can provide the following advantages:

- It helps you track your spending habits because the credit-card company sends you a monthly statement that includes an itemized list of all your card-related purchases. This list provides you with a paper trail of *what* you purchased that month and *when* you purchased it.
- It provides the convenience of making purchases online, which may save you some time and money that would otherwise be spent traveling to and from stores.
- It allows access to cash whenever and wherever you need, because any bank or ATM machine that displays your credit card's symbol will give you cash up to a certain limit, usually for a small transaction fee. Keep in mind that some credit-card companies charge a higher interest rate for cash advances than purchases.
- It enables you to establish a personal credit history. If you use a credit card responsibly, you can establish a good credit history that can be used later in life for big-ticket purchases such as a car or home. In effect, responsible use of a credit card shows others from whom you wish to seek credit (borrow money) that you're financially responsible.

Remember

Do not buy into the belief that the only way you can establish a good credit history is by using a credit card. It's not your only option; you can establish a good credit history through responsible use of a checking account and by paying your bills on time.

Strategies for Using Credit Cards Responsibly

While there may be advantages to using a credit card, you only reap those advantages if you use your card strategically. If not, the advantages of a credit card will be quickly and greatly outweighed by its disadvantages. Listed here are some key strategies for using a credit card in a way that maximizes its advantages and minimizes its disadvantages.

- **Use a credit card only as a convenience for making purchases and tracking the purchases you make; do not use it as a tool for obtaining a long-term loan.**

A credit card's main money-management advantage is that it allows you to make purchases with plastic instead of cash. The credit card allows you the convenience of not carrying around cash and enables you to receive a monthly statement of your purchases from the credit-card company, which makes it easier for you to track and analyze your spending habits.

The "credit" provided by a credit card should be seen simply as a short-term loan that must be paid back at the end of every month.

Remember

Do not use credit cards for long-term credit or long-term loans because their interest rates are outrageously high. Paying such a high rate of interest for a loan represents an ineffective (and irresponsible) money-management strategy.

- **Limit yourself to one card.**

The average college student has 2.8 credit cards (United College Marketing Service, cited in Pratt, 2008). More than one credit card just means more accounts to keep track of and more opportunities to accumulate debt. You don't need additional credit cards from department stores, gas stations, or any other profit-making business because they duplicate what your personal credit card already does (plus they charge extremely high interest rates for late payments).

- **Pay off your balance each month in full and on time.**

If you pay the full amount of your bill each month, this means that you're using your credit card effectively to obtain an interest-free, short-term (1-month) loan. You're just paying principal—the total amount of money borrowed and nothing more. However, if your payment is late and you need to pay interest, you end up paying more for the items you purchased than their actual ticket price. For instance, if you have an unpaid balance of $500 on your monthly credit bill for merchandise purchased the previous month and you are charged the typical 18 percent credit-card interest rate for late payment, you end up paying $590: $500 (merchandise) + $90 (18 percent interest to the credit-card company).

Credit-card companies make their money or profit from the interest they collect from cardholders who do not pay back their credit on time. Just as procrastinating about doing your work is a poor time-management habit, procrastinating about paying your credit-card bills is a poor money-management habit that can cost you dearly in the long run because of the high interest rate you pay.

Pay your total balance on time and avoid paying these huge interest rates to credit-card companies, which allow them to get rich at your expense. If you cannot pay the total amount owed at the end of the month, pay off as much of it as you possibly can—rather than making the minimum monthly payment. If you keep making only the minimum payment each month and continue using your credit card, you'll begin to pile up huge amounts of debt.

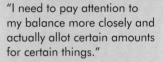

Student Perspective

"I need to pay attention to my balance more closely and actually allot certain amounts for certain things."

–First-year student

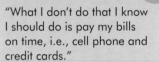

Student Perspective

"What I don't do that I know I should do is pay my bills on time, i.e., cell phone and credit cards."

–First-year student

"You'll never get your credit card debt paid off if you keep charging on your card and make only the minimum monthly payment. Paying only the minimum is like using a Dixie cup to bail water from a sinking boat."

–Eric Tyson, financial counselor and national best-selling author of *Personal Finance for Dummies* (2003)

!

Remember

If you keep charging on your credit card while you have an unpaid balance or debt, you no longer have a grace period to pay back your charges; instead, interest is charged immediately on all your purchases.

Take Action!

Credit Cardholders' Bill of Rights Act of 2009

7.1

Congress passed legislation in 2009 that enacted certain protections for consumers who use credit cards. Here are the specific reforms that affect college students:

- Creditors are forbidden from offering credit to consumers under the age of 18 (unless they are emancipated under state law, or the consumer's parent or legal guardian is the primary account holder).

- College students without a cosigner will have their credit line limited to the greater amount of 20 percent of their annual gross income or $500. The collective amount of credit available on all credit cards will be limited to 30 percent of the student's annual gross income.

- Creditors are not allowed to open a credit-card account for a college student who does not have a verifiable annual gross income or already has a credit-card account with that creditor or any of its affiliates (Chan, 2009).

THINK ABOUT IT Journal Entry **7.3**

1. Do you have a credit card? Do you have more than one?

_____

_____

2. If you have at least one credit card, do you pay off your entire balance each month?

_____

_____

3. If you don't pay off your entire balance each month, what would you say is your average unpaid balance per month?

_____

_____

4. What changes would you have to make in your money-management habits to be able to pay off your entire balance each month?

_____

_____

_____

_____

_____

Charge Card

A charge card works similar to a credit card in that you are given a short-term loan for 1 month; the only difference is that you must pay your bill in full at the end of each month and you cannot carry over any debt from one month to the next. Its major disadvantage relative to a credit card is that it has less flexibility—no matter what your expenses may be for a particular month, you must still pay up or lose your ability to acquire credit for the next month. For people who habitually fail to pay their monthly credit-card bill on time, this makes a charge card a smarter money-management tool than a credit card because the cardholder cannot continue to accumulate debt.

Debit Card

A debit card looks almost identical to a credit card (e.g., it has a MasterCard or Visa logo), but it works differently. When you use a debit card, money is immediately taken out or subtracted from your checking account. Thus, you're only using money that's already in your account (rather than borrowing money), and you don't receive a bill at the end of the month. If you attempt to purchase something with a debit card that costs more than the amount of money you have in your account, your card will not allow you to do so. Just like a bounced check, a debit card will not permit you to pay out any money that is not in your account. Like a check or ATM withdrawal, a purchase made with a debit card should immediately be subtracted from your balance.

Like a credit card, a major advantage of the debit card is that it provides you with the convenience of "plastic"; unlike a credit card, it prevents you from spending beyond your means and accumulating debt. For this reason, financial advisors often recommend using a debit card rather than a credit card (Knox, 2004; Tyson, 2003).

"Never spend your money before you have it."

–Thomas Jefferson, third president of the United States and founder of the University of Virginia

Snapshot Summary   7.1

Financial Literacy: Understanding the Language of Money Management

As you can tell from the variety of financial terms that have already been used in this chapter, you have to acquire a vocabulary of fiscal terms to be able to understand your financial options and transactions; in other words, you have to become financially literate. As you read the financial vocabulary terms listed here, place a checkmark next to any term whose meaning you didn't already know.

Account. A formal business arrangement in which a bank provides financial services to a customer (e.g., checking account or savings account).

Balance. The amount of money in an account or the amount of unpaid debt.

Budget. A plan for coordinating income and expenses such that sufficient money is available to cover or pay for expenses.

Credit. Money obtained with the understanding that it will be paid back, either with or without interest.

Credit Line (a.k.a. Credit Limit). The maximum amount of money (credit) made available to a borrower.

Debt. The amount of money owed.

Default. Failure to meet a financial obligation (e.g., a student who fails to repay a college loan defaults on that loan).

Deferred Student Payment Plan. A plan that allows student borrowers to temporarily defer or postpone loan payments for some acceptable reason (e.g., to pursue an internship or volunteer work after college).

Fixed Interest Rate. A loan with an interest rate that will remain the same for the entire term of the loan.

Grant. Money received that does not have to be repaid.

Gross Income. Income generated before taxes and other expenses have been deducted.

Insurance Premium. The amount paid in regular installments to an insurance company to remain insured.

Interest. The amount of money paid to a customer for deposited money (as in a bank account) or money paid by a customer for borrowed money (e.g., interest on a loan); interest is usually calculated as a percentage of the total amount of money deposited or borrowed.

Interest-Bearing Account. A bank account that earns interest if the customer keeps a sufficiently large sum of money in the bank.

Loan Consolidation. Consolidating (combining) separate student loans into one new, larger loan to make the process of tracking, budgeting, and repayment easier (loan consolidation typically requires the borrower to pay slightly more interest).

Loan Premium. The amount of money loaned without interest.

Merit-Based Scholarship. Money awarded to a student on the basis of performance or achievement that does not have to be repaid.

Need-Based Scholarship. Money awarded to a student on the basis of financial need that does not have to be repaid.

Net Income. Money remaining or earned after all expenses and taxes have been paid.

Principal. The total amount of money borrowed or deposited, not counting interest.

Variable Interest Rate. An interest rate on a loan that can vary or be changed by the lender.

Yield. Revenue or profit produced by an investment beyond the original amount invested (e.g., higher lifetime income and other monetary benefits acquired from a college education that exceed the amount of money invested in or spent on a college education).

THINK ABOUT IT   **Journal Entry** **7.4**

Which of the terms in the previous list were new to you?

_____

_____

_____

_____

_____

Do any of these terms apply to your current financial situation or money-management plans?

_____

_____

_____

_____

_____

_____

Sources of Income for Financing Your College Education

Free Application for Federal Student Aid

Free Application for Federal Student Aid (FASFA) is the application used by the U.S. Department of Education to determine aid eligibility for students. A formula is used to determine each student's estimated family contribution (EFC), which is the amount of money the government has determined a family can contribute to the educational costs of the student. No fee is charged to complete the application, and you should complete it annually to determine your eligibility to receive financial aid, whether you believe you are eligible or not. See the Financial Aid Office on your campus for the FAFSA form and for help in completing the form.

Scholarships

Scholarships are available from many sources, including the institution you choose to attend. They are awarded based on various criteria that may include a written essay, ACT or SAT scores, and high school grade point average (GPA). In addition to academic scholarships, scholarships are awarded based on organizations you may have been a part of, race or ethnicity, the region of the country you live in, athletics, artistic talents, and so on. It is important to remember that all scholarships are competitive and deadlines are observed by the awarding agencies or institution. Be aware of the application material deadlines and submit your materials well in advance of these deadlines.

You should contact the Financial Aid Office of the institution you are attending to find available scholarships. You can also conduct an Internet search to find many sites that offer scholarship information, but it is important to remember that you should not enter credit-card or bank account information on any site.

Grants

Grants are considered to be gift aids and generally are not required to be repaid. The Federal Pell Grant is the largest grant program and provides need-based aid to low-income undergraduate students. The amount of the grant depends on certain criteria such as (a) the anticipated contribution of the family to the student's education (EFC), (b) the cost of attending the postsecondary institution, (c) the enrollment status of the student (part time or full time), and (d) whether the student attends for a full academic year or less.

Loans

Student loans are required to be repaid once a student graduates from college. The Federal Perkins Loan is a 5 percent simple-interest loan awarded to exceptionally needy students. The repayment for this loan begins 9 months after a student is no longer enrolled at least half time.

The Federal Subsidized Stafford Loan is available to students enrolled at least half time and has a fixed interest rate that is established each year on July 1, which is based on the 91-day Treasury bill plus 2.5 percent. The federal government pays the interest on the loan while the student is enrolled. The repayment for this loan begins 6 months after a student is no longer enrolled half time.

The Federal Unsubsidized Stafford Loan is not based on need and has the same interest rate as the Federal Subsidized Stafford Loan. You are responsible for paying the interest on this loan while you're enrolled in college. The loan amount limits for Stafford loans are based on the classification of the student (e.g., freshman or sophomore). To apply for each of these loans, you must complete the FASFA form.

Keep in mind that federal and state regulations require that if you are receiving financial aid, you must maintain "satisfactory academic progress." In most cases this means that you must do the following:

1. Maintain a satisfactory GPA. (Your entire academic record will be reviewed, even if you have paid for any of the classes with your own resources.)
2. Make satisfactory academic progress. (Your academic progress will be evaluated at least once per year, usually at the end of each spring semester.)
3. Complete a degree or certificate program within an established period of time. (Check with your institution's Financial Aid Office for details.)

Take Action!

Federal Loan versus Private Loan: A Critical Difference

7.2

Private loans and federal loans are totally different and unrelated types of loans. Here are the key differences:

- Federal loans have fixed interest rates that are comparatively low (currently less than 7 percent).

- Private loans have variable interest rates that are very high (currently more than 15 percent) and can go higher at any time.

Warning: Despite the high cost of private loans, they are the fastest-growing type of loans taken out by college students, largely because of aggressive, misleading, and sometimes irresponsible or unethical advertising on loan-shopping websites. Students sometimes think they're getting a federal loan only to find out later they have taken on a more expensive private loan.

Source: Kristof (2008).

> **Remember**
>
> Private lenders are like credit-card companies; they charge extremely high interest rates, and they can go even higher at any time. They should not be used as a primary loan to help pay for college; they should only be used as a last resort—when no other options are available for covering your college expenses.

Salary Earnings

If you find yourself relying on your salary to pay for college tuition, check with your employer to see whether the company offers tuition reimbursement. You should also check with the Billing Office on your campus to determine whether payment plans are available for tuition costs. These plans may differ in terms of how much is due, deadlines for payments, and how any remaining debt owed to the institution is dealt with at the end of the term. You may find that the institution you are attending will not allow you to register for the following term until the previous term is completely paid for.

Research shows that when students work on campus (versus off campus) they are more likely to succeed in college (Astin, 1993; Pascarella & Terenzini, 1991, 2005). This is probably because students become more connected to the college when they work on campus (Tinto, 1993) and because on-campus employers are more flexible than off-campus employers in allowing students to meet their academic commitments while they are employed. For instance, campus employers are more willing to schedule students' work hours around their class schedule and allow students to modify their work schedule when their academic workload increases (e.g., midterm and finals). Thus, we strongly encourage you to seek on-campus employment and capitalize on its capacity to promote your academic success.

THINK ABOUT IT   **Journal Entry** **7.5**

Do you need to work part time to meet your college expenses?

_____

If yes, do you have to work more than 15 hours per week to make ends meet?

_____

If yes, is there anything you can do to change that?

_____

_____

_____

_____

_____

_____

Monetary Gifts from Family or Friends

Money received as a gift from family or friends who are supporting your education should be used wisely. Although necessities such as food and transportation support your academic goals, money given to you by friends or family members should be used to pay for tuition and textbooks first. Remaining funds can be used for other expenses.

Personal Savings

When possible, you should try to save a portion of your income for unforeseeable expenses that may occur (e.g., car repairs). Having money set aside may prevent you from being forced to use credit cards that put you in debt and may result in your paying interest on that debt until it is paid off.

"A penny saved is a penny earned."

–Benjamin Franklin, eighteenth-century inventor, newspaper writer, and cosigner of the *Declaration of Independence*

Financial Tools for Saving Money

If you're taking in more money than you're spending, you are saving money, and you can invest the money you've saved in an account that will allow you to earn interest on your savings. This account can help you build up a cash reserve that can be used for future needs or used immediately for emergencies. Two major financial tools available to you for earning interest on savings are:

1. Savings accounts; and
2. Money-market accounts.

Savings Account

A savings account can be opened at virtually any bank and will earn you interest on the money placed in your account. Usually, no minimum amount of money needs to be deposited to open a savings account, and you don't need to maintain a minimum amount of money in the account.

Money-Market Account

This account is just like a checking account; however, it allows you to write only a limited number of checks, and you're not charged for the checks you use. If you plan on writing no more than three checks per month and can continually maintain a minimum balance in your account, you're better off investing your savings in a money-market account than in a savings account because a money-market account will typically pay a higher rate of interest.

Money-Saving Strategies and Habits

The ultimate goal of money management is to save money and avoid debt. Here are some specific strategies for accomplishing this goal.

1. Prepare a personal budget.

A budget is simply a plan for coordinating income and expenses to ensure that your cash flow leaves you with sufficient money to cover your expenses. A budget helps you maintain awareness of your financial state or condition; it enables you to be your own accountant by keeping an accurate account of your money.

Just like managing and budgeting your time, the first step in managing and budgeting your money involves prioritizing. In the case of money management, prioritizing first involves identifying your most important expenses—necessities that are indispensable and that you must have to survive—as opposed to incidentals that are dispensable because you can live without them.

Some people can easily confuse essentials (needs) and incidentals (wants). For instance, if a piece of merchandise happens to be on sale, what this means is that it may be a great bargain for consumers who may want to purchase it; however, it doesn't mean that you need to consume (purchase) it before somebody else does.

> ### Student Perspective
>
> "I shouldn't buy random stuff (like hair dye) and other stuff when I don't need it."
>
> –First-year student

! Remember

Remaining consciously aware of the distinction between life's *essentials* that must be purchased and *incidentals* that may or may not be purchased is an important first step toward preparing an effective budget that enables you to save money and escape debt.

Personal Story

Since I was a student who had to manage my own college expenses, I became an expert in managing small budgets. The first thing I always took care of was my tuition. I was going to go to school even if I starved. The next thing I budgeted for was my housing, then food (since I worked in a grocery store, someone would feed me), and then transportation and clothing needs. If I ran out of money, I would then work additional hours if it did not interfere with my academics. I clearly understood, that I was working to make a better life for myself and not to just have money to spend at that time. To be successful, I had to be a great money manager because there was so little of it to manage. This took a lot of focus and strong will, but did it ever pay off? Absolutely.

—*Aaron Thompson*

You need to be aware of whether you're spending money on *impulse* and out of *habit* or out of need and after thoughtful reflection. The truth is that humans spend money for a host of psychological reasons (conscious or subconscious), many of which are unrelated to actual need. For example, they spend to build their self-esteem or self-image, to combat personal boredom, or to seek stimulation and an emotional "high" (Furnham & Argyle, 1998). Furthermore, people can become obsessed with spending money, shop compulsively, and become addicted to purchasing products. Just as Alcoholics Anonymous (AA) exists as a support group for alcoholics, Debtors Anonymous exists as a support group for shopaholics and includes a 12-step recovery program similar to AA.

> ### Student Perspective
>
> "I need to save money and not shop so much and impulse buy."
>
> –First-year student

2. Make all your bills visible and pay them off as soon as possible.

When your bills are visible, they become memorable and you're less likely to forget to pay them or forget to pay them on time. To increase the visibility of your bill payments, keep a financial calendar on which you record key fiscal deadlines for the academic year (e.g., due dates for tuition payments, residential bills, and financial-aid applications). Also, try to get in the habit of paying a bill as soon as you open it and have it in your hands, rather than setting it aside and running the risk of forgetting to pay it or losing it.

3. Live within your means.

This strategy is simple: Don't purchase what you can't afford. If you are spending more money than you're taking in, it means you're living *beyond* your means. To begin living *within* your means, you have two options:

a. Decrease your expenses (e.g., reduce your spending); or

b. Increase your income.

Since most college students are already working while attending college (Orszag & Whitmore, 2001) and working so many hours that it's interfering with their academic performance or progress (King, 2005), the best option for most college students who find themselves in debt is to reduce their spending and begin living within their means.

> "We choose to spend more money than we have today. Choose debt, or choose freedom, it's your choice."
>
> –Bill Pratt, *Extra Credit: The 7 Things Every College Student Needs to Know About Credit, Debt & Cash* (2008)

THINK ABOUT IT   Journal Entry **7.6**

Are you working while attending college?

_____

_____

If you're not working, are you sacrificing anything that you want or need because you lack money?

_____

_____

_____

_____

_____

_____

If you are working,

1. How many hours per week do you currently work?

_____

_____

2. Do you think that working is interfering with your academic performance or progress?

_____

_____

3. Would it be possible for you to reduce the number of weekly hours you now work and still be able to make ends meet?

_____

_____

> "It is preoccupation with possessions, more than anything else, that prevents us from living freely and nobly."
>
> –Bertrand Russell, British philosopher and mathematician

4. Economize.

By being intelligent consumers who use critical thinking skills when purchasing products, you can be frugal or thrifty without compromising the quality of your purchases. For example, you can pay less to see the same movie in the late afternoon than you would pay at night. Also, why pay more for brand name products that are the same as products with a different name? Why pay 33 percent more for Advil or Tylenol when the same amount of pain-relieving ingredient (ibuprofen or acetaminophen) is contained in generic brands? Often, what you're paying for when you buy brand name products is all the advertising these companies pay to the media and to celebrities to publicly promote their products. (That's why people instantly recognize them as familiar brand name products.)

Don't let peer pressure determine your spending habits.

! Remember

Advertising creates product familiarity, not product quality. The more money manufacturers pay for advertising and creating a well-known or "brand name" product, the more money you pay for the product—not necessarily because you're acquiring a product of higher quality but most often because you're covering its high cost of advertising.

5. Downsize.

Cut down or cut out spending for products that you don't need. Don't engage in conspicuous consumption just to "keep up with the Joneses" (your neighbors or friends), and don't allow peer pressure to determine your spending habits. Let your spending habits reflect your ability to think critically rather than your tendency to conform socially.

6. Live with others rather than living alone.

Although you lose privacy when you share living quarters with others, you save money; if you enjoy the company of those you live with, it also has social benefits.

7. Give gifts of time rather than money.

> "The richer your friends, the more they will cost you."
>
> –Elisabeth Marbury, legal agent for theatrical and literary stars in the late nineteenth and early twentieth centuries

Spending money on gifts for family, friends, and romantic partners is not the only way to show that you care. The point of gift giving is not to show others you aren't cheap or to show off your lavish spending skills. Instead, show off your social sensitivity by doing something special or making something meaningful for them. Gifts of time and kindness can often be more personal and more special than store-bought gifts.

Personal Story

When my wife (Mary) and I were first dating, she was aware that I was trying to gain weight because I was on the thin side. (All right, I was skinny.) One day when I came home from school, I found this hand-delivered package in front of my apartment door. I opened it up and there was a homemade loaf of whole wheat bread made from scratch by Mary. That gift didn't cost her much money, but she took the time to do it and remembered to do something that was important to me (gaining weight), which really touched me; it's a gift I've never forgotten. Since I eventually married Mary and we're still happily married, I guess you could say that inexpensive loaf of bread was the "gift that kept on giving."

—Joe Cuseo

---

8. Develop your own set of money-saving strategies and habits.

> "If you would be wealthy, think of saving as well as getting."
>
> –Benjamin Franklin, eighteenth-century inventor, newspaper writer, and cosigner of the *Declaration of Independence*

> "The safest way to double your money is to fold it over and put it in your pocket."
>
> –Kin Hubbard, American humorist, cartoonist, and journalist

You can save money by starting to do little things that eventually turn into regular money-saving habits, which can and do add up to big savings over time. Consider the following list of habit-forming tips for saving money that were suggested by students in a first-year seminar class:

- Don't carry a lot of extra money in your wallet. (It's just like food; if it's easy to get to, you'll be more likely to eat it up.)
- Shop with a list—get in, get what you need, and get out.
- Put all your extra change in a jar.
- Put extra cash in a piggy bank that requires you to smash the piggy to get at it.
- Seal your savings in an envelope.
- Immediately get extra money into the bank (and out of your hands).
- Bring (don't buy) your lunch.
- Take full advantage of your meal plan—you've already paid for it, so don't pay twice for your meals by buying food elsewhere.
- Use e-mail instead of the telephone.
- Hide your credit card or put it in the freezer so that you don't use it on impulse.
- Use cash (instead of credit cards) because you can give yourself a set amount of cash and can clearly see how much of it you have at the start of a week and how much is left at any point during the week.

THINK ABOUT IT   Journal Entry   **7.7**

Do you use any of the strategies on the preceding list?

_____

_____

_____

_____

_____

Have you developed any effective strategies that do not appear on the list?

_____

_____

_____

_____

_____

_____

Personal Story

When I was 4 years old living in the mountains of Kentucky, it was safe for a young lad to walk the railroad tracks and roads alone. My mother knew this and would send me to the general store to buy various small items we needed for our household. Since we had little money, she was aware of that we had to be cautious and only spend money on the essential necessities we needed to survive. I could only purchase items from the general store that I could carry back home by myself and the ones my mother strictly ordered me to purchase. Most of these items cost less than a dollar, and in many cases you could buy multiple items for that dollar in the early 1960s. At the store I would hand my mother's handwritten list to the owners. They would pick the items for me, and we would exchange the items for my money. On the checkout counter were jars with different kinds of candy or gum. You could buy two pieces for a penny. As a hardworking boy who was doing a good deed for his parents, I didn't think there would be any harm in rewarding myself with two pieces of candy after doing a good deed. After all, I could devour the evidence of my disobedience on my slow walk home. Upon my return, my mother, being the protector of the vault and the sergeant-of-arms in our household, would count each item I brought home to make sure I had been charged correctly. She always found that I had either been overcharged by 1 cent or that I had spent 1 cent. In those days, parents believed in behavior modification. After she gave me a scolding, she would say: "Boy, you better learn how to count your money if you're ever going to be successful in life." I learned the value of saving money and the discomfort of overspending at a young age.

—Aaron Thompson

9. When making purchases, always think in terms of their long-term total cost.

It's convenient and tempting for consumers to think in the short term ("I see it; I like it; I want it; and I want it now.") However, long-term thinking is one of the essential keys to successful money management and financial planning. Those small (monthly) installment plans that businesses offer to get you to buy expensive products may make the cost of those products appear attractive and affordable in the short run. However, when you factor in the interest rates you pay on monthly installment plans, plus the length of time (number of months) you're making installment payments, you get a more accurate picture of the product's total cost over the long run. This longer-range perspective can quickly alert you to the reality that a product's sticker price represents its partial and seemingly affordable short-term cost but its long-term total cost is much less affordable (and perhaps out of your league).

Furthermore, the long-term price for purchases sometimes involves additional "hidden costs" that don't relate directly to the product's initial price but that must be paid for the product's long-term use. For example, the sticker price you pay for clothes does not include the hidden, long-term costs that may be involved if those clothes require dry cleaning. By just taking a moment to check the inside label, you can save yourself this hidden, long-term cost by purchasing clothes that are machine washable. Or, to use an example of a big-ticket purchase, the extra money spent to purchase a new car (instead of a used car) includes not only paying a higher sticker price but also paying the higher hidden costs of licensing and insuring the new car, as well as any interest fees if the new car was purchased on an installment plan. When you count these hidden, long-term costs in a new car's total cost, buying a good used car is a more effective money-saving strategy than buying a new one.

> "Ask yourself how much of your income is being eaten up by car payments. It may be time to admit you made a mistake . . . sell it [and] replace it with an older or less sporty model."
>
> –Bill Pratt, *The 7 Things Every College Student Needs to Know About Credit, Debt & Cash* (2008)

! Remember

Avoid buying costly items impulsively. Instead, take time to reflect on the purchase you intend to make, do a cost analysis of its hidden or long-term costs, and then integrate these invisible costs with the product's sticker price to generate an accurate synthesis and clearer picture of the product's total cost.

Long-Range Financial Planning: Financing Your College Education

An effective money-management plan should be time sensitive and include the following financial-planning time frames:

- Short-range financial plan (e.g., weekly income and expenses)
- Mid-range financial plan (e.g., monthly income and expenses)
- Long-range financial plan (e.g., projected or anticipated income and expenses for the entire college experience)
- Extended long-range financial plan (e.g., expected income and debt after graduation, including a plan for repayment of any college loans)

Thus far, our discussion has focused primarily on short- and mid-range financial planning strategies that will keep you out of debt monthly or yearly. We turn now to issues involving long-term financial planning for your entire college experience. While no one "correct" strategy exists for financing a college education that works best for all students, some important research findings relate to the effectiveness of different financing strategies that college students have used, which you should be aware of when doing long-range financial planning for college and beyond.

Research shows that obtaining a student loan and working no more than 15 hours per week is an effective long-range strategy for students to finance their college education and meet their personal expenses. Students who use this strategy are more likely to graduate from college, graduate in less time, and graduate with higher grades than students who work part time for more than 15 hours per week while attending college full time, or students who work full time and attend college part time (King, 2002; Pascarella & Terenzini, 2005).

Studies also show that borrowing money in the form of a student loan and working part time for 15 or fewer hours per week is the most effective financial strategy for students at *all income levels*, and it is *especially effective for students with low incomes*. Unfortunately, less than 6 percent of all first-year students use this strategy. Instead, almost 50 percent of first-year students choose a strategy that research shows to be least associated with college success: borrowing nothing and trying to work more than 15 hours per week. Students who use this strategy increase their risk of lowering their grades significantly and withdrawing from college altogether (King, 2005), probably because they have difficulty finding enough time to handle the amount of academic work required by college on top of working outside of college for more than 15 hours per week. Thus, a good strategy for balancing learning and earning would be to try to limit work for pay to 15 hours per week (or as close to 15 hours as possible) because working longer hours may increase your temptation to switch from full-time to part-time enrollment, which can increase your risk of delaying graduation or not graduating (Pascarella & Terenzini, 2005).

Other students decide to finance their college education by working full time and going to college part time. These students believe it will be less expensive in the long run to attend college part time because it will allow them to avoid any debt from student loans. However, studies show that when students go to college part time so that they can work full time it significantly lengthens their time to degree completion and sharply reduces the likelihood that they will ever complete a college degree (Orszag, Orszag, & Whitmore, 2001).

Students who manage to eventually graduate from college, but take longer to do so because they have worked more than 15 hours per week for extra income, eventually lose money in the long run. The longer they take to graduate, the longer they must wait to "cash in" on their college degree and enter higher-paying, full-time positions that a college diploma would allow them to enter. The pay per hour for most part-time jobs that students hold while working in college is less than half what they will earn from working in a full-time position as a college graduate (King, 2005).

Compared to other loans, student loans have a much lower interest rate, and they don't need to be repaid until after students are awarded their college diploma—which, by the way, is awarded in its entirety after graduation—not in parts until the entire loan is repaid!

"My school sends me portions of my diploma as I make partial payments on my student loans."

Furthermore, studies show that two out of three college students have at least one credit card and nearly one-half of students with credit cards carry an average balance of more than $2,000 per month (Mae, 2005). Debt level this high is likely to push many students into working more than 15 hours a week to pay off their high level of debt. ("I owe, I owe, so off to work I go.") This often results in their taking a longer time to graduate and earn a college graduate's salary, because they enroll in fewer courses per term so that they have extra work time to earn enough money to pay off their credit-card debt.

Instead of these students paying almost 20 percent interest to credit-card companies for their monthly debt, they would be better off obtaining a student loan at a much lower interest rate and which they don't begin to pay back until 6 months after graduation—when they'll be making more money in full-time positions as college graduates. Despite the clear advantages of student loans compared to credit-card loans, only about 25 percent of college students who use credit cards take out a student loan (King, 2002).

! Remember

Student loans are provided by the American government with the intent of helping its citizens become better educated. In contrast, for-profit businesses such as credit-card companies lend students money with no intent or interest in helping them become better educated but with the intent of helping themselves make money—from the high rates of interest they collect from students who do not pay their debt in full at the end of each month.

Keep in mind that not all debt is bad. Debt can be good if it represents an investment in something that will appreciate with time (i.e., something that will gain in value and eventually turn into profit for the investor). Purchasing a college education on credit is a good investment because, over time, it will appreciate—in the form of higher salaries for the remainder of the life of the investor (the college graduate). In contrast, purchasing a new car is a bad long-term investment because it immediately begins to depreciate or lose monetary value once it is purchased. The instant you drive that new car off the dealer's lot, you immediately become the proud owner of a used car that's worth much less than what you just paid for it.

> **"**
> *"Unlike a car that depreciates in value each year that you drive it, an investment in education yields monetary, social, and intellectual profit. A car is more tangible in the short term, but an investment in education (even if it means borrowing money) gives you more bang for the buck in the long run."*
>
> –Eric Tyson, financial counselor and national best-selling author of *Personal Finance for Dummies* (2003)

THINK ABOUT IT   Journal Entry   **7.8**

In addition to college, what might be other good, long-term investments for you to make now or in the near future?

_____

_____

_____

_____

_____

_____

You may have heard the expression that "time is money." One way to interpret this expression is that the more money you spend, the more time you must spend making money. If you're going to college, spending more time to earn money to cover your spending habits often means spending less time studying, learning, completing classes, and earning good grades. You can avoid this vicious cycle by viewing academic work as work that "pays" you back in terms of completed courses and higher grades. If you put in more academic time to complete more courses within less time and earn better grades, you're paid back by increasing the likelihood you will graduate sooner and start earning the full-time salary of a college graduate—which will pay you about twice as much money per hour than you'll earn doing part-time work without a college degree (not to mention fringe benefits such as medical insurance, dental insurance, and paid vacation time). Furthermore, the time you put into earning higher grades while in college should pay off immediately in your first full-time position after college because research shows that students in the same field who graduate with higher grades are offered higher starting salaries (Pascarella & Terenzini, 2005).

> **"**
> *"I invested in myself—in study, in mastering my tools, in preparation. Many a man who is putting a few dollars a week into the bank would do much better to put it into himself."*
>
> –Henry Ford, founder of Ford Motor Co. and one of the richest people of his generation

!

Remember

Work for better grades now; work for better pay later.

You may need to delay your immediate material desires and consumer gratification by not purchasing high-priced products until later in life. Ultimately, financing a college education may require that you give serious thought to your current lifestyle choices and make firm decisions about what you can live without at the moment. For example, a new set of wheels or a more spacious apartment may have to wait until you graduate.

Finally, be sure you take full advantage of your Financial Aid Office during your time in college. This is the campus resource that has been designed specifically to help you finance your college education. If you are concerned about whether you are using the most effective strategy for financing your education, make an appointment to see a professional in your Financial Aid Office. Also, periodically check with this office to see whether you qualify for additional sources of income, such as:

• Part-time employment on campus;
• Low-interest loans;
• Grants; or
• Scholarships.

Keep a watchful eye out for notices posted near your Financial Aid Office about financial-aid reminders, application deadlines and updates, money-management workshops, and on-campus employment

◆Summary and Conclusion

The following key strategies for effectively managing money were recommended in this chapter:

• Develop financial self-awareness. Become aware of the amount of money you have flowing in and out.
• Develop a money-management plan. Ensure that the money coming in (income) is equal to or greater than the money going out (expenses).
• Use available financial tools and instruments to track your cash flow and manage your money, such as checking accounts, credit cards, charge cards, and debit cards.
• Explore all sources of income for financing your college education, including the FAFSA, scholarships, grants, loans, monetary gifts from family or friends, salary earnings, and personal savings.
• Use available financial tools for saving money, such as savings accounts and money-market accounts.
• Prepare a personal budget. A simple plan lets you coordinate income and expenses to ensure that your cash flow leaves you with sufficient money to cover your expenses. It enables you to be your own accountant by keeping an accurate account of your money.
• Make all your bills visible and pay them off quickly. When your bills are visible, you're less likely to forget to pay them on time.
• Live within your means. Don't purchase what you can't afford.
• Economize by using critical thinking skills when purchasing products. You can be frugal or thrifty without compromising quality.
• Downsize. Cut down or cut out spending for unneeded products. Let your spending habits reflect your ability to think critically rather than a tendency to be influenced by peer pressure.

- Live with others rather than living alone. Sharing translates to saving, and if you enjoy the company of those you live with, shared living quarters have social benefits.
- Give gifts of time rather than money. Gifts of time and kindness can often be more personal and more special than store-bought gifts.
- Work for better grades now; work for better pay later. Taking out a student loan and working part time for 15 or fewer hours per week is the most effective financial strategy for students at all income levels.
- Take full advantage of your Financial Aid Office during your time in college. Check periodically with this office to see whether you qualify for additional sources of income, such as part-time employment on campus, low-interest loans, grants, or scholarships.

Managing money is a key personal resource that can promote or sabotage your success in college and in life beyond college. Similar to time management, if you effectively manage your money and gain control of how you spend it, you can gain greater control over the quality of your life. On the other hand, if you ignore it or abuse it, you raise your level of debt and stress and lower your level of performance. Research shows that accumulating high levels of debt while in college is associated with higher levels of stress, lower academic performance, and greater risk of withdrawing from college. However, the good news is that students who learn to use effective money-management strategies are able to reduce unnecessary spending, accumulation of debt, and stress while improving the quality of their academic performance.

Internet-Based Resources for Further Information on Money Management

For additional information related to the ideas discussed in this chapter, we recommend the following Web sites:

www.360financialliteracy.org/In+Your+State/

www.youngmoney.com/money_management

www.students.gov

7.1 Self-Assessment of Financial Attitudes and Habits

Answer the following questions as accurately and honestly as possible.

		Agree	Disagree
1.	I pay my rent or mortgage on time each month.	_____	_____
2.	I avoid maxing out or going over the limit on my credit cards.	_____	_____
3.	I balance my checkbook each month.	_____	_____
4.	I set aside money each month for savings.	_____	_____
5.	I pay my phone and utility bills on time each month.	_____	_____
6.	I pay my credit-card bills in full each month to avoid interest charges.	_____	_____
7.	I believe it is important to buy the things I want when I want them.	_____	_____
8.	Borrowing money to pay for college is a smart thing to do.	_____	_____
9.	I have a monthly or weekly budget that I follow.	_____	_____
10.	The thing I enjoy most about making money is spending money.	_____	_____
11.	I limit myself to one credit card.	_____	_____
12.	Getting a degree will get me a good job and a good income.	_____	_____

Sources: Cude et al. (2006), Niederjohn (2008).

Give yourself one point for each item that you checked "agree"—except items 7, 9, and 10. For these items, give yourself a point if you checked "disagree."

A perfect score on this short survey would be 12.

Self-Assessment Questions

1. What was your total score?

2. Which items lowered your score?

3. Do you see any pattern across the items that lowered your score?

4. Do you see any realistic way or ways you could improve your score on this survey?

7.2 Financial Self-Awareness: Monitoring Money and Tracking Cash Flow

1. Use the worksheet on the next page to estimate what your income and expenses are per month, and enter them in column 2.

2. Track your actual income and expenses for a month and enter them in column 3. (To help you do this accurately, keep a file of your cash receipts, bills paid, and checking or credit records for the month.)

3. After 1 month of tracking your cash flow, answer the self-assessment questions.

Financial Self-Awareness Worksheet

	Estimate	Actual
Income Source:		
Parents/Family		
Work/Job		
Grants/Scholarships		
Loans		
Savings		
Others:		
TOTAL INCOME		
Essentials (Fixed Expenses)		
Living Expenses:		
Food/Groceries		
Rent/Room & Board		
Utilities (gas/electric)		
Clothing		
Laundry/Dry Cleaning		
Phone		
Computer		
Household Items (dishes, etc.)		
Medical Insurance Expenses		
Debt Payments (loans/credit cards)		
Others:		
School Expenses:		
Tuition		
Books		
Supplies (print cartridges, etc.)		
Special Fees (lab fees, etc.)		
Others:		
Transportation:		
Public Transportation (bus fees, etc.)		
Car Insurance		
Car Maintenance		
Fuel (gas)		
Car Payments		
Others:		
Incidentals (*Variable* Expenses)		
Entertainment:		
Movies/Concerts		
DVDs/CDs		
Restaurants (eating out)		
Personal Appearance/Accessories:		
Haircuts/Hairstyling		
Cosmetics/Manicures		
Fashionable Clothes		
Jewelry		
Others:		
Hobbies		
Travel (trips home, vacations)		
Gifts		
Others:		
TOTAL EXPENSES		

Self-Assessment Questions

1. Did you enter any sources of income or expenses that were not listed on the worksheet? (If yes, what were they?)

2. Were your estimates generally accurate?

3. What specific items or areas had the largest discrepancies between what you estimated they would be and what they actually were?

4. Comparing your bottom-line total for income and expenses, are you satisfied with how your monthly cash flow seems to be going?

5. What changes could you make to create more positive cash flow (i.e., to increase your income or savings and reduce your expenses or debt)?

6. How likely is it that you would actually make such changes?

Problems Paying for College

A college student posted the following message on the Internet:

I went to college for one semester, failed some my classes, and ended with 900 dollars in student loans. Now I can't even get financial aid or a loan because of some stupid thing that says if you fail a certain amount of classes you can't get aid or a loan. And now since I couldn't go to college this semester they want me to pay for my loans already, and I don't even have a job.

Any suggestions?

Reflection and Discussion Questions

1. What suggestions would you offer this student? Which should the student do right now? Which should the student do eventually?

2. What should the student have done to prevent this from happening?

3. Do you think that this student's situation is common or unusual? Why?

Social and Emotional Intelligence

8

Relating to Others and Regulating
Emotions

A once-popular song had the following lyrics: "People who need
people are the luckiest people in the world." Would you agree or disagree
with these lyrics? Why?

_____

_____

_____

_____

_____

_____

◆ **LEARNING GOAL**

To gain a set of social and
emotional skills that enhance
the quality of your interpersonal relationships and
mental health.

◆ The Importance of Interpersonal Relationships for Success, Health, and Happiness

Interpersonal relationships can be a source of social support that promotes success, or they may be a source of social conflict that distracts you from focusing
on and achieving your personal goals. As a new college student, you may find
yourself surrounded by multiple social opportunities. One of the adjustments
you'll need to make is finding a healthy middle ground between too much and
too little socializing, as well as forming solid interpersonal relationships that
support rather than sabotage your educational success.

Social intelligence, a.k.a. interpersonal intelligence, is the ability to relate
effectively to others and is considered to be a major form of human intelligence (Gardner, 1993; Goleman, 2006). Emotional intelligence is emotional
self-awareness or empathy (sensitivity to the emotions of others). Both social

Student Perspective

"I have often found conflict in
living a balanced academic
and social life. I feel that when
I am enjoying and succeeding
in one spectrum, I am lagging
in the other."

–First-year student

Student Perspective

"The Internet supposedly increases communication and brings humanity closer together. Instead, in my generation, I'm noticing quite the opposite. There seems to be less face-to-face communication. Everyone is hooked on social networking websites. We cowardly avoid interaction where there are no facial expressions or tones."

–First-year student

and emotional intelligence are better predictors of personal and professional success than is intellectual ability (Goleman, 1995, 2006).

Studies show that people who have stronger social support networks have a longer life expectancy (Giles, Glonek, Luszcz, & Andrews, 2005) and are more likely to report being happy (Myers, 1993). The development of a strong social support system is particularly important in today's high-tech world of virtual reality and online (vs. in-person) communication, both of which make it easier to avoid direct contact, not form human connections with others, and increase the risk of isolation, loneliness, and social avoidance (Putman, 2000).

| THINK ABOUT IT | Journal Entry | 8.2 |

Who are the people in your life that you tend to turn to for social support when you are experiencing stress or need personal encouragement?

_____

_____

_____

_____

_____

_____

◆ Improving the Quality of Interpersonal Relationships

The quality of your interpersonal relationships rests on two skills: (a) communication skills, or how well you send and receive information when interacting with others (verbally and nonverbally), and (b) human relations skills, or how well you relate to and treat people, i.e., "people skills."

Listed here are our top recommendations for strengthening your interpersonal communication skills. Some strategies may appear to be basic and obvious, but they're also powerful. It may be that because they are so basic people overlook look them and forget to use them consistently. Don't be fooled by the seeming simplicity of the following suggestions, and don't underestimate their social impact.

Strategies for Improving the Quality of Interpersonal Communication

1. Work hard at being a good listener.

Studies show that listening is the most frequent human communication activity, followed, in order, by reading, speaking, and writing (Newton, 1990; Purdy & Borisoff, 1996). One study found that college students spend an average of

52.5 percent of each day listening (Barker & Watson, 2000). Being a good listener is one of the top characteristics mentioned by people when they cite the positive features of their best friends (Berndt, 1992). Listening is also one of the top skills employers look for when hiring and promoting employees (Maes, Weldy, & Icenogle, 1997; Winsor, Curtis, & Stephens, 1997).

Human relations experts often recommend that people talk less, listen more, and listen more effectively (Nichols, 1995; Nichols & Stevens, 1957). Being a good listener is easier said than done because the ability to listen closely and sensitively is a challenging mental task. Studies show that listening comprehension for spoken messages is less than 50 percent (Nichols & Stevens, 1957; Wolvin & Coakley, 1993), which is not surprising considering that listeners have only one chance to understand words spoken to them. People cannot replay a message delivered in person like they can reread words in print. Studies also show that a person can understand spoken language at a rate almost four times faster than the average person speaks (Adler & Towne, 2001), which leaves our mind plenty of spare time to drift off to something else (e.g., think about what to say next). Since you're not actively doing something while listening, you can easily fall prey to passive listening, whereby you can give others the impression that you're focused on their words but your mind is partially somewhere else. When listening, you need to remain aware of this tendency to drift off and to actively fight it by devoting your full attention to others when they're speaking.

> **!**
>
> **Remember**
>
> When you listen closely to those who speak to you, you send them the message that you respect their ideas and that they're worthy of your undivided attention.

2. Be conscious of the nonverbal messages you send while listening.

Whether or not you're truly listening is often communicated silently through nonverbal body language. It's estimated that 90 percent of communication is nonverbal, because human body language often communicates stronger and truer messages than spoken language (Mehrabian, 1972). Researchers who study lying have identified one of the best ways to detect whether people are telling the truth: See whether their body language matches their spoken language. For example, if people say they're excited or enthusiastic about an idea you're communicating to them but their nonverbal communication indicates otherwise (e.g., their eyebrows don't raise and they sit motionless), you have good reason to doubt their sincerity (Eckman & Friesen, 1969).

When it comes to listening, body language may be the best way to communicate interest in the speaker's words, as well as interest in the person who's doing the speaking. Similarly, if you are speaking, awareness of your listeners' body language can provide important clues about whether you're holding or losing their interest.

A good mnemonic device (memory-improvement method) for remembering the nonverbal signals you should send others while listening is the acronym SOFTEN, in which each letter stands for an effective nonverbal message:

"We have been given two ears and but a single mouth in order that we may hear more and talk less."

–Zeno of Citium, ancient Greek philosopher and founder of Stoic philosophy

"Give every man thine ear, but few thy voice."

–William Shakespeare, English poet, playwright, and the most quoted writer in the English-speaking world

"The most important thing in communication is to hear what isn't being said."

–Peter F. Drucker, Austrian author and founder of the study of management

S = **Smiling.** Smile periodically but not continually, as if your smile is an artificial pose.

Sitting Still. Don't fidget and squirm, as if the speaker is making you feel anxious or bored.

O = **Opening Your Posture.** Avoid a closed posture with arms crossed or hands folded together, as if you're Superman or a Supreme Court justice who's about to pass judgment.

F = **Forward Leaning.** Leaning back can be interpreted as psychoanalyzing or evaluating the speaker.

Facing the Speaker Directly. Line up both shoulders with the speaker rather than turning one shoulder away, as if to give the speaker the "cold shoulder."

T = **Touching.** A light touch on the arm or hand can be a good way to communicate warmth, but no rubbing, stroking, or touching should be used in ways that could qualify as sexual harassment.

E = **Eye Contact.** Meet the speaker's eyes periodically but not continually, as if you're staring or glaring, and not infrequently, because the speaker may think that your lack of eye contact means you're looking around for something else more interesting or stimulating than the speaker.

N = **Nodding Your Head.** Nod slowly and every once in a while but not repeatedly and rapidly, because the latter sends the message that you want the speaker to hurry up and finish so that you can start talking.

Sending positive nonverbal signals when listening encourages others to become more self-confident and enthusiastic speakers, which not only benefits them but also benefits the listener. Listening to speakers who are more self-confident and animated makes listening less challenging and more stimulating.

An interesting exercise you can use to try to gain greater awareness of your nonverbal communication habits is to choose a couple of people whom you trust, and who know you well, and ask them to imitate your body language. This is an exercise that can often be revealing (and sometimes hilarious).

3. Be open to different topics of conversation.

Don't be a closed-minded or selective listener who listens to people like you're listening to the radio—selecting or tuning into only those conversational topics that reflect your favorite interests or personal points of view but tuning out everything else.

> **! Remember**
>
> People learn most from others whose interests and viewpoints don't necessarily match their own. Ignoring or blocking out information and ideas about topics that don't immediately interest you or support your particular perspective is not only a poor social skill but also a poor learning strategy.

If people express viewpoints that you don't agree with, you don't have to nod in agreement; however, you still owe them the courtesy of listening to what they have to say (rather than shaking your head, frowning, or interrupting them). This isn't just a matter of social etiquette; it's a matter of social ethics. After others finish expressing their point of view, you should then feel free to express your own. Your informed opinions are worth expressing, as long as you don't express them in an opinionated way—that is, stating them so strongly that it sounds like your viewpoints are the only rational or acceptable ones while all others are inferior or insane (Gibb, 1961). Opinionated expression is likely to immediately end a potentially useful discussion or a possible future relationship.

THINK ABOUT IT   Journal Entry   **8.3**

On what topics do you hold strong opinions?

_____

_____

_____

_____

_____

_____

When you express these opinions, how do others usually react to you?

_____

_____

_____

_____

_____

_____

Human Relations Skills (a.k.a. People Skills)

In addition to communicating and conversing well with others, one element of managing interpersonal relationships involves how well you relate to and treat people. You can use several strategies to improve this broader set of human relations or people skills.

1. Remember the names of people you meet.

Remembering people's names communicates to others that you know them as individuals. It makes each person you meet feel less like an anonymous face in a crowd and more like a special and unique individual with a distinctive identity.

Although people commonly claim they don't have a good memory for names, no evidence shows that the ability to remember names is an inherited trait that people are born with and have no control over; instead, it's a skill that

"We should be aware of the magic contained in a name. The name sets that individual apart; it makes him or her unique among all others. Remember that a person's name is to that person the sweetest and most important sound in any language."

–Dale Carnegie, author of the best-selling book _How to Win Friends and Influence People_ (1936) and founder of The Dale Carnegie Course, a worldwide program for business based on his teachings can be developed through personal effort and employment of effective learning and memory strategies.

You can use the following strategies for remembering names:

- Consciously pay attention to the name of each person you meet. Make a conscious effort to listen for the person's name rather than focus on the impression you're making on that person, the impression the individual is making on you, or what you're going to say next.
- Reinforce your memory for a new name by saying it or rehearsing it within a minute or two after you first hear it. For instance, if your friend Gertrude has just introduced you to Geraldine, you might say: "Geraldine, how long have you known Gertrude?" By using a person's name soon after you've heard it, you intercept memory loss when forgetting is most likely to occur—immediately after you acquire new information (Underwood, 1983).
- Strengthen your memory of an individual's name by associating it with other information learned about the person. For instance, you can associate the person's name with (a) your first impression of the individual's personality, (b) a physical characteristic of the person, (c) your topic of conversation, (d) the place where you met, or (e) a familiar word that rhymes with the person's name. By making a mental connection between the person's name and some other piece of information, you help your brain form a physical connection, which is the biological foundation of human memory.
- People write down things that they want to be sure to remember. You can use this same strategy for learning names by keeping a name journal that includes the names of new people you meet plus some information about them (e.g., what they do and what their interests are). You could make it a goal to meet one new person every day and make it a point to remember that person's name by recording it in your journal.

> "When I joined the bank, I started keeping a record of the people I met and put them on little cards, and I would indicate on the cards when I met them, and under what circumstances, and sometimes [make] a little notation which would help me remember a conversation."
>
> –David Rockefeller, prominent American banker, philanthropist, and former CEO of the Chase Manhattan Bank

! Remember

Developing the habit of remembering names not only is a social skill that can improve your interpersonal interactions and bring you friends but also is a powerful professional tool that can promote your career success in whatever field you may pursue.

In business, remembering people's names can help recruit and retain customers; in politics, it can win votes; and in education, it can promote the teacher's connection and rapport with students.

2. Refer to people by name when you greet and interact with them.

When you greet a person, be sure to use the person's name in your greeting. Saying, "Hi, Waldo," will mean a lot more to Waldo than simply saying "Hi" or, worse yet, saying "Hi, there"—which sounds like you're just acknowledging something "out there" that could be either a human or an inanimate object. By continuing to use people's names after you've learned them, you continue to send them the message that you haven't forgotten their unique identity and you continue to strengthen your memory of their names.

> "If we obey this law, [it] will bring us countless friends. The law is this: Always make the person feel important."
>
> –Dale Carnegie, How to Win Friends and Influence People (1936)

3. Show interest in others by remembering information about them.

Ask people questions about their personal interests, plans, and experiences. Listen closely to their answers, especially to what seems most important to them, what they care about, or what intrigues them, and introduce these topics when you have conversations with them. For one person that topic may be politics, for another it may be sports, and for another it may be relationships. When you see people again, ask them about something they brought up in your last conversation. Try to get beyond the standard, generic questions that people routinely ask after they say "Hello" (e.g., "What's going on?"). Instead, ask about something specific you discussed with them last time you spoke (e.g., "How did that math test go that you were worried about last week?"). This sends a clear message to others that you remember them and care about them. Your memory often reflects your priorities—you're most likely to remember what's most important to you. When you remember people's names and something about them, it lets them know that they're a high priority to you. Furthermore, you're likely to find that others start showing more interest in you after you show interest in them. Another surprising thing may happen when you ask questions that show interest in others: People are likely to say you're a great conversationalist and a good friend.

"You can make more friends in 2 months by becoming interested in other people than you can in 2 years by trying to get other people interested in you."

–Dale Carnegie, *How to Win Friends and Influence People* (1936)

Personal Story   One of my most successful teaching strategies is something I do on the first day of class. I ask my students to complete a student information sheet that includes their name and some information relating to their past experiences, future plans, and personal interests. I answer the same questions I ask my students, writing my information on the board while they write theirs on a sheet of paper. (This allows them to get to know me while I get to know them.) After I've collected all their information sheets, I call out the names of individual students, asking each student to raise a hand when his or her name is called so that I can associate the name and the student's face. To help me remember the names, as I call each name I rapidly jot down a quick word or abbreviated phrase next to the student's name for later review (e.g., a distinctive physical feature or where the student's seated).

I save the student information sheets and refer back to them throughout the term. For example, I record the student's name and strongest interest on a sticky note and attach the note onto my class notes near topics I'll be covering during the term that relate to the student's interest. When I get to that topic in class (which could be months later), I immediately see the student's name posted by it. When I begin to discuss the topic, I mention the name of the student who had expressed interest in it on the first day of class (e.g., "Gina, we're about to study your favorite topic."). Students often perk up when I mention their name in association with their preferred topic; plus, they're often amazed by my apparent ability to remember so much later in the term the personal interests that they shared on the first day of class. Students never ask how I remember their personal interests, so they're not aware of my sticky note strategy. Instead, they just think I have an extraordinary social memory and social sensitivity (which is just fine with me).

—Joe Cuseo

People with integrity also possess authenticity. They are genuine or "real"; how they appear to be is who they really are. It's noteworthy that the word "integrity" comes from the same word root as "integrate." This captures the idea that people with integrity have an integrated or unified sense of self. Their outer self (how they appear to others) is in harmony with their inner self (who

they really are). Said in another way, people with integrity have got it together; they are individuals whose inner character and outer personality come together to form an integrated and unified human.

How you see yourself is your self-concept or personal "identity," a word that derives from the Latin *identitas* for "being the same" (as in the words "identical" and "identify"). In contrast, your personality is how others see you. "Personality" originates from the Latin *persona*—a mask worn by actors who portrayed fictional characters in ancient Greek and Roman theater. People of integrity don't wear masks or play roles. Their public persona or outer personality is consistent with their private self or inner identity.

People with integrity also integrate their professed or stated values and their actual behavior. Their actions and commitments are aligned or in sync with their ideals and convictions. They are models of consistency rather than hypocrisy; they say what they mean, and they mean what they say. They don't give lip service to their values by just stating or announcing them; they embody them and live by them.

Individuals with integrity not only "talk the talk" but also "walk the talk" by practicing what they preach and remaining truthful to their values.

THINK ABOUT IT   Journal Entry **8.4**

How would you define love?

_____

_____

_____

_____

_____

Would you say that love is a feeling, an action, or both?

_____

_____

_____

_____

_____

_____

What do you think are the best signs that two people are in love?

_____

_____

_____

_____

_____

_____

What would you say is the most common reason people fall out of love?

_____

_____

_____

_____

_____

_____

Romantic Relationships

Research reveals that romantic love involves two stages: infatuation and mature love.

Passionate Love (Infatuation)

The first stage of romantic love is often characterized by the following features:

- **Impulsive.** Partners quickly or suddenly fall into love or are swept off their feet (e.g., "love at first sight").
- **Obsessive.** Partners can't stop thinking about each other.
- **Physical.** Heavy emphasis is placed on physical elements of the relationship. For example, lots of attention is focused on the partner's physical appearance or attractiveness, and the partners experience a high level of physical arousal and passion (i.e., erotic love in which lust and love are closely connected).
- **Emotional.** Intense emotion is characterized by a "rush" of chemical changes in the body (similar to a drug-induced state), including:
  1. Release of the hormone adrenalin that triggers faster rates of heartbeat and breathing; and
  2. Increased production of brain chemicals (e.g., dopamine) that triggers feelings of excitement, euphoria, joy, and general well-being (Bartels & Siki, 2000).

The intensity of this emotional and chemical experience decreases with time, typically leveling off within a year after the couple has been together. The decrease in emotional intensity experienced by romantic partners after their relationship continues for an extended period is similar to the buildup of tolerance to a drug after continued use (Peele & Brodsky, 1991).

- **Idealistic.** The partner and the relationship are perceived as perfect. For example, the partners may say things like "We're perfect for each other," "Nobody else has a relationship like ours," and "We'll be together forever." This is the stage where love can be "blind"—the partner's most obvious flaws and weaknesses aren't acknowledged or even seen. Similar to the psychological defense mechanism of denial, the lover pushes out of conscious awareness of any of the partner's personal shortcomings or any problems that may threaten the security of the relationship.

- **Attached and dependent.** The lovers feel insecure and cannot bear being separated (e.g., "I can't live without him"). This type of attachment and dependence follows the principle "I love you because I am loved" and "I love you because I need you." Thus, it may be difficult to determine whether the person is in love with the partner or is in love with the feeling of being in love or being loved (Fromm, 1970).

- **Possessive and jealous.** The lover expects exclusive rights to the partner and may become suspicious of the partner or those who interact with the partner in a friendly or affectionate manner. This suspiciousness can sometimes border on illogical or irrational; for example, "insane jealousy" may be experienced, whereby the lover suspects infidelity in the partner when none exists.

- **Despairing.** "Love sickness" is often experienced if the relationship breaks up. For example, an intense depression or "love withdrawal" may follow the breakup that is similar to withdrawal from a pleasure-producing drug. Studies show that the most common cause of despair or depression among college students is a romantic breakup (Foreman, 2009).

When partners are caught up in this intense stage of a romantic relationship, the quality of thinking can become seriously impaired, as reflected in expressions such as:

- "Madly in love." Losing ability to think rationally;
- "Love is blind." Failing to see obvious flaws in the partner; and
- "Insanely jealous." Having irrational thoughts about the partner "cheating" (Bassham, Irwin, Nardone, & Wallace, 2005; Ruggiero, 2004; Wade & Tavris, 1990).

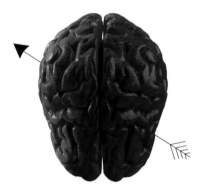

Despite expressions like "I love you with all my heart," romantic love takes place in the human brain and is accompanied by major changes in the production of brain chemicals.

*Happy Valentine's Day
I Love You with All My Brain!*

Mature Love

At the more advanced stage of a relationship, the partners gradually fall out of first-stage (puppy) love and gradually grow into a more mature stage of love that has the following characteristics:

- **Intimate.** Physical passion decreases. The "flames of the flesh" don't burn as intensely as in first-stage love, but a romantic afterglow continues. This afterglow is characterized by more emotional intimacy or closeness between the partners and greater self-disclosure, mutual trust, and honesty, which often enhance both the physical and the psychological qualities of the relationship (Viorst, 1998).

- **Balanced.** Less of an emotional high is experienced at this stage than during early stages of the relationship. For example, the mad rush of hormones and mass production of euphoria-producing brain chemicals is replaced by feelings of emotional serenity (mellowness) and emotional evenness (instead of emotional ups and downs). The love "rush" is replaced by a less intense but more consistently pleasant emotional state characterized by slightly elevated levels of different brain chemicals (endorphins rather than dopamine). Unlike infatuation or early-stage love, this pleasant emotional state doesn't decline with time; it may even grow stronger as the partners' relationship continues and matures (Bartels & Zeki, 2000).

- **Realistic.** At this more advanced stage of love, interest is focused broadly on the partner as a whole person rather than narrowly on the partner's physical qualities. Partners genuinely like one another as people and consider each other to be their "best" or "closest" friend. Partners have a realistic rather than an idealistic view of each other: Their respective strengths and weaknesses are recognized and accepted.

- **Altruistic.** The partners become less selfish and self-centered (egocentric) and become more selfless and other-centered (altruistic). Love moves beyond being just a noun—an emotion or feeling within the person (e.g., "I am in love"). It becomes an action verb—a way in which the partners act toward each other (e.g., "we love each other"). More emphasis is placed on caring for the partner than on being cared for. Mature love follows two principles:
  1. "I am loved because I love," not "I'm in love because I am loved"; and
  2. "I need you because I love you," not "I love you because I need you" (Fromme, 1980).

- **Trusting.** The partners have mutual trust and confidence in each other's commitment and aren't plagued by feelings of suspicion, distrust, or petty jealousy. Each partner may have interests and close friends outside the relationship without the other becoming jealous (Hatfield & Walster, 1985).

- **Independent and interdependent.** A complementary blend of independence and interdependence builds in the relationship—sometimes referred to as the paradox (contradiction) of love—whereby both partners maintain their independence and individuality yet both feel more complete and fulfilled when together. Both partners have their individual identity and do not expect the other to give them a personal identity and a sense of self-worth; however, together, their respective identities become more complete.

- **Caring.** The partners have mutual concern for each other's growth and fulfillment. Rather than being envious or competitive, they take joy in each other's personal success and accomplishments.

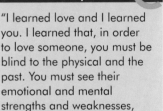

Student Perspective

"I learned love and I learned you. I learned that, in order to love someone, you must be blind to the physical and the past. You must see their emotional and mental strengths and weaknesses, passions and dislikes, hobbies and pastimes."

–Letter written by a first-year student

"Two become one, yet remain one."

–Erich Fromm, *The Art of Loving* (1970)

"If someone thinks that peace and love are just a cliché that must have been left behind in the 60s, that's a problem. Peace and love are eternal."

–John Lennon, musician, songwriter, peace activist, and co-founder of the Beatles

| **THINK ABOUT IT** | **Journal Entry** | **8.5** |

Rate your degree of agreement or disagreement with the following statements:

"All you need is love."

STRONGLY AGREE   AGREE   NOT SURE   DISAGREE   STRONGLY DISAGREE

Reason for rating:

_____

_____

_____

_____

_____

_____

_____

"Love is just a four-letter word."

STRONGLY AGREE   AGREE   NOT SURE   DISAGREE   STRONGLY DISAGREE

Reason for rating:

_____

_____

_____

_____

_____

_____

_____

"Love stinks."

STRONGLY AGREE   AGREE   NOT SURE   DISAGREE   STRONGLY DISAGREE

Reason for rating:

_____

_____

_____

_____

_____

_____

◆ Interpersonal Conflict

Disagreement and conflict among people are inevitable aspects of social life. Research shows that even the most happily married couples don't experience continual marital bliss but have occasional disagreements and conflicts (Gottman, 1994). Thus, conflict is something you cannot expect to escape or eliminate; you can only hope to contain it, defuse it, and prevent it from reaching unmanageable levels. The effective interpersonal communication and human relations skills discussed in this chapter can help minimize conflicts. In addition to these general skills, the following set of strategies may be used to handle interpersonal conflict constructively and humanely.

Minimizing and Resolving Interpersonal Conflicts

1. Pick the right place and time to resolve conflicts.

Don't discuss sensitive issues when you're fatigued, in a fit of anger, or in a hurry (Daniels & Horowitz, 1997), and don't discuss them in a public arena; deal with them only with the person involved. As the expression goes, "Don't air your dirty laundry in public." Addressing a conflict in public is akin to a public stoning; it's likely to embarrass or humiliate the person with whom you are in conflict and cause the other person to resist or resent you.

2. Decompress yourself before you express yourself.

When you have a conflict with someone, your ultimate objective should be to solve the problem, not to unload your anger and have an emotionally cathartic experience. Impulsively "dumping" on the other person may give you an immediate sense of relief, but it's not likely to produce permanent improvement in the other person's attitude or behavior toward you. Instead of unloading, take the load off—cool down and give yourself a little down time to reflect rationally—before you react emotionally. For example, count to 10 and give your emotions time to settle down before you begin to say anything. Pausing for reflection also communicates to the other person that you're giving careful thought and attention to the matter rather than lashing out randomly.

   If the conflict is so intense that you're feeling incensed or enraged, it may be a good idea to slow things down by writing out your thoughts ahead of time. This strategy will give you time to organize and clarify your ideas by first talking silently to yourself (on paper) before talking out loud to the other person (in person).

3. Give the person a chance to respond.

Just because you're angry doesn't mean that the person you're angry with must forfeit the right to free speech and self-defense. Giving the other person a chance to speak and be heard will increase the likelihood that you'll receive a cooperative response to your request. It will also prevent you from storming in, jumping the gun, and "pulling the trigger" too quickly before being sure you've got all the facts straight.

   After listening to the other person's response, check your understanding by summarizing it in your own words (e.g., "What I hear you saying is . . . "). This is an important first step in the conflict-resolution process because conflicts often revolve around a simple misunderstanding, failure to communicate,

"Seek first to understand, then to be understood."

–Stephen Covey, international best-selling author of *Seven Habits of Highly Effective People* (1990)

or a communication breakdown. Sometimes just taking the time to hear where the other person is coming from before launching into a full-scale complaint or criticism can reduce or resolve the conflict.

4. Acknowledge the person's perspectives and feelings.

After listening to the person's response, if you disagree with it don't dismiss or discount the person's feelings. For instance, don't say, "That's ridiculous" or "You're not making any sense." Instead, say, "I see how you might feel that way, but . . . " or "I feel badly that you are under pressure, but . . . "

5. If things begin to get nasty, call for a time-out or cease-fire, and postpone the discussion to allow both of you time to cool off.

When emotion and adrenalin run high, logic and reason often run low. This can result in someone saying something during a fit of anger, which, in turn, stimulates an angry response from the other person; then the anger of both combatants continues to escalate and turns into an intense volley of verbal punches and counterpunches. For example, the conversation may go something like this:

Person A: "You're out of control."
Person B: "No, I'm not out of control, you're just overreacting."

Person A: "*I'm* overreacting, you're the one who's yelling!"
Person B: "I'm not yelling, *you're* the one who's raising your voice!"

Blow-by-blow exchanges such as these are likely to turn up the emotional heat so high that resolving the conflict is out of the question until both fighters back off, retreat to their respective corners, cool down, and try again later when neither one of them is ready to throw a knockout punch.

6. Make your point assertively (not passively, aggressively, or passive–aggressively).

When you're passive, you don't stand up for your personal rights; you allow others to take advantage of you by allowing them to push you around. You say nothing when you should say something. You say "yes" when you want to say "no." When you handle conflict passively, you become angry, anxious, or resentful about doing nothing and keeping it all inside.

When you're aggressive, you stand up for your rights but you also violate the rights of the other person by threatening, dominating, humiliating, or bullying that person. You use intense, emotionally loaded words to attack the person (e.g., "You spoiled brat" or "You're a sociopath"). You manage to get what you want but at the other person's expense. Later, you tend to feel guilty about overreacting or coming on too strong (e.g., "I knew I shouldn't have said that").

When you're passive–aggressive, you get back or get even with the other person in an indirect and ineffective way by withholding or taking away something (e.g., not speaking to the other person or withdrawing all attention or affection).

In contrast, when you're assertive, you strike the middle ground between aggression and passivity. You handle conflict in a way that protects or restores your rights without taking away or stepping on the rights of the other person. You approach conflict in an even-tempered way rather than in an angry or agitated manner; you speak in a normal volume rather than yelling or screaming; and you communicate at a normal distance rather than getting up close and "into the face" of the other person involved in the conflict. You can resolve conflicts assertively by using the following four strategies:

a. Focus on the specific behavior causing the conflict, not the person's general character. Avoid labeling the person as "selfish," "mean," "inconsiderate," and so on. For instance, if you're upset because your roommate doesn't share in cleaning, stay away from aggressive labels such as "You slacker" or "You lazy bum." Attacking others with negative labels such as these does to the other person just what it sounds like: It gives the feeling of being attacked or verbally assaulted. This is likely to put the other person on the defensive and provoke a counterattack on one of your personal characteristics. Before you know it, you're likely to find yourself in a full-out war of words and mutual character assassinations that has escalated well beyond a small-scale skirmish about the specific behavior of one individual.

Rather than focusing on the person's general character, focus on the behaviors that are causing the problem (e.g., failing to do the dishes or leaving dirty laundry around the room). This will enable the other person to know exactly what actions need to be taken to take care of the problem. Furthermore, it's easier for others to change a specific behavior than it is to change their entire character, which would require a radical change in personality (or a frontal lobotomy).

b. Use "I" messages to focus on how the other person's behavior or action affects you. By using "I" messages, which focus on your perceptions and feelings, you send a message that's less accusatory and threatening (Narciso & Burkett, 1975). In contrast, "you" messages are more likely to make the other person defensive and put them on the offensive—ready to retaliate rather than cooperate (Gibb, 1991).

For instance, suppose you've received a course grade that's lower than what you think you earned or deserved and you decide to question your instructor about it. This conversation should not begin by saying to the instructor, "*You* gave me the wrong grade" or "*You* made a mistake." These messages are likely to make your professor immediately ready to defend the grade you received. Your professor will be less threatened and more likely to listen to and consider your complaint if you initiate the conversation with an "I" statement, such as "I don't believe I received the correct grade" or "I think an error may have been made in my final grade."

"I" messages are less aggressive because you're targeting an issue, not a person (Jakubowski & Lange, 1978). By saying, "I feel angry when . . . " rather than "You make me angry when . . . ," you send the message that you're taking responsibility for the way you feel rather than guilt-tripping the individual for making you feel that way (perhaps without the person even being aware of how you feel).

Lastly, when using "I" messages, try to describe what you're feeling as precisely as possible. Saying "I feel neglected when you don't write or call" more precisely identifies what you're feeling than saying "I wish you'd be more considerate." Describing what you feel in specific terms increases the persuasive power of your message and reduces the risk that the other person will misunderstand or discount it.

> "*Precision of communication is important, more important than ever, in our era of hair-trigger balances, when a false or misunderstood word may create as much disaster as a sudden thoughtless act.*"
>
> –James Thurber, U.S. author, humorist, and cartoonist

THINK ABOUT IT	Journal Entry	8.6

Your classmates aren't carrying their weight on a group project that you're all supposed to be working on as a team; you're getting frustrated and angry because you're doing most of the work. What might be an "I" message that you could use to communicate your concern in a nonthreatening way that's likely to resolve this conflict successfully?

_____

_____

_____

_____

_____

_____

c. Don't make absolute judgments or blanket statements. Compare the following three pairs of statements:

- "You're no help at all" versus "You don't help me enough."
- "You never try to understand how I feel" versus "You don't try hard enough to understand how I feel."
- "I always have to clean up" versus "I'm doing more than my fair share of the cleaning."

The first statement in each of the preceding pairs represents an absolute statement that covers all times, situations, and circumstances—without any room for possible exceptions. Such extreme, blanket criticisms are likely to put the criticized person on the defensive because they state that the person is lacking or deficient with respect to the behavior in question. The second statement in each pair states the criticism in terms of degree or amount, which is less likely to threaten the person's self-esteem (and is probably closer to the truth).

d. Focus on solving the problem, not winning the argument. Try not to approach conflict with the attitude that you're going to "get even" or "prove that you're right." Winning the argument but not persuading the person to change the behavior that's causing the conflict is like winning a battle but losing the war. Instead, approach the conflict with the attitude that it's a problem to be solved and that both parties can win—that is, both of you can end up with a better relationship in the long run if the issue is resolved.

"Don't find fault. Find a remedy."

–Henry Ford, founder of Ford Motor Co. and one of the richest people of his generation

7. Conclude your discussion of the conflict on a warm, constructive note.

By ending on a positive note, you assure that the other person knows there are no hard feelings and that you're optimistic the conflict can be resolved and your relationship can be improved.

8. If the conflict is resolved because of some change made by the other person, express your appreciation for the individual's effort.

Even if your complaint was legitimate and your request was justified, the person's effort to accommodate your request shouldn't be taken for granted. At the least, you shouldn't react to a positive change in behavior by rubbing it in with comments such as "That's more like it" or "It's about time!"

Expressing appreciation to the other person for making a change in response to your request is not only a socially sensitive thing to do but also a self-serving thing to do. By recognizing or reinforcing the other person's changed behavior, you increase the likelihood that the positive change in behavior will continue.

> "
>
> *"To keep your marriage brimming with love . . . when you're wrong, admit it; when you're right, shut up."*
>
> –Ogden Nash, American poet

The Importance of Emotional Intelligence for Educational and Personal Success

The term "intrapersonal" intelligence refers to the ability to be aware of your feelings or emotions (Gardner, 1983). More recently, the term "emotional intelligence" has been coined to describe the ability to identify and monitor your emotions and to be aware of how your emotions are influencing your thoughts and actions (Goleman, 1995; Salovey & Mayer, 1990). Emotional intelligence has been found to be a better predictor of personal and occupational success than is performance on intellectual intelligence tests (Goleman, 1995). Research on college students indicates that those with higher emotional intelligence, such as the ability to identify their emotions and moods, are (a) less likely to experience boredom (Harris, 2006) and (b) more able to focus their attention and get absorbed (in the zone) when completing challenging tasks (Wiederman, 2007). The connection between emotional intelligence and successful personal performance is further supported by research indicating that people who are able to control their emotions and use them to their advantage are more likely to persist longer at challenging tasks (Simunek, Schutte, Hollander, & McKenley, 2000) and to experience professional success (Goleman, 1995; Saarni, 1999). Success in college is a challenging task that will test your emotional strength and your ability to persist to task completion (graduation).

Research also indicates that experiencing positive emotions, such as optimism and excitement, promotes learning by increasing the brain's ability to take in, store, and retrieve information (Rosenfield, 1988). In one study involving nearly 4,000 first-year college students, it was found that students' level of optimism or hope for success during their first term on campus was a more accurate predictor of their first-year grades than was their SAT score or high school grade point average (GPA; Snyder et al., 1991). In contrast, negative emotions such as anxiety and fear can interfere with the brain's ability to (a) store memories (Jacobs & Nadel, 1985), (b) retrieve stored memories (O'Keefe & Nadel, 1985), and (c) engage in higher-level thinking (Caine & Caine, 1991).

College students who score higher on tests of emotional intelligence and emotional management have been found to achieve higher GPAs at the end of their first year (Schutte et al., 1998). Additional research shows that new college students who take seminars or college success courses, which include information on emotional control and emotional-skill development, are more likely to be successful during their first year of college (Schutte & Malouff, 2002).

◆ Stress and Anxiety

Among the most common emotions that humans have to monitor, manage, and regulate are stress and anxiety. College students report higher levels of stress while in college than they did before college (Bartlett, 2002; Sax, 2003), and students entering college in recent years report higher levels of stress (Astin, Parrot, Korn, & Sax, 1997; Sax, Astin, Korn, & Mahoney, 1999) and lower levels of mental health (Kadison & DiGeronimo, 2004) than they have in years past. This increased level of stress may reflect that you're living in a world experiencing an unprecedented rate of technological change and information overload. Terms such as "Internet addiction" and "information fatigue syndrome" are now being used by psychologists to diagnose disorders involving, respectively, psychological dependency on the Internet and excess stress relating to information overload (Waddington, 1996; Young, 1996).

What exactly is stress? The biology of stress originates from the fight-or-flight reaction that's been wired into your body for survival purposes. This automatic reaction prepares you to handle danger or threat by flooding your body with chemicals (e.g., adrenalin) in the same way that ancient humans had to handle threats by engaging in fight or flight (escape) when confronted by life-threatening predators.

The word "stress" derives from a Latin root that means "to draw tight." Thus, stress isn't necessarily bad. For example, a tightened guitar string provides better sound than a string that's too lax or loose, a tightened bow delivers a more powerful arrow shot, and a tightened muscle provides more strength or speed. Such productive stress is sometimes referred to as eustress—deriving from the root *eu* meaning

COUNSELING OFFICE Hours: 24–7

● Anxiety Disorders
Drug Addiction
Internet Addiction
Information Fatigue Syndrome

Today's technological revolution and information explosion may be making life particularly stressful.

The "fight-or-flight" reaction occurs when we're under stress because it's a throwback to the time when ancient humans needed to fight with or flee from potential predators. However, unlike other animals, stress doesn't cause our hair to rise up and appear more intimidating to foes (but we still can get "goose bumps" when we're nervous, and we still refer to scary events as "hair raising" experiences).

"good" (as in the words "euphoria," meaning good mood, and "eulogy," meaning good words).

If you keep college stress at a moderate level, it can be a productive emotion that will promote your learning and personal development. Stress in moderate amounts can benefit your:

- Physical performance (e.g., strength and speed);
- Mental performance (e.g., attention and memory); and
- Mood (e.g., hope and optimism).

THINK ABOUT IT   Journal Entry   **8.7**

Can you think of a situation in which you performed at a higher level because you were somewhat nervous or experienced a moderate amount of stress?

_____

_____

_____

_____

_____

_____

However, if stress is extreme and continues for a prolonged period, it moves from being a productive to a destructive feeling. Using the guitar string as an analogy, if a guitar is strung too tight, the string is likely to snap or break—which isn't productive. Unproductive stress is often referred to as distress—from the root *dis* meaning "bad" (as in the words "discomfort" and "disease"). Extreme stress can create feelings of intense anxiety or anxiety disorders (e.g., panic attacks), and if a high level of stress persists for a prolonged period, it can trigger psychosomatic illness—tension-induced bodily disorders (from *psyche*, meaning "mind," and *soma*, meaning "body"). For instance, prolonged distress can trigger indigestion by increasing secretion of stomach acids or contribute to high blood pressure, a.k.a. hypertension. Prolonged stress can also suppress the immune system, leaving you more vulnerable to flu, colds, and other infectious diseases. Studies show that the immune system of college students is suppressed (produces fewer antibodies) at stressful times during the academic term—such as midterms and finals (Jemott & Magloire, 1985; Kielcolt-Glaser & Glaser, 1986).

Excess stress can interfere with mental performance because the feelings and thoughts that accompany anxiety begin to preoccupy your mind and take up space in your working memory, leaving it with less capacity to process information you're trying to learn and retain. Studies also show that students experiencing higher levels of academic stress or performance anxiety are more likely to use ineffective surface approaches to learning that rely merely on

Research indicates that college students' stress levels tend to rise when they are experiencing a wave of exams, such as finals.

memorization (Ramsden & Entwistle, 1981) rather than effective deep-learning strategies that involve seeking meaning and understanding. Furthermore, high levels of test anxiety are more likely to result in careless concentration errors on exams (e.g., overlooking key words in test questions) and can interfere with memory for information that's been studied (Jacobs & Nadel, 1985; O'Keefe & Nadel, 1985; Tobias, 1985).

Although considerable research points to the negative effects of excess stress, you still need to keep in mind that stress can work either for or against you; you can be either energized or sabotaged by stress depending on its level of intensity and the length of time it continues. You can't expect to stop or eliminate stress, nor should you want to; you can only hope to contain it and maintain it at a level where it's more productive than destructive. Many years of research indicate that personal performance is best when it takes place under conditions of moderate stress because this creates a sense of challenge. On the other hand, too much stress creates performance anxiety, and too little stress results in loss of intensity or indifference (Sapolsky, 2004; Yerkes & Dodson, 1908). (See **Figure 8.1.**)

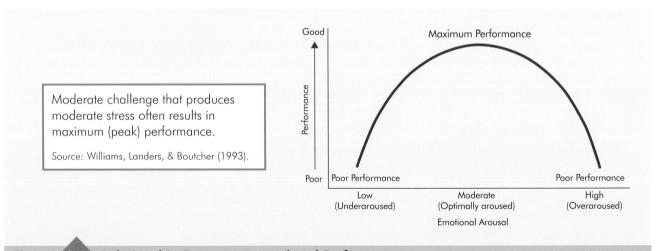

Moderate challenge that produces moderate stress often results in maximum (peak) performance.

Source: Williams, Landers, & Boutcher (1993).

Figure 8.1 Relationship Between Arousal and Performance

Box 8.1 provides a short summary of the signs or symptoms of extreme stress, which indicate that stress has climbed to a level where it's creating distress or anxiety. If these are experienced, particularly for an extended period during which symptoms continue to occur for 2 or more weeks, action should be taken to reduce them.

Take Action!   **8.1**

High Anxiety: Recognizing the Symptoms (Signs) of Distress

- Jitteriness or shaking—especially the hands
- Accelerated heart rate or heart palpitations—intense, irregular heartbeat
- Muscle tension—tightness in the chest, upper shoulders, or a tight feeling (lump) in the throat (the expressions "uptight" and "choking" stem from these symptoms of upper-body tension)
- Body aches—heightened muscle tension leading to tension headaches, backaches, or chest pain, which can become so extreme that it can feel as if a heart attack is taking place
- Sweating—especially sweaty (clammy) palms
- Cold, pale hands or feet—symptoms that led to the expressions "white knuckles" and "cold feet"
- Dry mouth—production of less saliva leading to a dry mouth (the expression "cotton mouth" stems from this loss of saliva)

- Stomach discomfort or indigestion—increased secretion of stomach acid that causes discomfort (the expression "feeling butterflies in my stomach" relates to this symptom)
- Elimination problems—constipation or diarrhea
- Feeling faint or dizzy—constriction of blood vessels decreasing oxygen flow to the brain
- Weakness and fatigue—sustained (chronic) state of arousal and prolonged muscle tension that becomes tiring
- Menstrual changes—missing periods or experiencing irregular menstrual periods
- Difficulty sleeping—insomnia or interrupted (fitful) sleep
- Increased susceptibility to colds, flu, and other infections—suppression of the body's immune system leading to more infections

---

THINK ABOUT IT   **Journal Entry**   **8.8**

How would you rate your level of anxiety in the following situations?

1. Taking tests or exams   high   moderate   low

2. Interacting in social situations   high   moderate   low

3. Making decisions about the future   high   moderate   low

Take Action!

Posttraumatic Stress Disorder: A Distinctive Form of Stress and Anxiety

8.2

Posttraumatic stress disorder (PTSD) is an anxiety disorder that arises after someone experiences a traumatic (dangerous or life-threatening) event, such as combat or sexual assault. It's natural to experience feelings of anxiety after such events, and the symptoms may last for weeks. However, if these feelings of anxiety do not gradually decline but remain or intensify over time and continue to interfere with the person's ability to carry out daily tasks, the person may be experiencing PTSD. Symptoms of PTSD include the following:

- Constantly feeling tense or "on edge"
- Finding it difficult to concentrate
- Being easily startled
- Having difficulty sleeping
- Experiencing emotional numbness

- Having sudden outbursts of anger
- Blocking memories of the traumatic experience and events around the time of the experience
- Having flashbacks—reliving the trauma repeatedly and experiencing frightening thoughts and physical symptoms (e.g., a racing heart or sweating) that may occur spontaneously or be triggered by sights, sounds, or dreams that serve as reminders of the original traumatic experience
- Avoiding places, events, or objects that are reminders of the traumatic experience

If the preceding symptoms are occurring 3 or more months after a traumatic event, professional help should be sought. A good place to start would be the Counseling Center on campus or the PTSD Information Line at (802) 296-6300 (e-mail: ncptsd@va.gov).

Source: National Institute of Mental Health (2009).

Student Perspective

"My stress has caused me to lose a lot of weight; my appetite is cut in half. My sleep pattern is off; I have trouble falling/staying asleep. No matter how stressed I was in high school, this never happened [before]. What can I do to de-stress?"

–First-term college student

Research-Based Techniques for Stress Management

If you perceive your level of stress to be reaching a point where it's beginning to interfere with the quality of your performance or life, you need to take steps to reduce it. Listed here are three stress-management methods whose positive effects have been well documented by research in psychology and biology (Benson & Klipper, 1990; Everly, 1989; Lehrer & Woolfolk, 1993).

Deep (Diaphragmatic) Breathing

The type of breathing associated with excessive stress is hyperventilation—fast, shallow, and irregular breathing—through the mouth rather than the chest. Breathing associated with relaxation is just the opposite—slow, deep, and regular breathing that originates from the stomach.

Breathing is something you usually do automatically or involuntarily; however, with some concentration and effort, you can control your breathing by controlling your diaphragm—the body's muscle that enables you to expand and contract your lungs. By voluntarily controlling your diaphragm muscle, you can slow your breathing rate, which, in turn, can bring down your stress level.

Your breathing rate is the pacesetter for the rate at which all other bodily systems operate. For example, when your breathing slows, your heart rate slows, your blood pressure goes down, and your muscle tension is reduced. Thus, if you slow your breathing, you produce a relaxation "wave" or "ripple effect" throughout your body. Deep breathing's ability to trigger relaxation across all systems of the body makes it one of the most powerful stress-management techniques available to you.

You can practice diaphragmatic breathing by inhaling and exhaling with your mouth closed (but without pressing your lips tightly together), keeping your chest still, and allowing your stomach to rise and fall at a slow, steady pace. To help you breathe this way, imagine a candle in front of you that you're blowing on and trying to make flicker without blowing it out. To be sure you're breathing through your stomach deeply and consistently, put one hand on your chest and make sure your chest remains still while you breathe; place your other hand on your stomach and make sure that it rises and falls as you breathe in and out, respectively.

By practicing diaphragmatic breathing consistently, it can soon become natural to you, and you'll be able to quickly shift into deep breathing anytime you feel yourself becoming anxious or tense (e.g., before a big exam or speech).

Progressive Muscle Relaxation

This stress-management method is similar to stretching exercises used to relax and loosen muscles before and after physical exercise. To achieve total-body (head-to-toe) muscle relaxation, progressively tense and release the five sets of muscles listed here. Hold the tension in each muscle area for about 5 seconds, and then release it slowly.

1. Wrinkle your forehead muscles, and then release them.
2. Shrug your shoulders up as if to touch your ears, and then drop them.
3. Make a fist with each hand, and then open both.
4. Tighten your stomach muscles, and then release them.
5. Tighten your toes by curling them under your feet, and then raise them as high as you can.

To help tense your muscles, imagine you're using them to push or lift a heavy object. When relaxing your muscles, take a deep breath and think or say the word "relax." By breathing deeply and thinking or hearing the word "relax" each time you release your muscles, the word becomes associated with your muscles becoming relaxed. Thus, if you find yourself in a stressful situation, you can take a deep breath, think or say the word "relax," and immediately release tension because that's what your muscles have been trained or conditioned to do.

Mental Imagery

You can use your visual imagination to create sensory experiences that promote relaxation. You can create your own relaxing "mental movie" or "imaginary DVD" by visually placing yourself in a calm, comfortable, and soothing setting. You can visualize ocean waves, floating clouds, floating in a warm sauna, or any sensory experience that tends to relax you. The more senses you use, the more real the scene will seem and the more powerful its relaxing effects will be (Fezler, 1989). Try to use all of your senses—try to see it, hear it, smell it, touch it, and feel it. You can also use musical imagination to create calming background music that accompanies your visual image.

Lastly, when using your visual imagination, close your eyes and move your eyeballs upward as if you're looking at the sky or ceiling. Research indicates that this upward eye movement tends to trigger alpha waves—brainwaves associated with a relaxed yet alert mental state (Liebertz, 2005a).

> ### Student Perspective
>
> "To relax, I like to stretch a lot."
>
> –First-year student

Personal Story

My wife, Mary, is a kindergarten teacher. Whenever her young students start misbehaving and the situation becomes stressful (e.g., during lunchtime when the kids are running wildly, arguing vociferously, and screaming at maximum volume), Mary "plays" relaxing songs in her head. She reports that her musical imagination always works to soothe her nerves, enabling her to remain calm and even tempered when she must confront children who need to be scolded or disciplined.

—Joe Cuseo

THINK ABOUT IT   Journal Entry   **8.9**

What are the most common sources of stress for you?

_____

_____

_____

_____

_____

_____

Would you say that you deal with stress well?

_____

_____

_____

_____

_____

_____

What strategies do you use to cope with stress?

_____

_____

_____

_____

_____

_____

_____

Stress-Reduction Strategies and Practices

In addition to formal stress-management techniques, such as diaphragmatic breathing, progressive muscle relaxation, and mental imagery, you can use other habits and simple strategies to reduce stress.

1. Reduce or eliminate intake of alcohol and caffeine.

Substances you put into your body physically can affect you emotionally. Because alcohol is a sedative or "downer" drug that slows the nervous system, people often turn to it as a strategy to cope with stress and promote relaxation (Carpenter & Hasin, 1998). However, if too much alcohol is consumed, it has just the opposite effect—it elevates tension because it triggers the release of cortisol, a hormone that activates and elevates the body's stress response.

Since stress can cause fatigue, people may also be tempted to use caffeine to regain energy. However, caffeine is a drug (a stimulant) that not only stimulates alertness but also activates the part of the involuntary nervous system that's associated with stress and arousal. Thus, caffeine is likely to increase feelings of nervous tension (hence the expression "coffee nerves"). If you already tend to get somewhat nervous or anxious in academic-performance situations, such as tests or speeches, the last thing you want to put into your system just before performance time is something that's going to elevate your tension level even further.

It's a myth that giving caffeine (e.g., a cup of coffee) to someone who's drunk will help sober that person up. Caffeine is a stimulant of the nervous system, but it doesn't lower the body's blood alcohol level and, therefore, will not lower the drunken person's level of intoxication. Caffeine will make a drunken person feel less sleepy but not any less drunk or any more capable of operating heavy machinery, such as driving a car. All it will do is create a wide-awake drunk (which may be more dangerous than a sleepy one).

2. Decrease your intake of simple sugars and increase your intake of foods high in complex carbohydrates.

Foods high in complex carbohydrates (e.g., brown rice, potatoes, pasta, legumes, whole grain bread, and cereals) increase release of a brain chemical called serotonin that triggers feelings of calmness and serenity. Although it may be tempting to put something sweet in your mouth when you're stressed and tired, simple sugars (e.g., chocolates, candies, and sugary sodas) will only deliver a short-term shot of nervous energy.

If you like to eat when you're stressed, choose something other than high-sugar, high-calorie foods (e.g., eat foods high in complex carbohydrates or chew a piece of sugarless gum) or try another way to relieve tension other than oral stimulation.

3. Start a journal.

Dealing with feelings by writing about them in a personal journal can provide a safe and regular outlet for releasing steam and coping with stress. Writing about your emotions also enables you to become more consciously aware of them, which reduces the risk of pushing them into your subconscious and denying them.

"There are thousands of causes for stress, and one antidote to stress is self-expression. That's what happens to me every day. My thoughts get off my chest, down my sleeves, and onto my pad."

–Garson Kanin, American writer, actor, and film director

4. Take time for humor and laughter.

Research on the power of humor for reducing tension is clear and convincing. In one research study, college students were unexpectedly given an assignment to deliver an impromptu (off the top of their head) speech. This unexpected assignment caused students' heart rate to elevate to an average of 110 beats per minute during their speech. However, if students watched humorous episodes of sitcoms before delivering their impromptu speech, their average heart rate was lower (80–85 beats per minute), which suggests that experiencing humor significantly lowers anxiety (O'Brien, cited in Howard, 2000). Research also shows that if your immune system is suppressed or weakened by stress, humor strengthens it by blocking the body's production of the stress hormone cortisol, the body chemical responsible for suppressing your immune system when you're stressed (Berk, cited in Liebertz, 2005b).

> "
>
> *"The arrival of a good clown exercises a more beneficial influence upon the health of a town than the arrival of twenty asses laden with drugs."*
>
> –Thomas Sydenham, seventeenth-century physician

◆ Depression

Along with anxiety, depression is the other emotional problem that most commonly afflicts humans and must be managed. Excess stress can turn into anxiety (a heightened state of tension, arousal, and nervous energy), or it can lead to depression (an emotional state characterized by a loss of optimism, hope, and energy). As its name implies, when people are depressed, their mood is "lowered" or "pushed down" (like depressing the accelerator in a car). In contrast to anxiety, which typically involves worrying about something that's currently happening or is about to happen (e.g., experiencing test anxiety before an upcoming exam), depression more often relates to something that's already happened. In particular, depression is often related to a loss, such as a lost relationship (e.g., departed friend, broken romance, or death of a family member) or a lost opportunity (e.g., losing a job, failing a course, or failing to be accepted into a major; Bowlby, 1980; Price, Choi, & Vinokur, 2002). It's natural and normal to feel dejected after losses such as these. However, if your dejection reaches a point where you can't concentrate and complete your day-to-day tasks, and if this continues for an extended period, you may be experiencing what psychologists call clinical depression (i.e., depression so serious that it requires professional help).

Box 8.3 provides a summary of symptoms or signs that may indicate the presence of depression. If these symptoms continue to occur for two or more weeks, action should be taken to relieve them.

!

Remember

There is a difference between feeling despondent or "down" and being depressed. When psychologists use the word "depression" they're usually referring to clinical depression—a mood state so low that it's interfering with a person's ability to cope with day-to-day life tasks, such as getting to school or going to work.

Take Action!

8.3

Recognizing the Symptoms (Signs) of Depression

- Low, down, dejected, sad, or blue feelings
- Pessimistic feelings about the future (e.g., expecting failure or feeling helpless or hopeless)
- Decreased sense of humor
- Difficulty finding pleasure, joy, or fun in anything
- Lack of concentration
- Loss of motivation or interest in things previously found to be exciting or stimulating
- Stooped posture (e.g., hung head or drawn face)
- Slower and softer speech rate

- Decreased animation and slower bodily movements
- Loss of energy
- Changes in sleeping patterns (e.g., sleeping more or less than usual)
- Changes in eating patterns (e.g., eating more or less than usual)
- Social withdrawal
- Neglect of physical appearance
- Consistently low self-esteem (e.g., thinking "I'm a loser")
- Strong feelings of worthlessness or guilt (e.g., thinking "I'm a failure")
- Suicidal thoughts (e.g., thinking "I can't take it anymore," "People would be better off without me," or "I don't deserve to live")

THINK ABOUT IT   Journal Entry   8.10

Have you, or a member of your family, ever experienced clinical depression?

_____

_____

_____

_____

_____

What do you think was the primary cause or factor that triggered it?

_____

_____

_____

_____

_____

_____

Strategies for Coping with Depression

Depression can vary widely in intensity. Moderate and severe forms of depression often require professional counseling or psychotherapy, and their cause often lies in genetic factors that involve inherited imbalances in brain chemistry.

The following strategies are offered primarily for milder cases of depression that are more amenable to self-help and self-control. These strategies may also be used with professional help or psychiatric medication to reduce the intensity and frequency of depression.

"Yesterday is gone. Tomorrow has not yet come. We have only today. Let us begin."

–Mother Teresa of Calcutta, Albanian, Catholic nun, and winner of the Nobel Peace Prize

1. Focus on the present and the future, not the past.

Consciously fight the tendency to dwell on past losses or failures because you can no longer change or control them. Instead, focus on things you can still control, which are occurring now and will occur in the future.

2. Deliberately make an effort to engage in positive or emotionally uplifting behavior when you're feeling down.

If your behavior is upbeat, your mind (mood) often follows suit. "Put on a happy face" may be an effective depression-reduction strategy because smiling produces certain changes in your facial muscles, which in turn, trigger changes in brain chemistry that improve your mood (Liebertz, 2005). In contrast, frowning activates a different set of facial muscles that reduces production of mood-elevating brain chemicals (Myers, 1993).

3. Continue to engage in activities that are fun and enjoyable for you.

For example, continue to socialize with friends and engage in your usual recreational activities. Falling into the downward spiral of withdrawing from doing the things that bring you joy because you're too down to do them will bring you down even further by taking away the very things that bring you up. Interestingly, the root of the word "recreation" means to re-create or create again, which suggests that recreation can revive, restore, and renew you—physically and emotionally.

4. Try to continue accomplishing things.

By staying busy and getting things done when you feel down, you help boost your mood by experiencing a sense of accomplishment and boosting your self-esteem. Doing something nice for someone less fortunate than yourself can be a particularly effective way to elevate your mood, because it helps you realize that your issues are often far less serious and more manageable than the problems faced by others.

"The best way to cheer yourself up is to try to cheer somebody else up."

–Samuel Clemens, a.k.a. Mark Twain, writer, lecturer, and humorist

5. Intentionally seek out humor and laughter.

In addition to reducing anxiety, laughter can lighten and brighten a dark mood. Furthermore, humor improves memory (Nielson, cited in Liebertz, 2005), which is an important advantage for people experiencing depression, because depression interferes with concentration and memory. Research supporting the benefits of humor for the body and mind is so well established that humor has become a legitimate academic field of study known as gelontology—the study of laughter (from the Greek word gelos for "laughter" and ology, meaning "study of").

> "If you can laugh at it, you can survive it."
>
> –Bill Cosby, American comedian, actor, and activist

6. Make a conscious effort to focus on your personal strengths and accomplishments.

Another way to drive away the blues is by keeping track of the good developments in your life. You can do this by keeping a positive events journal in which you note the good experiences in your life, including things you're grateful for, as well as your accomplishments and achievements. Positive journal entries will leave you with a visible, uplifting record that you can review anytime you're feeling down. Furthermore, a positive events journal can provide you with a starting point for developing a formal résumé, portfolio, and personal strengths sheet, which you can provide to those who serve as your personal references and who write your letters of recommendation.

7. If you're unable to overcome depression on your own, seek help from others.

College students are more likely than ever to seek professional help if they're feeling depressed (Kadison & DiGeronimo, 2004). This is good news because it suggests that seeking help is no longer viewed as a source of embarrassment or a sign of personal weakness; instead, today's college students are willing to share their feelings with others and improve the quality of their emotional life.

In some cases, you may be able to help yourself overcome emotional problems through personal effort and effective coping strategies. This is particularly true if you experience depression or anxiety in milder forms and for limited periods. However, overcoming more serious and long-lasting episodes of clinical depression or anxiety isn't as simple as people make it out to be when they glibly say, "Just deal with it," "Get over it," or "Snap out of it."

In mild cases of anxiety and depression, it's true that a person may be able to deal with or get over it, but in more serious cases, depression and anxiety may be strongly related to genetic factors that are beyond the person's control. The genes that trigger emotional problems often have a delayed effect; their influence doesn't kick in until the late teens and early 20s. Thus, individuals who may have experienced no emotional problems during childhood may begin to experience them for the first time while they're in college. These cases of depression and anxiety often cannot be solved by willpower alone because they're often related to underlying imbalances in brain chemicals caused by the individual's genetic makeup.

Certainly, you wouldn't tell a diabetic, "Come on; snap out of it. Get your insulin up." This sounds ridiculous because you know that this illness is caused by a chemical imbalance (shortage of insulin) in the body. Similarly, emotional disorders can be caused by a chemical imbalance (e.g., shortage of serotonin) in the brain. You wouldn't expect people suffering from diabetes to be able to exert self-control over a problem caused by their blood chemistry; similarly, you shouldn't expect people suffering from serious cases of emotional illness to be able to exert self-control over a problem caused by their brain chemistry.

© Galina Barskaya, 2010. Under license from Shutterstock, Inc.

One strategy for coping with depression is to write down the positive events in your life in a journal.

When professional assistance is needed for depression, anxiety, or any other emotional problem, an effective (and convenient) place to start is the Counseling Center on campus. Psychologists (who usually earned their doctoral degree in psychology, philosophy, or education) in this center are licensed to provide professional counseling, and they can make referrals to psychiatrists (who hold a doctorate in medicine) in case medication is needed.

Medications for emotional disorders are designed to compensate or correct chemical imbalances in the brain. Thus, taking medication for emotional disorders may be viewed as a way of helping the brain to produce chemicals that it should be producing on its own but isn't producing because of its genetic makeup. When humans experience intense physical pain, we understand and accept their need to take painkilling drugs (e.g., over-the-counter or prescription painkillers) to provide relief for their symptoms. Similarly, we should understand that humans experiencing intense emotional pain (e.g., depression or anxiety) may need to take psychiatric medication to provide relief for their symptoms.

THINK ABOUT IT   Journal Entry   **8.11**

If you thought you were experiencing a serious episode of anxiety or depression, would you feel comfortable seeking help from a professional?

_____

_____

If yes, why? If no, why not?

_____

_____

_____

_____

_____

◆ Summary and Conclusion

Interpersonal relationships are strengthened by communication skills (verbal and nonverbal), and human relations or people skills. You can improve the quality of your interpersonal communication and social relationships by:

- Being a good listener;
- Recognizing nonverbal messages you send while listening;
- Opening your mind to different topics of conversation;
- Recalling people's names;
- Greeting people by name when you interact with them; and
- Remembering information about others, thereby expressing interest in them.

Interpersonal conflict occurs throughout social life. However, you can minimize and manage such conflict by:

- Choosing the best place and time to resolve conflicts;
- Cooling off emotionally before expressing your thoughts verbally;
- Letting the person respond;
- Actively listening to the person's response;
- Make your point assertively rather than aggressively, passively, or both;
- Focusing on solving the problem rather than winning the argument;
- Ending the conversation on a warm, constructive note; and
- Expressing your appreciation for the person's effort to change in response to your request.

Today's college students report higher levels of stress than students in years past. Strategies that have been to be effective for reducing excessive stress or anxiety include:

- Deep (diaphragmatic) breathing;
- Progressive muscle relaxation;
- Mental imagery;
- Limited intake of or no alcohol and caffeine;
- Less intake of simple sugars (e.g., chocolates, candies, and sugary sodas);
- Greater intake of foods high in complex carbohydrates (e.g., brown rice, potatoes, pasta, legumes, whole grain bread, and cereals);
- Journaling; and
- Humor and laughter.

Depression is another common emotional problem that you must manage. Self-help strategies for coping with depression include:

- Focusing on the present and the future rather than the past;
- Intentionally improving your mood by engaging in enjoyable or emotionally uplifting activities;
- Continuing to accomplish things, especially those that benefit others who are less fortunate;
- Seeking out humor and experiencing laughter;
- Consciously focusing on personal strengths and accomplishments; and
- Seeking help from others, including professional help if your depression reaches a debilitating level.

Communicating and relating effectively with others are important life skills and forms of human intelligence. Similarly, emotional intelligence—the ability to identify and manage emotions when dealing with others and remain aware of how emotions influence thoughts and actions—has been found to be an important life skill that influences academic, personal, and professional success. The research and strategies discussed in this chapter point strongly to the conclusion that the quality of relationships and emotional life plays a pivotal role in promoting success, health, and happiness.

Internet-Based Resources for Further Information on Social and Emotional Intelligence

For additional information related to the ideas discussed in this chapter, we recommend the following Web sites:

Social Intelligence and Interpersonal Relationships:

www.Humanresources.about.com/od/interpersonalcommunication1/

www.articles911.com/Communication/Interpersonal_Communication/

www.hodu.com/ECS-Menu1.shtml

Emotional Intelligence and Mental Health:

www.socialresearchmethods.net/Gallery/Young/emotion.htm

www.eqi.org/eitoc.htm

www.nimh.nih.gov/publicat/index.cfm

Chapter 8 Exercises

8.1 Identifying Ways of Handling Interpersonal Conflict

Think of the social situation or relationship that is currently causing you the most conflict in your life. Describe how this conflict might be approached in each of the following ways:

1. Passively:

2. Aggressively:

3. Passive–aggressively:

4. Assertively:

(See **pp. 263–267** for descriptions of each of these approaches).

Consider practicing the assertive approach by role-playing it with a friend or classmate and then applying it to the actual situation or relationship in your life in which you're experiencing conflict.

8.2 College Stress: Identifying Potential Sources and Possible Solutions

Read through the following 29 college stressors and rate them in terms of how stressful each one is for you on a scale from 1 to 5 (1 = lowest, 5 = highest):

Potential Stressors		Stress Rating			
Tests and exams	1	2	3	4	5
Assignments	1	2	3	4	5
Class workload	1	2	3	4	5
Pace of courses	1	2	3	4	5
Performing up to expectations	1	2	3	4	5
Handling personal freedom	1	2	3	4	5
Time pressure (e.g., not enough time)	1	2	3	4	5
Organizational pressure (e.g., losing things)	1	2	3	4	5
Living independently	1	2	3	4	5
The future	1	2	3	4	5
Decisions about a major or career	1	2	3	4	5
Moral and ethical decisions	1	2	3	4	5
Finding meaning in life	1	2	3	4	5
Emotional issues	1	2	3	4	5
Physical health	1	2	3	4	5
Social life	1	2	3	4	5
Intimate relationships	1	2	3	4	5
Sexuality	1	2	3	4	5
Family responsibilities	1	2	3	4	5
Family conflicts	1	2	3	4	5
Family pressure	1	2	3	4	5
Peer pressure	1	2	3	4	5
Loneliness or isolation	1	2	3	4	5
Roommate conflicts	1	2	3	4	5
Conflict with professors	1	2	3	4	5
Campus policies or procedures	1	2	3	4	5
Transportation	1	2	3	4	5
Technology	1	2	3	4	5
Safety	1	2	3	4	5

Review your ratings and write down three of your top (highest-rated) stressors. Identify (a) a coping strategy you may use on your own to deal with that source of stress, and (b) a campus resource you could use to obtain help with that source of stress.

Stressor: _____

Individual coping strategy:

Campus coping resource:

Stressor: _____

Individual coping strategy:

Campus coping resource:

Stressor: _____

Individual coping strategy:

Campus coping resource:

Case Study

Lauren has been dating her new boyfriend (Nick) for about 2 months. She's convinced this is the "real thing" and that she's definitely "in love." Lately, Nick has been asking her to skip class to spend more time with him. He tells Lauren, "If you really love me, you would do it for our relationship." Lauren feels that Nick truly loves her and wouldn't do anything to hurt her or interfere with her goals. So she figures that skipping a few classes to spend time with her boyfriend is the right choice. However, Lauren's grades soon start to slip; at the same time, Nick starts to demand that she spend even more time with him.

Reflection and Discussion Questions

1. What concerns you most about Lauren's behavior?

   What concerns you most about Nick's behavior?

2. Would you agree with Lauren's decision to start skipping classes?

3. What might Lauren do to keep her grades up and still keep her relationship with Nick strong?

4. If you were Lauren's friend, what advice would you give her?

5. If you were Nick's friend, what advice would you give him?

Health and Wellness

9

THOUGHT STARTER **Journal Entry** **9.1**

What would you say are the three most important things that humans can do to preserve their health and promote their physical well-being?

1. _____

2. _____

3. _____

LEARNING GOAL

To acquire strategies for physical wellness that can be applied to promote your success during the first year of college and preserve wellness during your later years in college and beyond.

◆ What Is Wellness?

Wellness may be described as a state of good health and positive well-being that promotes peak mental and physical performance by enabling different dimensions of the self to work well together.

While experts disagree on the exact number and nature of the different dimensions of wellness (President's Council on Physical Fitness and Sports, 2001), we feel that wellness is best understood and developed in terms of the following dimensions of the self:

1. **Intellectual.** Knowledge, thoughts, and self-concept;
2. **Emotional.** Feelings, emotional adjustment, and mental health;
3. **Social.** Interpersonal interactions and relationships;
4. **Ethical.** Values and moral convictions;
5. **Physical.** Bodily health and wellness;
6. **Spiritual.** Beliefs about the meaning or purpose of life and the hereafter;
7. **Vocational (occupational).** Career development and satisfaction;
8. **Personal.** Self-concept, personal identity, and personal habits (e.g., how time and money are spent).

> "
> *"Wellness is an integrated method of functioning, which is oriented toward maximizing the potential of the individual."*
>
> –H. Joseph Dunn, originator of the term "wellness"

Your "self" is composed of multiple elements or dimensions, and each of them can affect your health, success, and happiness. As can be seen in **Figure 9.1**, numerous elements of the self join together to form the wellness wheel. The development of all these elements is a primary goal of wellness and that of a well-rounded college education.

People are not just thinking (intellectual) or working (vocational) beings; they are also social, emotional, physical, ethical, and spiritual beings. In Figure 9.1, these dimensions of the self are joined or linked to show they are interrelated and do not work independently; rather, they interdependently to affect an individual's development and well-being (Love & Love, 1995). For instance, your emotional state can be influenced by your social relationships (e.g., whether you feel lonely or loved); your intellectual performance can be influenced by your emotional state (e.g., whether you are relaxed or anxious); and your social relationships can be influenced by your physical condition (e.g., whether you have a positive or negative physical self-image). If one link in the chain is strengthened or weakened, other dimensions of the self are likely to be simultaneously strengthened or weakened.

Research strongly suggests that quality of life depends on attending to and integrating all important elements of the self. It has been found that people who are healthy (physically and mentally) and successful are typically individuals who have effectively attended to and blended all key dimensions of the self, enabling them to lead well-balanced and well-rounded lives (Covey, 1990; Goleman, 1995; Heath, 1977).

Since wholeness is essential for wellness, success, and happiness, read carefully the following descriptions and skills associated with each of the eight elements of holistic development. As you read the skills listed beneath each element, place a checkmark in the space next to any skill that is particularly important to you. You may check more than one skill within each area.

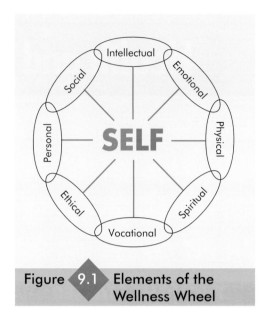

Figure 9.1 Elements of the Wellness Wheel

Skills and Abilities Associated with Each Element of Wellness

1. **Intellectual development.** Acquiring knowledge and learning how to learn deeply and how to think at a higher level.

Skills and abilities:
- Becoming aware of your intellectual abilities, interests, or learning styles
- Attaining and maintaining attention and concentration
- Using effective strategies for improving long-term learning and memory
- Moving beyond memorization to think at a higher level

- Using effective research skills to obtain information from various sources and systems
- Viewing issues from multiple angles or viewpoints (psychological, social, political, economic, etc.) to attain a balanced, comprehensive perspective
- Evaluating ideas critically in terms of their truth and value
- Thinking creatively or imaginatively
- Responding rationally and constructively to differing viewpoints or opposing arguments
- Resisting persuasion tactics that appeal to emotions and responding to them logically or rationally

2. **Emotional development.** Strengthening skills for understanding, controlling, and expressing emotions.

Skills and abilities:
- Dealing with emotions in an honest, nondefensive manner
- Maintaining a healthy balance between emotional control and emotional expression
- Responding with empathy and sensitivity to emotions experienced by others
- Dealing effectively with depression
- Dealing effectively with anger
- Using effective stress-management strategies to control anxiety or tension
- Responding positively to life changes and challenges
- Dealing effectively with fear of failure, criticism, or poor performance
- Accepting feedback in a constructive, nondefensive manner
- Maintaining optimism and enthusiasm

3. **Social development.** Enhancing the quality and depth of interpersonal relationships.

Skills and abilities:
- Using effective interpersonal communication skills
- Relating effectively to others in one-to-one, small-group, and large-group situations
- Overcoming shyness or loneliness and initiating new relationships
- Forming meaningful friendships
- Handling interpersonal conflict effectively in an assertive manner rather than in a passive or aggressive manner
- Providing advice and feedback to others in a constructive and considerate manner
- Using effective collaboration and teamwork skills to work productively with others
- Relating effectively to others from different cultural backgrounds and with different personal lifestyles
- Developing leadership skills

4. **Ethical development.** Acquiring a clear value system for guiding life choices and decisions and developing moral character, or the ability to make judgments and demonstrate consistency between moral convictions (beliefs) and moral commitments (actions).

Skills and abilities:
- Being self-aware of personal values and ethical assumptions

"*You know you've got to exercise your brain just like your muscles.*"

–Will Rogers, Native American humorist and actor

"*It's not stress that kills us; it is our reaction to it.*"

–Hans Selye, Canadian endocrinologist and author of *Stress Without Distress*

"*I look for people that take responsibility and are good team people over anything else. I can teach [them] the technical.*"

–Milwaukee business executive (Peter D. Hart Research Associates, 2006)

- Making important personal choices and life decisions based on a meaningful value system (e.g., decisions about majors, careers, and relationships)
- Having the courage to think and act with personal integrity or honesty, including honesty with respect to schoolwork, both inside and outside the classroom (academic integrity)
- Using electronic technology in an ethical and responsible manner
- Fulfilling personal commitments and responsibilities to others
- Knowing how to exercise individual freedom without infringing on the rights of others
- Developing concern and commitment for human rights and social justice
- Becoming a responsible citizen

5. **Physical development.** Applying knowledge about how the human body functions to prevent disease, maintain wellness, and promote peak performance.

Skills and abilities:
- Being aware of your physical condition and state of health
- Applying knowledge about exercise and fitness training to promote physical and mental health
- Understanding the role of rest and sleep patterns for promoting health and increasing energy
- Applying knowledge on nutrition and diet to enhance your health and physical performance
- Maintaining a healthy balance among work, relaxation, and recreation
- Having a healthy and positive body image
- Being aware of nutritional imbalances and eating disorders
- Being aware of the effects of drugs on the body and on physical and mental performance
- Being knowledgeable about the biology and psychology of human sexuality and sexually transmitted diseases
- Being knowledgeable about the physical and physiological differences between the sexes and their implications for male–female relationships and gender orientation

6. **Spiritual development.** Searching for an answer to the "big questions," such as the meaning or purpose of life and death and nonmaterial issues that transcend human life and the physical world.

Skills and abilities:
- Developing a personal philosophy or worldview about the meaning and purpose of human existence
- Appreciating what cannot be completely understood
- Appreciating the mysteries associated with the origin of the universe
- Exploring the connection between yourself and humanity
- Exploring the connection between yourself and the physical world that surrounds you
- Being open to examining questions relating to death and life after death
- Being open to examining questions about the possible existence of a supreme being or higher power

- Being aware of different approaches to spirituality and their underlying beliefs or assumptions
- Understanding the difference and relationship between faith and reason
- Being knowledgeable and tolerant of religious beliefs and practices

7. **Vocational development.** Exploring career options, making career choices wisely, and developing skills needed for lifelong career success.

Skills and abilities:
- Being knowledgeable about the relationship between college majors and careers
- Using effective strategies for exploring and identifying potential careers
- Selecting career options that are consistent with your personal values, interests, and talents
- Acquiring work experience in fields that relate to your career interests
- Developing an effective résumé and portfolio
- Adopting effective strategies for selecting individuals to serve as personal references and improving the quality of your letters of recommendation
- Developing effective job-search strategies
- Acquiring effective strategies for writing letters of inquiry and letters of application to potential employers
- Developing effective networking skills for making personal contacts with potential employers
- Learning strategies for effective job-interview preparation and performance

"Graduates entering the white-collar workforce are going to have to learn how to communicate effectively, both verbally and via the written word. Good writing skills and good public speaking skills are crucial to business success."

–Paul Dillon, *What Business Expects from Higher Education*

8. **Personal development.** Developing positive self-beliefs, personal attitudes, and personal habits.

Skills and abilities:
- Developing a sense of personal identity and a coherent self-concept (e.g., "Who am I?")
- Finding a sense of future direction and purpose (e.g., "Who am I becoming?")
- Developing self-respect and positive self-esteem
- Acquiring self-confidence
- Developing self-efficacy, or a strong belief that events and outcomes in life can be affected or influenced by personal initiative or effort
- Setting realistic goals
- Establishing personal priorities
- Becoming self-motivated and self-disciplined
- Developing the patience and perseverance to persist on tasks despite personal setbacks or frustration
- Learning practical skills for managing personal affairs effectively and efficiently
- Becoming independent and self-reliant

"The worst loneliness is not to be comfortable with yourself."

–Samuel Clemens, a.k.a. Mark Twain, writer, lecturer, and humorist

THINK ABOUT IT   Journal Entry   9.2

Look back and count the number of checkmarks you placed by each of the eight general areas of self-development. Did you find that you placed roughly the same number of checkmarks in all eight areas, or did you place more checkmarks in certain areas and fewer checkmarks in others?

_____

_____

_____

_____

_____

Based on the checkmarks you placed in each area, would you say that your interests in self-development are balanced across different elements of the self or are slanted toward strong interest in certain elements of development, with little interest in others?

_____

_____

_____

_____

_____

"Everyone is a house with four rooms: a physical, a mental, an emotional, and a spiritual. Most of us tend to live in one room most of the time, but unless we go into every room every day, even if only to keep it aired, we are not complete."

–Native American proverb

Buono salute é la vera ricchezza
("Good health is true wealth.")

–Italian proverb

"Health is a state of complete . . . well-being, and not merely the absence of disease or infirmity."

–World Health Organization

It could be said that physical health is the precondition or prerequisite that enables all other elements of wellness to take place. For instance, it's hard to develop intellectually or socially if you're not well physically, and it's hard to become wealthy and wise unless you're first healthy.

However, physical wellness isn't just the absence of illness or something that's done in reaction to illness (e.g., getting well after being sick); it's something that's done proactively to prevent illness from occurring (Corbin, Pangrazi, & Franks, 2000). Wellness puts into practice two classic proverbs: "Prevention is the best medicine" and "An ounce of prevention is worth a pound of cure."

As depicted in **Figure 9.2**, three potential interception points for preventing illness, maintaining health, and promoting peak performance range from the reactive (after illness) to proactive (before illness).

Wellness goes beyond merely maintaining physical health to attaining a quality of life to include personal satisfaction, happiness, vitality (energy and vigor), and longevity (a longer life span).

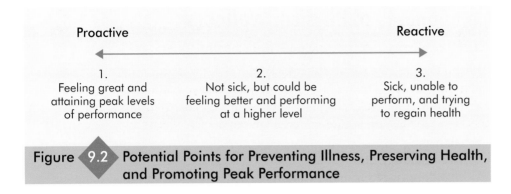

Figure 9.2 Potential Points for Preventing Illness, Preserving Health, and Promoting Peak Performance

◆ The Relevance of Wellness for Today's College Students

When students move directly from high school to college, and move from life at home to life on campus, they're making a major move toward taking sole responsibility for their own wellness.

In addition to receiving less guidance and supervision, new college students are making a major life transition; during times of change or transition, stress tends to increase. Bad health habits, such as poor eating habits, can further increase stress and moodiness (Khoshaba & Maddi, 1999–2004). In contrast, maintaining good health habits is one way to both cope effectively with college stress and promote peak performance.

Among the advantages experienced by college graduates are better physical health, longer lives, and higher levels of both psychological well-being (mental health) and personal happiness (life satisfaction). This suggests that students are learning something about wellness and how to promote it by the time they graduate from college. We want you to begin learning about wellness now so that you can experience its benefits immediately and continue to experience them throughout your college years.

THINK ABOUT IT   **Journal Entry** **9.3**

If you could single out one thing about your physical health as something you'd like to improve or learn more about, what would it be?

◆ Components of Physical Wellness

A healthy physical lifestyle includes five elements:

1. Supplying your body with effective fuel (nutrition);
2. Converting the fuel you consume into bodily energy (exercise);
3. Giving your body adequate rest (sleep) so that it can recover from the energy it has expended;
4. Managing stress and anxiety and controlling thoughts (positive or negative thinking); and
5. Avoiding risky substances and risky behaviors that can threaten your health and safety.

◆ Nutrition

Your body needs nutrients to replenish its natural biochemicals and repair its tissues. The food you put into your body supplies it with energy much like fuel does for a car. Just as high-quality gasoline can improve how well and how long your car runs, so can the consumption of high-quality (nutritious) food improve your body and mind, allowing them to function at peak capacity. Unfortunately humans often eat without any intentional planning about what they eat, choosing to pick up food on the run. America has become a fast-food nation, developing the habit of consuming food that can be accessed quickly, conveniently, cheaply, and in large (super-sized) portions (Schlosser, 2001).

Even when people slow down and take time to eat, they often consume food while their attention is divided and consumed by something else (e.g., conversation, reading, or watching TV).

Studies show that the least nutritious and healthy foods are the very ones that receive the most media advertising (Caroli, Argentieri, Cardone, & Masi, 2004; Hill, 2002). The most frequently advertised food items that people are consuming in the largest quantities tend to be junk food (i.e., food with the least nutrients, the most calories, and the highest health risks). The advertising, availability, and convenience of high-calorie, low-cost food is contributing to Americans being heavier now than at any other time in the nation's history. In 2003, approximately 65 percent of Americans 20 years and older were either overweight (20 percent more than the ideal body weight for their height and age) or obese (30 percent more than their ideal weight; American Obesity Association, 2002; Hill, Wyat, Reed, & Peters, 2003). The percentage of Americans who are overweight or obese has risen from 26 percent in 1976 (Hill et al., 2003). The most telling piece of evidence is the finding that when people from other countries move to America and begin to adopt American eating habits, they typically put on a significant amount of weight (Sundquist & Winkleby, 2000).

National surveys of first-year college students indicate that less than 40 percent report that they maintain a healthy diet (Sax, Lindholm, Astin, Korn, & Mahoney, 2004). The phrase "freshman 15" is commonly used to describe the 15-pound weight gain that some students experience during their first year of college (Brody, 2003; Levitsky, Nussbaum, Halbmaier, & Mrdjenovic, 2003). For some first-year students, this weight gain may be temporary and associated with the initial transition to the college eating lifestyle (e.g., all-you-can-eat dining halls, late-night pizzas, and junk-food snacks). However, for other students, it may signal the start of a longer-lasting pattern of gaining and carrying excess weight. The disadvantage of being overweight isn't merely a matter of appearance; it's also a matter of health and survival because excess weight increases susceptibility to the leading life-threatening diseases, such as diabetes, heart disease, and certain forms of cancer.

THINK ABOUT IT   **Journal Entry**   **9.4**

Have your eating habits changed since you've begun college?

_____

_____

If yes, in what way or ways have they changed?

_____

_____

_____

_____

_____

_____

Snapshot Summary   **9.1**

Eating Disorders

While some students experience the "freshman 15," others experience eating disorders related to lost weight and loss of control over their eating habits. The disorders described here are more common among females (National Institute of Mental Health, 2001). Studies show that approximately one of every three college females indicates that she worries about her weight, body image, or eating habits (Douglas et al., 1997; Haberman & Luffey, 1998). This is likely because Western cultures place more emphasis and pressure on females than males to maintain lighter body weight and body size. This is an unfortunate social standard (or double standard) because it subjects women to conflict between cultural expectations and biological realities. The female body is genetically constituted or naturally wired with more fat cells, which causes it to store fat more easily than the male body. It's likely that women have been naturally equipped with more ability to store fat because fat is a source of reserve energy that females, as the child-bearing sex, can draw upon during pregnancy to sustain their body, as well as the body of the fetus they're carrying.

What follows is a short summary of the major eating disorders experienced by college students. People experiencing these disorders often deny their problem, and their eating disorder is typically accompanied by emotional issues (e.g., depression and anxiety) that are serious enough to require professional treatment (American Psychiatric Association Work Group on Eating Disorders, 2000). The earlier these disorders are identified and treated, the better the prognosis or probability of complete and permanent recovery. The Counseling Center or Student Health Center is the key campus resource to begin the process of seeking help and treatment for any of the following eating disorders.

Anorexia Nervosa

The self-esteem of people who experience this disorder is often tied closely to their body weight or shape. They see themselves as overweight and have an intense fear of gaining weight, even though they're dangerously thin. Anorexics typically deny that they're severely underweight, and even if their weight drops to the point where they may look like walking skeletons, they may continue to be obsessed with losing weight, eating infrequently, and eating in extremely small portions. Anorexics may also use other methods to lose weight, such as compulsive exercise, diet pills, laxatives, diuretics, or enemas.

Bulimia Nervosa

This eating disorder is characterized by repeated episodes of binge eating—eating excessive amounts of food within a limited period. Bulimics tend to lose all sense of self-control during their binges; they then try to compensate for their overeating by engaging in extreme behavior that's designed to purge their guilt and prevent weight gain. For example, they may purge by self-induced vomiting, consuming excessive amounts of laxatives or diuretics, using enemas, or fasting. The binge–purge pattern typically takes place at least twice a week and continues for 3 or more months.

Unlike anorexia, bulimia is harder to detect because bulimics' binges and purges take place secretly and their body weight looks about normal for their age and height. However, similar to anorexics, bulimics fear gaining weight, aren't happy with their body, and have an intense desire to lose weight.

Binge-Eating Disorder

Like bulimia, this eating disorder involves repeated, out-of-control binging on large quantities of food. However, unlike bulimics, binge eaters don't purge after binging episodes. For someone to be diagnosed as suffering from binge-eating disorder, that person must demonstrate at least three of the following symptoms, two or more times per week, for several months:

1. Eating more rapidly than normal
2. Eating until becoming uncomfortably full
3. Eating large amounts of food when not physically hungry
4. Eating alone because of embarrassment about others seeing how much is eaten
5. Feeling guilty, disgusted, or depressed after overeating

Since those who suffer from these eating disorders usually don't recognize or admit their illness, friends and family members play a key role in helping them receive help before the disorder progresses to a life-threatening level. If someone you know is experiencing an eating disorder, consult with a professional at the Student Health Center or Counseling Center about strategies for approaching and encouraging this person to seek help.

Sources: American Psychiatric Association (1994); National Institute of Mental Health (2006).

Nutrition-Management Strategies

Consider this series of nutrition-management strategies for promoting your body's ability to stay well and perform well.

1. Develop a nutrition management plan to ensure your diet has variety and balance.

Take a look at **Figure 9.3**, which lists the basic food groups and the portions of each group recommended by the American Dietetic Association. The Food

Guide Pyramid divides food into six basic groups. Since foods vary in terms of the nature of nutrients they provide (carbohydrates, protein, and fat), no single food group can supply all nutrients your body needs. Therefore, your diet should be balanced to include all of these food groups but in different proportions or percentages. To find the daily amount of food you should be consuming from each of these major food groups (e.g., your age and gender), go to www.mypyramid.gov.

You can use the food pyramid to create a dietary plan that ensures you consume each of these food groups every day, which will result in a balanced diet that minimizes your risk of experiencing any nutritional deficits or deficiencies. If this guide to nutrition is followed, there should be no need for you to take vitamins or dietary supplements.

If you are confused as to what an appropriate portion size is for the categories in the food pyramid it may be easiest to consider the size of portions in terms of everyday items. A serving of meat should be about the size of a

Anatomy of MyPyramid

One size doesn't fit all
USDA's new MyPyramid symbolizes a personalized approach to healthy eating and physical activity. The symbol has been designed to be simple. It has been developed to remind consumers to make healthy food choices and to be active every day. The different parts of the symbol are described below.

Activity
Activity is represented by the steps and the person climbing them, as a reminder of the importance of daily physical activity.

Moderation
Moderation is represented by the narrowing of each food group from bottom to top. The wider base stands for foods with little or no solid fats or added sugars. These should be selected more often. The narrower top area stands for foods containing more added sugars and solid fats. The more active you are, the more of these foods can fit into your diet.

Personalization
Personalization is shown by the person on the steps, the slogan, and the URL. Find the kinds and amounts of food to eat each day at MyPyramid.gov.

Proportionality
Proportionality is shown by the different widths of the food group bands. The widths suggest how much food a person should choose from each group. The widths are just a general guide, not exact proportions. Check the Web site for how much is right for you.

Variety
Variety is symbolized by the 6 color bands representing the 5 food groups of the Pyramid and oils. This illustrates that foods from all groups are needed each day for good health.

Gradual Improvement
Gradual improvement is encouraged by the slogan. It suggests that individuals can benefit from taking small steps to improve their diet and lifestyle each day.

MyPyramid.gov
STEPS TO A HEALTHIER YOU

USDA U.S. Department of Agriculture
Center for Nutrition Policy
and Promotion
April 2005 CNPP-16

USDA is an equal opportunity provider and employer.

GRAINS VEGETABLES FRUITS OILS MILK MEAT& BEANS

 Figure 9.3 Food Guide Pyramid

deck of cards and a serving of vegetables or fruit should be about the size of a baseball. To assist you in consuming the appropriate portion size, use smaller bowls and plates and don't go back for seconds once you have consumed the serving. In addition, never eat directly from a bag; carton or any other type of container food is packaged in. This will give you a false sense of how much you are eating.

2. Minimize your consumption of foods whose nutritional value is low (or zero) and that increase your risk of heart disease and cancer.

- Reduce intake of fried and fatty foods such as pizza, hamburgers, French fries, donuts, butter, and margarine. These foods not only contain lots of calories but also can increase the risk of heart disease because they contain saturated fats and trans fats—"bad" fats that tend to stick to blood vessel walls and increase the risk of blocking normal blood flow. Saturated fats also increase the risk of certain forms of cancer, such as breast and bowel cancer. Saturated fats should comprise less than one-tenth of the total number of calories you consume (National Research Council, 1989).

- Reduce consumption of processed foods. Processed foods were originally natural foods, but synthetic ingredients have been added to them so that they can be preserved, packaged, jarred, canned, or bottled and sold later to the public in large or bulk quantities. Processed foods contain additives that supplement natural food to preserve its shelf life, make it more pleasing to the eye, or make it more pleasing to the taste buds. These additives typically have no nutritional value and may have unknown or possibly unhealthy effects on the body. For example, processed foods often contain added sugar and salt, which tend to promote weight gain and elevate blood pressure, respectively.

- Reduce consumption of high-fat dairy products (e.g., cheese, butter, margarine, cream, and whole milk). High-fat dairy products are high in saturated fat and sodium, both of which increase the risk of heart disease. The calcium contained in dairy products is good for you, but you're better off getting that calcium from low-fat dairy products, such as low-fat milk, yogurt, and cottage cheese.

- Minimize consumption of animal meat, particularly red meat such as hamburger and steak. Meat often contains a large amount of saturated fat, which poses a major risk for heart disease. Many people believe they must consume a substantial amount of red meat because the body needs protein. It's true that meat provides large amounts of protein, but protein should make up only 15 percent of your daily calories. Thus, Americans tend to consume about twice as much protein as their bodies need (National Research Council, 1989). Consequently, it's probably best to decrease the amount of protein you get from meat and increase the amount you get from sources that are low in saturated fat, such as plants (e.g., beans and peas), nuts (e.g., walnuts and almonds), and low-fat dairy products (e.g., low-fat milk and yogurt).

If or when you consume meat, you can reduce its health risk by eating lean meat that has less fat and by removing any fatty skin from the meat (e.g., removing the skin from chicken or turkey). You can also reduce the risk of meat's unhealthy effects by not frying it because the oils used in the frying process

> "Life expectancy would grow by leaps and bounds if green vegetables smelled as good as bacon."
>
> –Doug Larson, American cartoonist

increase the concentration of saturated fat in the meat. Instead of frying, roast, grill, bake, or broil the meat you eat.

3. Reduce calorie intake and control weight.

- Decrease or eliminate junk-food snacks. Replace sugary and salty snacks with healthier munchies, such as fruits, nuts, seeds, and raw vegetables. Many of these healthier snacks are as sweet, crispy, or crunchy as junk food snacks. Natural fruits can provide sweetness with more nutrients and fewer calories than processed sweets (e.g., candy bars and blended coffee drinks).

THINK ABOUT IT   **Journal Entry**   **9.5**

What type of junk food (if any) do you currently eat? Why?

_____

_____

_____

_____

_____

_____

_____

If you do eat junk food, what's the likelihood that you'll continue to do so? Why?

_____

_____

_____

_____

_____

_____

_____

- Decrease the tendency to pack most of your calories into one or two large meals per day. Most nutritionists recommend that people eat large meals less often and small meals more often. No research evidence or dietary rule supports the American habit of eating three times a day as the best nutritional practice. Six smaller meals or healthy snacks per day may be a more effective way to fuel the body than three, full-sized meals (Khoshaba & Maddi, 1999–2004).

- Reduce the total number of calories consumed during your evening meal. The meal you eat closest to bedtime should be your lightest meal with the fewest calories because you're soon going to be lying down and not expending much physical energy for 7 to 8 hours. Remember that calories are measures of the amount of energy contained in food. One calorie may be described as one unit or degree of energy. If you consume a unit of energy and don't use it, you don't lose it; instead, you save it or store it—as fat. In other words, much like money, if you don't spend your income (caloric intake), you tend to save it in your body's bank of fat cells. Eating lots of calories in the evening and then lying down and sleeping soon thereafter means those evening calories don't get burned as physical energy; instead, they get stored as body fat.

- Avoid rushing out at the beginning of the day and skipping or skimping on breakfast. As the term implies, a good breakfast provides energy that enables you to break your nighttime fast at the start of the day and sustain your energy throughout the day. (It also reduces your desire for unhealthy snacks later in the day.) Your first meal of the day should be the meal at which you consume most of your daily calories because you need energy for the next 16 or so hours that you'll be awake and moving.

4. Make a conscious attempt to increase consumption of natural foods that have been available to humans throughout natural history.

The following foods aren't processed foods but are natural foods that have been available to, and consumed by, humans for thousands of years. As a rule, the food that was good for our ancient ancestors and the survival of our species is good for us now. These are the foods that provide humans with the best protection against their two leading killers: heart disease and cancer.

- **Feast on fresh fruit.** Fruit has multiple nutritional benefits, including high amounts of vitamins (especially A and C) and minerals. Many fruits also contain high amounts of fiber, which helps purify the bloodstream, lowers the bad type of cholesterol that causes heart disease, and rids the body of toxins found in the intestine. Other fruits, such as berries, are rich in antioxidants—substances known to lower the risk of cancer by attacking oxidants (toxins) in the body that can damage genetic DNA and weaken the immune system. (Blueberries are thought to contain the most antioxidants, followed by blackberries, raspberries, and strawberries.) Keep in mind that fresh fruit is superior to canned fruit, which has been processed and artificially preserved. Also, if weight control is an issue for you, fresh fruit is superior to dried fruit, which contains more calories.

- **Go for fresh (or frozen) vegetables.** Fresh or frozen vegetables are superior to canned and processed vegetables. The natural oils in certain vegetables (e.g., olive, corn, avocado, and soy) are rich sources of unsaturated fat. Unsaturated fats, also known as essential fatty acids, are considered to be "good" fats because they don't congregate or coagulate in your bloodstream but remain in liquid form within your system; therefore, they don't degenerate into fat on the walls of blood vessels (Erasmus, 1993). Unsaturated fats also help wash away and flush out bad fats from your bloodstream. In addition to containing unsaturated fats, many vegetables—such as raw carrots and green beans—contain fiber that reduces the risk of heart disease and certain forms of cancer.

| **THINK ABOUT IT** | **Journal Entry** | **9.6** |

Do you eat fresh fruit and vegetables daily?

_____

_____

If yes, why?

_____

_____

_____

_____

_____

If no, why not?

_____

_____

_____

_____

_____

_____

- **Go wild on grains.** Whole-wheat bread and pasta, whole-grain cereals, oatmeal, and bran are examples of healthy grains. Note that the word "whole" should appear in the product's name (e.g., "whole-wheat bread" and "whole-grain cereal"). This is the key to determining that the grain is natural and not processed; for example, whole-wheat bread is made from a natural grain, but wheat or white bread has been processed.

  Natural grains contain complex carbohydrates, which the body uses to produce steady, ongoing energy. Complex carbohydrates are called "complex" because their molecular structure is harder for the body to digest and break down into blood sugar. Their more complex molecular structure slows the digestion process; as a result, they're absorbed into the bloodstream more slowly, which allows them to deliver energy to the body more gradually and evenly over an extended period (similar to a coated pill or time-released capsule). Thus, grains are an excellent source of food for producing steady, long-term energy (e.g., athletic activities that require endurance and stamina). Grains are also high in fiber, which helps fight heart disease and certain forms of cancer.

- **Feed freely on fish.** Fish are high in protein and low in saturated fat, and the natural oil in fish is high in unsaturated fat, which flushes out and washes away cholesterol-forming fats from the bloodstream (Khoshaba & Maddi, 1999–2004). Thus, a diet high in unsaturated fats (and low in saturated fats) reduces risk for cardiovascular disease such as high blood pressure, heart attacks, and strokes. However, be cautious about eating too much fish that could contain high levels of mercury—such as shark, swordfish, red snapper, and orange roughy. Eating a variety of fish will help minimize this risk (American Heart Association, 2006).

- **Consume lots of legumes.** The word "legumes" derives from the Latin root *legumend*, meaning "to gather." This group includes plants and seeds, such as beans (black, red, and navy), lentils, Brussels sprouts, peas, and peanuts. Such foods are great sources of fiber, protein, iron, and B vitamins; plus, they are naturally cholesterol free and low in saturated fat. The natural oil contained in these foods contains unsaturated fats—"good" fats that can reduce buildup of bad cholesterol in the bloodstream. It's interesting to note that in developing countries, where there is less affluence than in the United States, people rely mainly on legumes, grains, fruits, and vegetables. Despite their poorer economy and poorer medical care, people living in underdeveloped countries have significantly lower rates of heart disease and diet-related cancers than do people living (and eating) in the United States (U.S. Department of Health & Human Services, 2000).

- **Drink more water.** Most people don't get the recommended amount of water (seven 8-ounce glasses per day). You need to hydrate your body. The body uses water much like a car uses motor oil and transmission fluid to drive nutrients (fuel) to their proper destinations and to drive waste products out of the system. Water also improves your nervous system's ability to conduct electrochemical signals, which may benefit the brain's ability to process information more easily and more rapidly. In addition to its internal benefits, water has the cosmetic benefit of improving the appearance of your skin.

- **If you're a woman, make a conscious effort to consume more calcium.** Females should take in at least 1,200 mg of calcium per day (Gershoff & Whitney, 1996) to reduce the risk of osteoporosis (thinning of bones and loss of bone mass or density), which increases risk for fractures and curvature of the upper spine. Although osteoporosis can happen in men as well as women, it occurs more often among females. It's estimated that one of three women over the age of 40 will develop osteoporosis (Bohme & Budden, 2001). Low-fat, low-calorie dairy products, such as cottage cheese and low-fat yogurt, can contain lots of calcium without lots of calories. Sizable amounts of calcium are also found in other low-calorie foods, such as certain fish (e.g., salmon), vegetables (e.g., broccoli), and fruit (e.g., oranges; Gershoff & Whitney, 1996). Women can also ensure that they get their optimum level of calcium each day by taking calcium dietary supplements.

5. Maintain self-awareness of your eating habits.

The first step toward effective nutrition management is to become fully aware of your current eating habits. People often make decisions about what to eat without giving it much thought or even without conscious awareness. You can increase awareness of your eating habits by simply taking a little time to read the labels on the food products before you put them into your shopping cart and into your body. Keeping a nutritional log or journal of what you eat in a typical week to track its nutrients and caloric content is also an effective way to become self-aware of your eating habits.

Another thing to be aware of is your family history. Have members of your immediate and extended family shown tendencies toward heart disease? Diabetes? Cancer? If so, intentionally adopt a diet that will reduce your risk for developing the types of illnesses that you may have the genetic potential to develop.

THINK ABOUT IT   **Journal Entry**   **9.7**

Are you aware of any disease or illness that tends to run in your family?

_____

_____

If yes, is there anything you can do with respect to your diet that may decrease your risk of experiencing this disease or illness?

_____

_____

_____

_____

_____

_____

◆ Exercise and Fitness

Wellness depends not only on fueling the body but also on moving it. The benefits of physical exercise for improving the longevity and quality of human life are simply extraordinary. The health-promoting power of exercise is not surprising because physical activity was something that our early ancestors did daily to stay alive. They had no motorized vehicles to move them from point A to point B, and no one sold or served them food. Exercise was part of their daily survival routine of roaming and rummaging for fruit, nuts, and vegetables to eat or running after and tracking down animals for meat to eat. Just as eating natural (unprocessed) food is better for your health because it's

> "If exercise could be packaged into a pill, it would be the single most widely prescribed and beneficial medicine in the nation."
>
> –Robert N. Butler, former director of the National Institute of Aging

long been part of human history and has contributed to the survival of the human species, so too is exercise a "natural" health-promoting activity that has made the same contribution (Booth & Vyas, 2001). If done regularly, exercise may well be the most effective "medicine" available to humans for preventing disease and preserving lifelong health.

Personal Story

I kept in shape when I was young by playing sports such as basketball and baseball. Every chance that made itself available to my schedule, I would play these sports for hours at a time. I enjoyed it so much that I did not realize I was exercising. My body fat was practically nonexistent, energy was ever flowing, and my skills in basketball were always growing. As a middle-aged person, I realize I can no longer do the activities I did for fun as a young person because age has caught up with me. At this point in my life, I attempt to remain active to keep my body fat in a reasonable double-digit category. This takes good scheduling, forethought, and strong will.

—*Aaron Thompson*

Benefits of Exercise for the Body

1. Exercise promotes cardiovascular health.

Exercise makes for a healthy heart. The heart is a muscle, and like any other muscle in the body, its size and strength are increased by exercise. A bigger and stronger heart can pump more blood per beat, which reduces the risk for heart disease and stroke (loss of oxygen to the brain) by increasing circulation of oxygen-carrying blood throughout the body and by increasing the body's ability to dissolve blood clots (Khoshaba & Maddi, 1999–2004).

Exercise further reduces the risk of cardiovascular disease by decreasing the level of triglycerides (clot-forming fats) in the blood and by increasing the levels of "good" cholesterol (high-density lipoproteins) and preventing "bad" cholesterol (low-density lipoproteins) from sticking to and clogging up blood vessels.

2. Exercise stimulates the immune system.

Exercise improves the functioning of the immune system and enables you to better fight off infectious diseases (e.g., colds and the flu) for the following reasons:

- Exercise reduces stress, which normally weakens the immune system.
- Exercise increases breathing rate and blood flow throughout the body; which helps flush out germs from your system by increasing the circulation of antibodies carried through the bloodstream.
- Exercise increases body temperature, which helps kill germs—similar to how a low-grade fever kills germs when you're sick (May, 2004).

3. Exercise strengthens muscles and bones.

Exercise reduces muscle tension, which helps prevent muscle strain and pain. For example, strengthening abdominal muscles reduces the risk of developing lower back pain. Exercise also maintains bone density and reduces the risk of osteoporosis (brittle bones that bend and break easily). It's noteworthy that bone density before age 20 affects a person's bone density for the remainder of life. Thus, engaging in regular exercise early in life pays long-term dividends by preventing bone deterioration throughout life.

THINK ABOUT IT   Journal Entry   **9.8**

Have your exercise habits changed (for better or worse) since you've begun college?

_____

_____

If yes, why do you think this change has taken place?

_____

_____

_____

_____

_____

_____

4. Exercising promotes weight loss and weight management.

The increasing national trend toward weight gain is due not only to Americans consuming more calories but also to reduced levels of physical activity (American Obesity Association, 2002). Much of this reduction in physical activity results from the emergence of modern technological conveniences that have made it easier for humans to go about their daily business without exerting themselves in the slightest. Consequently, people are playing double jeopardy with their health by eating more and moving less.

Exercise is superior to dieting in one major respect: It raises the body's rate of metabolism (i.e., the rate at which consumed calories are burned as energy rather than stored as fat). In contrast, low-calorie dieting lowers the body's rate of metabolism (Leibel, Rosenbaum, & Hirsch, 1995) and slows the rate at which calories are burned. After 2 to 3 weeks of low-calorie dieting without exercising, the body saves more of the calories it does get by storing them as fat. This happens because long-term low-calorie dieting makes the body "think" it's starving; it therefore tries to compensate and increase its chances of survival by saving more calories as fat so that they can be used for future energy (Bennet & Gurin, 1983). In contrast, exercise speeds up basal metabolism—the body's rate of metabolism when it is resting. Thus, in addition to burning fat directly while exercising, exercise burns fat by continuing to keep the body's metabolic rate higher after you stop exercising and move on to do more sedentary things.

Benefits of Exercise for the Mind

In addition to the multiple benefits of exercise for the body are numerous benefits for the mind. What follows is a summary of the powerful benefits of physical exercise for mental health and mental performance. For people who believe that exercise isn't all that good for them and still cling to this belief after reading the following sections, it may be safe to conclude that they are in denial.

1. Exercise increases mental energy and improves mental performance.

Have you ever noticed how red your face gets when you engage in strenuous physical activity? This rosy complexion occurs because physical activity pumps enormous amounts of blood into your head region, resulting in more oxygen reaching your brain. Exercise increases the heart's ability to pump blood throughout the body and into the brain, and since the brain consumes more oxygen than any other part of the body, it's easy to see why it's the bodily organ that benefits the most from exercise. Moreover, exercise increases production of a brain chemical called norepinephrine, which helps form physical connections between brain cells (Howard, 2000). As mentioned in Chapter 4, these are the connections that provide the biological basis of learning and memory.

2. Exercise elevates mood.

> "It is exercise alone that supports the spirits, and keeps the mind in vigor."
>
> –Marcus Cicero, ancient Roman orator and philosopher

Exercise increases the release of endorphins (morphine-like chemicals found in the brain that produce a natural high) and serotonin (a mellowing brain chemical that reduces feelings of tension, anxiety, and depression). For these reasons, psychotherapists prescribe exercise for patients experiencing mild forms of anxiety or depression (Johnsgard, 2004). Studies show that people who exercise regularly tend to report feeling "happier" (Myers, 1993).

3. Exercise strengthens self-esteem.

Exercise improves self-esteem by giving you a sense of personal achievement or accomplishment by improving your physical self-image (e.g., improved weight control, body tone, and skin tone).

4. Exercise deepens and enriches the quality of sleep.

Research on the effects of exercise on sleep indicates that if exercise is engaged in at least 3 hours before bedtime it helps people fall asleep, stay asleep, and sleep more deeply (Singh, Clements, & Fiatarone, 1997). Therefore, exercise is a common component of treatment programs for people experiencing insomnia (Dement & Vaughan, 2000).

Guidelines and Strategies for Effective Exercise

Specific exercises vary in terms of what they do to and for the body. Nevertheless, some general guidelines and strategies, such as those discussed here, can be applied to any exercise routine or personal fitness program.

1. Warm up before exercising and cool down after exercising.

Start with a 10-minute warm up of low-intensity movements that are similar to the ones you'll be using in the actual exercise. This increases circulation of blood to the muscles that you'll be exercising and reduces muscle soreness and your risk of muscle pulls.

End your exercise routine with a 10-minute cool down, during which you stretch the muscles that you used while exercising. Stretch the muscle until it burns a little bit, and then release it. Cooling down after exercise improves circulation to the exercised muscles and enables them to return more gradually to a tension-free state, which will minimize the risk of muscle tightness, cramps, pulls, or tears.

2. Engage in cross-training to attain total body fitness.

A balanced, comprehensive fitness program is one that involves cross-training—combining different exercises to achieve overall bodily fitness. For instance, combine exercises that promote:

- Endurance and weight control (e.g., running, cycling, or swimming);
- Muscle strength and tone (e.g., weight training, push-ups, or sit-ups); and
- Flexibility (e.g., yoga, Pilates, or tai chi).

A total fitness plan also includes exercising various muscle groups rotationally (e.g., upper-body muscles one day, lower-body muscles the next), which allows your muscle tissue extra time to rest and fully repair itself before it's exercised again.

3. Exercising with regularity and consistency is as important as exercising with intensity.

Doing exercise regularly, and allowing strength and stamina to increase gradually, is the key to attaining fitness and avoiding injury. One strategy you can use to be sure that you're training your body, rather than straining and over-extending it, is to see whether you can talk while you're exercising. If you can't continue speaking without having to catch your breath, you may be overdoing it. Drop the intensity level and allow your body to adapt or adjust to a less strenuous level. After continuing at this lower level awhile, try again at the higher level while trying to talk simultaneously. If you can do both, then you're ready to continue at that level for some time. Thus, you can gradually increase the intensity, frequency, or duration of your exercise routine to a level that produces maximum benefits with minimal postexercise strain or pain.

4. Take advantage of exercise and fitness resources on your campus.

You paid for use of the campus gym or recreation center with your college tuition, so take advantage of this and other exercise resources on campus. Also, consider taking physical education courses offered by your college. They count toward your college degree, and typically they carry one unit of credit so that they can be easily added to your course schedule. If exercise-related groups or clubs meet on campus, consider joining them; they can provide you with a motivating support group that can convert your exercise routine from an experience that's done alone to a social experience with others.

Personal Story

I had a habit of exercising too intensely—to the point where I overfatigued my muscles and left my body feeling sore for days after I worked out. Like many people, I exercise while listening to music to make the exercise routine more stimulating. I've since discovered that listening to music through headphones while exercising may help me determine whether I'm overdoing it. If I can't sing along with the music without having to stop and catch my breath, then I know I'm overdoing it. This strategy has helped me manage my exercise-intensity level and reduce my day-after-exercise soreness. (Plus, I've gained more confidence as a singer. My singing sounds better to me when my ears are covered with headphones.)

—Joe Cuseo

---

5. Take a walk.

Many college campuses probably have a track available for you to walk or run laps. All you need is a good pair of tennis shoes. If you don't have a track available to you, there is always the option of using the many sidewalks that run through your campus to take a brisk walk for exercise.

6. Hit the green space or courts.

You most likely have basketball, racquetball and/or tennis courts available to you. These are a great way to enjoy fun exercise with friends or they allow you to meet new people should your friends not be interested in the activity.

7. Take advantage of natural opportunities for physical activity that present themselves during the day.

Exercise can take place outside a gym or fitness center and outside scheduled workout times. Opportunities for exercise often occur naturally as you go about your daily activities. For example, if you can walk or ride your bike to class, do that instead of driving a car or riding a bus. If you can climb some stairs instead of taking an elevator, take the route that's more physically challenging and requires more bodily activity.

8. Use exercise as a strategy for improving your academic performance.

Two simple strategies can be used to combine physical activity with mental activity in a way that may improve your academic performance:

- Take study breaks that involve physical activity (e.g., a short jog or brisk walk). Study breaks that include physical activity not only refresh the mind by giving it a break from studying but also stimulate the mind by increasing blood flow to your brain, which will help you retain what you've already studied and regain concentration for what you're about to study.
- Before exams, take a brisk walk. This will increase mental alertness by increasing oxygen flow to the brain; it will also decrease tension by increasing the brain's production of emotionally "mellowing" brain chemicals (e.g., serotonin and endorphins).

THINK ABOUT IT | **Journal Entry** | **9.9**

Do you have a regular exercise routine?

_____

_____

If no, why not?

_____

_____

_____

_____

_____

If yes, what do you do and how often do you do it?

_____

_____

_____

_____

_____

◆ Rest and Sleep

Sleep experts agree that humans in today's information-loaded, multitasking world aren't getting the quantity and quality of sleep needed to perform at peak levels (Mitler, Dinges, & Dement, 1994).

The Value and Purpose of Sleep

Resting and reenergizing the body are the most obvious purposes of sleep (Dement & Vaughan, 1999). However, other benefits of sleep are less well known but equally important for physical and mental health (Dement & Vaughan, 2000; Horne, 1988). Some of these key, less-apparent benefits of sleep are described here.

1. Sleep restores and preserves the power of the immune system.

Studies show that when humans and other animals lose sleep their production of disease-fighting antibodies is reduced and they become more susceptible to illness, such as common colds and the flu (Blakeslee, 1993).

> "
> "Sleep deprivation is a major epidemic in our society. Americans spend so much time and energy chasing the American dream that they don't have much time left for actual dreaming."
>
> —William Dement, pioneering sleep researcher and founder of the American Sleep Disorders Association

2. Sleep helps you cope with daily stress.

Sleep research shows that the percentage of time people spend in dream sleep increases when they are experiencing stress (Greenberg, Pillard, & Pearlman, 1972). When you lose dream sleep, emotional problems such as anxiety and depression worsen (Voelker, 2004). It's thought that the biochemical changes that take place in your brain during dream sleep restore imbalances in brain chemistry that trigger feelings of anxiety or depression. Getting quality sleep, especially dream sleep, is essential for maintaining a good mood and a positive frame of mind. Indeed, research reveals that people who sleep well are more likely to report that they are happy (Myers, 1993).

3. Sleep helps the brain form and store memories.

Studies show that loss of dream sleep at night results in poorer memory for information learned earlier in the day (Peigneux, Laureys, Delbeuck, & Maquet, 2001). For instance, adolescents who get minimal sleep have a more difficult time retaining new information learned in school (Horne, 1988).

Importance of Sleep for College Students

College students, in particular, tend to have poor sleep habits. Heavier academic workloads, more opportunities to socialize, and course schedules that provide more opportunity to procrastinate can result in last-minute, late-night, or all-night study binges that lead to irregular sleep schedules and regular sleep loss.

How much sleep do you need or should you get? The answer to this question lies in your genes and varies from person to person. On average, adults need 7 to 8 hours of sleep each day and teenagers need slightly more—about 9 hours (Roffwarg, Muzio, & Dement, 1966). Research shows that college students get an average of less than 7 hours of sleep each night (Hicks, cited in Zimbardo, Johnson, & Weber, 2006), which means that they're not getting the amount of sleep needed for optimal academic performance.

Attempting to train your body to sleep less is likely to be an exercise in futility, because what you're actually trying to do is force your body to do something that it's not naturally (genetically) inclined to do. Eventually, you pay the price for the sleep you've lost with lower energy and poorer performance. When your body is deprived of its needed amount of sleep, it accumulates "sleep debt," which, like financial debt, must be eventually paid back to your body at a later time (Dement & Vaughan, 1999). If your sleep debt isn't repaid, it will catch up with you and you will pay the consequences in terms of impaired health, mood, and performance (Van Dongen, Maislin, Mullington, & Dinges, 2003). For example, studies show that the effects of sleep loss on driving an automobile are similar to the effects of alcohol (Arnett, Wilde, Munt, & MacLean, 2001; Fletcher, Lamond, van den Heuvel, & Dawson, 2003), and sleep-deprived students have been found to earn lower grades than students who get sufficient sleep (Spinweber, cited in Zimbardo et al., 2006).

Student Perspective

"I 'binge' sleep. I don't sleep often and then I hibernate for like a day or two."

—First-year student

Student Perspective

"I'm not getting enough sleep. I've been getting roughly 6–7 hours of sleep on weekdays. In high school, I would get 8–9 hours of sleep."

—First-year student

Student Perspective

"First of all, you should probably know that your body will not function without sleep. I learned that the hard way."

—Words written by a first-year student in a letter of advice to new college students

What amount of sleep per night do you think you need to perform at your highest level?

_____
_____
_____
_____
_____

How many nights per week do you typically get this amount of sleep?

_____
_____
_____
_____
_____

If you're not getting this optimal amount of sleep each night, what is preventing you from doing so?

_____
_____
_____
_____
_____
_____

Strategies for Improving Sleep Quality

Since sleep has powerful benefits for both the body and the mind, if you can improve the quality of your sleep, you can improve your physical and mental well-being. Listed here is a series of strategies for improving sleep quality that should also improve your health and performance.

1. Increase awareness of your sleep habits by keeping a sleep log or sleep journal.

In your sleep journal, note nights when you slept well or poorly and what you did before going to bed on those nights. Tracking your sleep experiences in a journal may enable you to find patterns that reveal relationships among certain things you do (or don't do) during the day on those nights you sleep well. If you detect such a pattern, you may have detected a routine you could follow regularly to ensure that you consistently get high-quality sleep.

2. Attempt to get into a regular sleep schedule by going to sleep and getting up about the same times each day.

Irregular sleep schedules can disrupt the quality of sleep. This is what happens to people who experience jet lag. Traveling to a new time zone often requires travelers to change their sleep schedule to accommodate the time shift, which can disrupt the quality of their sleep (Rader & Hicks, 1987). Your body likes to work on a biological rhythm of set cycles; if you can get your body on a regular sleep schedule, you're more likely to establish a biological rhythm that makes it easier for you to fall asleep, stay asleep, and wake up naturally from sleep according to your internal alarm clock.

Establishing a stable sleep schedule is particularly important around midterms and finals. Unfortunately, these are the times during the term when students often disrupt their normal sleep patterns by cramming in last-minute studying, staying up later, getting up earlier, or not going to sleep. Sleep research shows that if you want to be at your physical and mental best for upcoming exams, you should get yourself on a regular sleep schedule of going to bed about the same time and getting up about the same time for at least 1 week before your exams (Dement, 1999).

THINK ABOUT IT   **Journal Entry** 9.11

Do you have or need an alarm clock to wake up in the morning?

_____

_____

Why?

_____

_____

_____

_____

_____

_____

---

3. Sleep in the same place each night.

People are creatures of habit, and if the brain gets in the habit of associating the same environmental cues (e.g., sights, smells, and sounds) with falling asleep, you're more likely to fall asleep when you find yourself in that same environment. By repeatedly sleeping in the same environment (e.g., the same room, the same side of the bed, and the same sound of a humming fan), these sensations become repeatedly paired or associated with sleep and your body is more likely to respond to those associations by falling asleep (Hauri & Linde, 1996).

4. Attempt to get into a relaxing bedtime ritual each night.

Taking a hot bath or shower, consuming hot milk, or listening to relaxing music are bedtime rituals that can get you into a worry-free state and help you fall asleep sooner. Also, making a list of things you intend to do the next day before going to bed may help you relax and fall asleep because you can go bed with the peace of mind that comes from being organized and ready to handle the following day's tasks.

Light studying or reviewing previously studied material may also be good to do at bedtime because sleep can help you better retain what you've experienced just before going to sleep. Many years of studies show that the best thing you can do after attempting to learn something is to "sleep on it," probably because your brain can then focus on processing it without interference from outside distractions (Jenkins & Dallenbach, 1924).

5. Make sure the temperature of your sleep room is not too warm (no higher than 70 degrees).

Warm temperatures often make people feel sleepy, but they usually don't help them stay asleep or sleep well. This is why people have trouble sleeping on hot summer evenings. High-quality, uninterrupted sleep is more likely to take place at cooler, more comfortable room temperatures (Coates, 1977).

6. Avoid intense mental activity just before going to sleep.

Light mental work may serve as a relaxing presleep ritual, but cramming intensely for a difficult exam or doing intensive writing before bedtime is likely to generate a state of mental arousal, which will interfere with your ability to "wind down" and fall asleep.

7. Avoid intense physical exercise before going to sleep.

Physical exercise generates an increase in muscle tension and mental energy (oxygen flow to the brain), which energizes you and keeps you from falling asleep. If you're going to exercise in the evening, it should be done at least 3 hours before bedtime (Hauri & Linde, 1996).

8. Avoid consuming sleep-interfering foods, beverages, or drugs in late afternoon or evening.

In particular, avoid the following substances near bedtime:

- **Caffeine.** By working as a stimulant drug for most people, caffeine is likely to stimulate your nervous system and keep you awake.
- **Nicotine.** This stimulant drug is also likely to reduce the depth and quality of your sleep.
- **Alcohol.** This drug will make you feel sleepy in larger doses, but smaller doses can have a stimulating effect; furthermore, alcohol in all doses disrupts the quality of sleep by reducing the amount of time you spend in dream-stage sleep (marijuana does the same).
- **Gas-producing foods.** Avoid late intake of, for example, peanuts, beans, fruits, raw vegetables, or high-fat snacks, because your stomach has to work hard to digest them, and this internal energy (and noise) can interrupt or

disrupt your sleep. Eating anything near bedtime isn't a good idea because the internal activity your body engages in to digest the food is likely to interfere with the quality of your sleep.

> **! Remember**
>
> Things that make you feel sleepy (e.g., warm room temperature or alcohol consumption) often won't improve the depth and quality of your sleep.

◆ Stress and Anxiety

Students entering college today are reporting higher levels of stress (Astin, Parrot, Korn, & Sax, 1997; Sax, et al., 1999) and lower levels of mental health (Kadison & DiGeronimo, 2004) than they have in years past. This increased level of stress may reflect the fact that we're now living in an era of rapid technological change and information overload. In fact, psychiatric terms such as "Internet addiction" and "information fatigue syndrome" are now being used to refer to emotional disorders relating to psychological dependency on the Internet and excessive stress relating to information overload (Waddington, 1996; Young, 1996).

What exactly is *stress*? The etymology of the word "stress" derives from a Latin root that means, "to draw tight." Thus, stress isn't necessarily bad. For example, a tightened guitar string provides better sound than a string that's too lax or loose. Such productive stress is sometimes referred to as *eustress*—which is derived from the root "eu" meaning "good" (as in the word euphoria—good mood).

If stress occurs for a short period of time and in a manageable amount, it can benefit us by improving:

1. Our physical performance (e.g., strength and speed),
2. Our mental performance (e.g., attention and memory), and
3. Our mood (e.g., hope and optimism).

"Eustress" can provide the needed motivation for you to plan, set deadlines, and accomplish tasks. The body reacts to short-term stress with a sudden boost of energy caused by adrenaline which in turn can help you perform tasks more efficiently. Good stress challenges you but allows you to feel you have a sense of control. The accomplishment of tasks that occurs during these periods of stress in turn increases your self-esteem.

However, if stress is extreme or excessive, and continues for a prolonged period of time, it moves from being productive to being destructive. Such unproductive stress is often referred to as *distress*—from the root "dis" meaning "bad" (as in the words discomfort and disease). Extreme stress produces intense anxiety or anxiety disorders (e.g., panic attacks), and if a high level of stress persists for a prolonged period of time, it can trigger certain illnesses such as high blood pressure. Also, prolonged stress can suppress our immune system, leaving us more vulnerable to flu, colds, and other infectious diseases. Studies show that college students' immune systems produce fewer antibodies at very stressful times during the academic term, such as during periods of intense testing (e.g., midterms and finals) (Jemott & Magloire, 1985; Kielcolt-Glaser & Glaser, 1986).

Although there is considerable research pointing to the negative effects of excess stress, we still need to keep in mind that stress can work either for or against us; we can be either energized or sabotaged by stress depending on its level of intensity and the length of time it continues. Many years of research indicate that personal performance is best when it takes place under conditions of *moderate stress*, which creates a sense of challenge, rather than too much stress, which creates performance anxiety, or too little stress, which results in lack of intensity or indifference (Sapolsky, 2004; Yerkes & Dodson, 1908).

Snapshot Summary 9.2 provides a short summary of the key signs or symptoms of extreme stress that may indicate that stress has reached a level of distress or high anxiety. If these symptoms continue to occur for two or more weeks, action should be taken to reduce it.

Snapshot Summary

9.2

High Anxiety: Signs of Distress

- Jitteriness or shaking—especially the hands
- Accelerated heart rate or heart palpitations—intense, irregular heartbeat
- Muscle tension—tightness in the chest, upper shoulders, or a tight feeling ("lump") in the throat
- Body aches—due to increased muscle tension (e.g., "tension headaches" in the back of the head; lower backache), or chest pain—which can become so extreme that the person may feel that a heart attack is taking place
- Sweating—e.g., sweaty (clammy) palms
- Cold, pale hands or feet
- Dry mouth—due to production of less saliva
- Stomach discomfort or indigestion—due to increased secretion of stomach acid

- Elimination problems—e.g., constipation or diarrhea
- Feeling faint or dizzy—due to constriction of blood vessels that decreases oxygen flow to the brain
- Weakness and fatigue—due to being in a sustained (chronic) state of arousal and muscle tension
- Menstrual changes—such as missing periods or experiencing irregular menstrual periods
- Difficulty sleeping—such as insomnia, or interrupted (fitful) sleep
- Increased susceptibility to colds, flu, and other infections—due to suppression of the body's immune system

Stress-Reduction Strategies and Practices

Following are some simple strategies or practices that can be used to reduce stress.

1. Reduce or avoid intake of alcohol and caffeine.

The substances we put into our body physically can affect us emotionally. Because alcohol is a sedative or "downer" drug that slows down the nervous system, people often turn to it as a strategy to cope with stress and promote relaxation (Carpenter & Hasin, 1998). However, if too much alcohol is consumed, it has just the opposite effect because it stimulates release of cortisol—a hormone that activates and elevates the body's stress response.

Since stress can cause fatigue, people may also be tempted to use caffeine to regain energy. However, caffeine is a stimulant drug that not only stimulates alertness, it also stimulates the part of our involuntary nervous system that's associated with stress and arousal. Thus, caffeine is likely to increase feelings of nervous tension.

Decrease your intake of simple sugars (e.g., chocolates, candies, sugary sodas), and increase your intake of foods that are high in complex carbohydrates.

Foods high in complex carbohydrates (e.g., brown rice, potatoes, pasta, legumes, whole grain bread, and cereals) elevate a brain chemical called serotonin, which increases feelings of calmness and serenity. Although it may be tempting to put something sweet in your mouth when you're stressed and tired, simple sugars will only deliver a short-term shot of nervous energy.

2. Journaling

Dealing with stressful feelings by writing about them in a personal journal can provide a safe and regular outlet for releasing steam and coping with stress. Also, writing about our emotions enables us to deal with them more consciously and rationally, reducing the risk that we'll suppress or repress them into our subconscious.

3. Take time for humor and laughter.

Research on the power of humor for reducing tension is clear and convincing. For example, one research study involved college students who were unexpectedly given an assignment to deliver an impromptu (off the top of their head) speech. This sudden assignment resulted in the students' heart rate elevating to an average of 110 beats per minute during their speech. However, students who watched humorous episodes of sitcoms before delivering their impromptu speeches displayed a lower average heart rate of 80–85 beats per minute, indicating that humor served to lower their level of anxiety (O'Brien, cited in Howard, 2000).

◆ Alcohol, Drugs, and Risky Behavior

In addition to putting healthy nutrients into our body, exercising, and resting our body, another key aspect of physical wellness is keeping risky substances out of our body and keeping away from risky behaviors that can jeopardize our health and impair our performance.

Alcohol Use Among College Students

Alcohol is "legal" for people 21 years of age and older. However, whether you're of legal age or not, it's likely that alcohol has already been available to you and will continue to be available to you in college. Since alcohol is a substance seen frequently at college parties and social gatherings, it's likely that you will be confronted with decisions about alcohol, which is likely to involve two choices:

1. To drink or not to drink; and
2. To drink responsibly or irresponsibly.

Obviously, the best way to avoid irresponsible drinking is not to drink at all. This is the safest option, particularly if there is a history of alcohol abuse in your family. If you choose to drink, make sure that it's *your* choice and not a choice that others are making for you, due to social pressure or peer conformity. College students tend to overestimate the number of their peers who drink and the amount they drink. This overestimation can lead students to believe that if they don't drink, they're not doing what's expected or "normal" (DeJong & Linkenback, 1999).

Alcohol Abuse Among College Students

Unfortunately, irresponsible drinking is the number one drug problem on college campuses. Although alcohol is a "legal" substance (if you're 21 years of age or older), and it is a liquid or beverage that people drink rather than inject, smoke, or snort, the fact still remains that alcohol is a mind-altering drug when it's consumed in a large enough quantity (dose).

Also, like any other drug, alcohol abuse is a form of drug abuse. Approximately 7 to 8 percent of people who drink develop alcohol addiction or dependency (alcoholism) (Julien, 2004). However, among college students, the most frequent form of alcohol abuse is *binge drinking*—consuming large amounts of alcohol in a short amount of time, resulting in a state of intoxication or inebriation (a.k.a., a drunken state).

Binge drinking is a form of alcohol abuse that more than two of every five college students engage in (Substance Abuse and Mental Health Services Administration, 2006). It has direct, negative effects on the drinker's:

1. **Body.** It results in acute alcohol withdrawal syndrome (better known as a "hangover"), and
2. **Mind.** It results in memory loss (in extreme form, known as "blackouts").
3. **Behavior.** For example, class absence (Engs, 1977; Engs & Hanson, 1986). Research indicates that repeatedly getting drunk can reduce the size and effectiveness of the part of the brain involved with memory formation (Brown, et al., 2000), which suggests that the more often we get drunk, the dumber we get (Weschsler & Wuethrich, 2002).

Furthermore, binge drinking can have indirect negative effects on an individual's health and safety by reducing the drinker's inhibitions about engaging in risk-taking behavior, which increases the risk of personal accidents, injuries, and illnesses. Arguably, no other drug reduces a person's inhibitions as dramatically as alcohol. After consuming significant amounts of alcohol, humans can become much less cautious about doing things they normally wouldn't do. This chemically induced sense of courage (sometimes referred to as "liquid courage") can override the process of logical thinking and decision-making, thereby increasing the drinker's willingness to engage in irrationally risky behavior. Essentially, when some people drink, they begin to think they're invincible, immortal, and infertile.

Also, drinking increases the risk of aggressive behavior, such as: fighting, damaging property, sexual assault (e.g., date rape), and sexual harassment (Abbey, 2002; Bushman & Cooper, 1990).

Alcohol-related incidents among college students between the ages of 18–24 are staggering in their numbers: 1,700 deaths occur annually from unintentional injuries (including car accidents); 599,000 are unintentionally injured while under the influence of alcohol; 696,000 are physically assaulted by another student who has been drinking; 97,000 are victims of alcohol-related sexual assault or date rape; 400,000 have unprotected sex with more than 100,000 reporting they were too intoxicated to know whether they consented to having sex (Hingson, Heeren, Zakocs, Kopstein, & Wechsler 2005).

Since alcohol is a depressant drug that depresses or slows down the human nervous system, it increases aggressive and sexual behavior by slowing down signals normally sent from the front part of the upper brain (the "human brain"), which is responsible for rational thinking and normally inhibits or controls the lower, middle part of the brain (the "animal brain"), which is responsible for basic animal drives, such as sex and aggression.

Illegal Drugs

In addition to alcohol, there are other substances likely to be encountered on college campuses that are illegal for anyone to use at any age. Among the most commonly used illegal drugs by college students are the following:

- **Marijuana** (a.k.a. "weed" or "pot"). Primarily a depressant or sedative drug that slows down the nervous system and produces a "mellow" feeling of relaxation. In 2006, 16.7 percent of college students reported having used marijuana within the last month (University of Michigan, 2007).
- **Ecstasy** (a.k.a. "X"). A stimulant typically taken in pill form that speeds up the nervous system and reduces social inhibitions.
- **Cocaine** (a.k.a. "coke" or "crack"). A stimulant that's typically snorted or smoked, and produces a strong "rush" of euphoria. In 2006, 1.8 percent of college students reported having used cocaine within the last month (University of Michigan, 2007).
- **Amphetamines** (a.k.a. "speed" or "meth"). A strong stimulant that increases energy and general arousal, which is usually taken in pill form, but may also be smoked or injected.
- **Hallucinogens** (a.k.a. "psychedelics"). Drugs that alter or distort perception, which are typically swallowed—e.g., LSD (a.k.a., "acid") and hallucinogenic mushrooms (a.k.a. "shrooms").
- **Narcotics** (e.g., heroin and prescription pain pills). Depressant or sedative drugs that slow down the nervous system and produce feelings of relaxation; heroin is injected or smoked, and it typically produces an intense "rush" of euphoria.

All of these drugs are potentially habit forming. If they are injected (shot directly into a vein) or smoked (inhaled through the lungs), they can be particularly risky because these routes allow the drug to reach the brain faster and with greater impact. Thus, a "higher" peak effect is experienced and is experienced more rapidly, which is followed by a sharp drop or "crash" after the drug produces its peak effect. This roller-coaster effect produces a greater desire or craving to use the drug again, which increases the risk of dependency or addiction.

Listed below are common signs that use of any drug (including alcohol) is moving in the direction of drug dependency or addiction:

- Increasing frequency of use
- Increasing the amount (dose) used
- Difficulty cutting back (e.g., unable to use less frequently or in smaller amounts)
- Difficulty controlling or limiting the amount taken after starting
- Using the drug alone
- Hiding or hoarding the drug
- Lying about drug use
- Reacting angrily or defensively when questioned about drug use
- Being in denial about abusing the drug (e.g., "I don't have a problem.")
- Rationalizing drug abuse (e.g., "Everyone's doing it; it's no big deal.")
- When continuing to use the drug means more to the user than the personal and interpersonal problems caused by its use

Addiction is a potential problem and major motive for repeated use of any drug. However, there are multiple motives or reasons for using drugs besides addiction. Being aware of what motivates humans to use drugs can help promote self-awareness of motives for personal use, and it can also promote awareness of healthier ways to experience the same psychological effects produced by drugs.

Drug Use among College Students: Common Causes and Major Motives

1. **Social pressure.** Using drugs to fit in or be cool (for example, smoking marijuana because it's available at parties and everyone else is doing it).
2. **Recreational ("party") use.** Taking a drug for fun or pleasure (e.g., drinking alcohol at parties to loosen inhibitions and have a good time.).
3. **Experimental use.** Using a drug out of curiosity—to test out its effects (e.g., trying LSD to see what it's like to have a psychedelic or hallucinogenic experience).
4. **Therapeutic use.** Taking a prescription or over-the-counter drug as treatment for a mental or emotional disorder (e.g., taking Prozac for depression or Ritalin to treat attention deficit disorder).
5. **Performance enhancement.** Taking a drug to improve physical or mental performance (e.g., taking steroids to improve athletic performance or stimulants to stay awake all night and cram for an exam).
6. **Escapism.** Using a drug to escape or eliminate a personal problem or an unpleasant emotional state (e.g., taking amphetamines to escape depression or boredom).
7. **Addiction.** Habitual use of a drug that's motivated by physical or psychological dependence.

Threats to Sexual Wellness: Aggressive Sexual Behavior

Sexual Assault, a.k.a. Sexual Violence

Rape is a form of sexual assault, which is defined legally as nonconsensual (unwanted) sexual penetration that is obtained through physical force, by threat of bodily harm, or when the victim is incapable of giving consent due to alcohol or drug intoxication (Fenske, Miller, & Trivedi, 1996). Rape occurs in two major forms:

1. **Stranger rape.** When a total stranger forces sexual intercourse on the victim.
2. **Acquaintance rape or date rape.** When the victim knows, or is dating, the person who forces unwanted sexual intercourse. It's estimated that about 85 percent of reported rapes are committed by an acquaintance (Dobkin & Sippy, 1995). Alcohol is frequently associated with acquaintance rapes because it lowers the rapist's inhibitions and reduces the victim's ability to judge whether s/he is in a potentially dangerous situation. Since the victim is familiar with the offender, s/he may feel at fault or conclude that what happened is not sexual assault.

Recommendations for reducing the risk of rape and sexual assault:

- Don't drink to excess or associate with others who drink to excess.
- Go to parties with at least one other friend so you can keep an eye out for each other.
- Clearly and firmly communicate your sexual intentions and limits (e.g., If you say "no," make absolutely sure that he knows that you mean what you say and you say what you mean).
- Distinguish lust from love. If you just met someone who makes sexual advances toward you, that person lusts after you but doesn't love you.
- Take a self-defense class.
- Carry mace or pepper spray.
- Don't assume someone wants to have sex just because they are:
  a. very friendly,
  b. dressed in a certain way, or
  c. drinking alcohol.
- If someone says "no," don't assume that she really means "yes."
- Don't interpret sexual rejection as personal rejection.

Fifty percent of sexual assaults involving college students are attributed to alcohol abuse. Research has found that women feel more responsible for an incident of sexual assault if they have been consuming alcohol prior to the assault. In addition, sixty two percent of men blame alcohol for committing rape (Abbey, 2002).

Abusive Relationships

An abusive relationship may be defined as one in which one partner abuses the other—physically, verbally, or emotionally. Abusive individuals often are dependent on their partners for their sense of self-worth. They commonly have low self-esteem and fear their partner will abandon them, so they attempt to prevent this abandonment by over-controlling their partner. Frequently, abusers feel powerless or weak in other areas of their life and overcompensate by attempting to gain power, personal strength, and exerting power over their partner.

Potential Signs of Abuse:

1. Abuser tries to dominate or control all aspects of the partner's life,
2. Abuser frequently yells, shouts, intimidates, or makes physical threats,
3. Abuser constantly puts down the partner and damages the partner's self-esteem,
4. Abuser displays intense and irrational jealousy,
5. Abuser demands affection or sex when the partner is not interested,

6. The abused partner behaves differently and is more inhibited when the abuser is around, or

7. The abused partner fears the abuser.

Strategies for Avoiding or Escaping Abusive Relationships

- Avoid isolation by continuing to maintain social ties with others outside of the relationship.
- Do not seek your own sense of self-worth through a relationship with someone else.
- Understand that a partner who is overly attentive may not be doing it to enhance your own life, but rather to begin controlling you or aspects of your life.
- To help you see your relationship more clearly, ask friends for feedback on how they see it. (Love can sometimes be "blind"; it's possible to be in denial about an abusive relationship and not see what is really going on.)
- Speak with a professional counselor on campus to help you see your relationships more objectively and help you cope or escape from any relationship that you sense is becoming abusive.

References: ETR Associates (2000). *Acquaintance rape*. Santa Cruz, CA. ETR Associates (2001). *Sexual harassment*. Santa Cruz, CA.

http://sexualviolence.uchicago.edu/daterape.shtml

http://webpages.marshall.edu/~presssman1/rape.html.

http://www.uhs.berkeley.edu/home/healthtopics/sexual_assault/saalcohol. shtml

Minimize Your Risk of Contracting Sexually Transmitted Infections (STIs)

STIs represent a group of contagious infections that are spread through sexual contact. More than 25 different types of STIs have been identified, and virtually all of them are easily treated if detected early. (See Box XX for a summary of the major types of STIs.) However, if STIs are ignored, some of them can progress to the point where they cause internal infections and possible infertility (Cates, Herndon, Schulz, & Darroch, 2004).

The Center for Disease Control estimates there are approximately 19 million new infections of STIs annually, with almost half of them among those ages 15–24.

Experiencing pain during or after urination, or have unusual discharge from the penis or vaginal areas, may be early signs of an STI. However, sometimes the symptoms can be subtle; so if you have any doubt, play it safe and check it out immediately by visiting the Health Center on your campus. Any advice or treatment you receive there will remain completely confidential.

If you're a male and sexually active, you can reduce your risk and your partner's risk of contracting a STI by using a latex condom (Holmes, Levine, & Weaver, 2004) (polyurethane could be an alternative if there is an allergic reaction to latex). If you're a sexually active female, insist that your partner use a latex condom. You can reduce your risk of catching a sexually transmitted infection by having sex with fewer partners.

Naturally, the easiest and most foolproof way to eliminate risk for STI (and unwanted pregnancy) is by not engaging in sexual intercourse. While having sexual feelings is normal and healthy, it doesn't mean you have to act on these feelings by expressing and satisfying them through sexual intercourse. You can choose abstinence, which doesn't mean that you cannot express physical affection or that you've decided never to have sex; it just means that you're choosing not to have sexual intercourse at this point in your life.

If you decide to have sex and happen to contract an STI, immediately inform anyone you've had sex with, so that he or she may receive early treatment before the disease progresses. This isn't just a nice or polite thing to do; it's the right (ethical) thing to do.

Sexually Transmitted Infections

STIs represent a group of contagious infections that are spread through sexual contact. The more sexual partners you have, the greater the risk of contracting an STI. Latex condoms provide the best protection.

More than 25 different types of STIs have been identified, but the following bacteria and viruses account for the majority of infections. These infections are typically very treatable, but if they are ignored, they can lead to internal infections and possible infertility.

STIs Caused by Bacteria

Gonorrhea

This is a common STI with few symptoms but serious consequences if it is left untreated. In 2007, there were 355,991 cases reported, however the Center for Disease Control (CDC) estimates there are nearly twice as many infections annually than the number reported (Weinstock, Berman, & Cates, Jr., 2004). Men typically experience creamy, yellow-colored, pus-like discharge from the penis, and burning when urinating. Women experience few early symptoms, but the disease can lead to later pelvic infections and possible infertility. The best way to detect gonorrhea, or any other STI that produces early symptoms that are not visible, is to have a laboratory test done by a doctor or healthcare provider. Gonorrhea can be treated and completely cured with antibiotics.

Chlamydia

This is the number-one bacterial STI; it's estimated to infect more than 10 percent of college students. In 2007, there were 1,108,374 chlamydia diagnoses reported, the largest number of cases ever reported to the CDC for any condition. However, the CDC estimates that there are approximately 2.8 million new cases of chlamydia annually, meaning more than half of new cases go undiagnosed and unreported (Weinstock, et al., 2004). Symptoms include a clear, mucous-like discharge and a burning sensation when urinating. Men may experience pain in the testes, and women may experience pain in the abdomen. However, women typically experience few or no early symptoms.

Genital Herpes

Typically produces painful blisters on the genitals or in the anus, which may itch and burn, especially during and following urination. Symptoms may disappear and come back, but are never cured. Later attacks tend to be less severe than the first attack. The frequency and intensity of outbreaks can be reduced with prescription medication (e.g., acyclovir capsules).

Syphilis

Men first experience ulcers (open sores) on the penis. Women may first develop ulcers in the vagina, but they can be overlooked, allowing the disease to progress. Syphilis is totally curable with antibiotics.

STIs Caused by Viruses

Human Papilloma Virus (HPV)

Overall, this is the most common STI among young, sexually active people. HPV is a virus that may cause warts in the genital area, but it typically does not produce noticeable symptoms in its early stages. Sometimes, the disease may also cause lesions (abnormal tissue changes) that are not visible, but when they appear, they look like small hard, cauliflower-like spots. Men can experience warts on the penis. HPV is treatable with laser or chemical treatment, which basically burn off the lesions. If untreated, HPV can lead to cancer of the cervix in women.

Human Immunodeficiency Virus (HIV)

Early symptoms include fever, night sweats, swollen lymph nodes, diarrhea, chronic fatigue, and weight loss. About one-half of people with HIV experience these flu-like symptoms, but one-half show no symptoms at all. Thus, the disease may go undetected until the person is given a blood test for some other reason. Most cases of HIV are transmitted through sexual contact; however, the disease may also be contracted through the sharing of intravenous needles. The most serious form of HIV is *Acquired Immune Deficiency Syndrome (AIDS)*, which is a life-threatening condition, because the person's immune system becomes severely impaired and leaves the infected person vulnerable to cancer and diseases of the nervous system.

Hepatitis B or *Hepatitis C*

About one-half of the people with hepatitis experience flu-like symptoms, and one-half show no symptoms at all. Thus, the disease may go undetected until the person is given a blood test for some other reason.

Pubic Lice (a.k.a. "Crabs")

Caused by tiny lice that are called "crabs" (because they look like sea crabs), which breed in pubic hair around the genitals. These creatures are not dangerous but can cause intense itching.

Strategies for Minimizing or Eliminating the Negative Effects of Alcohol, Drugs, and Risky Behavior

Don't let yourself be pressured into drinking.

College students tend to overestimate the number of their peers who drink, so don't feel you're uncool, unusual, or abnormal if you prefer not to drink.

If you decide to drink, maintain awareness of how much you're drinking on any occasion, and continually monitor your physical and mental state.

Don't continue to drink after you've reached a state of moderate relaxation or a mild loss of inhibition. Drinking to the point where you're drunk, or bordering on intoxication, doesn't promote your physical health or your social life. The key to drinking responsibly and in moderation is to have a plan in mind for managing your drinking. Such a plan can include strategies such as:

1. Drinking slowly,
2. Eating while drinking,
3. Alternating between drinking alcoholic and non-alcoholic beverages, and
4. Tapering off your drinking after the first hour of a party or social gathering (Vogler & Bartyz, 1992).

Lastly, don't forget that alcohol is costly, both in terms of money and calories. Thus, reducing or eliminating your drinking is a good money-management and weight-management strategy.

If you're a woman who drinks, or who frequents places where other people drink, remain aware of the possibility of date-rape drugs being dropped into your drink.

Drugs such as Gamma-hydroxybutyric acid (a.k.a., "GHB" or "G") and Rohypnol (a.k.a., "roofies" or "roaches") induce sleep and memory loss, and they are particularly powerful when taken with alcohol. To guard against this risk, don't let others give you drinks and hold onto your drink at all times.

If you find yourself in a situation where an illegal drug is available to you, our bottom-line recommendation is this: Don't check it out. If you're in doubt, keep it out—don't put anything you're unsure about into your body.

We acknowledge that the college years are a time for exploring and experimenting with different ideas, experiences, feelings, and states of consciousness. However, doing illegal drugs just isn't worth the risk. Even if you're aware of how an illegal drug affects people in general, you don't know how it's going to affect you in particular because each individual has a unique genetic makeup. Unlike legal drugs that have to pass through rigorous testing by the FDA (Federal Drug Administration) before they are approved for public consumption, you can't be sure how an illegal drug has been produced and packaged from one time to the next; and you don't know if, or what, it may have been "cut" (mixed) with during the production process. Thus, you're not just taking a criminal risk by using a drug that's illegal; you're also taking a physical risk by consuming a drug that may have unpredictable effects on your body and mind.

If you haven't smoked cigarettes, don't even think about starting.

The active ingredient in cigarettes, *nicotine*, is one of the most highly addictive drugs known to man (Jarvik, 1995). There are people who've been able to beat alcohol addiction and heroin addiction, but have not been able to kick their nicotine habit (Stolerman & Jarvis, 1995). In addition to its high potential for addiction, the health disadvantages of cigarette smoking are numerous and serious, which include increased susceptibility to our two leading killers: heart disease and cancer (Freund, Belanger, D'Agostino, & Kannel, 1993).

It's noteworthy that some women use cigarette smoking as a weight-control strategy because it elevates metabolism and burns calories. However, cigarette smoking produces only about a 7 percent increase in the rate of metabolism; in contrast, physical exercise increases the rate of metabolism by an average of 15 percent (Audrain, et al., 1995).

◆ Summary and Conclusion

The research studies and scholarly wisdom reviewed in this chapter suggest that physical wellness is most effectively promoted if you adopt the following strategies with respect to your body:

- **Pay more attention to nutrition.** In particular, you should increase consumption of natural fruits, vegetables, legumes, whole grains, fish, and water and decrease consumption of processed, fatty, and fried foods. Although the expression, "you are what you eat" may be a bit of an exaggeration, it contains a kernel of truth because the food you consume influences your health, your emotions, and your performance.

- **Become more physically active.** To counteract the sedentary lifestyle created by life in modern society and to attain total fitness, you should engage in a balanced blend of exercises that build stamina, strength, and flexibility.

- **Be careful not to cheat on sleep.** Humans typically do not get enough sleep to perform at their highest levels. College students, in particular, need to get more sleep and develop more regular or consistent sleep habits.

- **Maintain awareness of emotions and monitor stress.** Develop a set of self-help strategies for coping with the two most troublesome human emotions: anxiety and depression.

- **Drink alcohol responsibly or not at all.** Avoid excess consumption of alcohol or use of other mind-altering substances that can threaten our physical health, impair our mental judgment, and increase our tendency to engage in dangerous, risk-taking behavior.

Internet-Based Resources for Further Information on Health and Wellness

For additional information related to the ideas discussed in this chapter, we recommend the following Web sites:

www.eatright.org

www.fitness.gov/home_resources.htm

www.sleepfoundation.org

www.nida.nih.gov

9.1 Nutritional Self-Assessment and Self-Improvement

1. Go online to www.mypyramid.gov.

2. In the boxes on the right side of the screen, fill in your age, gender, and daily level of physical activity.

3. Click "select" to get a nutritional guide that is customized to your age, gender, and exercise habits.

4. For each of the five food groups listed here, record the amount recommended for you to consume daily, and next to it, estimate the amount you now consume.

Basic Food Type	*Amount Recommended*	*Amount Consumed*
Grains		
Vegetables		
Fruits		
Milk Products		
Meat and Beans		

5. For any food group that you're consuming less than the recommended amounts, click on that group to find foods you could consume to meet the recommended daily amount. In the space that follows, record any items that you'd be willing to consume in greater amounts to meet the daily recommendation.

    _____

    _____

    _____

    _____

6. How likely is it that you'll add these food items to your regular diet?

    Very likely   Possibly   Unlikely

7. If you didn't answer "very likely," what would interfere or prevent you from adding these food items to your regular diet?

9.2 Wellness Self-Assessment and Self-Improvement

For each aspect of wellness listed here, rate yourself in terms of how close you think you are to doing what you should be doing (1 = furthest from the ideal, 5 = closest to the ideal).

	Nowhere Close to What I Should Be Doing		Not Bad but Should Be Better		Right Where I Should Be
	1	2	3	4	5
Nutrition	1	2	3	4	5
Exercise	1	2	3	4	5
Sleep	1	2	3	4	5
Alcohol and Drugs	1	2	3	4	5

For each area in which there's a wide gap between where you are now and where you should be, identify the best action you could take to reduce or eliminate this gap.

Concerns about Eating: Too Much or Too Little?

The following e-mail message was sent by an underweight, 25-year-old female (Nancy) who was seeking advice.

I have a big worry: I eat normally during the day but I eat two scoops of ice cream at the end of the day followed by a large package of cookies. I am not exaggerating the situation. Last week, I could only stuff myself with 2 scoops of Häagen-Dazs after dinner, but these days it's getting worse—now that I can add bread and buttery cookies (a whole packet—not those mini ones, mind you). What should I do? I know that I should gain weight but I should be getting the extra pounds by more normal means like meat or milk—and I am really worried that once this binge and indulgence becomes a habit, it's difficult to get rid of.

Nancy goes on to ask the following questions about her condition. As you read each question, respond to it with the advice you think would be best.

1. Is it OK that I eat that much at the end of each day rather than distributing it equally throughout the day? (Though the former way seems better, I can tell myself, "Hey, girl, after all, you are eating less than your sister!")

2. I am eating junk food—ice cream, loads of biscuits, bread, those Garden chocolate roll cakes, chocolate fingers, chocolate McVita's, buttery cookies . . . . It seems that this is not as healthy as gaining weight by eating meat, milk, or carbohydrates. Is this true?

3. Is it unhealthy to eat just before bed?

4. Could it become difficult to stop?

5. Am I controlled by food?

6. Now that I am eating more than my sister, I am really scared, very scared indeed, not only because I am eating far more than my sister but also because I am having fat deposited in undesirable parts of my body and getting a totally worse figure than she has—that fat which I had tried so hard for 3 years to get rid of. Any advice?

Source: Chan & Ma (2002).

Educational Planning and Decision Making

Making Wise Choices about Your Courses, Major, and Degree Plans

THOUGHT STARTER   Journal Entry   **10.1**

Are you decided or undecided about a college major?

_____

_____

If you are undecided, list any subjects that might be possibilities:

_____

_____

_____

_____

_____

If you are decided, what is your choice and why did you choose this major?

_____

_____

_____

_____

_____

Indicate how sure you are about that choice by circling one of the following options:

ABSOLUTELY SURE   FAIRLY SURE   NOT TOO SURE   LIKELY TO CHANGE

◆ When Should You Decide Whether to Pursue a 4-Year Degree and What Your Major Should Be?

As a new student, you may be undecided for a variety of good reasons. For instance, you may be undecided because you have interests in various subjects. This is a healthy form of indecision because it shows that you have a broad range of interests and a high level of motivation to learn about different subjects. You may also be undecided because you are a careful, reflective thinker whose decision-making style is to gather more information before making any long-term commitments.

Similarly, changing your original educational plans is not necessarily a bad thing. It may mean that you have discovered another field that's more interesting to you or that's more compatible with your personal interests and talents. It's okay to start off not knowing what your major will be or whether you want to pursue a 4-year degree or a shorter-range educational goal, such as an associate degree or vocational–technical certificate. You still have time to make up your mind and to change your mind. Don't think that you must lock yourself into a particular plan and must either stick with it or drop out of college if your plans change. You can take courses that will count toward graduation, regardless of what major or educational track you end up taking.

Changing your educational plan has one downside: If you make that change late in your college experience, it can result in more time to graduation (and more tuition) because you may need to complete additional courses required for your newly chosen field.

! Remember

As a rule, you should reach a fairly firm decision about your major during your second (sophomore) year in college. However, to reach a good decision within this time frame, the process of exploring and planning should begin now—during your first term in college.

THINK ABOUT IT   **Journal Entry** **10.2**

If you've already chosen a major or specialized program, what led
you to this choice?

_____

_____

_____

_____

_____

_____

◆ The Importance of Long-Range Educational Planning

College will allow you many choices about what courses to enroll in and what
field to specialize in. By looking ahead and developing a tentative plan for
your courses beyond the first term of college, you will position yourself to
view your college experience as a full-length movie and get a sneak preview of
the total picture. In contrast, scheduling your classes one term at a time just
before each registration period (when everyone else is making a mad rush to
get their advisor's signature for the following term's classes) forces you to view
your academic experience as a series of short, separate snapshots that lack connection or direction.

Long-range educational planning also enables you to take a proactive approach to your future. Being proactive means you are taking early, preventa-
tive action that anticipates events before they sneak up on you, forcing you to
react to events in your life without time to plan your best strategy. As the old
saying goes, "If you fail to plan, you plan to fail." Through advanced planning,
you can actively take charge of your academic future and make it happen _for_
you, rather than waiting and passively letting it happen _to_ you.

> "
> "When you have to make a
> choice and don't make it, that
> is in itself a choice."
>
> –William James, philosopher and one of
> the founders of American psychology

!

Remember

Any long-range plan you develop is not set in stone; it can change depending on
changes in your academic interests and future plans. The purpose of long-range
planning is not to lock you into a particular plan but to free you from shortsighted-
ness, procrastination, or denial about choosing to take charge of your life.

Don't take the denial and avoidance approach to planning your educational future.

THINK ABOUT IT · Journal Entry 10.3

Choosing a major is a life-changing decision because it will determine what you do for the rest of your life. Would you agree or disagree with this statement?

_____

_____

Why?

_____

_____

_____

_____

_____

_____

One important element of long-range educational planning is deciding whether you're going to continue your education beyond your community college experience by transferring to a 4-year college or university and when you plan to make that transfer transition. Some community college students plan to transfer to a 4-year college before completing their associate degree at their community college. However, we strongly recommend that you complete your general education program before attempting to transfer, because multiple advantages are associated with completing 60 or more units at a 2-year college and attaining an associate degree. These advantages are listed in the next section.

Advantages of Completing an Associate Degree Before Transferring to a 4-Year College or University

1. You will acquire a college degree before completing a bachelor's degree.

Regardless of whether you receive academic or cocurricular distinctions and awards, completion of an associate degree is an achievement in itself for two reasons:

a. It indicates that you have survived the two most critical years of the college experience. Research shows that almost 75 percent of those students who withdraw from college do so during the freshman and sophomore years (American College Testing, 2009). The associate degree is evidence to 4-year colleges and future employers that you have persisted through, and completed, these two critical years.

b. The associate degree signifies that you have successfully completed the general education component of the college experience. In some ways, this is the most important component of the college experience because it represents the acquisition of breadth of knowledge and the development of essential learning skills (e.g., written and oral communication). Surveys indicate that employers look for and value these skills the most in their employees (National Association of Colleges & Employers, 2003).

Having your associate degree after your sophomore year will also improve your job prospects during your junior and senior years of college (e.g., your chances of obtaining an internship, part-time employment during the academic year, or full-time employment during the summers between your sophomore and your junior years and between your junior and your senior years). In addition, those with an associate degree, on average, earn more than $13,000 more per year than individuals with a high school diploma (College Board, 2008). Thus, the 2-year degree not only should increase your chances of being hired but also should increase the amount of pay you receive. Furthermore, this vocational advantage of earning an associate degree will be particularly important if, for some reason, you're unable to complete the bachelor's (or baccalaureate) degree or if you have to postpone its completion.

2. You will complete general education requirements, basic skills courses, and premajor requirements before transferring.

Completing an associate degree will enable you to finish up general education requirements and skill-building courses (e.g., writing and math) in smaller classes where you are likely to receive more individual attention and more personalized feedback from instructors and academic support. Thus, you will have a broader base of knowledge and a more highly developed set of academic skills before transferring. Studies show that students who transfer to 4-year institutions after completing just one year at a 2-year college have a greater "dip" or drop in grade point average (GPA) than students who transfer after two years (Cuseo, 2003; Diaz, 1992). The bigger drop in GPA for early transfers may also be due to greater culture shock experienced by students who transfer after one year because they enter 4-year institutions neither as freshmen nor as juniors—the two years when most other students enter 4-year colleges. Thus, sophomore-year transfers begin their 4-year college experience as interlopers or "betweeners." This can make it difficult for sophomore transfers to fit into the student culture because they have fewer peers entering with them and because orientation activities are more likely to be geared toward entering freshmen and junior transfers.

3. You will have extra time and advisement for deciding on an academic major and a 4-year college.

For students who are not sure about what their particular major will be or what particular 4-year institution they should transfer to, returning to their community college for the sophomore year will provide an additional year of time and advisor contact that can be used to reach both of these important decisions. Making these two decisions is a complex and interrelated process. What major you eventually decide on may influence what college you should attend. Some academic majors may not be offered at all colleges, and the nature and quality of the same major may vary from one college to another. For example, the psychology major at College X may require different courses and have a different career-preparation emphasis than the psychology major at college Y. Also, transfer students may report different levels of satisfaction with the psychology program and the professors in the psychology department at College X than they do at College Y.

Since so many of the courses you will be taking during your last two years of college will be courses in your major, when you choose a 4-year college for transfer, you're also choosing the particular department within the college that houses your particular major. Your second year at a community college can supply you with the time needed to finalize your decision about what major to declare and to consult with a network of advisors concerning what 4-year colleges would be best for your particular major and your future career goals.

4. You may have a higher college GPA at the end of your sophomore year.

It's likely that your GPA will be higher after your sophomore year at your community college than it is after your freshman year because you've made the critical first-year adjustment and have gained greater experience with the system. A higher GPA when you transfer will increase the likelihood that you will be accepted, particularly if you're applying for admission into "impacted" majors (i.e., majors that are competitive and hard to get into because they are overcrowded).

5. There will be less emphasis on high school grades and SAT scores by 4-year colleges.

Four-year colleges and universities are likely to place less emphasis on high school grades and SAT scores when reviewing the applications of students who've completed two full years of college than they are for students who attempt to transfer earlier. Some 4-year campuses require SAT scores for high school seniors and for students attempting to transfer after one year of college but will not require SAT scores from transfer students who have completed two full years of college and hold an associate degree.

6. You will have more opportunity to receive academic recognition and awards before transferring.

If you're doing well academically during your first year at your community college, returning for the sophomore year will enable you to enter the community college's Honors program, take honors courses, and become a member of the National Collegiate Honors Council and Phi Theta Kappa—an international honor society for 2-year college students. If you then complete your associate degree at a community college, you become eligible for academic honors at graduation, such as graduating magna cum laude (with high distinction) or summa cum laude (with highest distinction). These awards can increase your prospects for acceptance at 4-year colleges, as well as your chances for scholarships and other types of merit-based financial aid that are earmarked for junior-transfer students. These academic achievements will be listed on your transcript and will provide you with a distinctive advantage for acceptance at 4-year schools, as well as increase your eligibility for entry into their Honors programs. Furthermore, these accomplishments will remain on your permanent college record after you graduate with a 4-year (bachelor's) degree, which should increase your job prospects after graduation and your chances for acceptance at graduate schools (e.g., to pursue a master's or doctoral degree) and professional schools (e.g., to pursue a law or medical degree).

7. You will have opportunities and recognition for leadership activities before transferring.

If you are a first-year college student with leadership potential, or if you are committed to developing your leadership skills, you may become eligible for various résumé- and character-building leadership opportunities during your sophomore year at a community college (e.g., peer tutoring or peer mentoring). At 4-year colleges, sophomores are often unable to assume these leadership positions because they may be reserved for more experienced upper-division students (juniors and seniors). At your community college, you can get these experiences as sophomores and use them to (a) increase your chances of acceptance at 4-year colleges, (b) qualify for similar leadership positions at the 4-year college to which you transfer, and (c) enhance your job prospects during your last two years of college and after you complete your bachelor's degree.

8. You will have a chance to participate in a graduation ceremony after completing the associate degree program.

Completion of an associate degree will also enable you to participate in your community college's graduation ceremony. The significance of this celebratory event should not be underestimated. This is an opportunity for you to be recognized publicly—in front of family, friends, faculty, and fellow students—for your completion of general education and for any academic and cocurricular awards you achieved along the way.

Research indicates that student involvement in college rituals or ceremonial events (such as graduation) reinforces students' motivation and commitment to continue their education and promotes their ability to persist or persevere until achieving their final degree objective (Kuh et al., 1991, 2005). Thus, participation in your community college's graduation ceremony may not only celebrate your attainment of the associate degree but also strengthen or stimulate your drive to achieve a bachelor's degree.

Proof of the power of the graduation experience is illustrated in the following excerpt of a letter written by a student who graduated from a 2-year college and transferred to a 4-year campus to complete her bachelor's degree.

Personal Story

I graduated with my associate degree [several years ago] and I just wanted to get in touch and let you know how I am doing. I successfully graduated from USF [University of San Francisco] in four years (including the two before I transferred). During the graduation ceremony after my sophomore year, I saw some fellow students wearing the yellow shawl that represented walking with honors. I thought to myself, "I am going to walk with honors when I get my B.A." And that I did! Who would have ever thought? [Now] I have decided that I want to go to graduate school.

—Letter from a 2-year college graduate received by Joe Cuseo

Take Action!

10.1

Tips for Students Transferring to 4-Year Colleges and Universities

The following criteria are those that most likely will be used by 4-year colleges to evaluate your application and decide on your acceptance:

- **Academic Record.** Colleges will look at your overall GPA and grades for courses in your chosen major.
- **Out-of-Class Experiences.** For example, your involvement in leadership activities and volunteer experience in the community or on campus can play a role in your acceptance to a 4-year college.
- **Letters of Recommendation.** Letters can come, for example, from course instructors and academic advisors. Provide the following courtesies for those you ask to write letters of recommendation for you:
  - A *fact sheet* about yourself that will enable them to cite concrete examples or evidence of your achievements and contributions (which will make the letter more powerful)
  - A *stamped, addressed* envelope (a personal courtesy that makes the job a little easier for your reference)
  - A *thank-you note* close to the date that the letter is due (not only a nice thing to do but also a reminder in case the person has forgotten about your letter or has not yet set aside time to write it)
- **Personal Statement.** In your letter of application for admission, which you write when applying to a school, try to demonstrate your knowledge of:
  - *yourself* (e.g., your personal interests, abilities, and values);
  - your intended *major* (e.g., why you're interested in it and what you might do with it after graduation); and
  - the *college* to which you're applying by showing that you know something specific about the school (e.g., its mission, philosophy, and programs—especially the particular program to which you're applying).

To maximize your success at 4-year colleges and universities, take the initiative to connect with people who can contribute to your success, including the following:

- **Faculty.** Make sure they know who you are (e.g., sit in front of class, come up to speak with them after class, visit them in their office, or volunteer to help them with research they're doing that you find interesting or relevant to your career interests).
- **Students in Your Major.** Connect with them in study groups and major clubs (psychology club, history club, etc.).

- **Career Development Specialists.** Connect with these professionals on strategies for enhancing your marketability after graduation. Ask them about what graduates (alumni) with your major have gone on to do and whether they can connect you with an alum in a career that you intend to pursue.

Take Action!

A Checklist of Course-Registration Reminders for Community College Students

Achieving your educational goals requires both long- and short-range planning. Your long-range plan involves completing your degree, and your short-range plan involves continuing your enrollment in college from term to term. When planning to register for the next academic term, keep the following list of reminders handy to ensure that your term-to-term transition proceeds smoothly.

- ✓ Check the registration dates and be prepared to register at the earliest date that's available to you.
- ✓ Check with an academic advisor to be sure that you're planning to take the right classes for your program, major, and any 4-year school that you plan to transfer to.

- ✓ Let your advisor know what your educational goals are and if you've changed your goals since the last time you registered.
- ✓ Let your advisor know the total number of hours per week you plan to work so that you create a schedule that will allow you to successfully balance schoolwork and for-pay work.
- ✓ If you're receiving financial aid, meet with a financial aid counselor or advisor to be sure that you have adequate funds to cover next term's tuition, book costs, and parking fees.
- ✓ Once you've registered, periodically check the status of your courses because last-minute changes can occur in the time and day when courses meet and it's possible that one of your courses might be canceled (e.g., due to insufficient enrollment).

> **! Remember**
>
> Unlike high school, summer school in college isn't something you do to make up for courses that were failed or should have been taken during the "regular" school year (fall and spring terms). Instead, it's an additional term that you can use to make further progress toward your college degree and reduce the total time it takes to complete your degree.

◆ Myths About the Relationship Between Majors and Careers

Good decisions are based not on misconceptions or myths but on accurate information. Effective planning for a college major requires accurate information about the relationship between majors and careers. Unfortunately, several popular myths about the relationship between majors and careers can lead to uninformed or unrealistic choices of a college major.

Myth 1. When You Choose Your Major, You're Choosing Your Career

While some majors lead directly to a particular career, most do not. Majors leading directly to specific careers are called preprofessional or prevocational majors, and they include such fields as accounting, engineering, and nursing. However, most college majors don't channel you directly down one particular career path; instead, they leave you with various career options. All physics majors don't become physicists, all philosophy majors don't become philosophers, all history majors do not become historians, and all English majors do not become Englishmen (or Englishwomen). The career path of most college graduates is not a straight line that runs directly from their major to their career. The trip from college to career or careers is more like climbing a tree. As illustrated in **Figure 10.1**, you begin with the tree's trunk—the foundation

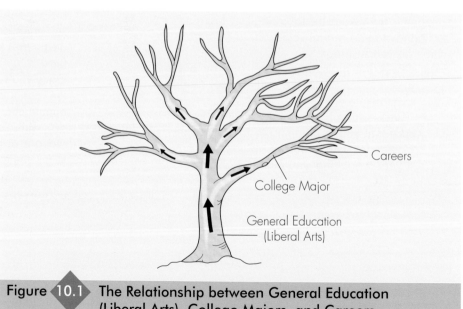

Figure 10.1 **The Relationship between General Education (Liberal Arts), College Majors, and Careers**

of general education (courses required of all college students, whatever their major may be) that grows into separate limbs (different college majors) that, in turn, lead to different branches (different career paths or options).

Note that the career branches grow from the same limb. Likewise, the same major leads to a "family" of related careers. For example, an English major often leads to careers that involve use of the written language (e.g., editing, journalism, and publishing), while a major in art leads to careers that involve use of visual media (e.g., illustration, graphic design, and art therapy). (Note that the Web site www.mymajors.com provides useful and free information on groups or families of jobs that tend to be related to different majors.)

Also, different majors can lead to the same career. For instance, many majors can lead a student to law school and to an eventual career as a lawyer; there is no undergraduate major in law or prelaw. Similarly, premed isn't a major. Although most students interested in going to medical school after college major in some field in the natural sciences (e.g., biology or chemistry), it's possible for students to go to medical school with majors in other fields, particularly if they take and do well in certain science courses that are emphasized in medical school (e.g., general biology, general chemistry, and organic and inorganic chemistry).

Thus, don't presume that your major is your career or that your major automatically turns into your career. This is one reason some students procrastinate about choosing a major; they think they are making a lifelong decision and fear that if they make the "wrong" choice they'll be stuck doing something they hate for the rest of their lives. The belief that your major becomes your career may also account for 58 percent of college graduates choosing to major in a preprofessional or prevocational field (e.g., nursing, accounting, or engineering; Association of American Colleges & Universities, 2007). These majors have a career obviously connected to them, which reassures students (and their family members) that they will have a job after graduation. However, although students in prevocational majors may be more likely to be hired immediately after graduation, tracking college graduates with other college majors has shown that six months after graduation they too have jobs; thus, they are not more likely to be unemployed (Pascarella & Terenzini, 2005).

> **Student Perspective**
>
> "Things like picking majors and careers really scare me a lot! I don't know exactly what I want to do with my life."
>
> –First-year student

! Remember

Don't assume that choosing your college major means that you're choosing what you'll be doing for as long as you'll be living.

Research on college graduates indicates that they change careers numerous times and the further they continue along their career path, the more likely they are to work in a field that is unrelated to their college major (Millard, 2004). Remember that the general education curriculum is a significant part of a college education. It allows students to acquire knowledge in diverse subjects and to develop durable, transferable skills (e.g., writing, speaking, and organizing) that qualify college graduates for a diversity of careers, regardless of what their particular major happened to be.

The order in which decisions about majors and careers are covered in this book reflects the order in which they are likely to be made in your life. For most college majors, students first decide on their major; later, they decide on their career. Although it is important to think about the relationship between your choice of major and your choice of career or careers, these are different choices that are usually made at different times. Both choices relate to your future goals, but they involve different time frames: Choosing your major is a short-range goal, whereas choosing your career is a long-range goal.

> **!**
>
> **Remember**
>
> Choosing a major and choosing a career are not always the same decision; they are often separate decisions that don't have to be made at the same time.

Myth 2. After a Bachelor's Degree, Any Further Education Must Be in the Same Field as Your College Major

After college graduation, you have two main options or alternative paths available to you:

1. You can enter a career immediately.
2. You can continue your education in graduate school or professional school. (See **Figure 10.2** for a visual map of the signposts or stages in the college experience and the basic paths available to you after college graduation.)

Once you complete a bachelor's degree, it's possible to continue your education in a field that's not directly related to your college major. This is particularly true for students who are majoring in preprofessional careers that funnel them directly into a particular career after graduation (Pascarella & Terenzini, 2005). For example, if you major in English, you can still go to graduate school in a subject other than English; you could go to law school or get a master's degree in business administration. It's common to find graduate students in master's of business administration programs who were not business majors in college (Dupuy & Vance, 1996).

THINK ABOUT IT   **Journal Entry**   **10.4**

Reflect on the timeline on the next page and **Figure 10.2**, which suggests that it will take you two years to complete an associate degree and 4 years to complete a bachelor's degree.

1. Do you see yourself completing an associate degree in two years? A bachelor's degree in 4 years?

_____

_____

_____

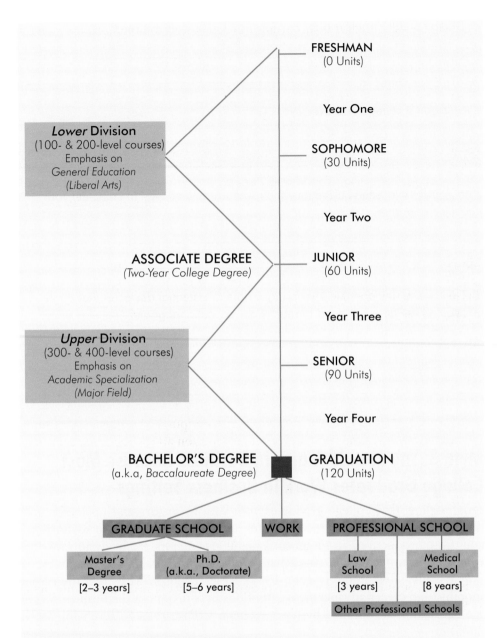

FRESHMAN
(0 Units)

Year One

SOPHOMORE
(30 Units)

Year Two

JUNIOR
(60 Units)

Year Three

SENIOR
(90 Units)

Year Four

Lower **Division**
(100- & 200-level courses)
Emphasis on
General Education
(Liberal Arts)

ASSOCIATE DEGREE
(Two-Year College Degree)

Upper **Division**
(300- & 400-level courses)
Emphasis on
Academic Specialization
(Major Field)

BACHELOR'S DEGREE
(a.k.a, *Baccalaureate Degree*)

GRADUATION
(120 Units)

GRADUATE SCHOOL   **WORK**   **PROFESSIONAL SCHOOL**

Master's
Degree

[2–3 years]

Ph.D.
(a.k.a., Doctorate)

[5–6 years]

Law
School

[3 years]

Medical
School

[8 years]

Other Professional Schools

Notes

1. The total number of *general education* units and the total number of units needed to **graduate** with a bachelor's degree may vary somewhat from school to school. Also, the total number of units required for a *major* will vary somewhat from major to major and from school to school.

2. It often takes college students longer than four years to graduate due to a variety of reasons, such as working part-time and taking fewer courses per term, needing to repeat courses that were failed or dropped, or making a late change to a different major and needing to fulfill additional requirements for the new major.

3. *Graduate* and *professional* schools are options for continuing to higher levels of education after completion of an undergraduate (college) education.

4. Compared to graduate school, *professional* school involves advanced education in more "applied" professions (e.g., pharmacy or public administration).

Figure 10.2   Timeline to the Future: A Snapshot of the College Experience and Beyond

"We should not underestimate the ability of people to eventually obtain their college degrees. Nor should we minimize the diversity of behaviors which lead individuals to leave and eventually to return to complete their college degree programs."

–Vincent Tinto, nationally known researcher and scholar on college-student success

2. Do you plan to transfer after completing an associate degree?

_____

_____

If yes, to what college or university?

_____

_____

If no, do you ever see yourself eventually returning to college to complete your bachelor's degree?

_____

_____

3. Do you see any possible interfering factors or potential obstacles that might prolong the time you need to reach your educational goals?

_____

_____

_____

_____

"Employers are far more interested in the prospect's ability to think and to think clearly, to write and speak well, and how (s)he works with others than in his major or the name of the school (s)he went to. Several college investigating teams found that these were the qualities on which all kinds of employers, government and private, base their decisions."

–Lauren Pope, *Looking beyond the Ivy League* (1990)

Myth 3. You Should Major in Business Because Most College Graduates Work in Business Settings

Studies show that college graduates with various majors end up working in business settings. For instance, engineering majors are likely to work in accounting, production, and finance. Liberal arts majors are likely to move on to positions in business settings that involve marketing, human resources, or public affairs (Bok, 2006; Useem, 1989). Research also reveals that the career mobility and career advancement of nonbusiness majors in the business world are equal to those attained by business majors (Pascarella & Terenzini, 1991, 2005).

Don't restrict your choices of a major to business by believing in the myth that you must major in business to work for a business after graduation.

Student Perspective

"They asked me during my interview why I was right for the job and I told them because I can read well, write well and I can think. They really liked that because those were the skills they were looking for."

–English major hired by a public relations firm (*Los Angeles Times*, April 4, 2004)

Myth 4. If You Major in a Liberal Arts Field, the Only Career Available Is Teaching

Liberal arts majors are not restricted to teaching careers. Many college graduates with majors in liberal arts fields have proceeded to, and succeeded in, careers other than teaching. Among these graduates are such notable people as:

- Jill Barad (English major), CEO, Mattel Toys;
- Steve Case (political science major), CEO, America Online;
- Brian Lamb (speech major), CEO, C-Span; and
- Willie Brown (liberal studies major), mayor, San Francisco.

Source: Indiana University (2004).

Studies show that college graduates in liberal arts majors are just as likely to advance to the highest levels of corporate leadership as graduates majoring in preprofessional fields, such as business and engineering (Pascarella & Terenzini, 2005). If you are considering a major in a liberal arts field, you should not be dismayed or discouraged by those who may question your choice by asking, "What are you going to do with a degree in *that* major?"

Note: A good career-information Web site for liberal arts majors can be found at www.eace.org/networks/liberalarts.html.

Myth 5. Specialized Skills Are More Important for Career Success Than General Skills

You may find that general education (liberal arts) courses are sometimes viewed by students as unnecessary requirements that they have to "get out of the way" before they can "get into what's really important"—their major or academic specialization. However, general education courses develop practical, durable, and transferable skills that supply a strong foundation for success in any career.

Also, don't forget that the general skills and qualities developed by the liberal arts increase career advancement (your ability to move up the career ladder) and career mobility (your ability to move into different career paths). Specific, technical skills may be important for getting into a career, but general educational skills are more important for moving up the career ladder. The courses you take as part of your general education will prepare you for your advanced career positions, not just your first one (Boyer, 1987; Miller, 2003). Furthermore, general professional skills are growing even more important for college graduates entering the workforce in the twenty-first century because the demand for upper-level positions in management and leadership will exceed the supply of workers available to fill these positions (Herman, 2000).

THINK ABOUT IT   **Journal Entry**   **10.5**

In what ways do you think your general education courses will improve your work performance in the career field you may pursue?

_____

_____

_____

_____

_____

_____

Factors to Consider When Choosing Your Major or Field of Study

Gaining self-awareness is the critical first step in making decisions about a college major, or any other important decision. You must know yourself before you can know what choice is best for you. While this may seem obvious, self-awareness and self-discovery are often overlooked aspects of the decision-making process. In particular, you need awareness of your:

- **Interests.** What you like doing;
- **Abilities.** What you're good at doing; and
- **Values.** What you feel good about doing.

| **THINK ABOUT IT** | **Journal Entry** | **10.6** |

In Chapter 2 (**pp. 44–49**), you answered self-awareness questions related to each of these three elements of self. Review your answers to these questions. Do you notice anything about your entries that suggests there might be certain majors or fields of study that match your interests, abilities, and values?

_____

_____

_____

_____

_____

_____

Multiple Intelligences: Identifying Personal Abilities and Talents

One element of your self that you should be aware of when choosing a major is your mental strengths, abilities, or talents. Intelligence was once considered to be one general trait that could be detected and measured by an intelligence quotient (IQ) test. Now, the singular word "intelligence" has been replaced by the plural word "intelligences" to reflect that humans can display intelligence or mental ability in many forms other than their paper-and-pencil performance on an IQ test.

Listed in **Box 10.3** are forms of intelligence identified by Howard Gardner (1983, 1993) from studies of gifted and talented individuals, experts in different lines of work, and various other sources. As you read through the types of intelligence, place a checkmark next to the type that you think represents your strongest ability or talent. (You can possess more than one type.) Keep your type or types of intelligence in mind when you're choosing a college major. Ideally, you want to select a major that taps into and builds on your strongest skills or talents. Choosing a major that's compatible with your abilities should enable you to master the concepts and skills required by your major more rapidly and deeply. Furthermore, if you follow your academic talents, you're likely to succeed or excel in what you do, which will bolster your academic self-confidence and motivation.

Multiple Forms of Intelligence

10.3

- **Linguistic Intelligence.** Ability to communicate through words or language (e.g., verbal skills in the areas of speaking, writing, listening, or reading)
- **Logical–Mathematical Intelligence.** Ability to reason logically and succeed in tasks that involve mathematical problem solving (e.g., the skill for making logical arguments and following logical reasoning or the ability to think effectively with numbers and make quantitative calculations)
- **Spatial Intelligence.** Ability to visualize relationships among objects arranged in different spatial positions and ability to perceive or create visual images (e.g., forming mental images of three-dimensional objects; detecting detail in objects or drawings; artistic talent for drawing, painting, sculpting, and graphic design; or skills related to sense of direction and navigation)
- **Musical Intelligence.** Ability to appreciate or create rhythmical and melodic sounds (e.g., playing, writing, or arranging music)
- **Interpersonal (Social) Intelligence.** Ability to relate to others; to accurately identify others' needs, feelings, or emotional states of mind; and to effectively express emotions and feelings to others (e.g., interpersonal communication skills or the ability to accurately "read" the feelings of others or to meet their emotional needs)
- **Intrapersonal (Self) Intelligence.** Ability to self-reflect, become aware of, and understand your own thoughts, feelings, and behavior (e.g., capacity for personal reflection, emotional self-awareness, and self-insight into personal strengths and weaknesses)
- **Bodily–Kinesthetic (Psychomotor) Intelligence.** Ability to use your own body skillfully and to acquire knowledge through bodily sensations or movements (e.g., skill at tasks involving physical coordination, the ability to work well with hands, mechanical skills, talent for building models and assembling things, or skills relating to technology)
- **Naturalist Intelligence.** Ability to carefully observe and appreciate features of the natural environment (e.g., keen awareness of nature or natural surroundings or the ability to understand causes or results of events occurring in the natural world)

Source: Gardner (1993).

THINK ABOUT IT   **Journal Entry**   **10.7**

Which type or types of intelligence listed in **Box 10.3** represent your strongest area or areas?

_____

_____

_____

_____

_____

_____

Which majors or fields of study do you think may be the best match for your natural talents?

_____

_____

_____

_____

_____

_____

Learning Styles: Identifying Your Learning Preferences

Your learning style is another important personal characteristic you should be aware of when choosing your major. Learning styles refer to individual differences in learning preferences—that is, ways in which individuals prefer to perceive information (receive or take it in) and process information (deal with it after taking it in). Individuals may differ in terms of whether they prefer to take in information by reading about it, listening to it, seeing an image or diagram of it, or physically touching and manipulating it. Individuals may also vary in terms of whether they like to receive information in a structured and orderly format or in an unstructured form that allows them the freedom to explore, play with, and restructure it in their own way. Once information has been received, individuals may also differ in terms of how they prefer to process or deal with it mentally. Some might like to think about it on their own; others may prefer to discuss it with someone else, make an outline of it, or draw a picture of it.

Personal Story

In my family, whenever there's something that needs to be assembled or set up (e.g., a ping-pong table or new electronic equipment), I've noticed that my wife, my son, and myself have different learning styles in terms of how we go about doing it. I like to read the manual's instructions carefully and completely before I even attempt to touch anything. My son prefers to look at the pictures or diagrams in the manual and uses them as models to find parts; then he begins to assemble those parts. My wife seems to prefer not to look at the manual. Instead, she likes to figure things out as she goes along by grabbing different parts from the box and trying to assemble those parts that look like they should fit together—piecing them together as if she were completing a jigsaw puzzle.

—Joe Cuseo

You can take specially designed tests to assess your particular learning style and how it compares with others. If you're interested in taking one, the Learning Center or Career Development Center are the two most likely sites on campus where you will be able to do so.

Probably the most frequently used learning styles test is the Myers-Briggs Type Indicator (MBTI; Myers, 1976; Myers & McCaulley, 1985), which is based on the personality theory of psychologist Carl Jung. The tests consist of four pairs of opposing traits and assesses how people vary on a scale (low to high) for each of these four sets of traits. The four sets of opposing traits are illustrated in **Figure 10.3.**

Extraversion	*Introversion*
Prefer to focus on "outer" world of persons, actions, or objects	Prefer to focus on "inner" world of thoughts and ideas
Sensing	*Intuition*
Prefer interacting with the world directly through concrete, sensory experiences	Prefer dealing with symbolic meanings and imagining possibilities
Thinking	*Feeling*
Prefer to rely on logic and rational thinking when making decisions	Prefer to rely on human needs and feelings when making decisions
Judging	*Perceiving*
Prefer to plan for and control events	Prefer flexibility and spontaneity

Figure 10.3 Traits and Learning Styles Measured by the Myers-Briggs Type Indicator (MBTI)

As you read the following four pairs of opposite traits, place a mark along the line where you think you fall with respect to each set of traits. For example, place a mark in the middle of the line if you think you are midway between these opposing traits, or place a mark at the far left or far right if you think you lean strongly toward the trait listed on either end.

THINK ABOUT IT   **Journal Entry 10.8**

For each of the following four sets of opposing traits, make a note about where you fall—middle, far left, or far right.

	Far Left	Middle	Far Right
Extraversion–introversion			
Sensing–intuition			
Thinking–feeling			
Judging–perceiving			

What majors or fields of study do you think are most compatible with your personality traits?

_____

_____

_____

_____

It has been found that college students who score differently on the MBTI have different learning preferences when it comes to the style of writing and type of writing assignments (Jensen & Ti Tiberio, cited in Bean, 2001). See **Figure 10.4** for the details on the findings.

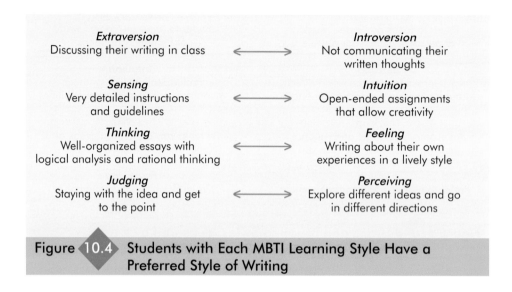

Figure 10.4   **Students with Each MBTI Learning Style Have a Preferred Style of Writing**

These results clearly indicate that students have different learning styles, which, in turn, influence the type of writing assignments they feel most comfortable performing. This may be important to keep in mind when choosing your major because different academic fields emphasize different styles of writing. Some fields place heavy emphasis on writing that is structured and tightly focused (e.g., science and business), while other fields encourage writing with personal style, flair, or creativity (e.g., English and art). How your writing style meshes with the style emphasized by an academic field may be an important factor to consider when making decisions about your college major.

Another popular learning styles test is the Learning Styles Inventory (Dunn, Dunn, & Price, 1990), which was originally developed by David Kolb, a professor of philosophy (Kolb, 1976, 1985). It is based on how individuals differ with respect to the following two elements of the learning process:

How Information Is *Perceived* (Taken in)

Concrete Experience	*Reflective Observation*
Learning through direct involvement or personal experience	Learning by watching or observing

How Information Is *Processed* (Dealt with after it has been taken in)

Abstract Conceptualization	*Active Experimentation*
Learning by thinking about things and drawing logical conclusions	Learning by taking chances and trying things out

When these two dimensions are crisscrossed to form intersecting lines, four sectors (areas) are created, each of which represents a different learning style, as illustrated in **Figure 10.5**. As you look at the four areas (styles) in the figure, circle the style that you think reflects your most preferred way of learning.

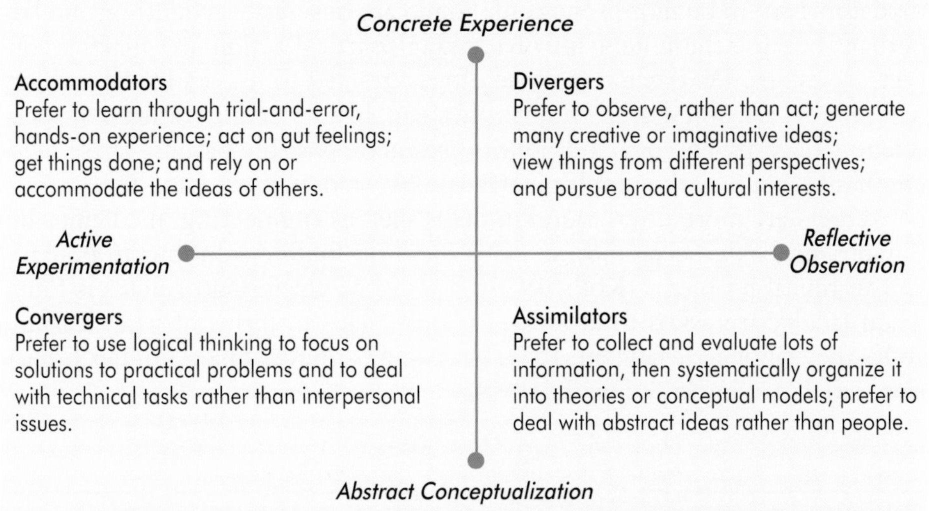

Concrete Experience

Accommodators
Prefer to learn through trial-and-error, hands-on experience; act on gut feelings; get things done; and rely on or accommodate the ideas of others.

Divergers
Prefer to observe, rather than act; generate many creative or imaginative ideas; view things from different perspectives; and pursue broad cultural interests.

Active Experimentation   *Reflective Observation*

Convergers
Prefer to use logical thinking to focus on solutions to practical problems and to deal with technical tasks rather than interpersonal issues.

Assimilators
Prefer to collect and evaluate lots of information, then systematically organize it into theories or conceptual models; prefer to deal with abstract ideas rather than people.

Abstract Conceptualization

Figure 10.5 Learning Styles Measured by the *Learning Styles Inventory (LSI)*

THINK ABOUT IT   Journal Entry 10.9

Which one of the four learning styles appears to most closely match your learning style? (Check one of the following boxes.)

☐ Accommodator

☐ Diverger

☐ Converger

☐ Assimilator

What majors or fields of study do you think would be a good match for your learning style?

_____

_____

_____

_____

_____

_____

Research indicates that students majoring in different fields tend to display differences in these four learning styles (Svinicki & Dixon, 1987). For instance, assimilators are more often found majoring in mathematics and natural sciences (e.g., chemistry and physics), probably because these subjects stress reflection and abstract thinking. In contrast, academic fields where accommodators tend to be more commonly found are business, accounting, and law, perhaps because these fields involve taking practical action and making concrete decisions. Divergers are more often attracted to majors in the fine arts (e.g., music, art, and drama), humanities (e.g., history and literature), or social sciences (e.g., psychology and political science), possibly because these fields emphasize appreciating multiple viewpoints and perspectives. In contrast, convergers are more often found in fields such as engineering, medicine, and nursing, probably because these fields focus on finding solutions to practical and technical problems (Kolb, 1976). This same clustering of fields is found when faculty are asked to classify academic fields in terms of what learning styles they emphasize (Biglan, 1973; Carnegie Commission on Higher Education, cited in Svinicki & Dixon, 1987).

Personal Story

I first noticed that students in different academic fields may have different learning styles when I was teaching a psychology course that was required for students majoring in nursing and social work. I noticed that some students in class seemed to lose interest (and patience) when we got involved in lengthy class discussions about controversial issues or theories, while others seemed to love it. On the other hand, whenever I lectured or delivered information for an extended period, some students seemed to lose interest (and attention), while others seemed to get into it and took great notes. After one class period that involved quite a bit of class discussion, I began thinking about which students seemed most involved in the discussion and which seemed to drift off or lose interest. I suddenly realized that the students who did most of the talking and seemed most enthused during the class discussion were the students majoring in social work. On the other hand, most of the students who appeared disinterested or a bit frustrated were the nursing majors.

When I began to think about why this happened, it dawned on me that the nursing students were accustomed to gathering factual information and learning practical skills in their major courses and were expecting to use that learning style in my psychology course. The nursing majors felt more comfortable with structured class sessions in which they received lots of factual, practical information from the professor. On the other hand, the social work majors were more comfortable with unstructured class discussions because courses in their major often emphasized debating social issues and hearing viewpoints or perspectives.

As I left class that day, I asked myself: Did the nursing students and social work students select or gravitate toward their major because the type of learning emphasized in the field tended to match their preferred style of learning?

—Joe Cuseo

Since students have different learning styles and academic fields emphasize different styles of learning, it's important to consider how your learning style meshes with the style of learning emphasized by the field you're considering as a major. If the match seems to be close or compatible, then the marriage between you and that major could be one that leads to a satisfying and successful learning experience.

We recommend taking a trip to the Learning Center or Career Development Center on your campus to take a learning styles test. Even if the test doesn't help you choose a particular major, it will at least help you become more aware of your particular learning style. This alone could contribute to your academic success, because studies show that when college students gain greater self-awareness of their learning styles, they improve their academic performance (Claxton & Murrell, 1988).

THINK ABOUT IT   **Journal Entry**   **10.10**

In addition to taking formal tests to assess your learning style, you can gain awareness of your learning styles through some simple introspection or self-examination. Take a moment to complete the following sentences that are designed to stimulate personal reflection on your learning style:

I learn best if . . . .

_____

_____

_____

_____

I learn most from . . . .

_____

_____

_____

_____

I enjoy learning when . . . .

_____

_____

_____

_____

> "Minds differ still more than faces."
>
> –Voltaire, eighteenth-century French author and philosopher

To sum up, the most important factor to consider when reaching decisions about a major is whether it is compatible with four characteristics of your self: your (1) learning style, (2) your abilities, (3) your personal interests, and (4) your values (see **Figure 10.6**). These four pillars provide the foundation for effective decisions about a college major.

Strategies for Discovering a Major Compatible with Your Interests, Talents, and Values

If you're undecided about a major, there's no need to feel anxious or guilty. You're at an early stage in your college experience. Although you've decided to postpone your decision about a major, this doesn't mean you're a clueless procrastinator as long as you have a plan for exploring and narrowing down

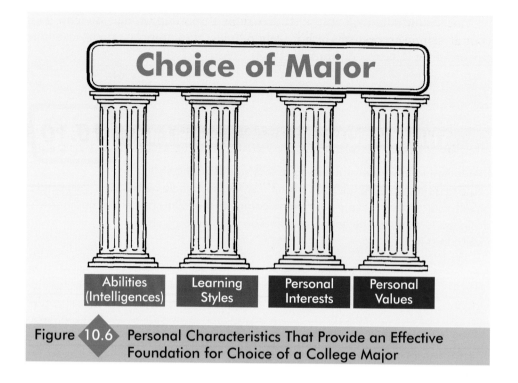

Figure 10.6 Personal Characteristics That Provide an Effective Foundation for Choice of a College Major

your options. Just be sure that you don't put all thoughts about your major on the back burner and simply drift along until you have no choice but to make a choice. Start exploring and developing a game plan now that will lead you to a wise decision about your major.

Similarly, if you've already chosen a major, this doesn't mean that you'll never have to give any more thought to that decision or that you can just shift into cruise control and motor along a mindless ride in the major you've selected. Instead, you should continue the exploration process by carefully testing your first choice, making sure it's a choice that is compatible with your abilities, interests, and values. In other words, take the approach that it's your *current* choice; whether it becomes your firm and *final* choice will depend on how well you perform, and how interested you are, in the first courses you take in the field.

To explore and identify majors that are compatible with your personal strengths and interests, use the following strategies.

1. Use past experience to help you choose a major.

Think about the subjects that you experienced during high school and your early time in college. As the old saying goes, "Nothing succeeds like success itself." If you have done well and continue to do well in a certain field of study, this may indicate that your natural abilities and learning style correspond well with the academic skills required by that particular field. This could translate into future success and satisfaction in the field if you decide to pursue it as a college major.

You can enter information about your academic performance with high school courses at a Web site (www.mymajors.com), which will analyze it and provide you with college majors that may be a good match for you (based on your academic experiences in high school).

2. Use your elective courses to test your interests and abilities in subjects that you might consider as a major.

As its name implies, "elective" courses are those that you elect or choose to take. In college, electives come in two forms: free electives and restricted electives.

Free electives are courses that you may elect (choose) to enroll in; they count toward your college degree but are not required for general education or your major.

Restricted electives are courses that you must take, but you choose them from a restricted list of possible courses that have been specified by your college as fulfilling a requirement in general education or your major. For example, your campus may have a general education requirement in social or behavioral sciences that requires you to take two courses in this field, but you're allowed to choose those two courses from a menu of options in the field, such as anthropology, economics, political science, psychology, or sociology. If you're considering one of these subjects as a possible major, you can take an introductory course in this subject and test your interest in it while simultaneously fulfilling a general education requirement needed for graduation. This strategy will allow you to use general education as the main highway for travel toward your final destination (a college degree) and give you the opportunity to explore potential majors along the way.

You can also use your free electives to select courses in fields that you are considering as possible majors. By using some of your free and restricted electives in this way, you can test your interest and ability in these fields; if you find one that is a good match, you may have found yourself a major.

Naturally, you don't have to use all your electives for the purpose of exploring majors. As many as one-third of your courses in college may be electives. This leaves you with a great deal of freedom to shape your college experience in a way that best meets your personal needs and future interests. For suggestions on how to make the best use of your free electives, see **Box 10.4**.

3. Be sure you know the courses that are required for the major you're considering.

In college, it's expected that students may know the requirements for the major they've chosen. These requirements vary considerably from one major to another. Be sure to review your college catalog carefully to determine what courses are required for the major you're considering. If you have trouble tracking down the requirements in your college catalog, don't become frustrated. These catalogs are often written in a technical manner that can sometimes be hard to interpret. If you need help identifying and understanding the requirements for a major that you are considering, don't be embarrassed about seeking assistance from a professional in your school's Academic Advisement Center.

Personal Story   As an academic advisor, I often see students who are confused about what they want to major in, especially traditionally aged (18 to 24 years old) students. I can relate to these students because I changed my major multiple times before I reached a final decision. The first piece of advice I give students about choosing majors is to use their resources (e.g., academic advisement) and to do some research on the courses required for the majors they're considering. Over the last few years, I've seen many students who want to major in forensic science—largely due to the popularity of the *CSI* shows. I then ask them how they feel about science and math, and many of these students tell me they hate those subjects. When I inform them that becoming a forensic scientist often involves a minimum of a master's in chemistry, they decide to look at other majors. Fewer surprises like this would occur if students did at least some research on what courses are required for the majors and careers they're considering.

—Julie McLaughlin

Take Action!

Top 10 Suggestions for Making the Most of Your College Electives

Your elective courses give you academic freedom and personal control of your college coursework. You can exercise this freedom strategically by selecting electives in a way that enables you to make the most of your college experience and college degree. As you read these 10 suggestions, identify your two primary strategies for using your electives.

You can use your electives for the following purposes:

1. Complete a minor or build an area of concentration. Your electives can complement and strengthen your major or allow you to pursue a field of interest other than your major.

2. Help you choose a career path. Just as you can use electives to test your interest in a college major, you can use them to test your interest in a career. For instance, you could enroll in:
   - Career planning or career development courses; and
   - Courses that involve internships or service learning experiences in a field that you're considering as a possible career (e.g., health, education, or business).

3. Strengthen your skills in areas that may appeal to future employers. For example, courses in foreign language, leadership development, and argumentation or debate develop skills that are attractive to future employers and may improve your employment prospects.

4. Develop practical life skills that you can use now or in the near future. You could take courses in managing personal finances, marriage and family, or child development to help you manage your money and your future family.

5. Seek balance in your life and develop yourself as a whole person. You can use your electives strategically to cover all key dimensions of self-development. For instance, you could take courses that promote your emotional development (e.g., stress management), social development (e.g., interpersonal relationships), mental development (e.g., critical thinking), physical development (e.g., nutrition, self-defense), and spiritual development (e.g., world religions or death and dying).

10.4

Remember

Choose courses that contribute not only to your major and career but also to your quality of life.

6. Make connections across different academic disciplines (subject areas). Courses designed specifically to integrate two or more academic disciplines are referred to as interdisciplinary courses. For example, psychobiology is an interdisciplinary course that combines or integrates the fields of psychology (focusing on the mind) and biology (focusing on the body) and thus helps you see how the mind influences the body, and vice versa. Making connections across subjects and seeing how they can be combined to create a more complete understanding of a subject or issue can be a stimulating mental experience. Furthermore, the presence of interdisciplinary courses on your college transcript may be attractive to future employers because responsibilities and issues in the work world are not neatly packaged into separate majors; they require the ability to combine skills acquired from different fields of study.

7. Help you develop broader perspectives on life and the world in which we live. You can take courses that progressively widen your perspectives. For example, you could select courses that provide you with a societal perspective (e.g., sociology), a national perspective (e.g., political science), an international perspective (e.g., cultural geography), and a global perspective (e.g., ecol-

ogy). These broadening perspectives widen your scope of knowledge and deepen your understanding of the world.

8. Appreciate different cultural viewpoints and improve your ability to communicate with people from diverse cultural backgrounds. You could take courses relating to differences across nations (international diversity), such as international relations, and you could take courses relating to ethnic and racial differences in America (domestic diversity).

9. Stretch beyond your familiar or customary learning style to experience different ways of learning or develop new skills. Your college curriculum is likely to include courses that were never previously available to you and that focus on skills you've never had the opportunity to test or develop. These courses can stretch your mind and allow you to explore new ideas and acquire new perspectives.

10. Learn something about which you were always curious or simply wanted to know more about. For instance, if you've always been curious about how members of the other sex think and feel, you could take a course on the psychology of men and women. Or if you've always been fascinated by movies and how they are made, you might elect to take a course in filmmaking or cinematography.

THINK ABOUT IT   **Journal Entry**   **10.11**

What were the two primary strategies you selected from the list in **Box 10.4**?

_____

_____

_____

_____

Write a short explanation about why you chose each of these strategies.

_____

_____

_____

_____

_____

_____

_____

_____

———————————————————————————————————————

Keep in mind that college majors often require courses in fields outside of the major. Such courses are designed to support the major. For instance, psychology majors are often required to take at least one course in biology, and business majors are often required to take calculus. If you are interested in majoring in a particular subject area, be sure you are fully aware of such outside requirements and are comfortable with them.

Once you've accurately identified all courses required for the major you're considering, ask yourself the following two questions:

a. Do the course titles and descriptions appeal to my interests and values?
b. Do I have the abilities or skills needed to do well in these courses?

You don't want to be surprised by unexpected requirements after you have already committed to a major, particularly if these unanticipated requirements do not match your personal abilities, interests, or learning styles.

4. Look over an introductory textbook in the field you're considering as a major.

Find an introductory book in a major that you're considering, review its table of contents, and ask yourself whether the topics are compatible with your academic interests and talents. Also, read a few pages of the text to get some sense of the writing style used in the field and how comfortable you are with it. You should find introductory textbooks for all courses in your college bookstore, in the college library, or with a faculty member in that field.

5. Talk with students majoring in the field you are considering and ask them about their experiences.

Try to speak with several students in the field so that you get a balanced perspective that goes beyond the opinion of one individual. A good way to find students in the major you're considering is to visit student clubs on campus related to the major (e.g., psychology club or history club). You could also check the class schedule to see when and where classes in your major are meeting and then go the classroom where these classes meet and speak with students about the major, either before class begins or after class lets out. The following questions may be good ones to ask students in a major that you're considering:

• What first attracted you to this major?
• What would you say are the advantages and disadvantages of majoring in this field?
• Knowing what you know now, would you choose the same major again?

Also, ask students about the quality of teaching and advising in the department. Studies show that different departments within the same college or university can vary greatly in terms of the quality of teaching, as well as their educational philosophy and attitude toward students (Pascarella & Terenzini, 1991).

6. Sit in on some classes in the field you are considering as a major.

If the class you want to visit is large, you probably could just slip into the back row and listen. However, if the class is small, you should ask the instructor's permission. When visiting a class, focus on the content or ideas being covered in class rather than the instructor's personality or teaching style. (Keep in mind that you're trying to decide whether you will major in the subject, not in the teacher.)

7. Discuss the major you're considering with an academic advisor.

It's probably best to speak with an academic advisor who advises students in various majors rather than to someone who advises only students in their particular academic department or field. You want to be sure to discuss the major with an advisor who is neutral and will give you unbiased feedback about the pros and cons of majoring in that field.

8. Speak with some faculty members in the department that you're considering as a major.

Consider asking them the following questions:

- What academic skills or qualities are needed for a student to be successful in your field?
- What are the greatest challenges faced by students majoring in your field?
- What do students seem to like most and least about majoring in your field?
- What can students do with a major in your field after college graduation?
- What types of graduate programs or professional schools would a student in your major be well prepared to enter?

9. Visit your Career Development Center.

See whether information is available on college graduates who've majored in the field you're considering and what they've gone on to do with that major after graduation. This will give you an idea about the type of careers the major can lead to or what graduate and professional school programs students often enter after completing a major in the field that you're considering.

10. Surf the Web site of the professional organization associated with the field that you're considering as a major.

For example, if you're thinking about becoming an anthropology major, check out the Web site of the American Anthropological Association. If you're considering history as a major, look at the Web site of the American Historical Association. The Web site of a professional organization often contains useful information for students who are considering that field as a major. For example, the Web site of the American Philosophical Association contains information about nonacademic careers for philosophy majors, and the American Sociological Association's Web site identifies various careers that sociology majors are qualified to pursue after college graduation. To locate the professional Web site of the field that you might want to explore as a possible major, ask a faculty member in that field or complete a search on the Web by simply entering the name of the field followed by the word "association."

11. Be sure you know what academic standards must be met for you to be accepted for entry into a major.

Because of their popularity, certain college majors may be impacted or over-subscribed, which means that more students are interested in majoring in these fields than there are openings for them. For instance, preprofessional majors that lead directly to a particular career are often the ones that often become oversubscribed (e.g., accounting, education, engineering, premed, nursing, or physical therapy). On some campuses, these majors are called restricted majors, meaning that departments control their enrollment by limiting the number of students they let into the major. For example, departments may restrict entry to their major by admitting only students who have achieved an overall GPA of 3.0 or higher in certain introductory courses required by the majors, or they may take all students who apply for the major, rank them by their GPA, and then count down until they have filled their maximum number of available spaces (Strommer, 1993).

Be sure you know whether the major you're considering is impacted or oversubscribed and whether it requires certain academic standards to be met before you can be admitted. As you complete courses and receive grades, check to see whether you are meeting these standards. If you find yourself failing to meet these standards, you may need to increase the amount of time and effort you devote to your studies and seek assistance from your campus Learning Center. If you're working at your maximum level of effort and are regularly using the learning assistance services available on your campus but are still not meeting the academic standards of your intended major, consult with an academic advisor to help you identify an alternative field that may be closely related to the restricted major you were hoping to enter.

THINK ABOUT IT   **Journal Entry   10.12**

Do you think that the major you're considering is likely to be oversubscribed (i.e., there are more students wanting to major in the field than there are openings in the courses)?

_____

_____

_____

_____

_____

_____

_____

_____

12. Consider the possibility of a college minor in a field that complements your major.

A college minor usually requires about one-half the number of credits (units) required for a major. Most campuses allow you the option of completing a minor with your major. Check with your academic advisor or the course catalog of the school you're considering to transfer to; if the school offers a minor that interests you, find out what courses are required to complete it.

If you have strong interests in two different fields, a minor will allow you to major in one of these fields while minoring in the other. Thus, you can pursue two fields that interest you without having to sacrifice one for the other. Furthermore, a minor can be completed at the same time as most college majors without delaying your time to graduation. (In contrast, a double major will typically lengthen your time to graduation because you must complete the separate requirements of two different majors.) You can also pursue a second field of study alongside your major without increasing your time to graduation by completing a cognate area—a specialization that requires fewer courses to complete than a minor (e.g., four to five courses instead of seven to eight courses). A concentration area may have even fewer requirements (only two to three courses).

Taking a cluster of courses in a field outside your major can be an effective way to strengthen your résumé and increase your employment prospects because it demonstrates your versatility and allows you to gain experience in areas that may be missing or underemphasized in your major. For example, students majoring in the fine arts (e.g., music or theater) or humanities (e.g., English or history) may take courses in the fields of mathematics (e.g., statistics), technology (e.g., computer science), and business (e.g., economics)—all of which are not emphasized by their major.

◆ Summary and Conclusion

Here is a snapshot of the points that were made in this chapter:

- Changing your educational goal is not necessarily a bad thing; it may represent your discovery of another field that's more interesting to you or that's more compatible with your personal interests and talents.
- Several myths exist about the relationship between college majors and careers that need to be dispelled:
  - **Myth 1.** When you choose your major, you're choosing your career.
  - **Myth 2.** After a bachelor's degree, any further education must be in the same field as your college major.
  - **Myth 3.** You should major in business because most college graduates work in business settings.
  - **Myth 4.** If you major in a liberal arts field, the only career available is teaching.
  - **Myth 5.** Specialized skills are more important for career success than general skills.

You should be aware of two important elements when choosing your major: your form or forms of multiple intelligence (your mental strengths or talents) and your learning style (your preferred way of learning).

Strategically select your courses in a way that contributes most to your educational, personal, and professional development. Choose your elective courses with one or more of the following purposes in mind:

- Choose a major or confirm whether your first choice is a good one.
- Acquire a minor or build a concentration that will complement your major.
- Broaden your perspectives on the world around you.
- Become a more balanced or complete person.
- Handle the practical life tasks that face you now and in the future.
- Strengthen your career development and employment prospects after graduation.

With "higher" education comes a higher degree of freedom of choice and a greater opportunity to determine your own academic course of action. Employ it and enjoy it—use your freedom strategically to make the most of your college experience and college degree.

Internet-Based Resources for Further Information on Educational Planning and Decision Making

For additional information related to the ideas discussed in this chapter, we recommend the following Web sites:

www.mymajors.com

www.princetonreview.com/majors.aspx

www.eace.org/networks/liberalarts.html

Chapter 10 Exercises

10.1 Planning General Education

- Look at your college catalog. If you don't have a copy, you may be able to access it online or obtain a copy from your academic advisor or Registrar's Office. Use the index in the catalog to find the general education requirements at your college. You're likely to find that general education requirements are organized into academic divisions of knowledge that make up the college curriculum, such as humanities, fine arts, and natural sciences. Within each of these academic divisions, you'll see courses listed that fulfill the general education requirement for that particular division. In some cases, you'll have no choice about what courses you must take to fulfill the general education requirement, but in most cases, you'll have the freedom to choose from a group of courses. Read the course descriptions to get an idea about what each course covers, and choose those courses that are most relevant to your educational and career plans or to your interests in fields that you might consider choosing as a major.
- Record the courses you plan to take to fulfill your general education requirements on the following form. (Remember that courses you are taking this term may be fulfilling certain general education requirements, so be sure to include them on the form.)

General Education Planning Form

Academic Division: _____

General education courses you plan to take to fulfill requirements in this division: (Record the course number and course title)

Academic Division: _____

General education courses you plan to take to fulfill requirements in this division:

Academic Division: _____

General education courses you plan to take to fulfill requirements in this division:

Academic Division: _____

General education courses you plan to take to fulfill requirements in this division:

Academic Division: _____
General education courses you plan to take to fulfill requirements in this division:

Academic Division: _____
General education courses you plan to take to fulfill requirements in this division:

10.2 Planning for a College Major and Transfer to a 4-Year College

In the preceding exercise, you made a plan for the general education component of your college experience. Now consider developing a tentative plan for a college major or specialized field of study. Even if you don't think you're going to transfer to a 4-year college and complete a bachelor's degree, it's still a good idea to complete this exercise because it'll give you an idea about what it would take to get such a degree. It's possible that when you see it all laid out in a plan you might be motivated to pursue a bachelor's degree—if not right now then perhaps at a later point in your life.

1. Go to your college catalog and use its index to locate pages containing information related to the major you have chosen or are considering. If you are undecided, select a field that you might consider as a possibility. To help you identify possible majors, you can use your catalog or go online and complete the short interview at the www.mymajors.com Web site.

   The point of this exercise is not to force you to commit to a major now but to familiarize you with the process of developing a plan, thereby putting you in a position to apply this knowledge when you reach a final decision about the major you intend to pursue. Even if you don't yet know what your final destination may be with respect to a college major, creating this educational plan will keep you moving in the right direction.

2. Once you've selected a major for this assignment, look at the catalog of the 4-year college to which you plan to transfer to identify the courses that are required for the major you have selected. Use the form that follows to list the number and title of each course required by the major.

   You'll find that you must take certain courses for the major; these are often called core requirements. For instance, at most colleges, all business majors must take microeconomics. You will likely discover that you can choose other required courses from a menu or list of options (e.g., "choose any three courses from the following list of six courses"). Such courses are often called restricted electives in the major. When you find restricted electives in the major you've selected, read the course descriptions and choose those courses from the list that appeal most to you. Simply list the numbers and titles of these courses on the planning form. (You don't need to write down all choices listed in the catalog.)

   College catalogs can sometimes be tricky to navigate or interpret, so if you run into any difficulty, don't panic. Seek help from an academic advisor. Your campus may also have a degree audit program available, which allows you to track major requirements electronically. If so, take advantage of it.

College Major Planning Form

Major Selected: _____

Core Requirements in the Major
(Courses in your major that you must take)

Course #	Course Title	Course #	Course Title

Restricted Electives in the Major
(Courses required for your major that you choose to take from a specified list)

Course #	Course Title	Course #	Course Title

Self-Assessment Questions

1. Looking over the courses required for the major you've selected, would you still be interested in majoring in this field?

2. Were there courses required by the major that you were surprised to see or that you did not expect would be required?

3. Are there questions that you still have about this major?

10.3 Developing a Comprehensive Transfer and Graduation Plan

A comprehensive, long-range graduation plan includes all three types of courses you need to complete a college degree:

1. General education requirements

2. Major requirements

3. Free electives

In the preceding exercises, you planned for your required general education courses and required courses in your major. The third set of courses you'll take in college that count toward your degree consists of courses called free electives—courses that are not required for general education or your major but that you freely choose from any of the courses listed in your college catalog. By combining your general education courses, major courses, and free-elective courses, you can create a comprehensive, long-term transfer and graduation plan.

Use the form on **p. 371** to develop this complete educational plan. Use the slots to pencil in the general education courses you're planning to take to fulfill your general education requirements, your major requirements, and your free electives. (For ideas on choosing your free electives, see **Box 10.4 on p. 356**.) Since this may be a tentative plan, it's probably best to use a pencil when completing it in case you need to make modifications to it.

Notes

1. If you have not decided on a major, a good strategy might be to concentrate on taking liberal arts courses to fulfill your general education requirements during your first year of college. This will open more slots in your course schedule during your sophomore year. By that time, you may have a better idea of what you want to major in, and you can fill these open slots with courses required by your major. This may be a particularly effective strategy if you choose to major in a field that has many lower-division (freshman and sophomore) requirements that have to be completed before you can be accepted as a transfer student in that major. (These lower-division requirements are often referred to as premajor requirements.)

2. Keep in mind that the course number indicates the year in the college experience that the course is usually taken. Courses numbered in the 100s (or below) are typically taken in the first year of college, 200-numbered courses in the sophomore year, 300-numbered courses in the junior year, and 400-numbered courses in the senior year. Also, be sure to check whether the course you're planning to take has any prerequisites—courses that need to be completed before you can enroll in the course you're planning to take. For example, if you are planning to take a course in literature, it is likely that you cannot enroll in it until you have completed at least one prerequisite course in writing or English composition.

3. To complete a college degree in 4 years, you should complete about 30 credits each academic year. Summer term is considered part of an academic year, and we encourage you to use that term to help keep you on a 4-year timeline.

4. Check with an academic advisor to see whether your college and the 4-year college to which you're planning to transfer have developed a projected plan of scheduled courses, which indicates the academic term when courses listed in the catalog are scheduled to be offered (e.g., fall, spring, or summer) for the next two to three years. If such a long-range plan of scheduled courses is available, take advantage of it because it will enable you to develop a personal educational plan that includes not only what courses you will take but also when you will take them. This can be an important advantage because some courses you may need for graduation will not be offered every term. We strongly encourage you to inquire about and acquire any long-range plan of scheduled courses that may be available and use it when developing your long-range graduation plan.

5. Don't forget to include out-of-class learning experiences as part of your educational plan, such as volunteer service, internships, and study abroad. (For information on these learning experiences, see Chapter 11.)

Your long-range graduation plan is not something set in stone that can never be modified. Like clay, its shape can be molded and changed into a different form as you gain more experience with the college curriculum. Nevertheless, your creation of this initial plan will be useful because it will provide you with a blueprint to work from. Once you have created slots specifically for your general education requirements, your major courses, and your electives, you have accounted for all the categories of courses you will need to complete to graduate. Thus, if changes need to be made to your plan, they can be easily accommodated by simply substituting different courses into the slots you've already created for these three categories.

! Remember

The purpose of this long-range planning assignment is not to lock you into a rigid plan but to give you a telescope for viewing your educational future and a map for reaching your educational goals.

Long-Range Transfer and Graduation Planning Form

STUDENT: ID NO.:

MAJOR: MINOR:

TERM		TERM		TERM		TERM	
Course	Units	Course	Units	Course	Units	Course	Units
TOTAL		TOTAL		TOTAL		TOTAL	

TERM		TERM		TERM		TERM	
Course	Units	Course	Units	Course	Units	Course	Units
TOTAL		TOTAL		TOTAL		TOTAL	

TERM		TERM		TERM		TERM	
Course	Units	Course	Units	Course	Units	Course	Units
TOTAL		TOTAL		TOTAL		TOTAL	

TERM		TERM		TERM		TERM	
Course	Units	Course	Units	Course	Units	Course	Units
TOTAL		TOTAL		TOTAL		TOTAL	

		COCURRICULAR EXPERIENCES	SERVICE LEARNING AND INTERNSHIP EXPERIENCES
Advisor's Signature	Date:		
Student's Signature	Date:		
Notes:			

Self-Assessment Questions

1. Do you think this was a useful assignment? Why or why not?

2. Do you see any way in which this assignment could be improved or strengthened?

3. Did completing this long-range graduation plan influence your educational plans in any way?

Dazed and Confused: General Education versus Career Specialization

Joe Tech was looking forward to college because he thought he would have freedom to select the courses he wanted and the opportunity to get into the major of his choice (computer science). However, he is shocked and disappointed with his first-term schedule of classes because it consists mostly of required general education courses that do not seem to relate to his major, and some of these courses are about subjects that he already took in high school (English, history, and biology). He's beginning to think he would be better off moving off the transfer track and getting a technical degree so that he could finish sooner, get into the computer industry, and start earning money.

Reflection and Discussion Questions

1. What do you see as the potential advantages and disadvantages of Joe pursuing a technical degree instead of a 4-year college degree?

2. Can you relate to Joe, or do you know of students who feel as he does?

3. Do you see any way Joe might strike a balance between pursuing his career interest and obtaining his college degree so that he can pursue both goals at the same time?

Career Exploration, Planning, and Preparation

11

LEARNING GOAL

To acquire strategies that can be used now and throughout the remaining years of your college experience for effective career exploration, preparation, and development.

Before you start to dig into this chapter, take a moment to answer the following questions:

1. Have you decided on a career, or are you leaning strongly toward one?

_____

_____

2. If yes, why have you chosen this career? (Was your decision influenced by anybody or anything?)

_____

_____

_____

_____

_____

_____

3. If no, are there any careers you're considering as possibilities?

_____

_____

_____

_____

_____

_____

◆ The Importance of Career Planning

College graduates in the twenty-first century are likely to continue working until age 75 (Herman, 2000). Once you enter the workforce full time, you'll spend most of the remaining waking hours of your life working. The only other single activity that you'll spend more time doing in your lifetime is sleeping. When you consider that such a sizable portion of your life is spent working and that your career can strongly influence your sense of personal identity and self-esteem, it becomes apparent that career choice is a critical process that should begin early in your college experience.

> **! Remember**
>
> When you're doing *career* planning, you're also doing *life* planning because you are planning how you will spend most of the waking hours of your future.

Even if you've decided on a career that you were dreaming about since you were a preschooler, the process of career exploration and planning is not complete because you still need to decide on what specialization within that career you'll pursue. For example, if you're interested in pursuing a career in law, you'll need to eventually decide what branch of law you wish to practice (e.g., criminal law, corporate law, or family law). You'll also need to decide what employment sector or type of industry you would like to work in, such as nonprofit, for-profit, education, or government. Thus, no matter how certain or uncertain you are about your career path, you'll need to begin exploring career options and start taking your first steps toward formulating a career development plan.

◆ Strategies for Career Exploration and Development

Reaching an effective decision about a career involves the same four steps you used in the goal-setting process (see Chapter 2):

> 1. **Awareness of yourself.** Your personal abilities, interests, needs, and values

> 2. **Awareness of your options.** The variety of career fields available to you

> 3. **Awareness of what best "fits" you.** The careers that best match your personal abilities, interests, needs, and values

> 4. **Awareness of the process.** How to prepare for and gain entry into the career of your choice

Step 1. Self-Awareness

The more you know about yourself, the better your choices and decisions will be. Self-awareness is a particularly important step to take when making career decisions because the career you choose says a lot about who you are and what you want from life. Your personal identity and life goals should not be based on or built around your career choice; it should be the other way around.

> **Remember**
>
> Your personal attributes and goals should be considered first because they provide the foundation on which you build your career choice and future life.

One way to gain greater self-awareness of your career interests is by taking psychological tests or assessments. These assessments allow you to see how your interests in certain career fields compare with those of other students and professionals who've experienced career satisfaction and success. These comparative perspectives can give you important reference points for assessing whether your level of interest in a career is high, average, or low relative to other students and working professionals. Your Career Development Center is the place on campus where you can find these career-interest tests, as well as other instruments that allow you to assess your career-related abilities and values.

When making choices about a career, you may have to consider one other important aspect of yourself: your personal needs. A "need" may be described as something stronger than an interest. When you satisfy a personal need, you are doing something that makes your life more satisfying or fulfilling. Psychologists have identified several important human needs that vary in strength or intensity from person to person. Listed in **Box 11.1** are personal needs that are especially important to consider when making a career choice.

Take Action!

Personal Needs to Consider When Making Career Choices

As you read the needs listed here, make a note after each one, indicating how strong the need is for you (high, moderate, or low).

1. Autonomy. Need to work independently without close supervision or control. Individuals high in this need may experience greater satisfaction working in careers that allow them to be their own boss, make their own decisions, and control their own work schedule. Individuals low in this need may experience greater satisfaction working in careers that are more structured and involve working with a supervisor who provides direction, assistance, and frequent feedback.

11.1

2. **Affiliation.** Need for social interaction, a sense of belonging, and the opportunity to collaborate with others. Individuals high in this need may experience greater satisfaction working in careers that involve frequent interpersonal interaction and teamwork with colleagues or coworkers. Individuals low in this need may be more satisfied working alone or in competition with others.

3. **Achievement.** Need to experience challenge and a sense of personal accomplishment. Individuals high in this need may be more satisfied working in careers that push them to solve problems, generate creative ideas, and continually learn new information or master new skills. Individuals low in this need may be more satisfied with careers that don't continually test their abilities and don't repeatedly challenge them to stretch their skills with new tasks and different responsibilities.

4. **Recognition.** Need for high rank, status, and respect from others. Individuals high in this need may crave careers that are prestigious in the eyes of friends, family, or society. Individuals with a low need for recognition would feel comfortable working in a career that they find personally fulfilling, without being concerned about how impressive or enviable their career appears to others.

5. **Sensory Stimulation.** Need to experience variety, change, and risk. Individuals high in this need may be more satisfied working in careers that involve frequent changes of pace and place (e.g., travel), unpredictable events (e.g., work tasks that vary considerably), and moderate stress (e.g., working under pressure of competition or deadlines). Individuals with a low need for sensory stimulation may feel more comfortable working in careers that involve regular routines, predictable situations, and minimal amounts of risk or stress.

THINK ABOUT IT   Journal Entry   **11.2**

Which of the five needs in **Box 11.1** did you indicate as being strong personal needs?

_____

_____

_____

_____

_____

What career or careers do you think would best match your strongest needs?

_____

_____

_____

_____

_____

_____

Personal Story   While enrolled in my third year of college with half of my degree completed, I had an eye-opening experience. I wish this experience had happened in my first year, but better late than never. Although I had chosen a career during my first year of college, my decision-making process was not systematic and didn't involve critical thinking. I chose a major based on what sounded prestigious and would pay me the most money. Although these are not necessarily bad factors, my failure to use a systematic and reflective process to evaluate these factors was bad. In my junior year of college I asked one of my professors why he decided to get his Ph.D and become a professor. He simply answered, "I wanted autonomy." This was an epiphany for me. He explained that when he looked at his life he determined that he needed a career that offered independence, so he began looking at career options that would offer that. After that explanation, "autonomy" became my favorite word, and this story became a guiding force in my life. After going through a critical self-awareness process, I determined that autonomy was exactly what I desired and a professor is what I became.

—Aaron Thompson

Taken altogether, four aspects of yourself should be considered when exploring careers: your personal abilities, interests, values, and needs. As illustrated in **Figure 11.1**, these four pillars provide a solid foundation for effective career choices and decisions. You want to choose a career that you're good at, interested in, and passionate about and that fulfills your personal needs.

Lastly, since a career choice is a long-range decision that involves life beyond college, self-awareness should involve not only reflection on who you are now but also self-projection—reflecting on how you see yourself in the future. When you engage in the process of self-projection, you begin to see a connection between where you are now and where you want or hope to be.

Student Perspective

"I think that a good career has to be meaningful for a person. It should be enjoyable for the most part [and] it has to give a person a sense of fulfillment."

—First-year student

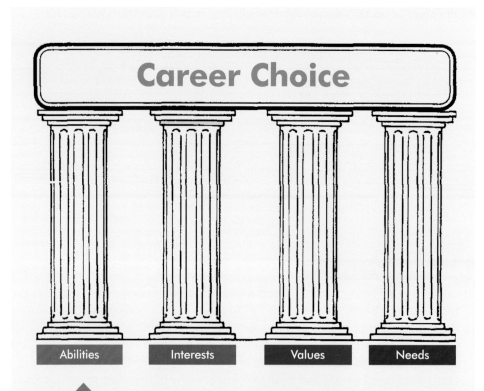

Figure 11.1 Personal Characteristics Providing the Foundation for Effective Career Choice

THINK ABOUT IT   Journal Entry 11.3

Project yourself 10 years into the future and visualize your ideal career and life.

1. What are you spending most of your time doing during your typical workday?

_____

_____

_____

_____

2. Where and with whom are you working?

_____

_____

_____

_____

3. How many hours are you working per week?

_____

_____

4. Where are you living?

_____

_____

5. Are you married? Do you have children?

_____

_____

6. How does your work influence your home life?

_____

_____

_____

_____

_____

Ideally, your choice of a career should be one that leads to the best-case future scenario in which your typical day goes something like this: You wake up in the morning and hop out of bed enthusiastically—eagerly looking forward to what you'll be doing at work that day. When you're at work, time flies by, and before you know it, the day's over. When you return to bed that night and look back on your day, you feel good about what you did and how well you did it. For this ideal scenario to have any chance of becoming a reality, or even coming close to reality, you have to select a career path that is true to yourself—a path that leads you to a career that closely matches your abilities (what you do well), your interests (what you like to do), your values (what you feel good about doing), and your needs (what brings you satisfaction and fulfillment in life).

Step 2. Awareness of Your Options

To make effective decisions about your career path, you need to have accurate knowledge about the nature of different careers and the realities of the work world. The Career Development Center is the first place to go for this information and help with career exploration and planning. In addition to helping you explore your personal career interests and abilities, the Career Development Center is your key campus resource for learning about the nature of different careers and for strategies on locating career-related work experiences.

If you were to ask people to name as many careers as they can, they wouldn't come close to naming the 900 career titles listed by the federal government in its Occupational Information Network. Many of these careers you may have never heard of, but some of them may represent good career options for you. You can learn about careers through nine major routes or avenues:

- Reading about them in books or online
- Becoming involved in cocurricular programs on campus related to career development

- Taking career development courses
- Interviewing people in different career fields
- Observing (shadowing) people at work in different careers
- Interning
- Participating in a co-op program
- Volunteering
- Working part time

There are many more career choices in today's work world than there were for our early ancestors.

Resources on Careers

Your Career Development Center and your College Library are campus resources where you can find a wealth of reading material on careers, either in print or online. Listed here are some of the most useful sources of written information on careers:

- *Dictionary of Occupational Titles* (www.occupationalinfo.org). This is the largest printed resource on careers; it contains concise definitions of over 17,000 jobs. It also includes information on:
  - Work tasks that people in the career typically perform regularly;
  - Types of knowledge, skills, and abilities that are required for different careers;
  - Interests, values, and needs of individuals who find working in particular careers to be personally rewarding; and
  - Background experiences of people working in different careers that qualified them for their positions.

- *Occupational Outlook Handbook* (**www.bls.gov/oco**). This is one of the most widely available and used resources on careers. It contains descriptions of approximately 250 positions, including information on the nature of work, work conditions, places of employment, training or education required for career entry and advancement, salaries, careers in related fields, and additional sources of information about particular careers (e.g., professional organizations and governmental agencies). A distinctive feature of this resource is that it contains information about the future employment outlook for different careers.
- *Encyclopedia of Careers and Vocational Guidance* (**Chicago: Ferguson Press**). As the name suggests, this is an encyclopedia of information on qualifications, salaries, and advancement opportunities for various careers.
- **Occupational Information Network (O*NET) Online (online.onet-center.org).** This is America's most comprehensive source of online information about careers. It contains an up-to-date set of descriptions for almost 1,000 careers, plus lots of other information similar to what you would find in the *Dictionary of Occupational Titles.*

In addition to these general sources of information, your Career Development Center and College Library should have books and other published materials related to specific careers or occupations (e.g., careers for English majors).

You can also learn a lot about careers by simply reading advertisements for position openings in your local newspaper or online, such as at www.careerbuilder.com and www.monstertrak.com. When reading position descriptions, make special note of the tasks, duties, or responsibilities they involve and ask yourself whether these positions are compatible with your personal profile of abilities, interests, needs, and values.

Career Planning and Development Programs

Periodically during the academic year, cocurricular programs devoted to career exploration and career preparation are likely to be offered on your campus. For example, the Career Development Center may sponsor career exploration or career planning workshops that you can attend for free. Also, the Career Development Center may organize a career fair on campus at which professionals working in different career fields are given booths on campus where you can visit with them and ask questions about their careers. Research indicates that career development workshops offered on campus are effective for helping students plan for and decide on a career (Brown & Krane, 2000; Hildenbrand & Gore, 2005).

Career Development Courses

Many colleges offer career development courses for elective credit. These courses typically include self-assessment of your career interests, information about different careers, and strategies for career preparation. You should be doing career planning, so why not do it by taking a career development course that rewards you with college credit for doing it? Studies show that students who participate in career development courses experience significant benefits in terms of their career choice and career development (Pascarella & Terenzini, 2005).

Information Interviews

One of the best and most overlooked ways to get accurate information about careers is to interview professionals who are working in career fields. Career development specialists refer to this strategy as information interviewing. Don't assume that working professionals would not be interested in taking time out of their day to speak with a student. Most are willing to be interviewed about their careers; they often enjoy it (Crosby, 2002).

Information interviews provide you inside information about what careers are like because you're getting that information directly from the horse's mouth. It also helps you gain experience and confidence in interview situations, which may help you prepare for future job interviews. Furthermore, if you make a good impression during information interviews, the people you interview may suggest that you contact them again after graduation in case there are position openings. If there are openings, you might find yourself being the interviewee instead of the interviewer (and you might find yourself a job).

Because interviews are a valuable source of information about careers and provide possible contacts for future employment, we strongly recommend that you complete the information interview assignment included at the end of this chapter.

THINK ABOUT IT   **Journal Entry 11.4**

If you were to observe or interview a working professional in a career that interests you, what position would that person hold?

_____

_____

_____

_____

_____

Career Observation (Shadowing)

In addition to learning about careers from reading and interviews, you can experience careers more directly by placing yourself in workplace situations or work environments that allow you to observe workers performing their daily duties. Two college-sponsored programs may be available on your campus that would allow you to observe working professionals:

- **Job Shadowing Programs.** These programs allow you to follow ("shadow") and observe a professional during a typical workday.
- **Externship Programs.** An externship is basically an extended form of job shadowing, which lasts for a longer period (e.g., 2–3 days).

Visit your Career Development Center to learn about what job shadowing or externship programs may be available on your college campus. If none are available in a career field that interests you, consider finding one on your own by using strategies similar to those we recommend for information interviews at the end of this chapter. The only difference is that instead of asking the person for an interview, you'd be asking whether you could observe that person at work. The same person who gave you an information interview might be willing to allow such observation. Keep in mind that just 1 or 2 days of observation will give you some firsthand information about a career but will not give you firsthand experience in that career.

Internships

In contrast to job shadowing or externships, whereby you observe someone at work, an internship program immerses you in the work itself and gives you the opportunity to perform career-related work duties. A distinguishing feature of internships is that you can receive academic credit and sometimes financial compensation for the work you do. An internship usually totals 120 to 150 work hours, which may be completed at the same time you're enrolled in a full schedule of classes when you're not taking classes (e.g., during summer term). An advantage of an internship is that it enables college students to avoid the classic catch-22 situation they often run into when interviewing for their first career position after graduation. The interview scenario usually goes something like this: The potential employer asks the college graduate, "What work experience have you had in this field?" The recent graduate replies, "I haven't had any work experience because I've been a full-time college student." This scenario can be avoided if you

> "Got Experience?"—The "killer question" that college graduates can't answer after college unless they've had some career-related work experience during college (e.g., internships or volunteer service).

complete an internship during your college experience, which allows you to say, "Yes, I do have work experience in this field." We encourage you to participate in an internship while in college because it will enable you to beat the "no experience" rap after graduation and distinguish yourself from many other college graduates. Research shows that students who have internships while in college are more likely to develop career-relevant work skills and find employment immediately after college graduation (Pascarella & Terenzini, 2005).

Internships are typically available to college students during their junior or senior year; however, there may be internships available to first- and second-year students on your campus. You can also pursue internships on your own. Published guides describe various career-related internships, along with information on how to apply for them (e.g., *Peterson's Internships* and the *Vault Guide to Top Internships*). You could also search for internships on the Web (e.g., www.internships.com and www.vaultreports.com). Another good resource for possible information on internships is the local chamber of commerce in the town or city where your college is located or in your hometown.

Another option for gaining firsthand work experiences is by enrolling in courses that allow you to engage in hands-on learning related to your career interest. For instance, if you're interested in working with children, courses in child psychology or early childhood education may offer experiential learning opportunities in a preschool or daycare center on campus.

Cooperative Education (Co-op) Programs

A co-op is similar to an internship but involves work experience that lasts longer than one academic term and often requires students to stop their course-work temporarily to participate in the program. However, some co-op programs allow you to continue to take classes while working part time at a co-op position; these are sometimes referred to as parallel co-ops. Students are paid for participating in co-op programs but do not receive academic credit—just a notation on their college transcript (Smith, 2005).

Typically, co-ops are only available to juniors or seniors, but you can begin now to explore co-op programs by reviewing your college catalog and visiting your Career Development Center to see whether your school offers co-op programs in career areas that may interest you. If you find any, plan to get involved with one because it can provide you with authentic and extensive career-related work experience.

The value of co-ops and internships is strongly supported by research, which indicates that students who have these experiences during college:

- Are more likely to report that their college education was relevant to their career;
- Receive higher evaluations from employers who recruit them on campus;
- Have less difficulty finding an initial position after graduation;
- Are more satisfied with their first career position after college;
- Obtain more prestigious positions after graduation; and
- Report greater job satisfaction (Gardner, 1991; Knouse, Tanner, & Harris, 1999; Pascarella & Terenzini, 1991, 2005).

In one statewide survey that asked employers to rank various factors they considered important when hiring new college graduates, internship or co-operative education programs received the highest ranking (Education Commission of the States, 1995). Furthermore, employers report that if full-time positions open up in their organization or company, they usually turn first to their own interns and co-op students (National Association of Colleges & Employers, 2003).

Volunteer Service

Engaging in volunteerism not only helps your community but also helps you by giving you the opportunity to explore different work environments and gain work experience in career fields that relate to your area of service. For example, volunteer service to different age groups (e.g., children, adolescents, or the elderly) and service in different environments (e.g., hospital, school, or laboratory) can provide you with firsthand work experience and simultaneously give you a chance to test your interest in possibly pursuing future careers related to these different age groups and work environments. (To get a sense of the range of service opportunities that may be available to you, go to www. usa.service.org.)

Personal Story

As an academic advisor, I was once working with two first-year students, Kim and Christopher. Kim was thinking about becoming a physical therapist, and Chris was thinking about becoming an elementary school teacher. I suggested to Kim that she visit the hospital nearby our college to see whether she could do volunteer work in the physical therapy unit. The hospital did need volunteers, so she volunteered in the physical therapy unit and loved it. That volunteer experience confirmed for her that physical therapy is what she should pursue as a career. She completed a degree in physical therapy and is now a professional physical therapist.

I suggested to Chris, the student who was thinking about becoming an elementary school teacher, that he visit some local schools to see whether they could use a volunteer teacher's aide. One of the schools did need his services, and Chris volunteered as a teacher's aide for about 10 weeks. At the halfway point during his volunteer experience, he came into my office to tell me that the kids were just about driving him crazy and that he no longer had any interest in becoming a teacher. He ended up majoring in communications.

Kim and Chris were the first two students I advised to get involved in volunteer work to test their career interests. Their volunteer experiences proved so valuable for helping both of them make a career decision that I now encourage all students I advise to get volunteer experience in the field they're considering as a future career.

—Joe Cuseo

Volunteer service also enables you to network with professionals outside of college who may serve as excellent references and resources for letters of recommendation for you. Furthermore, if these professionals are impressed with your volunteer work, they may become interested in hiring you part time while you're still in college or full time when you graduate.

It may be possible to do volunteer work on campus by serving as an informal teaching assistant or research assistant to a faculty member. Such experiences are particularly valuable for students intending to go to graduate school. If you have a good relationship with any faculty members who are working in an academic field that interests you, consider asking them whether they would like some assistance (e.g., with their teaching or research responsibilities). Your volunteer work for a college professor could lead to making a presentation with your professor at a professional conference or may even result in your name being included as a coauthor on an article published by the professor.

THINK ABOUT IT   Journal Entry   **11.5**

Have you done volunteer work? If you have, did you learn anything
from your volunteer experiences that might help you decide which types of work
best match your interests or talents?

_____

_____

_____

_____

Part-Time Work

Jobs that you hold during the academic year or during summer break should not be overlooked as potential sources of career information and as résumé-building experience. Part-time work can provide opportunities to learn or develop skills that may be relevant to your future career, such as organizational skills, communication skills, and ability to work effectively with co-workers from diverse backgrounds or culture.

Also, work in a part-time position may eventually turn into a full-time career. The following personal story illustrates how this can happen.

Personal Story   One student of mine, an English major, worked part time for an organization that provides special assistance to mentally handicapped children. After he completed his English degree, he was offered a full-time position in this organization, which he accepted. While working at his full-time position with handicapped children, he decided to go to graduate school part time and eventually completed a master's degree in special education, which qualified him for a promotion to a more advanced position in the organization, which he also accepted.

—Joe Cuseo

It might also be possible for you to obtain part-time work experience on campus through your school's work–study program. A work–study job allows you to work at your college in various work settings, such as the Financial Aid Office, College Library, Public Relations Office, or Computer Services Center, and often allows you to build your employment schedule around your academic schedule. On-campus work can provide you with valuable career-exploration and résumé-building experiences, and the professionals for whom you work can serve as excellent references for letters of recommendation to future employers. To see whether you are eligible for your school's work–study program, visit the Financial Aid Office on your campus.

Learning about careers through firsthand experience in actual work settings (e.g., shadowing, internships, volunteer services, and part-time work) is critical to successful career exploration and preparation. You can take a career-interest test, or you can test your career interest through actual work experiences. There is simply no substitute for direct, hands-on experience for gaining knowledge about careers. These firsthand experiences represent the ultimate career-reality test. They allow you direct access to information about what careers are really like—as opposed to how they are portrayed on TV or in the movies, which often paint an inaccurate or unrealistic picture of careers, making them appear more exciting or glamorous than they are.

In summary, firsthand experiences in actual work settings equip you with five powerful career advantages, which enable you to:

- Learn about what work is like in a particular field;
- Test your interest and skills for certain types of work;
- Strengthen your résumé by adding experiential learning to academic (classroom) learning;
- Acquire contacts for letters of recommendation; and
- Network with employers who may refer or hire you for a position after graduation.

Be sure to use your campus resources (e.g., the Career Development Center and Financial Aid Office), your local resources (e.g., chamber of commerce), and your personal contacts (family and friends) to locate and participate in work experiences that relate to your career interests. When you land an internship, work hard at it, learn as much as you can from it, and build relationships with as many people as possible at your internship site because these are the people who can provide you with future contacts, references, and referrals.

> *"Give me a history major who has done internships and a business major who hasn't, and I'll hire the history major every time."*
>
> —William Ardery, senior vice president, investor communications company (quoted in *The New York Times*)

THINK ABOUT IT   Journal Entry **11.6**

1. Have you learned anything from your firsthand work experiences that may influence your future career plans?

_____

_____

_____

_____

_____

_____

2. If you could get firsthand work experience in any career field right now, what career would it be?

_____

_____

_____

_____

_____

_____

Step 3. Awareness of What Best Fits You

When considering career options, don't buy into either of the following common myths about careers, which can lead students to poor career decisions.

Myth 1. Once you've decided on a career, you have decided on what you'll be doing for the rest of your life.

This is simply and totally false. The term "career" derives from the same root word as "racecourse." Like a racecourse, a career involves movement that typically takes different turns and twists, and like any race, it's not how fast you start but how strong you finish that matters most. This ability to move and change direction is what distinguishes a professional career from a dead-end job. Americans average four careers in a lifetime; it's also estimated that today's college graduates will change jobs 12 to 15 times, which will span three to five career fields (U.S. Bureau of Labor Statistics, 2005). These statistics may be surprising because you're probably going to college with the idea that you're preparing for a particular career. However, these results become less surprising when you consider that the general education component of your college experience provides you with versatile, transferable skills that can qualify you for different positions in various career fields.

Myth 2. You need to pick a career that's in demand and that will get you a job with a good starting salary right after graduation.

Looking only at careers that are "hot" now and have high starting salaries can distract you from looking at yourself and cause you to overlook a more important question: Are these careers truly compatible with your personal abilities, interests, needs, and values? Starting salaries and available job openings are external factors that can be easily seen and counted; thus, they may get more attention and receive more weight in the decision-making process than qualities that are harder to see and put a number on—such as inner characteristics. In the case of career decision making, this can result in college students choosing careers based exclusively on external factors (salaries and openings) without giving equal (or any) attention to such internal factors as personal abilities, interests, and values. This can lead some college graduates to enter careers that eventually leave them bored, frustrated, or dissatisfied.

The number of job offers you receive immediately after graduation and the number of dollars you earn as a starting salary in your first position are short-term (and short-sighted) standards for judging whether you've made a good career choice. Remember that there's a critical difference between career *entry* and career *advancement*. Some college graduates may not bolt out of the starting gate and begin their career path with a well-paying first position, but they will steadily work their way up the career ladder and be promoted to a more advanced position than graduates who start out with higher salaries.

Criteria (Standards) to Consider When Evaluating Career Options

Effective decision making requires you to identify all important factors that should be considered when evaluating your options and determine how much weight (influence) each of these factors should carry. As we emphasize throughout this chapter, the factor that should carry the greatest weight in career decision making is the match between your choice and your personal abilities, interests, needs, and values.

Suppose you discover more than one career option that's compatible with these four dimensions of yourself. What other aspects of a career should be considered to help you reach a decision and make a selection? Many people would probably say salary, but as the length of the following list suggests, other important aspects or characteristics of careers should be factored into your decision-making process.

- **Work Conditions.** Work conditions include such considerations as:
  - The nature of the work environment (e.g., physical and social environment);
  - The geographical location of the work (e.g., urban, suburban, or rural);

- The work schedule (e.g., number of hours per week and flexibility of hours); and
- Work-related travel (e.g., opportunities to travel, frequency of travel, and locations traveled to).
- **Career Entry.** Can you enter into the career without much difficulty, or does the supply of people pursuing the career far exceed the demand (e.g., professional acting)? If a career is highly competitive and difficult to gain entry into, it doesn't mean you should automatically give up on it; however, it does mean you should have an alternative career to fall back on until you can (or in case you can't) catch a break that will allow you to break into your ideal career.
- **Career Advancement (Promotion).** An ideal first job educates and prepares you to advance to an even better one. Will the career you're considering provide you with opportunities for promotion to more advanced positions?
- **Career Mobility.** Is it easy to move out of the career and into a different career path? This may be an important factor to consider because careers may rise or fall in demand; furthermore, your career interests or values may change as you gain more work and life experience.
- **Financial Benefits.** Financial considerations include salary— both starting salary and expected salary increases with greater work experience or advancement to higher positions. However, it also includes fringe benefits, such as health insurance, paid vacation time, paid sick-leave time, paid maternity- or paternity-leave time, paid tuition for seeking advanced education, and retirement benefits.
- **Impact of the Career on Your Personal Life.** How would the career affect your family life, your physical and mental health, and your self-concept or self-esteem? Remember that your life should not be built around your career; your career should be built around your life. Your means of making a living and other important aspects of yourself need to be considered simultaneously when making career choices, because the nature of your work will affect the nature (and quality) of your life.

JupiterImages Corporation.

When evaluating career options, be sure to take into account things like the amount of travel required.

"The French work to live, but the Swiss live to work."

–French proverb

! Remember

A good career decision should involve more than salary and should take into consideration how the career will affect all dimensions of your self (social, emotional, physical, etc.) throughout all stages of your adult life: young adulthood, middle age, and late adulthood. It's almost inevitable that your career will affect your identity, the type of person you become, how you will balance the demands of work and family, and how well you will serve others beyond yourself. An effective career decision-making process requires you to make tough and thoughtful decisions about what matters most to you.

"Money is a good servant but a bad master."

–French proverb

THINK ABOUT IT   **Journal Entry** **11.7**

Answer the following questions about a career that you're considering or have chosen:

1. Why are you considering this career? (What led or caused you to become interested in it?)

_____

_____

_____

_____

_____

_____

2. Would you say that your interest in this career is motivated primarily by intrinsic factors—that is, factors "inside" of you, such as your personal abilities, interests, needs, and values? Or, would you say that your interest in the career is influenced more heavily by extrinsic factors—that is, factors "outside" of you, such as starting salary, pleasing parents, meeting family expectations, or meeting an expected role for your gender (male role or female role)?

_____

_____

_____

_____

_____

_____

3. If money were not an issue and you could earn a comfortable living in any career, would you choose the same career?

_____

_____

_____

_____

_____

_____

Step 4. Awareness of the Process

Whether you're keeping your career options open, or if you think you've already decided on a particular career, you can start taking steps to prepare for career success by using the following strategies to prepare for successful career entry and advancement.

Self-Monitoring: Watching and Tracking Your Personal Skills and Positive Qualities

Don't forget that *learning* skills are also *earning* skills. The skills you're acquiring in college may appear to be just *academic* skills, but they're also *career* skills. For instance, when you're in the process of completing academic tasks such as taking tests and writing papers, you're using various career-relevant skills (e.g., analyzing, organizing, communicating, and problem solving).

Many students think that a college diploma or certificate is an automatic passport to a good job and career success (Ellin, 1993; Sullivan, 1993). However, for most employers of college graduates, what matters most is not only the credential but also the skills and personal strengths an applicant brings to the position (Education Commission of the States, 1995). You can start building these skills and strengths by self-monitoring (i.e., watching yourself and keeping track of the skills you're using and developing during your college experience). Skills are mental habits, and like all other habits that are repeatedly practiced, their development can be so gradual that you may not even notice how much growth is taking place—perhaps somewhat like watching grass grow. Thus, career development specialists recommend that you consciously track your skills to remain aware of them and to put you in a position to "sell" them to potential employers (Lock, 2000).

One strategy you can use to track your developing skills is to keep a career-development journal in which you note academic tasks and assignments you've completed, along with the skills you used to complete them. Be sure to record skills in your journal that you've developed in nonacademic situations, such as those skills used while performing part-time jobs, personal hobbies, cocurricular activities, or volunteer services. Since skills are actions, it's best to record them as action verbs in your career-development journal.

The key to discovering career-relevant skills and qualities is to get in the habit of stepping back from your academic and out-of-class experiences to reflect on what skills and qualities these experiences entailed and then get them down in writing before they slip your mind. You're likely to find that many personal skills you develop in college will be the same ones that employers will seek in the workforce. **Box 11.2** contains some important career-success skills that you're likely to develop during your college experience.

Personal Skills Relevant to Successful Career Performance 11.2

The following behaviors represent a sample of useful skills that are relevant to success in various careers (Bolles, 1998). As you read these skills, underline or highlight any of them that you have performed, either inside or outside of school. As you read these traits, underline or highlight any of them that you feel you possess or will soon possess.

advising	assembling	calculating	coaching	coordinating
creating	delegating	designing	evaluating	explaining
initiating	mediating	measuring	motivating	negotiating
operating	planning	producing	proving	researching
resolving	sorting	summarizing	supervising	synthesizing
translating				

Personal Story

After class one day, I had a conversation with a student (Max) about his personal interests. He said he was considering a career in the music industry and was now working part time as a disc jockey at a night club. I asked him what it took to be a good disc jockey, and in less than 5 minutes of conversation, we discovered many more skills were involved in doing his job than either of us had realized. He was responsible for organizing 3 to 4 hours of music each night he worked; he had to read the reactions of his audience (customers) and adapt or adjust his selections to their musical tastes; he had to arrange his selections in a sequence that periodically varied the tempo (speed) of the music he played throughout the night; and he had to continually research and update his music collection to track the latest trends in hits and popular artists. Max also said that he had to overcome his fear of public speaking to deliver announcements that were a required part of his job.

Although we were just having a short, friendly conversation after class about his part-time job, Max wound up reflecting on and identifying multiple skills he was using on the job. We both agreed that it would be a good idea to get these skills down in writing so that he could use them as selling points for future jobs in the music industry or in any industry.

—Joe Cuseo

In addition to tracking your developing skills, track your positive traits or personal qualities. While it's best to record your skills as action verbs because they represent actions that you can perform for anyone who hires you, it may be best to track your attributes as adjectives because they describe who you are and what personal qualities you can bring to the job. **Box 11.3** gives a sample of personal traits and qualities that are relevant to success in multiple careers. As you read these traits, underline or highlight any of them that you feel you possess or will soon possess.

Take Action!

Personal Traits and Qualities Relevant to Successful Career Performance 11.3

broad minded	cheerful	congenial	conscientious	considerate
courteous	curious	dependable	determined	energetic
enthusiastic	ethical	flexible	imaginative	industrious
loyal	observant	open minded	outgoing	patient
prepared	persistent	persuasive	positive	precise
productive	punctual	reasonable	reflective	sincere
tactful	thorough			

THINK ABOUT IT   **Journal Entry** **11.8**

Look back at the personal skills and traits listed in **Boxes 11.2**
and **11.3** that you noted you possess or will soon possess.

1. Do you see your personal skills and traits as being relevant to the career or
   careers you're considering?

   _____

   _____

   _____

2. Do you see these skills and traits being as relevant, or more relevant, to any
   career or careers that you haven't yet considered?

   _____

   _____

   _____

   _____

! Remember

Keeping track of your developing skills and your positive qualities is as important
to your successful entry into a future career as completing courses and compiling
credits.

Self-Marketing: Packaging and Presenting Your Personal Strengths and Achievements

To convert your college experience into immediate employment, it might be
useful to view yourself (a college graduate) as a product and employers as intentional customers who may be interested in making a purchase (of your skills

and attributes). As a first-year student, it could be said that you're in the early stages of the product-development process. Now is the time to begin the process so that by the time you graduate your finished product (you) will be one that employers notice and become interested in purchasing.

An effective self-marketing plan is one that gives employers a clear idea of what you can bring to the table and do for them. This should increase the number of job offers you receive and increase your chances of finding a position that best matches your interests, talents, and values.

You can effectively advertise or market your personal skills, qualities, and achievements to future employers through the following channels:

- College transcript
- Cocurricular experiences
- Personal portfolio
- Personal résumé
- Letters of application (a.k.a. cover letters)
- Letters of recommendation (a.k.a. letters of reference)
- Networking
- Personal interview

These are the primary tools you will use to showcase yourself to employers and employers will use to evaluate you. Here's how you can strategically prepare for and sharpen these tools to maximize their effectiveness.

College Transcript

A college transcript is a listing of all courses you enrolled in and the grades you received in those courses. Two pieces of information included on your college transcript can influence employers' hiring decisions or admissions committee decisions about your acceptance to a 4-year college, graduate, or professional school: (a) the grades you earned in your courses and (b) the types of courses you completed.

Simply stated, the better your grades in college, the better your employment prospects after college. Research on college graduates indicates that the higher their grades, the higher:

- The prestige of their first job;
- Their total earnings; and
- Their job mobility.

This relationship between college grades and career success exists for students at all types of colleges and universities, regardless of the reputation or prestige of the institution they attend (Pascarella & Terenzini, 1991, 2005).

The particular types of courses listed on your college transcript can also influence employment and acceptance decisions. Listed here are the types of courses that should strengthen your college transcript.

- **Honors Courses.** If you achieve excellent grades during your first year, you may apply or be recommended for the Honors program at your campus and take more academically challenging courses. If you qualify for the Honors program, we recommend that you accept the challenge. Even though A grades may be more difficult to achieve in honors courses, the presence of these courses on your college transcript clearly shows that you were admitted to the Honors program and were willing to accept this academic challenge.

- **Leadership Courses.** Many employers hire college graduates with the hope or expectation that they will advance and eventually assume important leadership positions in the company or organization. Although a leadership course is not likely to be required for general education, or for your major, it is an elective course that will develop your leadership skills and the impressiveness of your college transcript.

- **International and Cross-Cultural Courses.** Courses whose content crosses national and cultural boundaries are often referred to as international and cross-cultural courses. These courses are particularly pertinent to success in today's world, in which there is more international travel, more interaction among citizens from different countries, and more economic interdependence among nations than at any other time in world history (Office of Research, 1994). As a result of these developments, employers now place higher value on employees with international knowledge and foreign language skills (Fixman, 1990; Office of Research, 1994). Taking courses that have an international focus, or that focus on cross-cultural comparisons, helps you develop a global perspective that can improve the quality of your college degree and increase the attractiveness of your college transcript to potential employers.

- **Diversity (Multicultural) Courses.** America's workforce is more ethnically and racially diverse today than at any other time in the nation's history, and it will grow even more so in the years ahead (U.S. Bureau of Labor Statistics, 2005). Successful career performance in today's diverse workforce requires sensitivity to human differences and the ability to relate to people from different cultural backgrounds (National Association of Colleges & Employers, 2003; Smith, 1997). College courses relating to diversity awareness and appreciation, or courses emphasizing multicultural interaction and communication, can be valuable additions to your college transcript that should strengthen your career preparation, placement, and advancement.

Cocurricular Experiences

Participation in student clubs, campus organizations, and other types of cocurricular activities can be a valuable source of experiential learning that can complement classroom-based learning and contribute to your career preparation and development. A sizable body of research supports the value of cocurricular experiences for career success (Astin, 1993; Kuh, 1993; Pascarella & Terenzini, 1991, 2005). Strongly consider getting involved in cocurricular life on your campus, especially involvement with cocurricular experiences that:

- Allow you to develop leadership and helping skills (e.g., leadership retreats, student government, college committees, peer counseling, or peer tutoring);
- Enable you to interact with others from diverse ethnic and racial groups (e.g., multicultural club or international club), and
- Provide you with out-of-class experiences related to your academic major or career interests (e.g., student clubs in your college major or intended career field).

Keep in mind that cocurricular experiences are also résumé-building experiences that provide solid evidence of your commit-

Participation in campus organizations can be a valuable source of experience that contributes to your career preparation and development.

ment to the college community outside the classroom. Be sure to showcase these experiences to prospective employers.

Also, the campus professionals with whom you may interact while participating in cocurricular activities (e.g., the director of student activities or dean of students) can serve as valuable references for letters of recommendation to future employers or graduate and professional schools.

Personal Portfolio

You may have heard the word "portfolio" as a collection of artwork that professional artists put together to showcase or advertise their artistic talents. However, a portfolio can be a collection of any materials or products that illustrates an individual's skills and talents or demonstrates an individual's educational and personal development. For example, a portfolio could include such items as:

- Outstanding papers, exam performances, research projects, or lab reports;
- Art work, photos from study abroad, service learning, or internships experiences;
- Video footage of oral presentations or theatrical performances;
- CDs of musical performances;
- Assessments from employers or coaches; and
- Letters of recognition or commendation.

You can start the process of portfolio development right now by saving your best work and performances. Store them in a traditional portfolio folder, or save them on a computer disc to create an electronic portfolio. Another option would be to create a Web site and upload your materials there. Eventually, you should be able to build a well-stocked portfolio that documents your skills and demonstrates your development to future employers or future schools.

The ritual of burning completed coursework in high school is not recommended in college. (Instead, save your best work, and include it in a personal portfolio.)

You can start to develop an electronic portfolio now by completing the Creating an Electronic Portfolio exercise at the end of this chapter.

THINK ABOUT IT   **Journal Entry** **11.9**

What do you predict will be your best "work products" in college—those that are most likely to appear in your portfolio?

_____

_____

_____

_____

_____

_____

Why?

_____

_____

_____

_____

_____

Personal Résumé

Unlike a portfolio, which contains actual products or samples of your work, a résumé may be described as a listed summary of your most important accomplishments, skills, and credentials. If you have just graduated from high school, you may not have accumulated enough experiences to construct a fully developed résumé. However, you can start to build a skeletal résumé that contains major categories or headings (the skeleton) under which you'll eventually include your experiences and accomplishments. (See **Box 11.4** for a sample skeleton résumé.) As you acquire experiences, you can flesh out the résumé's skeleton by gradually filling in its general categories with skills, accomplishments, and credentials.

Constructing a Résumé

Use this skeletal résumé as an outline or template for beginning construction of your own résumé and for setting your future goals. (If you have already developed a résumé, use this template to identify and add categories that may be missing from your current one.)

Name (First, Middle, Last)

Current Addresses: Permanent Addresses:
Postal Address   Postal Address
E-mail address   E-mail address
Phone no.   Phone no.

EDUCATION: Name of College or University, City, State
                Degree Name (e.g., Bachelor of Science)
                College Major (e.g., Accounting)
                Graduation Date, GPA

RELATED WORK   Position Title, City, State   Start and stop dates
EXPERIENCES: (Begin the list with the most recent
(List skills used or developed.)   position dates held.)

VOLUNTEER (COMMUNITY SERVICE)
EXPERIENCES:
(List skills used or developed.)

NOTABLE COURSEWORK:
(e.g., leadership, international, or interdisciplinary courses)

COCURRICULAR EXPERIENCES:
(e.g., student government or peer leadership)
(List skills used or developed.)

PERSONAL SKILLS AND POSITIVE QUALITIES:
(List as bullets. Be sure to include those that are especially relevant to the position for which you're applying.)

HONORS/AWARDS: (In addition to those received in college, you may include those received
                     in high school.)

PERSONAL INTERESTS: (Include items that showcase any special hobbies or talents that are not
                       directly related to school or work.)

Letters of Application (a.k.a. Cover Letters)

You write a letter of application when applying for a position opening or for acceptance to a school. When writing these letters, be sure that you demonstrate awareness and knowledge of:

- Yourself (e.g., your personal interests, abilities, and values);
- The organization or institution to which you are applying (e.g., showing that you know something specific about its purpose, philosophy, programs, and the position you are applying for); and
- The match or fit between you and the organization (e.g., between the skills and qualities you possess and those that the position requires).

Focusing on these three major points should make your letter complete and will allow the letter to flow sequentially from a focus on *you*, to a focus on *them*, to a focus on the *relationship* between you and them. Here are some suggestions for developing each of these three points in your letter of application.

- **Organize information about yourself into a past–present–future sequence of personal development.** For instance, point out the following:
  - Where you have been—your past history or background experiences that qualify you to apply for the position (academic, cocurricular, and work experiences)
  - Where you are now—why you've decided to apply for the position today
  - Where you intend to go—what you hope to do or accomplish for the employer once you get there

  Taking this past–present–future approach to organizing your letter should result in a smooth, well-sequenced flow of information about you and your development. Also, by focusing on where you've been and where you're going, you demonstrate your ability to reflect on the past and project to the future.

  When describing yourself, try to identify specific examples or concrete illustrations of your positive qualities and areas in which you have grown or improved in recent years. While it is important to highlight all your major strengths, this doesn't necessarily mean you should ignore or cover up areas in which you feel you still need to improve or develop. No human is perfect; one indication of someone with a healthy self-concept is that person's ability to recognize and acknowledge both personal strengths and areas in which further improvement or development is needed. Including a touch of honest self-assessment in your letter of application demonstrates both sincerity and integrity. It should also reduce the risk that your letter will be perceived as a "snow job" that pours on mounds and pounds of self-flattery without an ounce of personal humility.

- **Do some advanced research about the particular organization to which you're applying.** In your letter of application, mention some aspects or characteristics of the organization that you've learned about, such as one of its programs that impressed you or attracted your interest. This sends the message that you have taken the time and initiative to learn something about the organization, which says something positive about you.

- **Make it clear why you feel there is a good fit or match between you and the organization to which you've applied.** When applying for a position, your first objective is to focus on what you can do for the organization rather than what it can do for you or what's in it for you.

Point out how your qualities, skills, interests, or values are in line with the organization's needs or goals. By doing some research on the particular institution or organization that you're applying to, and by including this information in your letter of application, you also distinguish your application from the swarms of standard "form letters" that companies receive from other applicants.

Letters of Recommendation (a.k.a. Letters of Reference)

Personal letters of recommendation can be a powerful way to document your strengths and selling points. To maximize the power of your personal recommendations, give careful thought to:

- Who should serve as your references;
- How to approach them; and
- What to provide them.

Strategies for improving the quality of your letters of recommendation are suggested in **Box 11.5.**

Take Action!

11.5

The Art and Science of Requesting Letters of Recommendation: Effective Strategies and Common Courtesies

1. Select recommendations from people who know you well. Think about individuals with whom you've had an ongoing relationship, who know your name, and who know your strengths; for example, an instructor who you've had for more than one class, an academic advisor whom you see often, or an employer whom you've worked for over an extended period.

2. Seek a balanced blend of letters from people who have observed you perform in different settings or situations. The following are settings in which you may have performed well and people who may have observed your performance in these settings:

   - The classroom—a professor who can speak to your academic performance
   - On campus—a student life professional for a cocurricular reference who can comment on your contributions outside the classroom
   - Off campus—a professional for whom

you've performed volunteer service, part-time work, or an internship

3. Pick the right time and place to make your request. Be sure to make your request well in advance of the letter's deadline date (e.g., at least 2 weeks). First ask whether the person is willing to write the letter, and then come back with forms and envelopes. Do not approach the person with these materials in hand because this may send the message that you have assumed or presumed the person will automatically say "yes." (This is not the most socially sensitive message to send someone whom you're about to ask for a favor.) Lastly, pick a place where the person can give full attention to your request. For instance, make a personal visit to the person's office, rather than making the request in a busy hallway or in front of a classroom full of students.

4. Waive your right to see the letter. If the school or organization to which you're applying has a reference-letter form that asks whether or not you want to waive (give up) your right to see the letter, waive your right—as long as you feel reasonably certain that you will be receiving a good letter of recommendation.

By waiving your right to see your letter of recommendation, you show confidence that the letter to be written about you will be positive, and you assure the person who reads the letter that you didn't inspect or screen it to make sure it was a good one before sending it.

5. Provide your references with a fact sheet about yourself. Include your experiences and achievements—both inside and outside the classroom. This will help make your references' job a little easier by providing points to focus on. More importantly, it will help you because your letter becomes more powerful when it contains concrete examples or illustrations of your positive qualities and accomplishments. On your fact sheet, be sure to include any exceptionally high grades you may have earned in certain courses, as well as volunteer services, leadership experiences, special awards or forms of recognition, and special interests or talents that relate to your academic major and career choice. Your fact sheet is the place and time for you to "toot your own horn," so don't be afraid of coming across as a braggart or egotist. You're not being conceited; you're just showcasing your strengths.

6. Provide your references with a stamped, addressed envelope. This is a simple courtesy that makes their job a little easier and demonstrates your social sensitivity.

7. Follow up with a thank-you note. Thank your references about the time your letter of recommendation should be sent. This is the right thing to do because it shows your appreciation; it's also the smart thing to do because if the letter hasn't been written yet the thank-you note serves as a gentle reminder for your reference to write the letter.

8. Let your references know the outcome of your application. (e.g., your admission to a school or acceptance of a job offer). This is the courteous thing to do, and your references are likely to remember your courtesy, which could strengthen the quality of any future letters they may write for you.

THINK ABOUT IT   Journal Entry   **11.10**

Have you met a faculty member or other professional on campus who knows you well enough to write a personal letter of recommendation for you?

_____

_____

If yes, who is this person, and what position does he or she hold on campus?

_____

_____

_____

_____

_____

_____

Networking

Would it surprise you to learn that 80 percent of jobs are never advertised? This means that the jobs you see listed in a classified section of the newspaper and posted in a Career Development Center or employment center represent only 20 percent of available openings at any given time. Almost one-half of all job hunters find employment through people they know or have met, such as friends, family members, and casual acquaintances. When it comes to locating positions, *who* you know can be as important as *what* you know or how good your résumé looks. Consequently, it's important to continually expand the circle of people who are aware of your career interests and abilities, because they can be a valuable source of information about employment opportunities.

Also, be sure to share copies of your résumé with friends and family members, just in case they come in contact with employers who are looking for somebody with your career interests and qualifications.

Personal Interview

A personal interview is your opportunity to make a positive in-person impression. You can make a strong first impression during any interview by showing that you've done your homework and have come prepared. In particular, you should come to the interview with knowledge about yourself and your audience.

You can demonstrate knowledge about yourself by bringing a mental list of your strongest selling points to the interview and being ready to speak about them when the opportunity arises. You can demonstrate knowledge of your audience by doing some homework on the organization you are applying to, the people who are likely to be interviewing you, and the questions they are likely to ask you. Try to acquire as much information about the organization and its key employees as is available to you online and in print. When you know your audience (who your interviewers are likely to be and what they're likely to ask), and when you know yourself well (what about yourself you're going to say), you should then be ready to answer what probably is the most important interview question of all: "What can *you* do for *us?*"

To prepare for interviews, visit your Career Development Center and inquire about questions that are commonly asked during personal interviews. You might also try to speak with seniors who have interviewed with recruiters and ask them whether certain questions tended to be frequently asked. Once you begin to participate in actual interviews, make note of the questions you are asked. Although you may be able to anticipate some of the more general questions that are asked in almost any interview, there likely will be unique questions asked of you that relate specifically to your personal qualifications and experiences. If these questions are asked in one of your interviews, there's a good chance they'll be asked in a future interview. As soon as you complete an interview, mentally review it and attempt to recall the major questions you were asked before they slip your mind. Consider developing an index-card catalog of questions that you've been asked during interviews—with the question on one side and your prepared response on the reverse side. By being better prepared for personal interviews, you'll increase the quality of your answers and decrease your level of anxiety.

Lastly, remember to send a thank-you note to the person who interviewed you. This is not only the courteous thing to do; it's also the smart thing to do because it demonstrates your interpersonal sensitivity and reinforces the person's memory of you.

◆ Summary and Conclusion

In national surveys, employers rank attitude of the job applicant as the number one factor in making hiring decisions; they rate it higher in importance than such factors as reputation of the applicant's school, previous work experience, and recommendations of former employers (Education Commission of the States, 1995; Institute for Research on Higher Education, 1995). Graduating from college with a diploma or certificate may make you a more competitive job candidate, but you still have to compete by documenting and selling your strengths and skills. Your diploma or certificate doesn't work like a merit badge or passport that you flash to gain automatic access to an ideal job. Your college experience will open career doors, but it's your attitude, initiative, and effort that will enable you to step through those doors and into a successful career.

Internet-Based Resources for Further Information on Careers

For additional information related to the ideas discussed in this chapter, we recommend the following Web sites:

www.bls.gov/oco

www.internships.com

www.vaultreports.com

www.mapping-your-future.org/planning/

www.monster.com

www.salary.com

Chapter 11 Exercises

11.1 Conducting an Information Interview

To learn accurate information about a career that interests you, interview working professionals in that career—a career-exploration strategy known as information interviewing. An information interview enables you to:

- Learn what a career is really like;

- Network with professionals in the field; and

- Become confident in interview situations and prepare for later job interviews.

    1. Select a career that you may be interested in pursuing. Even if you are currently keeping your career options open, pick a career that might be a possibility. You can use the resources cited on **p. 406** in this chapter to help you identify a career that may be most appealing to you.

    2. Find someone who is working in the career you selected and set up an information interview with that person. To help locate possible interview candidates, consider members of your family, friends of your family members, and family members of your friends. Any of these people may be working in the career you selected and may be good interview candidates, or they may know others who could be good candidates. The Career Development Center on your campus may also be able to provide you with graduates of your college or professionals working in the local community near your college who are willing to talk about their careers with students. Lastly, you might consider using the Yellow Pages or the Internet to find names and addresses of possible candidates. Send them a short letter or e-mail asking about the possibility of scheduling a short interview. Mention that you would be willing to conduct the interview in person or by phone, whichever would be more convenient for them. If you do not hear back within a reasonable period (e.g., within a couple of weeks), send a follow-up message; if you do not receive a response to the follow-up message, then consider contacting someone else.

    3. Conduct an information interview with the professional who has agreed to speak with you. Consider using the following suggested strategies.

Suggested Strategies for Conducting Information Interviews

- **First, thank the person for taking the time to speak with you.** This should be the first thing you do after meeting the person—before you officially begin the interview.

- **Prepare your interview questions in advance.** Here are some questions that you might consider asking:

    1. How did you decide on your career?

    2. What qualifications or prior experiences did you have that enabled you to enter your career?

    3. How does someone find out about openings in your field?

    4. What steps did you take to find your current position?

    5. What advice would you give to beginning college students about things they could start doing now to help them prepare to enter your career?

    6. During a typical day's work, what do you spend most of your time doing?

    7. What do you like most about your career?

    8. What are the most difficult or frustrating aspects of your career?

    9. What personal skills or qualities do you see as being critical for success in your career?

10. How does someone advance in your career?

11. Are there any moral issues or ethical challenges that tend to arise in your career?

12. Are members of diverse groups likely to be found in your career? (This is an especially important question to ask if you are a member of an ethnic, racial, or gender group that is underrepresented in the career field.)

13. What impact does your career have on your home life or personal life outside of work?

14. If you had to do it all over again, would you choose the same career?

15. Would you recommend that I speak with anyone else to obtain additional information or a different perspective on this career field? (If the answer is "yes," you may follow up by asking: "May I mention that you referred me?") This question is recommended because it's always a good idea to obtain more than one person's perspective before making an important choice or decision, especially one that can have a major influence on your life—such as your career choice.

- **Take notes during the interview.** This not only benefits you by helping you remember what was said; it also sends a positive message to the person you're interviewing by showing that the person's ideas are important and worth writing down.

If the interview goes well, you could ask whether it might be possible to observe or shadow your interviewee during a day at work.

Self-Assessment Questions

After completing your interview, take a moment to reflect on it and answer the following questions:

1. What information did you receive that impressed you about this career?

2. What information did you receive that distressed (or depressed) you about this career?

3. What was the most useful thing you learned from conducting this interview?

4. Knowing what you know now, would you still be interested in pursuing this career? (If yes, why?) (If no, why not?)

11.2 Creating an Electronic Portfolio

Using Folio180, create an electronic portfolio of your accomplishments and activities. In this assignment, you will collect information related to the following four areas:

1. Interests

2. Work and Professional Experiences

3. Awards, Honors, and Commendations

4. Academic Work

You will also have the opportunity to support your entries with documents (e.g., Word, Excel, and PowerPoint files) as well as electronic photos, videos, and recordings. When completed, you will have a professional-looking electronic portfolio that you can use to showcase in applications for jobs, internships, scholarships, and admission to graduate and professional schools.

Detailed instructions for this assignment are found at http://www.folio180.com/customer/KH-Cuseo/Thriving2_11_portfolio1.htm. Just type in this URL in your Internet browser, and follow the instructions.

Career Choice: Conflict and Confusion

Josh is a first-year student whose family has made a great financial sacrifice to send him to college. He deeply appreciates the tremendous commitment his family has made to his education and wants to pay them back as soon as possible. Consequently, he has been looking into careers that offer the highest starting salaries to college students immediately after graduation. Unfortunately, none of these careers seem to match Josh's natural abilities and personal interests, so he's conflicted, confused, and starting to get stressed out. He knows he'll have to make a decision soon because the careers with high starting salaries involve majors that have many course requirements, and if he expects to graduate in a reasonable period, he'll have to start taking some of these courses during his first year.

Reflection and Discussion Questions

1. If you were Josh, what would you do?

2. Do you see any way that Josh might balance his desire to pay back his parents as soon as possible with his desire to pursue a career that's compatible with his interests and talents?

3. What other questions or factors do you think Josh should consider before making his decision?

Glossary

Ability (Aptitude) the capacity to do something well or to have the potential to do it well.

Academic Advisor a professional who advises college students on course selection, helps students understand college procedures, and helps guide their academic progress toward completion of a college degree.

Academic Dismissal denying a student continued college enrollment because of a cumulative GPA that remains below a minimum level (e.g., below 2.0).

Academic Probation a period (usually one term) during which students with a GPA that is too low (e.g., less than 2.0) are given a chance to improve their grades; if the student's GPA does not meet or exceed the college's minimum requirement after this probationary period, that student may be academically dismissed from the college.

Academic Support Center the place on campus where students can obtain individual assistance from professionals and trained peers to support and strengthen their academic performance.

Active Involvement the amount of personal time devoted to learning in college and the degree of personal effort or energy (mental and physical) put into the learning process.

Administrator someone whose primary responsibility is the governance of the college or a unit within the college, such as an academic department or student support service.

Career the sum total of vocational experiences throughout an individual's work life.

Career Advancement working up the career ladder to higher levels of decision-making responsibility and socioeconomic status.

Career Development Center a key campus resource for learning about the nature of different careers and strategies on how to locate career-related work experiences.

Career Development Course a college course that typically includes self-assessment of career interests, information about different careers, and strategies for career preparation.

Career Entry gaining entry into a career and beginning a career path.

Citation an acknowledgment of the source of any piece of information included in a written paper or oral report that doesn't represent original work or thoughts.

Cocurricular Experience the learning and development that occur outside the classroom.

Collaboration the process of two or more people working interdependently toward a common goal that involves true teamwork, whereby teammates support one another's success and take equal responsibility for helping the team move toward its shared goal.

Communication Skills skills necessary for accurate comprehension and articulate expression of ideas, which include reading, writing, speaking, listening, and multimedia skills.

Commuter Student a college student who does not live on campus.

Concentration a cluster of approximately three courses in the same subject area.

Concept a larger system or network of related ideas.

Concept (Idea) Map a visual diagram that represents or maps out main categories of ideas and their relationships in a visual–spatial format.

Cooperative Education (Co-op) Program a program in which students gain work experience relating to their college major, either by stopping their coursework temporarily to work full time at the co-op position or by continuing to take classes while working part time at the co-op position.

Core Course a course required of all students, regardless of their particular major.

Counseling Services the personal counseling provided by professionals on campus that is designed to promote self-awareness and self-development in emotional and social aspects of life.

Cover (Application) Letter a letter written by an applicant who is applying for an employment position or admission to a school.

Cramming packing study time into one study session immediately before an exam.

Creative Thinking a form of higher-level thinking that involves producing a new and different idea, method, strategy, or work product.

Critical Thinking a form of higher-level thinking that involves making well-informed evaluations or judgments.

Culture a distinctive pattern of beliefs and values learned by a group of people who share the same social heritage and traditions.

Cum Laude graduating with honors (e.g., achieving a cumulative GPA of at least 3.3).

Cumulative Grade Point Average a student's GPA for all academic terms combined.

Curriculum the total set of courses offered by a college or university.

Dean's List achieving an outstanding GPA for a particular term (e.g., 3.5 or higher).

Diversity interacting with and learning from peers of varied backgrounds and lifestyles.

Diversity Appreciation valuing the experiences of different groups of people and interest in learning more about them.

Diversity (Multicultural) Course a course designed to promote diversity awareness and appreciation of multiple cultures.

Documentation information sources that serve as references to support or reinforce conclusions in a written paper or oral presentation.

Elective a course that students are not required to take but that they elect or choose to take.

Ethnic Group (Ethnicity) a group of people who share the same culture.

Experiential Learning out-of-class experiences that promote learning and development.

Faculty the collection of instructors on campus whose primary role is to teach courses that comprise the college curriculum.

Free Elective a course that students may elect to enroll in, which counts toward a college degree but is not required for either general education or academic major.

Freshman 15 a phrase commonly used to describe the 15-pound weight gain that some students experience during their first year of college.

Full-Time Student a student who typically enrolls in and completes at least 24 units per academic year.

Grade Points the amount of points earned for a course, which is calculated by multiplying the course grade by the number of credits carried by the course.

Grade Point Average (GPA) the translation of students' letter grades into a numerical system, whereby the total number of grade points earned in all courses is divided by total number of course units.

Graduate School a university-related education pursued after completing a bachelor's degree.

Grant money received that does not have to be repaid.

Higher-Level Thinking thinking at a higher or more complex level than merely acquiring factual knowledge or memorizing information.

Holistic (or Whole-Person) Development the development of the total self, which includes intellectual, social, emotional, physical, spiritual, ethical, vocational, and personal development.

Human Diversity the variety of differences that exist among people who comprise humanity (the human species).

Humanity the common elements of the human experience shared by all humans.

Illustrate to provide concrete examples or specific instances.

Information Interview an interview with a professional working in a career to obtain inside information on what the career is like.

Information Literacy the ability to find, evaluate, and use information.

Intellectual (Cognitive) Development acquiring knowledge and learning how to learn and how to think deeply.

Interest something someone likes or enjoys doing.

International Student a student attending college in one nation who is a citizen of another nation.

International Study (Study Abroad) Program doing coursework at a college or university in another country.

Internship a work experience related to a college major for which students receive academic credit and, in some cases, financial compensation.

Interpret to draw a conclusion about something and support that conclusion with evidence.

Introspection turning inward to gain deeper self-awareness of what has been done, what is being done, or what will be done.

Job Shadowing a program that allows a student to follow (shadow) and observe a professional during a typical workday.

Justify to back up arguments and viewpoints with evidence.

Leadership the ability to influence people in a positive way (e.g., motivating peers to do their best) or the ability to produce positive change in an organization or institution (e.g., improving the quality of a school, business, or political organization).

Leadership Course a course in which students learn how to advance and eventually assume important leadership positions in a company or organization.

Learning Community a program in which the same group of students takes the same block of courses together during the same academic term.

Learning Habit the usual approach, method, or technique a student uses while attempting to learn.

Learning Style the way in which individuals prefer to perceive information (receive or take it in) and process information (deal with it once it has been taken in).

Liberal Arts the component of a college education that provides the essential foundation or backbone for the college curriculum and is designed to equip students with a versatile set of skills to promote their success in any academic major or career.

Lifelong Learning Skills skills that include learning how to learn and how to continue learning that can be used throughout the remainder of personal and professional life.

Magna Cum Laude graduating with high honors (e.g., achieving a cumulative GPA of at least 3.5).

Major the academic field students choose to specialize in while in college.

Mentor someone who serves as a role model and personal guide to help students reach their educational or occupational goals.

Merit-Based Scholarship money awarded on the basis of performance or achievement that does not have to be repaid.

Metacognition thinking about the process of thinking.

Midterm the midpoint of an academic term.

Minor a second field of study that is designed to complement and strengthen a major, which usually consists of about half the number of courses required for a college major (e.g., six to seven courses are usually needed for a minor).

MLA Style a style of citing references in a research report that is endorsed by the Modern Language Association and is commonly used by academic fields in the humanities and fine arts (e.g., English and philosophy).

Mnemonic Device (Mnemonics) a specific memory-improvement method designed to prevent forgetting, which often involves such memory-improvement principles as meaning, organization, visualization, or rhythm and rhyme.

Multicultural Center a place on campus designed to provide space for interaction among members of diverse cultural groups.

Multicultural Competence the ability to understand cultural differences and to interact effectively with people from multiple cultural backgrounds.

Multidimensional Thinking a form of higher-level thinking that involves taking multiple perspectives and considering multiple theories.

Multiple Intelligences the notion that humans display intelligence or mental skills in many other forms besides their ability to perform on intellectual tests such as IQ and SAT tests.

Need a key element of life planning that represents something stronger than an interest and makes a person's life more satisfying or fulfilling.

Need-Based Scholarship money awarded to students on the basis of financial need that does not have to be repaid.

Netiquette applying the principles of social etiquette and interpersonal sensitivity when communicating online.

Non-Traditional-Age (Reentry) Student a student entering college who is not directly out of high school.

Online Resource a resource that can be used to search for and locate information, including online card catalogs, Internet search engines, and electronic databases.

Oral Communication Skills the ability to speak in a concise, confident, and eloquent fashion.

Oversubscribed (Impacted) Major a major that has more students interested in it than there are openings for students to be accepted.

Paraphrase restating or rephrasing information in original words.

Part-to-Whole Method a study strategy that involves dividing study time into smaller parts or units and then learning these parts in several short, separate study sessions in advance of exams.

Part-Time Student a student who typically enrolls in and completes less than 24 units per academic year.

Personal Reflection the process deliberately and thoughtfully reviewing what has been learned and connecting it to what is already known.

Persuasive Speech an oral presentation intended to persuade or convince the audience to agree with a certain conclusion or position by providing supporting evidence.

Plagiarism the deliberate or unintentional use of someone else's work without acknowledging it, giving the impression that it is original work.

Portfolio a collection of work materials or products that illustrates an individual's skills and talents or demonstrates that individual's educational and personal development.

Prewriting an early stage in the writing process where the focus is on generating and organizing ideas rather than expressing or communicating ideas to someone else.

Prejudice to prejudge members of the same group in the same way.

Primary Source the information obtained from a firsthand source or original document.

Process-of-Elimination Method a multiple-choice test-taking strategy that involves weeding out or eliminating choices that are clearly wrong and continuing to do so until the choices are narrowed down to one answer that seems to be the best choice available.

Procrastination the tendency to postpone making a decision or taking action until the last moment.

Professional School a formal education pursued after a bachelor's degree in school that prepares students for an "applied" profession (e.g., pharmacy, medicine, or law).

Prerequisite Course a course that must be completed before students can enroll in a more advanced course.

Proofreading a final microscopic form of editing that focuses on detecting mechanical errors relating to such things as referencing, grammar, punctuation, and spelling.

Race (Racial Group) a group of people who share some distinctive physical traits, such as skin color or other facial characteristics.

Recall Test Question a type of test question that requires students to generate or produce the correct answer on their own, such as a short-answer question or an essay question.

Recitation (Reciting) a study strategy that involves verbally stating information to be remembered without looking at it.

Recognition Test Question a type of test question that requires students to select or choose a correct answer from answers that are provided to them (e.g., multiple-choice, true–false, and matching questions).

Reconstruction a process of rebuilding a memory part by part or piece by piece.

Reentry Student a student who matriculated as a traditional (just out of high school) student but who left college to meet other job or family demands and has returned to complete a degree or obtain job training.

Reference (Referral) Letter a letter of reference typically written by a faculty member, advisor, or employer for students who are applying for entry into positions or schools after college or for students during the college experience when they apply for special academic programs, student leadership positions on campus, or part-time employment.

Reflection a thoughtful, personal review of what a person has already done, is in the process of doing, or is planning to do.

Research Skills the ability to locate, access, retrieve, organize, and evaluate information from various sources, including library- and technology-based (computer) systems.

Restricted Elective a course that falls into an area of study students must complete but can be chosen from a restricted set or list of possible courses that have been specified by the college.

Résumé a written summary or outline that effectively organizes and highlights an individual's strongest qualities, personal accomplishments, and skills, as well as personal credentials and awards.

Rough Draft an early stage in the writing process whereby a first (rough) draft is created that converts the writer's major ideas into sentences, without worrying about the mechanics of writing (e.g., punctuation, grammar, or spelling).

Scholarly a criterion or standard for critically evaluating the quality of an information source; typically, a source is considered to be scholarly if it has been reviewed by a panel or board of impartial experts in the field before being published.

Secondary Source a publication that relies on or responds to a primary source that has been previously published (e.g., a textbook that draws its information from published research studies or an article that critically reviews a published novel or movie).

Self-Assessment the process of reflecting on and evaluating personal characteristics, such as personality traits, learning habits, and personal strengths or weaknesses.

Self-Monitoring the ability to watch yourself and maintain self-awareness of how you're learning, what you're learning, and whether you're learning.

Semester (Term) Grade Point Average a GPA for one semester or academic term.

Service Learning a form of experiential learning in which students serve or help others while they acquire skills through hands-on experience that can be used to strengthen their résumé and explore fields of work that may relate to their future career interests.

Shallow (Surface-Oriented) Learning an approach to learning in which students spend most of their study time repeating and memorizing information in the exact form that it was presented to them.

Socially Constructed Knowledge the acquisition of knowledge built through interaction and dialogue with others.

Stereotyping viewing individuals of the same type (group) in the same (fixed) way.

Stigmatizing associating inferior or unfavorable traits with people who belong to the same group.

Student Development (Cocurricular) Transcript an official document issued by the college that validates a student's cocurricular achievements, which the student can have sent to prospective employers or schools.

Student Development Services (Student Affairs) a division of the college that provides student support on issues relating to social and emotional adjustment, involvement in campus life outside the classroom, and leadership development.

Student Handbook an official publication of a college or university that identifies student roles and responsibilities, violations of college rules and policies, and opportunities for student involvement in cocurricular programs, such as student clubs, campus organizations, and student leadership positions.

Summa Cum Laude graduating with highest honors (e.g., achieving a cumulative GPA of at least 3.8).

Syllabus an academic document that serves as a contract between instructor and student, which outlines course requirements, attendance policies, grading scale, course topic outlines by date, dates of tests and for completing reading and other assignments, and information about the instructor (e.g., office location and office hours).

Synthesis a form of higher-level thinking that involves building up ideas by integrating (connecting) separate pieces of information to form a whole or more comprehensive product.

Test Anxiety a state of emotional tension that can weaken test performance by interfering with memory and thinking.

Test Wise the ability to use the characteristics of the test question itself (such as its wording or format) to increase the probability of choosing the correct answer.

Theory a body of conceptually related concepts and general principles that help in organizing, understanding, and applying knowledge that has been acquired in a particular field of study.

Thesis Statement an important sentence in the introduction of a paper that is a one-sentence summary of the key point or main argument a writer intends to make, and support with evidence, in the body of the paper.

Transferable Skills skills that can be transferred or applied across a range of subjects, careers, and life situations.

Values what a person strongly believes in and cares about or feels is important to do and should be done.

Visual Aids charts, graphs, diagrams, or concept maps that improve learning and memory by enabling the learner to visualize information as a picture or image and connect separate pieces of information to form a meaningful whole.

Visual Memory memory that relies on the sense of vision.

Visualization a memory-improvement strategy that involves creating a mental image or picture of what is to be remembered or by imagining it being placed at a familiar site or location.

Vocational (Occupational) Development exploring career options, making career choices wisely, and developing skills needed for career success.

Waive to give up a right to access information (e.g., waiving the right to see a letter of recommendation).

Wellness a state of optimal health, peak performance, and positive well-being that is produced when different dimensions of the self (body, spirit, and mind) are attended to and effectively integrated.

Work–Study Program a federal program that supplies colleges and universities with funds to provide on-campus employment for students who are in financial need.

Written Communication Skills the ability to write in a clear, creative, or persuasive manner.

Dictionary of College Vocabulary

Academic Affairs unit or division of the college that deals primarily with the college curriculum, course instruction, and campus services that support academic success (e.g., library and learning center).

Academic Calendar the scheduling system used by a college or university to divide the academic year into shorter terms (e.g., semesters, trimesters, or quarters).

Academic Credits (Units) what students are credited with after completing courses that are counted toward completion of their college degree; course credit is typically counted in terms of how many hours the class meets each week (e.g., a course meets for three hours per week counts for 3 credits).

Academic Standing where a student stands academically (cumulative GPA) at a given point in their college experience (e.g., after one term or one year).

Academic Transcript a list of all courses a student has enrolled in, the grades received in those courses, and the student's grade-point average.

Advanced Placement (AP) Tests tests designed to measure college-level work that are taken while a student is in high school; if the student scores high enough, then college credit is awarded in the subject area tested or the student is granted advanced placement in a college course.

Analysis (Analytical Thinking) a form of higher-level thinking skill, which involves breaking down information and identifying its key parts or underlying elements and detecting what is most important or relevant.

APA Style a particular style of citing references in a research report or term paper that is endorsed by the American Psychological Association (APA) and is most commonly used in fields that comprise the Behavioral Sciences (e.g., Psychology and Sociology) and Natural Sciences (e.g., Biology and Chemistry).

Associate Degree (A.A./A.S. Degree) two-year college degree that represents completion of general education requirements and prepares students for transfer to a four-year college or university.

Bachelor's (Baccalaureate) Degree degree awarded by four-year colleges and universities, which represents the completion of general education requirements plus completion of an academic specialization in a particular major.

Breadth Requirements required general-education courses that span a wide-range of different subject areas.

Certificate credential received by students at a community college or technical college who have completed a one- or two-year vocational or occupational training program, which allows them entry into a specific occupation or career.

College Catalog (a.k.a., College Bulletin) an official publication of a college or university that identifies its mission, curriculum, academic policies and procedures, as well as the names and educational background of the faculty.

Combined bachelor/graduate degree program a program offered by some universities that allows students to apply for simultaneous admission to both undergraduate and graduate school in a particular field and to receive both a bachelor's degree and a graduate degree in that field after completing the combined program (e.g., a Bachelor's and Master's degree in physical therapy).

Counseling Services personal counseling provided by professionals on campus, that is designed to promote self-awareness and self-development in emotional and social aspects of life.

Cross-registration a collaborative program offered by two colleges or universities that allow students who are enrolled at one institution to register for and take courses at another institution.

Dean a college or university administrator who is responsible for running a particular unit of the college.

Distance Learning enrolling in and completing courses online rather than in person.

Doctoral Degree an advanced degree obtained after completion of the bachelor's (baccalaureate) degree, which typically requires 5 to 6 years of full-time study in graduate school, including completion of a thesis or doctoral dissertation.

Double Major attaining a bachelor's degree in two majors by meeting the course requirements of both academic fields.

Drop/Add the process of changing an academic schedule by dropping courses or adding courses to a pre-existing schedule; at most colleges and universities, adding and dropping courses can be done during the first week of the academic term.

Fine Arts a division of the liberal arts curriculum that focuses largely on artistic performance and appreciation of artistic expression by pursuing such questions as: What is beautiful? How do humans express and appreciate aesthetic (sensory) experiences, imagination, creativity, style, grace, and elegance?

Full-time Student a student who typically enrolls and completes at least 24 units per academic year.

General-Education Curriculum collection of courses designed to provide a "general" or "broad" rather than narrow education, and develop skills needed for success in any major or career.

Graduate Record Examination (GRE) a standardized test for admission to graduate schools, which is used in a manner similar to the way that the SAT and ACT tests are used for admission to undergraduate colleges and universities.

Graduate Assistant (GA) a graduate student who receives financial assistance to pursue graduate studies by working in a university office or college professor.

Graduate Student student who has completed a 4-year (Bachelor's) degree and is enrolled in graduate school to obtain an advanced degree (e.g., Master's or Ph.D.).

Greek Life a term that refers to both fraternities (usually all male) and sororities (usually all female).

Hazing a rite of induction to a social or other organization, most commonly associated with fraternities.

Health Services on-campus services provided to help students who are experiencing physical illnesses or injuries, and to educate students on matters relating to health and wellness.

Higher Education formal education beyond high school.

Honors Program a special program of courses and other learning experiences designed for college students who have demonstrated exceptionally high levels of academic achievement.

Humanities division of the liberal arts curriculum that focuses on the human experience, human culture, and questions that arise in a human's life, such as: Why are we here? What is the meaning or purpose of our existence? How should we live? What is the good life? Is there life after death?

Impacted Major an academic major in which there are more students wishing to enter the program than there are spaces available in the program; thus, students must formally apply and qualify for admission to the major by going through a competitive screening process.

Independent Study a project that allows a student to receive academic credit for an in-depth study of a topic of his or her choice by working independently with a faculty member without enrolling in a formal course that meets in a classroom according to a set schedule.

Interdisciplinary courses or programs that are designed to help students integrate knowledge from two or more academic disciplines (fields of study).

Inter-Term (a.k.a., January Interim or Maymester) a short academic term, typically running 3 to 4 weeks during which students enroll in only one course, which is studied intensively.

Learning Habits the usual approaches, methods, or techniques a student uses while attempting to learn.

Living-Learning Environment on-campus student residence that is designed and organized in such a way that student learning experiences are integrated into their living environment (e.g., study groups, tutoring, and student development workshops).

Lower-Division Courses courses taken by college students during their freshman and sophomore years.

Master's Degree degree obtained after completion of the bachelor's (baccalaureate) degree, which typically requires 2 to 3 years of full-time study in graduate school.

Matriculation the process of initially enrolling in or registering for college. (The term is derived from the term, "matricula"—a list or register of persons belonging to a society or community.)

Multicultural Center place on campus that is designed to provide a place for interaction among and between members of diverse cultural groups.

Natural Sciences a division of the liberal arts curriculum that focuses on observing the physical world and explaining natural phenomena, asking such questions as: What causes physical events in the natural world? How can we predict and control physical events and improve the quality of interaction between humans and the natural environment?

Non-Resident Status out-of-state students who typically pay higher tuition than in-state students because they are not residents of the state in which their college is located.

Orientation an educational program designed to help students make a smooth transition to college that is delivered to students before their first academic term.

Part-Time Student a student who typically enrolls and completes less than 24 units per academic year.

Pass/Fail (Credit/No Credit) Grading a grading option offered in some courses whereby students do not receive a letter grade (A–F), but only a grade of "pass" (credit) or "fail" (no credit).

Phi Beta Kappa a national honor society that recognizes outstanding academic achievement of students at 4-year colleges and universities.

Phi Theta Kappa a national honor society that recognizes outstanding academic achievement of students at 2-year colleges.

Placement Tests tests administered to new students upon entry to a college or university designed to assess their basic academic skills (e.g., reading, writing, mathematics) in order to place them in courses that are neither too advanced nor too elementary for their particular level of skill development.

Postsecondary Education formal education beyond secondary (high school) education.

Pre-professional Coursework undergraduate courses that are required or strongly recommended for gaining entry into professional school (e.g., medical school or law school).

Proficiency Tests tests given to college students before graduation that are designed to assess whether they can perform certain academic skills (e.g., writing) at a level advanced enough to qualify them for college graduation.

Quarter System a system for scheduling courses in which the academic year is divided into four quarters (fall, winter, spring, and summer terms), each of which lasts approximately 10–11 weeks.

Registrar's Office campus office that maintains college transcripts and other official records associated with student coursework and academic performance.

Resident Assistant undergraduate student (sophomore, junior or senior) whose role is to enforce rules in student residences and help new students adjust successfully to residence hall life.

Resident Director student development professional who is in charge of residential (dormitory) life and the person to whom resident assistants report.

Resident Status in-state students who typically pay lower tuition than out-of-state students because they are residents of the state in which their college is located.

Residential Students students who live on campus or in a housing unit owned and operated by the college.

Semester System a system for scheduling courses in which the academic year is divided into two terms (fall and spring) that are approximately 15–16 weeks long.

Self-Regulation adjusting learning strategies in a way that best meets the specific demands of the subject being learned.

Senior Seminar (Capstone) Course course designed to put a "cap" or final touch on the college experience, helping seniors to tie ideas together in their major and/or make a smooth transition from college to life after college.

Shadow Majors students who have been admitted to their college or university, but have not yet been admitted to their intended major.

Social and Behavioral Sciences a division of the liberal arts curriculum that focuses on the observation of human behavior, individually and in groups, asking such questions as: What causes humans to behave the way they do? How can we predict, control, or improve human behavior and interpersonal interaction?

Student Activities co-curricular experiences offered outside the classroom that are designed to promote student learning and student involvement in campus life.

Student-Designed (Interdisciplinary) Major an academic program offered at some colleges and universities in which a student works with a college representative or committee to develop a major that is not officially offered by the institution.

Student Development Services (Student Affairs) division of the college that provides student support on issues relating to social and emotional adjustment, involvement in campus life outside the classroom, and leadership development.

Student Handbook an official publication of a college or university that identifies student roles and responsibilities, violations of college rules and policies, and opportunities for student involvement in co-curricular programs, such as student clubs, campus organizations, and student leadership positions.

Summer Session courses offered during the summer between spring and fall terms that typically run for 4 to 6 weeks.

Teaching Assistant (TA) a graduate student who receives financial assistance to pursue graduate studies by teaching undergraduate courses, leading course discussions, and/or helping professors grade papers or conduct labs.

Transfer Program two-year college program that provides general education and pre-major coursework to prepare students for successful transfer to a four-year college or university.

Trimester System a system for scheduling courses in which the academic year is divided into three terms (fall, winter, spring) that are approximately 12–13 weeks long.

Undeclared students who have not committed to a college major.

Undergraduate student who is enrolled in a 2-year or 4-year college.

University an educational institution that offers not only undergraduate degrees, but graduate degrees as well.

Upper-division Courses courses taken by college students during their junior and senior years.

Vocational/Technical Programs community college programs of study that train students for a particular occupation or trade and immediate employment after completing a two-year associate degree (e.g., Associate of Applied Science) or a one-year certificate program.

Volunteerism volunteering personal time to help others.

Withdrawal dropping a class after the drop/add deadline, which results in a student receiving a "W" for the course and no academic credit.

Writing Center a campus support service where students can receive assistance at any stage of the writing process, whether it be collecting and organizing ideas, composing a first draft, or proofreading a final draft.

References

Academic Integrity at Princeton. (2003). *Examples of plagiarism*. Retrieved October 21, 2006, from http://www.princeton.du/pr/pub/integrity/pages/plagiarism.html

Acredolo, C., & O'Connor, J. (1991). On the difficulty of detecting cognitive uncertainty. *Human Development, 34*, 204–223.

Adler, R. B., & Towne, M. (2001). *Looking out, looking in: Interpersonal communication* (10th ed.). Orlando, FL: Harcourt Brace.

Ainslie, G. (1975). Specious reward: A behavioral theory of impulsiveness and impulse control. *Psychological Bulletin, 82*, 463–496.

Ainslie, G. (1992). *Picoeconomics: The strategic interaction of successive motivational states within the person*. New York: Cambridge University Press.

Alkon, D. L. (1992). *Memory's voice: Deciphering the brain-mind code*. New York: HarperCollins.

Allport, G. W. (1954). *The nature of prejudice*. Cambridge, MA: Addison-Wesley.

Amabile, T., Hadley, C. N., & Kramer, S. J. (2002). Creativity under the gun. *Harvard Business Review, 80*(8), 52–61.

American College Testing. (2009). *National college dropout and graduation rates, 2008*. Retrieved June 4, 2009, from http://www.act.org/news

American Council on Education. (2008). *Making the case for affirmative action*. Retrieved January 13, 2007, from http://acenet.edu/bookstore/descsriptions/making_the_case/works/research.cfm

American Heart Association. (2006). *Fish, levels of mercury and omega-3 fatty acids*. Retrieved January 13, 2007, from http://americanheart.org/presenter.jthml?identifier=3013797

American Obesity Association. (2002). *Obesity in the U.S.* Retrieved April 26, 2006, from http://www.obesity.org/subs/fastfacts/obesity_US.shtml

American Psychiatric Association. (1994). *Diagnostic and Statistical Manual for Mental Disorders* (4th ed., DSM-IV). Washington, DC: American Psychiatric Press.

American Psychiatric Association. Work Group on Eating Disorders. (2000). Practice guidelines for the treatment of patients with eating disorders. *American Journal of Psychiatry, 157*, 1–39.

Amir, Y. (1976). The role of intergroup contact in change of prejudice and ethnic relations. In P. A. Katz (Ed.), *Towards the elimination of racism* (pp. 245–308). New York: Pergamon Press.

Anderson, C. J. (2003). The psychology of doing nothing: Forms of decision avoidance result from reason and emotion. *Psychological Bulletin, 129*, 139–167.

Anderson, J. R., & Bower, G. H. (1974). Interference in memory for multiple contexts. *Memory and Cognition, 2*, 509–514.

Anderson, M., & Fienberg, S. E. (2000). Race and ethnicity and the controversy over the U.S. census. *Current Sociology, 48*(3), 87–110.

Appleby, D. C. (2008, June). *Diagnosing and treating the deadly 13th grade syndrome*. Paper presented at the Association of Psychological Science Convention, Chicago, IL.

Arnedt, J. T., Wilde, G. J. S., Munt, P. W., & MacLean, A. W. (2001). How do prolonged wakefulness and alcohol compare in the decrements they produce on a simulated driving task? *Accident Analysis and Prevention, 33*, 337–344.

Astin, A. W. (1993). *What matters in college?* San Francisco: Jossey-Bass.

Astin, A. W., Parrot, S. A., Korn, W. S., & Sax, L. J. (1997). *The American freshman: Thirty year trends, 1966–1996*. Los Angeles: Higher Education Research Institute, University of California.

Ausubel, D. P. (1978). The facilitation of meaningful verbal learning in the classroom. *Educational Psychologist, 12*, 251-257.

Bandura, A. (1986). *Social foundations of thought and action: A social cognitive theory*. Englewood Cliffs, NJ: Prentice Hall.

Bandura, A. (1994). Self-efficacy. In V. S. Ramachaudran (Ed.), *Encyclopedia of human behavior* (Vol. 4, pp. 71–81). New York: Academic Press.

Bandura, A. (1997). *Self-efficacy: The exercise of control*. New York: Freeman.

Bandura, A., & Cervone, D. (1983). Self-evaluative and self-efficacy mechanisms governing the motivational effects of goal systems. *Journal of Personality and Social Psychology, 45*(5), 1017–1028.

Barefoot, B. O., Warnock, C. L., Dickinson, M. P., Richardson, S. E., & Roberts, M. R. (Eds.). (1998). *Exploring the evidence: Vol. 2. Reporting outcomes of first-year seminars* (Monograph No. 29). Columbia: National Resource Center for the First-Year Experience and Students in Transition, University of South Carolina.

Bargdill, R. W. (2000). A phenomenological investigation of being bored with life. *Psychological Reports, 86,* 493–494.

Barker, L., & Watson, K. W. (2000). *Listen up: How to improve relationships, reduce stress, and be more productive by using the power of listening.* New York: St. Martin's Press.

Bartels, A., & Zeki, S. (2000). The neural basis of romantic love. *European Journal of Neuroscience, 12,* 172–193.

Bartlett, T. (2002). Freshman pay, mentally and physically, as they adjust to college life. *Chronicle of Higher Education, 48,* 35–37.

Basadur, M., Runco, M. A., & Vega, L. A. (2000). Understanding how creative thinking skills, attitudes, and behaviors work together. *Journal of Creative Behavior, 34*(2), 77–100.

Bassham, G., Irwin, W., Nardone, H., & Wallace, J. M. (2005). *Critical thinking* (2nd ed.). New York: McGraw-Hill.

Bates, G. A. (1994). *The next step: College.* Bloomington, IN: Phi Delta Kappa.

Baumeister, R. F., Heatherton, T. F., & Tice, D. M. (1994). *Losing control: How and why people fail at self-regulation.* San Diego, CA: Academic Press.

Bean, J. C. (2003). *Engaging ideas.* San Francisco: Jossey-Bass.

Beck, B. L., Koons, S. R., & Milgram, D. L. (2000). Correlates and consequences of behavioral procrastination: The effects of academic procrastination, self-consciousness, self-esteem and self-handicapping. *Journal of Social Behavior and Personality, 15,* 3–13.

Benjamin, L. T., Jr., Cavell, T. A., & Shallenberger, W. R., III. (1984). Staying with initial answers on objective tests: Is it a myth? *Teaching of Psychology, 11,* 133–141.

Benjamin, M., McKeachie, W. J., Lin, Y.-G., & Holinger, D. (1981). Test anxiety: Deficits in information processing. *Journal of Educational Psychology, 73,* 816–824.

Bennet, W., & Gurin, J. (1983). *The dieter's dilemma.* New York: Basic Books.

Benson, H., & Klipper, M. Z. (1990). *The relaxation response.* New York: Avon.

Berndt, T. J. (1992). Friendship and friends' influence in adolescence. *Current Directions in Psychological Science, 1*(5), 156–159.

Biglan, A. (1973). The characteristics of subject matter in different academic areas. *Journal of Applied Psychology, 57,* 195–203.

Bjork, R. (1994). Memory and metamemory considerations in the training of human beings. In J. Metcalfe & A. P. Shimamura (Eds.), *Metacognition: Knowing about knowing* (pp. 185–206). Cambridge, MA: MIT Press.

Blakeslee, S. (1993, August 3). Mystery of sleep yields as studies reveal immune tie. *The New York Times,* pp. C1, C6.

Boekaerts, M., Pintrich, P. R., & Zeidner, M. (2000). *Handbook of self-regulation.* San Diego: Academic Press.

Bohme, K., & Budden, F. (2001). *The silent thief: Osteoporosis, exercises and strategies for prevention and treatment.* Buffalo, NY: Firefly.

Bok, D. (2006). *Our underachieving colleges.* Princeton, NJ: Princeton University Press.

Bolles, R. N. (1998). *The new quick job-hunting map.* Toronto, Ontario, Canada: Ten Speed Press.

Booth, F. W., & Vyas, D. R. (2001). Genes, environment, and exercise. *Advances in Experimental Medicine and Biology, 502,* 13–20.

Boudreau, C., & Kromrey, J. (1994). A longitudinal study of the retention and academic performance of participants in a freshman orientation course. *Journal of College Student Development, 35,* 444–449.

Bowen, H. R. (1977). *Investment in learning: The individual and social value of American higher education.* San Francisco: Jossey-Bass.

Bowen, H. R. (1997). *Investment in learning: The individual and social value of American higher education* (2nd ed.). Baltimore: Johns Hopkins Press.

Bowlby, J. (1980). *Attachment and loss: Vol. 3. Loss, sadness, and depression.* New York: Basic Books.

Boyer, E. L. (1987). *College: The undergraduate experience in America.* New York: Harper & Row.

Bradshaw, D. (1995). Learning theory: Harnessing the strength of a neglected resource. In D. C. A. Bradshaw (Ed.), *Bringing learning to life: The learning revolution, the economy and the individual* (pp. 79–92). London: Falmer Press.

Bransford, J. D., Brown, A. L., & Cocking, R. R. (1999). *How people learn: Brain, mind, experience and school.* Washington, DC: National Academy Press.

Bridgeman, B. (2003). *Psychology and evolution: The origins of mind.* Thousand Oaks, CA: Sage.

Brody, J. E. (2003, August 18). Skipping a college course: Weight gain 101. *The New York Times*, p. D7.

Brown, R. D. (1988). Self-quiz on testing and grading issues. *Teaching at UNL (University of Nebraska–Lincoln)*, *10*(2), 1–3.

Brown, S. D., & Krane, N. E. R. (2000). Four (or five) sessions and a cloud of dust: Old assumptions and new observations about career counseling. In S. D. Brown & R. W. Lent (Eds.), *Handbook of counseling psychology* (3rd ed., pp. 740–766). New York: Wiley.

Bruffee, K. A. (1993). *Collaborative learning: Higher education, interdependence, and the authority of knowledge*. Baltimore: Johns Hopkins University Press.

Burka, J. B., & Yuen, L. M. (1983). *Procrastination: Why you do it, what to do about it*. Reading, MA: Addison-Wesley.

Caine, R. N., & Caine, G. (1991). *Teaching and the human brain*. Alexandria, VA: Association for Supervision and Curriculum Development.

Cameron, L. (2003). *Metaphor in educational discourse*. London: Continuum.

Campbell, T. A., & Campbell, D. E. (1997, December). Faculty/student mentor program: Effects on academic performance and retention. *Research in Higher Education*, *38*, 727–742.

Caplan, P. J., & Caplan, J. B. (1994). *Thinking critically about research on sex and gender*. New York: HarperCollins College Publishers.

Carnegie, D. (1936). *How to win friends and influence people*.

Caroli, M., Argentieri, L., Cardone, M., & Masi, A. (2004). Role of television in childhood obesity prevention. *International Journal of Obesity Related Metabolic Disorders*, *28*(Suppl. 3), S104–S108.

Carpenter, K. M., & Hasin, D. S. (1998). A prospective evaluation of the relationship between reasons for drinking and DSM-IV alcohol-use disorders. *Addictive Behaviors*, *23*(1), 41–46.

Carter, R. (1998). *Mapping the mind*. Berkeley: University of California Press.

Chan, Z. C. Y., & Ma, J. L. C. (2002, December). Anorexic eating: Two case studies in Hong Kong. *Qualitative Report*, *7*(4). Retrieved October 24, 2009, from http://www.nova.edu/ssss/QR/QR7-4/chan.html

Chi, M., de Leeuw, N., Chiu, M. H., & LaVancher, C. (1994). Eliciting self-explanations improves understanding. *Cognitive Science*, *18*, 439–477.

Chickering, A. W., & Schlossberg, N. K. (1998). Moving on: Seniors as people in transition. In J. N. Gardner, G. Van der Veer, et al. (Eds.), *The senior year experience* (pp. 37–50). San Francisco: Jossey-Bass.

Chronicle of Higher Education. (2003, August 30). Almanac 2003–04. *Chronicle of Higher Education*, *49*(1).

Cianciotto, J. (2005). *Hispanic and latino same sex-couple households in the United States: A report from the 2000 Census*. New York: The National Gay and Lesbian Task Force Policy Institute and the National Latino/a Coalition for Justice.

Claxton, C. S., & Murrell, P. H. (1988). *Learning styles: Implications for improving practice*. ASHE-ERIC Educational Report No. 4. Washington, DC: Association for the Study of Higher Education.

Coates, T. J. (1977). *How to sleep better: A drug-free program for overcoming insomnia*. Englewood Cliffs, NJ: Prentice Hall.

College Board. (2006). *Education pays update*. Washington, DC: Author.

College Board. (2008). *Education pays 2007*. Washington, DC: Author.

Collins, A. M., & Loftus, E. F. (1975). A spreading activation theory of semantic processing. *Psychological Review*, *82*, 407–428.

Colombo, G., Cullen, R., & Lisle, B. (1995). *Rereading America: Cultural contexts for critical thinking and writing*. Boston: Bedford Books of St. Martin's Press.

Conaway, M. A. (1982). Listening: Learning tool and retention agent. In A. S. Algier & K. W. Algier (Eds.), *Improving reading and study skills* (pp. 51–63). San Francisco: Jossey-Bass.

Corbin, C. B., Pangrazi, R. P., & Franks, B. D. (2000). Definitions: Health, fitness, and physical activity. *President's Council on Physical Fitness and Sports Research Digest*, *3*(9), 1–8.

Covey, S. R. (1990). *Seven habits of highly effective people* (2nd ed.). New York: Fireside.

Crawford, H. J., & Strapp, C. H. (1994). Effects of vocal and instrumental music on visuospatial and verbal performance as moderated by studying preference and personality. *Personality and Individual Differences*, *16*(2), 237–245.

Crosby, O. (2002). Informational interviewing: Get the scoop on careers. *Occupational Outlook Quarterly* (Summer), 32–37.

Csikszentmihalyi, M. (1996). *Creativity: Flow and the psychology of discovery and invention*. New York: HarperCollins.

Cude, B. J., Lawrence, F. C., Lyons, A. C., Metzger, K., LeJeune, E., Marks, L., & Machtmes, K. (2006). College students and financial literacy: What they know and what we need to learn. *Proceedings of the Eastern Family Economics and Resource Management Association Conference* (pp. 102–109).

Cuseo, J. B. (1996). *Cooperative learning: A pedagogy for addressing contemporary challenges and critical issues in higher education.* Stillwater, OK: New Forums Press.

Cuseo, J. B. (2003a). Comprehensive academic support for students during the first year of college. In G. L. Kramer et al. (Eds.), *Student academic services: An integrated approach* (pp. 271–310). San Francisco: Jossey-Bass.

Cuseo, J. B. (2003b, November). *The transfer transition.* Preconference workshop conducted at the Tenth National Conference on Students in Transition, Lake Buena Vista, FL.

Cuseo, J. B. (2005). "Decided," "undecided," and "in transition": Implications for academic advisement, career counseling, and student retention. In R. S. Feldman (Ed.), *Improving the first year of college: Research and practice* (pp. 27–50). Mahwah, NJ: Lawrence Erlbaum.

Cuseo, J. B., & Barefoot, B. O. (1996). A natural marriage: The extended orientation seminar and the community college. In J. Henkin (Ed.), *The community college: Opportunity and access for America's first-year students* (pp. 59–68). Columbia: National Resource Center for the First-Year Experience and Students in Transition, University of South Carolina.

Damrad-Frye, R., & Laird, J. (1989). The experience of boredom: The role of self-perception of attention. *Journal of Personality & Social Psychology, 57,* 315–320.

Daniels, D., & Horowitz, L. J. (1997). *Being and caring: A psychology for living.* Prospect Heights, IL: Waveland Press.

Dee, T. (2004). Are there civic returns to education? *Journal of Public Economics, 88,* 1697–1720.

Dement, W. C., & Vaughan, C. (1999). *The promise of sleep.* New York: Delacorte Press.

Dement, W. C., & Vaughan, C. (2000). *The promise of sleep: A pioneer in sleep medicine explores the vital connection between health, happiness, and a good night's sleep.* New York: Dell.

Demmert, W. G., Jr., & Towner, J. C. (2003). *A review of the research literature on the influences of culturally based education on the academic performance of Native American students.* Retrieved from the Northwest Regional Educational Laboratory, Portland, Oregon, Web site: http://www.nrel.org/indianaed/cbe.pdf

DesMaisons, K. (1998). *Potatoes not Prozac.* London: Simon & Schuster.

Diaz, P. (1992). Effects of transfer on academic performance of community college students at the four-year institution. *Community Junior College Quarterly of Research and Practice, 16*(3), 279–291.

Douglas, K. A., Collins, J. L., Warren, C., Kahn, L., Gold, R., Clayton, S., et al. (1997). Results from the 1995 national college health risk behavior survey. *Journal of American College Health, 46,* 55–66.

Doyle, S., Edison, M., & Pascarella, E. (1998). *The "seven principles of good practice in undergraduate education" as process indicators of cognitive development in college: A longitudinal study.* Paper presented at the annual meeting of the Association for the Study of Higher Education, Miami, FL.

Druckman, D., & Bjork, R. A. (Eds.). (1991). *In the mind's eye: Enhancing human performance.* Washington, DC: National Academy Press.

Dryden, G., & Vos, J. (1999). *The learning revolution: To change the way the world learns.* Torrance, CA: Learning Web.

Dunn, R., Dunn, K., & Price, G. (1990). *Learning style inventory.* Lawrence, KS: Price Systems.

Dupuy, G. M., & Vance, R. M. (1996, October). *Launching your career: A transition module for seniors.* Paper presented at the Second National Conference on Students in Transition, San Antonio, TX.

Eaton, S. B., & Konner, M. (1985). Paleolithic nutrition: A consideration of its nature and current implications. *New England Journal of Medicine, 312,* 283.

Eckman, P., & Friesen, W. V. (1969). Nonverbal leakage and clues to deception. *Psychiatry, 32,* 88–106.

Education Commission of the States. (1995). *Making quality count in undergraduate education.* Denver, CO: ECS Distribution Center.

Education Commission of the States. (1996). *Bridging the gap between neuroscience and education.* Denver, CO: Author.

Einstein, G. O., Morris, J., & Smith, S. (1985). Note-taking, individual differences, and memory for lecture information. *Journal of Educational Psychology, 77*(5), 522–532.

Ellin, A. (1993, September). Post-parchment depression. *Boston Phoenix*.

Ellis, A. (1995). Changing rational-emotive therapy (RET) to rational emotive behavior therapy (REBT). *Journal of Rational-Emotive & Cognitive Behavior Therapy, 13*(2), 85–89.

Ellis, A., & Knaus, W. J. (1977). *Overcoming procrastination*. New York: Signet Books.

Elster, J., & Lowenstein, G. (Eds.). (1992). *Choice over time*. New York: Russell Sage Foundation.

Erasmus, U. (1993). *Fats that heal, fats that kill*. Burnaby, British Columbia, Canada: Alive Books.

Erickson, B. L., Peters, C. B., & Strommer, D. W. (2006). *Teaching first-year college students*. San Francisco: Jossey-Bass.

Erickson, B. L., & Strommer, D. W. (1991). *Teaching college freshmen*. San Francisco: Jossey-Bass.

Erickson, B. L., & Strommer, D. W. (2005). Inside the first-year classroom: Challenges and constraints. In J. L. Upcraft, J. N. Gardner, & B. O. Barefoot, *Challenging and supporting the first-year student* (pp. 241–256). San Francisco: Jossey-Bass.

Ericsson, K. A., & Charness, N. (1994). Expert performance. *American Psychologist, 49*(8), 725–747.

Everly, G. S. (1989). *A clinical guide to the treatment of the human stress response*. New York: Plenum Press.

Ewell, P. T. (1997). Organizing for learning. *AAHE Bulletin, 50*(4), 3–6.

Family Care Foundation. (2005). *If the world were a village of 100 people*. Retrieved December 19, 2006, from http://www.familycare.org.news/if_the_world.htm

Feldman, K. A., & Newcomb, T. M. (1994). *The impact of college on students*. New Brunswick, NJ: Transaction Publishers. (Original work published 1969).

Feskens, E. J., & Kromhout, D. (1993). Epidemiologic studies on Eskimos and fish intake. *Annals of the New York Academy of Science, 683*, 9–15.

Fidler, P., & Godwin, M. (1994). Retaining African-American students through the freshman seminar. *Journal of Developmental Education, 17*, 34–41.

Fisher, J. L., Harris, J. L., & Harris, M. B. (1973). Effect of note-taking and review on recall. *Journal of Educational Psychology, 65*(3), 321–325.

Fixman, C. S. (1990). The foreign language needs of U.S.-based corporations. *Annals of the American Academy of Political and Social Science, 511*, 25–46.

Flavell, J. H. (1985). *Cognitive development* (2nd ed.). Englewood Cliffs, NJ: Prentice Hall.

Fletcher, A., Lamond, N., van den Heuvel, C. J., & Dawson, D. (2003). Prediction of performance during sleep deprivation and alcohol intoxication using a quantitative model of work-related fatigue. *Sleep Research Online, 5*, 67–75.

Flett, G. L., Blankstein, K. R., Hewitt, P. L., & Koledin, S. (1992). Components of perfectionism and procrastination in college students. *Social Behavior & Personality, 20*, 85–94.

Flowers, L., Osterlind, S., Pascarella, E., & Pierson, C. (2001). How much do students learn in college? Cross-sectional estimates using the College Basic Academic Subjects Examination. *Journal of Higher Education, 72*, 565–583.

Foreman, J. (2009, March 2). Students, don't blame college for your misery. *Los Angeles Times*, p. F3.

Franklin, K. F. (2002). Conversations with Metropolitan University first-year students. *Journal of the First-Year Experience & Students in Transition, 14*(2), 57–88.

Fromm, E. (1970). *The art of loving*. New York: Bantam.

Fromme, A. (1980). *The ability to love*. Chatsworth, CA: Wilshire Book Company.

Frost, S. H. (1991). *Academic advising for student success: A system of shared responsibility* (ASHE-ERIC Higher Education Report, No. 3). Washington, DC: School of Education and Human Development, George Washington University.

Furnham, A., & Argyle, M. (1998). *The psychology of money*. New York: Routledge.

Gardner, H. (1983). *Frames of mind: The theory of multiple intelligences*. New York: Basic Books.

Gardner, H. (1993). *Frames of mind: The theory of multiple intelligences* (2nd ed.). New York: Basic Books.

Gardner, P. D. (1991, March). *Learning the ropes: Socialization and assimilation into the workplace*. Paper presented at the Second National Conference on the Senior Year Experience, San Antonio, TX.

Gershoff, S., & Whitney, C. (1996). *The Tufts University guide to total nutrition*. New York: Harper Perennial.

Gibb, J. R. (1961, September). Defensive communication. *Journal of Communication, 11*, 3.

Gibb, H. R. (1991). *Trust: A new vision of human relationships for business, education, family, and personal living* (2nd ed.). North Hollywood, CA: Newcastle.

Giles, L. C., Glonek, F. V., Luszcz, M. A., & Andrews, G. R. (2005). Effect of social networks on 10-year survival in very old Australians: The Australia longitudinal study of aging. *Journal of Epidemiology and Community Health, 59*, 574–579.

Gladwell, M. (2008). *Outliers: The story of success*. New York: Little, Brown.

Glass, J., & Garrett, M. (1995). Student participation in a college orientation course: Retention, and grade point average. *Community College Journal of Research and Practice, 19*, 117–132.

Glenberg, A. M., Bradley, M. M., Kraus, T. A., & Renzaglia, G. J. (1983). Studies of the long-term recency effect: Support for a contextually guided retrieval hypothesis. *Journal of Experimental Psychology: Learning, Memory, and Cognition, 9*, 231–255.

Glenberg, A. M., Schroeder, J. L., & Robertson, D. A. (1998). Averting the gaze disengages the environment and facilitates remembering. *Memory & Cognition, 26*(4), 651–658.

Goleman, D. (1995). *Emotional intelligence: Why it can matter more than IQ*. New York: Random House.

Gottman, J. (1994). *Why marriages succeed and fail*. New York: Fireside.

Graf, P. (1982). The memorial consequence of generation and transformation. *Journal of Verbal Learning and Verbal Behavior, 21*, 539–548.

Green, M. G. (Ed.). (1989). *Minorities on campus: A handbook for enhancing diversity*. Washington, DC: American Council on Education.

Greenberg, R., Pillard, R., & Pearlman, C. (1972). The effect of dream (stage REM) deprivation on adaptation to stress. *Psychosomatic Medicine, 34*, 257–262.

Grunder, P., & Hellmich, D. (1996). Academic persistence and achievement of remedial students in a community college's success program. *Community College Review, 24*, 21–33.

Haberman, S., & Luffey, D. (1998). Weighing in college students' diet and exercise behaviors. *Journal of American College Health, 46*, 189–191.

Hall, R. M., & Sandler, B. R. (1982). *The classroom climate: A chilly one for women*. Project on the Status of Women. Washington, DC: Association of American Colleges.

Hall, R. M., & Sandler, B. R. (1984). *Out of the classroom: A chilly campus climate for women*. Project on the Status of Women. Washington, DC: Association of American Colleges.

Harriott, J., & Ferrari, J. R. (1996). Prevalence of procrastination among samples of adults. *Psychological Reports, 78*, 611–616.

Harris, M. B. (2000). Correlates and characteristics of boredom and proneness to boredom. *Journal of Applied Social Psychology, 30*(3), 576–598.

Hartley, J. (1998). *Learning and studying: A research perspective*. London: Routledge.

Hartley, J., & Marshall, S. (1974). On notes and note taking. *Universities Quarterly, 28*, 225–235.

Hashaw, R. M., Hammond, C. J., & Rogers, P. H. (1990). Academic locus of control and the collegiate experience. *Research & Teaching in Developmental Education, 7*(1), 45–54.

Hatfield, E., & Walster, G. W. (1985). *A new look at love*. Lanham, MD: University Press of America.

Hauri, P., & Linde, S. (1996). *No more sleepless nights*. New York: John Wiley & Sons.

Haven't filed yet? Tackle those taxes. (2003, April 11). *USA Today*, p. 3b.

Health, C., & Soll, J. (1996). Mental budgeting and consumer decisions. *Journal of Consumer Research, 23*, 40–52.

Heath, H. (1977). *Maturity and competence: A transcultural view*. New York: Halsted Press.

Herman, R. E. (2000, November). Liberal arts: The key to the future. *USA Today Magazine, 129*, 34.

Higbee, K. L. (2001). *Your memory: How it works and how to improve it*. New York: Marlowe.

Higher Education Research Institute. (2004). *The spiritual life of college students: A national study of college students' search for meaning and purpose*. Los Angeles: Author, Graduate School of Education & Information Studies, University of California.

Hildenbrand, M., & Gore, P. A., Jr. (2005). Career development in the first-year seminar: Best practice versus actual practice. In P. A. Gore (Ed.), *Facilitating the career development of students in transition* (Monograph No. 43, pp. 45–60). Columbia: National Resource Center for the First-Year Experience and Students in Transition, University of South Carolina.

Hill, A. J. (2002). Developmental issues in attitudes toward food and diet. *Proceedings of the Nutrition Society, 61*(2), 259–268.

Hill, J. O., Wyat, H. R., Reed, G. W., & Peters, J. C. (2003). Obesity and environment: Where do we go from here? *Science, 299*, 853–855.

Hobson, J. A. (1988). *The dreaming brain*. New York: Basic Books.

Hollenbeck, J. R., Williams, C. R., & Klein, H. J. (1989). An empirical examination of the antecedents of commitment to difficult goals. *Journal of Applied Psychology, 74*(1), 18–23.

Horne, J. (1988). *Why we sleep: The functions of sleep in humans and other mammals.* New York: Oxford University Press.

Howard, P. J. (2000). *The owner's manual for the brain: Everyday applications of mind-brain research* (2nd ed.). Atlanta: Bard Press.

Howe, M. J. (1970). Note-taking strategy, review, and long-term retention of verbal information. *Journal of Educational Psychology, 63,* 285.

Hunter, M. A., & Linder, C. W. (2005). First-year seminars. In M. L. Upcraft, J. N. Gardner, B. O. Barefoot, et al. (Eds.), *Challenging and supporting the first-year student: A handbook for improving the first year of college* (pp. 275–291). San Francisco: Jossey-Bass.

Indiana University. (2004). *Selling your liberal arts degree to employers.* Retrieved July 7, 2004, from http://www.indiana.edu/~career/fulltime/selling_liberal_arts.html

Institute for Research on Higher Education. (1995). Connecting schools and employers: Work-related education and training. *Change, 27*(3), 39–46.

Internal Revenue Service. (2004). *Statistics of income 2001–2003.* Washington, DC: Author.

Jablonski, N. G., & Chaplin, G. (2002). Skin deep. *Scientific American* (October), 75–81.

Jacobs, W. J., & Nadel, L. (1985). Stress-induced recovery of fears and phobias. *Psychological Review, 92*(4), 512–531.

Jakubowski, P., & Lange, A. J. (1978). *The assertive option: Your rights and responsibilities.* Champaign, IL: Research Press.

Janis, I. L. (1982). *Groupthink: Psychological studies of policy decisions and fiascoes* (2nd ed.). Boston: Houghton Mifflin.

Jemott, J. B., & Magloire, K. (1988). Academic stress, social support, and secretory immunoglobulin. *Journal of Personality and Social Psychology, 55,* 803–810.

Jenkins, J. G., & Dallenbach, K. M. (1924). Oblivescence during sleep and waking. *American Journal of Psychology, 35,* 605–612.

Jensen, E. (1998). *Teaching with the brain in mind.* Alexandria, VA: Association for Supervision and Curriculum Development.

Johnsgard, K. W. (2004). *Conquering depression and anxiety through exercise.* New York: Prometheus.

Johnstone, A. H., & Su, W. Y. (1994). Lectures: A learning experience? *Education in Chemistry, 31*(1), 65–76, 79.

Jones, L., & Petruzzi, D. C. (1995). Test anxiety: A review of theory and current treatment. *Journal of College Student Psychotherapy, 10*(1), 3–15.

Kachgal, M. M., Hansen, L. S., & Nutter, K. J. (2001). Academic procrastination prevention/intervention: Strategies and recommendations. *Journal of Developmental Education, 25,* 14–24.

Kadison, R. D., & DiGeronimo, T. F. (2004). *College of the overwhelmed: The campus mental health crisis and what to do about it.* San Francisco: Jossey-Bass.

Kagan, S., & Kagan, M. (1998). *Multiple intelligences: The complete MI book.* San Clemente, CA: Kagan Cooperative Learning.

Kasper, G. (2004, March). *Tax procrastination: Survey finds 29% have yet to begin taxes.* Retrieved June 6, 2006, from http://www.preweb.com/releases/2004/3/prweb114250.htm

Khoshaba, D. M., & Maddi, S. R. (1999–2004). *HardiTraining: Managing stressful change.* Newport Beach, CA: Hardiness Institute.

Kielcolt-Glaser, J. K., & Glaser, R. (1986). Psychological influences on immunity. *Psychosomatics, 27,* 621–625.

Kiecolt, J. K., Glaser, R., Strain, E., Stout, J., Tarr, K., Holliday, J., & Speicher, C. (1986). Modulation of cellular immunity in medical students. *Journal of Behavioral Medicine, 9,* 5–21.

Kiewra, K. A. (1985). Students' note-taking behaviors and the efficacy of providing the instructor's notes for review. *Contemporary Educational Psychology, 10,* 378–386.

Kierwa, K. A. (2000). Fish giver or fishing teacher? The lure of strategy instruction. *Teaching at UNL (University of Nebraska–Lincoln), 22*(3), 1–3.

Kierwa, K. A., DuBois, N., Christian, D., McShane, A., Meyerhoffer, M., & Roskelley, D. (1991). Note-taking functions and techniques. *Journal of Educational Psychology, 83*(2), 240–245.

Kiewra, K. A., & Fletcher, H. J. (1984). The relationship between notetaking variables and achievement measures. *Human Learning, 3,* 273–280.

Kiewra, K. A., Hart, K., Scoular, J., Stephen, M., Sterup, G., & Tyler, B. (2000). Fish giver or fishing teacher? The lure of strategy instruction. *Teaching at UNL (University of Nebraska–Lincoln), 22*(3).

King, A. (1990). Enhancing peer interaction and learning in the classroom through reciprocal questioning. *American Educational Research Journal, 27*(4), 664–687.

King, A. (1995). Guided peer questioning: A cooperative learning approach to critical thinking. *Cooperative Learning and College Teaching, 5*(2), 15–19.

King, J. E. (2002). *Crucial choices: How students' financial decisions affect their academic success.* Washington, DC: American Council on Education.

King, J. E. (2005). Academic success and financial decisions: Helping students make crucial choices. In R. S. Feldman (Ed.), *Improving the first year of college: Research and practice* (pp. 3–26). Mahwah, NJ: Lawrence Erlbaum.

Kintsch, W. (1968). Recognition and free recall of organized lists. *Journal of Experimental Psychology, 78,* 481–487.

Kintsch, W. (1970). *Learning, memory, and conceptual processes.* Hoboken, NJ: John Wiley & Sons.

Kintsch, W. (1994). Text comprehension, memory, and learning. *American Psychologist, 49,* 294–303.

Klein, S. P., & Hart, F. M. (1968). Chance and systematic factors affecting essay grades. *Journal of Educational Measurement, 5,* 197–206.

Knouse, S., Tanner, J., & Harris, E. (1999). The relation of college internships, college performance, and subsequent job opportunity. *Journal of Employment Counseling, 36,* 35–43.

Knox, S. (2004). *Financial basics: A money management guide for students.* Columbus: Ohio State University Press.

Kolb, D. A. (1976). Management and learning process. *California Management Review, 18*(3), 21–31.

Kolb, D. A. (1985). *Learning styles inventory.* Boston: McBer.

Kristof, K. M. (2008, December 27). Hooked on debt: Students learn too late the costs of private loans. *Los Angeles Times,* pp. A1, A18–A19.

Kruger, J., Wirtz, D., & Miller, D. (2005). Counterfactual thinking and the first instinct fallacy. *Journal of Personality and Social Psychology, 88,* 725–735.

Kuh, G. D. (1993). In their own words: What students learn outside the classroom. *American Educational Research Journal, 30,* 277–304.

Kuh, G. D., Kinzie, J., Schuh, J. H., Whitt, E. J., et al. (2005). *Student success in college: Creating conditions that matter.* San Francisco: Jossey-Bass.

Kuh, G. D., Schuh, J. H., Whitt, E., et al. (1991). *Involving colleges.* San Francisco: Jossey-Bass.

Kuhn, L. (1988). What should we tell students about answer changing? *Research Serving Teaching, 1*(8).

Kurfiss, J. G. (1988). *Critical thinking: Theory, research, practice, and possibilities.* ASHE-ERIC, Report No. 2. Washington, DC: Association for the Study of Higher Education.

Ladas, H. S. (1980). Note-taking on lectures: An information-processing approach. *Educational Psychologist, 15*(1), 44–53.

Lakein, A. (1973). *How to get control of your time and your life.* New York: New American Library.

Lay, C. H., & Silverman, S. (1996). Trait procrastination, time management, and dilatory behavior. *Personality & Individual Differences, 21,* 61–67.

Latané, B., Liu, J. H., Nowak, A., Bonevento, N., & Zheng, L. (1995). Distance matters: Physical space and social impact. *Personality and Social Psychology Bulletin, 21,* 795–805.

LeDoux, J. E. (1996). *The emotional brain: The mysterious underpinnings of emotional life.* New York: Touchstone.

Lefcourt, H. M. (1982). *Locus of control: Current trends in theory and research.* Hillsdale, NJ: Erlbaum.

Lehrer, P. M., & Woolfolk, R. L. (1993). *Principles and practice of stress management* (Vol. 2). New York: Guilford Press.

Leibel, R. L., Rosenbaum, M., & Hirsch, J. (1995). Changes in energy expenditure resulting from altered body weight. *New England Journal of Medicine, 332,* 621–628.

Letvin, D. J. (2006). *This is your brain on music: The science of a human obsession.* New York: Dutton.

Levine, A., & Cureton, J. S. (1998). *When hopes and fears collide.* San Francisco: Jossey-Bass.

Levitsky, D. A., Nussbaum, M., Halbmaier, C. A., & Mrdjenovic, G. (2003, July). *The freshman 15: A model for the study of techniques to curb the "epidemic" of obesity.* Annual meeting of the Society of the Study of Ingestive Behavior, University of Groningen, Haren, The Netherlands.

Lewin, K. (1935). *A dynamic theory of personality.* New York: McGraw-Hill.

Liebertz, C. (2005a). Want clear thinking? Relax. *Scientific American Mind, 16*(3), 88–89.

Liebertz, C. (2005b). A healthy laugh. *Scientific American Mind, 16*(3), 90–91.

Light, R. L. (1990). *The Harvard assessment seminars.* Cambridge, MA: Harvard University Press.

Light, R. L. (1992). *The Harvard assessment seminars, second report.* Cambridge, MA: Harvard University Press.

Light, R. J. (2001). *Making the most of college: Students speak their minds.* Cambridge, MA: Harvard University Press.

Linn, R. L., & Gronlund, N. E. (1995). *Measurement and assessment in teaching* (7th ed.). Englewood Cliffs, NJ: Prentice Hall.

Lock, R. D. (2000). *Taking charge of your career direction* (4th ed.). Belmont, CA: Wadsworth/Thomson Learning.

Locke, E. (1977). An empirical study of lecture note-taking among college students. *Journal of Educational Research, 77*, 93–99.

Locke, E. A., & Latham, G. P. (1990). *A theory of goal setting and task performance*. Englewood Cliffs, NJ: Prentice Hall.

Love, P., & Love, A. G. (1995). *Enhancing student learning: Intellectual, social, and emotional integration*. ASHE-ERIC Higher Education Report No. 4. Washington, DC: Graduate School of Education and Human Development, George Washington University.

Maddi, S. R. (2002). The story of hardiness: Twenty years of theorizing, research, and practice. *Consulting Psychology Journal: Practice and Research, 54*(3), 175–185.

Mae, N. (2005). *Undergraduate students and credit cards in 2004: An analysis of usage rates and trend*. Wilkes-Barre, PA: Nellie Mae Corp.

Maes, J. D., Weldy, T. G., & Icenogle, M. L. (1997). A managerial perspective: Oral communication competency is most important for business students in the workplace. *Journal of Business Communication, 34*(1), 67–80.

Malvasi, M., Rudowsky, C., & Valencia, J. M. (2009). *Library Rx: Measuring and treating library anxiety, a research study*. Chicago: Association of College and Research Libraries.

Marzano, R. J., Pickering, D. J., & Pollock, J. (2001). *Classroom instruction that works: Research-based strategies for increasing student achievement*. Alexandria, VA: Association for Supervision and Curriculum Development.

Maslow, A. H. (1954). *Motivation and personality*. New York: Harper & Row.

McCance, N., & Pychyl, T. A. (2003, August). *From task avoidance to action: An experience sampling study of undergraduate students' thoughts, feelings and coping strategies in relation to academic procrastination*. Paper presented at the Third Annual Conference for Counseling Procrastinators in the Academic Context, University of Ohio, Columbus.

McGuiness, D., & Pribram, K. (1980). The neurophysiology of attention: Emotional and motivational controls. In M. D. Wittrock (Ed.), *The brain and psychology* (pp. 95–139). New York: Academic Press.

Mehrabian, A. (1972). *Nonverbal communication*. Chicago: Adline-Atherton.

Middleton, F., & Strick, P. (1994). Anatomical evidence for cerebellar and basal ganglia involvement in higher brain function. *Science, 226*(51584), 458–461.

Millard, B. (2004, November). *A purpose-based approach to navigating college transitions*. Preconference workshop presented at the Eleventh National Conference on Students in Transition, Nashville, TN.

Miller, M. A. (2003, September/October). The meaning of the baccalaureate. *About Campus*, pp. 2–8.

Millman, J., Bishop, C., & Ebel, R. (1965). An analysis of test-wiseness. *Educational and Psychological Measurement, 25*, 707–727.

Milton, O. (1982). *Will that be on the final?* Springfield, IL: Charles C. Thomas.

Minninger, J. (1984). *Total recall: How to boost your memory power*. Emmaus, PA: Rodale.

Mitler, M. M., Dinges, D. F., & Dement, W. C. (1994). Sleep medicine, public policy, and public health. In M. H. Kryger, T. Roth, & W. C. Dement (Eds.), *Principles and practice of sleep medicine* (2nd ed.). Philadelphia: Saunders.

Moeller, M. L. (1999). History, concept and position of self-help groups in Germany. *Group Analysis, 32*(2), 181–194.

Molnar, S. (1991). *Human variation: Race, type, and ethnic groups* (3rd ed.). Englewood Cliffs, NJ: Prentice Hall.

Monk, T. H. (2005). The post-lunch dip in performance. *Clinical Sports Medicine, 24*(2), 15–23.

Multon, K. D., Brown, S. D., & Lent, R. W. (1991). Relation of self-efficacy beliefs to academic outcomes: A meta-analytic investigation. *Journal of Counseling Psychology, 38*(1), 30–38.

Murname, K., & Shiffrin, R. M. (1991). Interference and the representation of events in memory. *Journal of Experimental Psychology: Learning, Memory, & Cognition, 17*, 855–874.

Myers, D. G. (1993). *The pursuit of happiness: Who is happy—and why?* New York: Morrow.

Myers, D. G., & McCaulley, N. H. (1985). *Manual: A guide to the development and use of the Myers-Briggs Type Indicator*. Palo Alto, CA: Consulting Psychologists Press.

Nagda, B. R., Gurin, P., & Johnson, S. M. (2005). Living, doing and thinking diversity: How does pre-college diversity experience affect first-year students' engagement with college diversity? In R. S. Feldman (Ed.), *Improving the first year of college: Research and practice* (pp. 73–110). Mahwah, NJ: Lawrence Erlbaum.

Narciso, J., & Burkett, D. (1975). *Disclose yourself: Discover the "me" in relationships.* Englewood Cliffs, NJ: Prentice Hall.

Natale, V., & Ciogna, P. (1996). Circadian regulation of subjective alertness in morning and evening types. *Environmental Design Research Association, 20*(4), 491–497.

National Association of Colleges & Employers. (2003). *Job Outlook 2003 survey.* Bethlehem, PA: Author.

National Institute of Mental Health. (2001). *Eating disorders: Facts about eating disorders and the search for solutions.* Retrieved August 7, 2006, from http://www.nimh.nih.gov/publicat/eating disorders.cfm

National Institute of Mental Health. (2006). *The numbers count: Mental disorders in America.* Retrieved December 16, 2006, from http://www.nimh.nih.gov.pulicat/numbers.cfm

National Research Council. (1989). *Diet and health: Implications for reducing chronic disease risk.* Washington, DC: Committee on Diet and Health, National Academy Press.

Newell, A., & Rosenbloom, P. S. (1981). Mechanisms of skill acquisition of the law of practice. In J. R. Anderson (Ed.), *Cognitive skills and their acquisition.* Hillsdale, NJ: Erlbaum.

Newton, T. (1990, September). *Improving students' listening skills.* IDEA Paper No. 23. Manhattan, KS: Center for Faculty Evaluation and Development.

Nichols, M. P. (1995). *The lost art of listening.* New York: Guilford Press.

Nichols, R. G., & Stevens, L. A. (1957). *Are you listening?* New York: McGraw-Hill.

Niederjohn, M. S. (2008). First-year experience course improves students' financial literacy. *ESource for College Transitions* (electronic newsletter published by the National Resource Center for the First-Year Experience and Students in Transition), *6*(1), 9–11.

Norman, D. A. (1982). *Learning and memory.* San Francisco: W. H. Freeman.

Obama, B. (2006). *The audacity of hope: Thoughts on reclaiming the American dream.* New York: Three Rivers Press.

Office of Research. (1994). *What employers expect of college graduates: International knowledge and second language skills.* Washington, DC: Office of

Educational Research and Improvement (OERI), U.S. Department of Education.

O'Keefe, J., & Nadel, L. (1985). *The hippocampus as a cognitive map.* Oxford, England: Clarendon Press.

Onwuegbuzie, A. J. (2000). Academic procrastinators and perfectionistic tendencies among graduate students. *Journal of Social Behavior and Personality, 15,* 103–109.

Orszag, J. M., Orszag, P. R., & Whitmore, D. M. (2001). *Learning and earning: Working in college.* Retrieved July 19, 2006, from http://www.brockport.edu/career01/upromise.htm

Pace, C. R. (1990a). Measuring the quality of student effort [Monograph]. *Current Issues in Higher Education, 2*(1).

Pace, C. R. (1990b). *The undergraduates.* Los Angeles: Center for the Study of Evaluation, University of California.

Paivio, A. (1990). *Mental representations: A dual coding approach.* New York: Oxford University Press.

Park, O. (1984). Example comparison strategy versus attribute identification strategy in concept learning. *American Educational Research Journal, 21*(1), 145–162.

Pascarella, E. T. (2001, November/December). Cognitive growth in college: Surprising and reassuring findings from The National Study of Student Learning. *Change,* pp. 21–27.

Pascarella, E., & Terenzini, P. (1991). *How college affects students: Findings and insights from twenty years of research.* San Francisco: Jossey-Bass.

Pascarella, E., & Terenzini, P. (2005). *How college affects students: A third decade of research* (Vol. 2). San Francisco: Jossey-Bass.

Paul, R., & Elder, L. (2004). *The nature and functions of critical and creative thinking.* Dillon Beach, CA: Foundation for Critical Thinking.

Peele, S., & Brodsky, A. (1991). *Love and addiction.* New York: Signet Books.

Peigneux, P. P., Laureys, S., Delbeuck, X., & Maquet, P. (2001, December 21). Sleeping brain, learning brain: The role of sleep for memory systems. *NeuroReport, 12*(18), A111–A124.

Pennsylvania State University. (2005). *How to avoid plagiarism.* Retrieved October 15, 2005, from http://tlt.its.psu/suggestions/cyberplag/cyberplagexamples.html

Peter D. Hart Research Associates. (2006). *How should colleges prepare students to succeed in today's global economy?* Based on surveys among employers and recent college graduates conducted on behalf of the Association of American Colleges and Universities. Washington, DC: Author.

Peterson, C., & Seligman, M. E. P. (2004). *Character strengths and virtues: A handbook and classification.* New York: Oxford University Press.

Pettigrew, T. F. (1998). Intergroup contact theory. *Annual Review of Psychology, 49,* 65–85.

Piaget, J. (1978). *Success and understanding.* Cambridge, MA: Harvard University Press.

Piaget, J. (1985). *The equilibration of cognitive structures: The central problem of intellectual development.* Chicago, IL: University of Chicago Press.

Pinker, S. (1994). *The language instinct.* New York: HarperCollins.

Pintrich, P. R. (Ed.). (1995). *Understanding self-regulated learning* (New Directions for Teaching and Learning No. 63). San Francisco: Jossey-Bass.

Pope, L. (1990). *Looking beyond the Ivy League.* New York: Penguin Press.

Porter, S. R., & Swing, R. L. (2006). Understanding how first-year seminars affect persistence. *Research in Higher Education, 47*(1), 89–109.

Potts, J. T. (1987). Predicting procrastination on academic tasks with self-report personality measures (Doctoral dissertation, Hofstra University). *Dissertation Abstracts International, 48,* 1543.

President's Council on Physical Fitness and Sports. (2001). Toward a uniform definition of wellness: A commentary. *Research Digest, 3*(15), 1–8.

Pribram, K. H. (1991). *Brain and perception: Holonomy and structure in figural processing.* Hillsdale, NJ: Erlbaum.

Pratt, B. (2008). *Extra credit: The 7 things every college student needs to know about credit, debt, and cash.* Keedysville, MD: ExtraCreditBook.com.

Price, R. H., Choi, J. N., & Vinokur, A. D. (2002). Links in the chain of adversity following job loss: How financial strain and loss of personal control lead to depression, impaired functioning, and poor health. *Journal of Occupational Health Psychology, 7*(4), 302–312.

Purdue University Online Writing Lab. (1995–2004). *Writing a research paper.* Retrieved August 18, 2005, from http://owl.english.purdue.edu/workshops/hypertext/ResearchW/notes.html

Purdy, M., & Borisoff, D. (Eds.). (1996). *Listening in everyday life: A personal and professional approach.* Lanham, MD: University Press of America.

Putman, R. D. (2000). *Bowling alone: The collapse and revival of American community.* New York: Simon & Schuster.

Rader, P. E., & Hicks, R. A. (1987, April). *Jet lag desynchronization and self-assessment of business-related performance.* Paper presented at the meeting of the Western Psychological Association, Long Beach, CA.

Ramsden, P. (2003). *Learning to teach in higher education* (2nd ed.). London: RoutledgeFalmer.

Ramsden, P., & Entwistle, N. J. (1981). Effects of academic departments on students' approaches to studying. *British Journal of Educational Psychology, 51,* 368–383.

Reed, S. K. (1996). *Cognition: Theory and applications* (3rd ed.). Pacific Grove, CA: Brooks/Cole.

Rennels, M. R., & Chaudhair, R. B. (1988). *Eye-contact and grade distribution. Perceptual and Motor Skills, 67* (October), 627–632.

Resnick, L. B. (1986). *Education and learning to think, Special Report.* Pittsburgh: Commission on Behavioral and Social Sciences Education, University of Pittsburgh.

Rhoads, J. (2005). *The transition to college: Top ten issues identified by students.* Retrieved June 30, 2006, from http://advising.wichita.edu/lasac/pubs/aah/trans.htm

Riesman, D., Glazer, N., & Denney, R. (2001). *The lonely crowd: A study of the changing American character* (rev. ed.). New Haven, CT: Yale University Press.

Ring, T. (1997, October). Issuers face a visit to the dean's office. *Credit Card Management, 10,* 34–39.

Roffwarg, H. P., Muzio, J. N., & Dement, W. C. (1966). Ontogenetic development of the human sleep-dream cycle. *Science, 152,* 604–619.

Roos, L. L., Wise, S. L., Yoes, M. E., & Rocklin, T. R. (1996). Conducting self-adapted testing using MicroCAT. *Educational and Psychological Measurement, 56,* 821–827.

Rosenfield, I. (1988). *The invention of memory: A new view of the brain.* New York: Basic Books.

Rothblum, E. D., Solomon, L. J., & Murakami, J. (1986). Affective, cognitive, and behavioral differences between high and low procrastinators. *Journal of Counseling Psychology, 33*(4), 387–394.

Rotter, J. (1966). Generalized expectancies for internal versus external controls of reinforcement. *Psychological Monographs: General and Applied, 80*(609), 1–28.

Ruggiero, V. R. (2004). *Beyond feelings: A guide to critical thinking.* New York: McGraw-Hill.

Runco, M. A. (2004). Creativity. *Annual Review of Psychology, 55,* 657–687.

Saarni, C. (1999). *The development of emotional competence*. New York: Guilford.

Sadker, M., & Sadker, D. (1994). *Failing at fairness: How America's schools cheat girls*. New York: Charles Scribner's Sons.

Salovey, P., & Mayer, J. D. (1990). Emotional intelligence. *Imagination, Cognition, and Personality, 9*, 185–211.

Sapolsky, R. (2004). *Why zebras don't get ulcers*. New York: W. H. Freeman.

Savitz, F. (1985). Effects of easy examination questions placed at the beginning of science multiple-choice examinations. *Journal of Instructional Psychology, 12*(1), 6–10.

Sax, L. J. (2003, July–August). Our incoming students: What are they like? *About Campus*, pp. 15–20.

Sax, L. J., Astin, A. W., Korn, W. S., & Mahoney, K. M. (1999). *The American freshman: National norms for fall 1999*. Los Angeles: Higher Education Research Institute, Graduate School of Education & Information Studies, University of California.

Sax, L. J., Bryant, A. N., & Gilmartin, S. K. (2004). A longitudinal investigation of emotional health among male and female first-year college students. *Journal of the First-Year Experience & Students in Transition, 16*(2), 29–65.

Sax, L. J., Lindholm, J. A., Astin, A. W., Korn, W. S., & Mahoney, K. M. (2004). *The American freshman: National norms for fall, 2004*. Los Angeles: Higher Education Research Institute, University of California.

Schacter, D. L. (1992). Understanding implicit memory. *American Psychologist, 47*(4), 559–569.

Schlosser, E. (2001). *Fast food nation: The dark side of the all-American meal*. Boston: Houghton Mifflin.

Schneider, W., & Chein, J. M. (2003). Controlled and automatic processing: Behavior, theory, and biological mechanisms. *Cognitive Science, 27*, 525–559.

Schunk, D. H. (1995). Self-efficacy and education and instruction. In J. E. Maddux (Ed.), *Self-efficacy, adaptation, and adjustment: Theory, research, and application* (pp. 281–303). New York: Plenum Press.

Schutte, N. S., Malouff, J. M., et al. (1998). Development and validation of emotional intelligence. *Personality and Individual Differences, 26*, 167–177.

Schutte, N. S., & Malouff, J. M. (2002). Incorporating emotional skills content in a college transition course enhances student retention. *Journal of the First-Year Experience, 14*(1), 7–21.

Sedlacek, W. (1987). Black students on White campuses: 20 years of research. *Journal of College Student Personnel, 28*, 484–495.

Segall, M. H., Campbell, D. T., & Herskovits, M. J. (1966). *The influence of culture on visual perception*. Indianapolis: Bobbs-Merrill.

Seligman, M. E. P. (1991). *Learned optimism*. New York: Knopf.

Shanley, M., & Witten, C. (1990). University 101 freshman seminar course: A longitudinal study of persistence, retention, and graduation rates. *NASPA Journal, 27*, 344–352.

Shatz, M. A., & Best, J. B. (1987). Students' reasons for changing answers on objective tests. *Teaching of Psychology, 14*(4), 241–242.

Shelton, J. T., Elliot, E. M., Eaves, S. D., & Exner, A. L. (2009). The distracting effects of a ringing cell phone: An investigation of the laboratory and the classroom setting. *Journal of Environmental Psychology*, (March). Retrieved October 25, 2009, from http://news-info.wustl.edu/news/page/normal/14225.html

Sidle, M., & McReynolds, J. (1999). The freshman year experience: Student retention and student success. *NASPA Journal, 36*, 288–300.

Simopoulos, A. P., & Pavlou, K. N. (Eds.). (1997). Genetic variation and dietary response. *World Review of Nutrition and Dietics*. Basel, Switzerland: S. Karger.

Simunek, M., Schutte, N. S., Hollander, S., & McKenley, J. (2000). *The relationship between ability to understand and regulate emotions, mood, and self-esteem*. Paper presented at the Conference of the American Psychological Society, Miami, FL.

Singh, N. A., Clements, K. M., & Fiatarone, M. A. (1997). A randomized controlled trial of the effect of exercise on sleep. *Sleep, 20*, 95–101.

Smith, D. (1997). How diversity influences learning. *Liberal Education, 83*(2), 42–48.

Smith, D. D. (2005). Experiential learning, service learning, and career development. In P. A. Gore (Ed.), *Facilitating the career development of students in transition* (Monograph No. 43, pp. 205–222). Columbia: National Resource Center for the First-Year Experience and Students in Transition, University of South Carolina.

Smith, R. L. (1994). The world of business. In W. C. Hartel, S. W. Schwartz, S. D. Blume, & J. N. Gardner (Eds.), *Ready for the real world* (pp. 123–135). Belmont, CA: Wadsworth Publishing.

Smith, T., Snyder, C. R., & Handelsman, M. M. (1982). On the self-serving function of an academic wooden leg: Test anxiety as a self-handi-capping strategy. *Journal of Personality & Social Psychology, 42,* 314–321.

Snyder, C. R. (1995). Conceptualizing, measuring, and nurturing hope. *Journal of Counseling and Development, 73* (January/February), 355–360.

Snyder, C. R., Harris, C., Anderson, J. R., Holleran, S. A., Irving, L. M., Sigmon, S. T., et al. (1991). The will and the ways: Development and vali-dation of an individual-differences measure of hope. *Journal of Personality and Social Psychology, 60,* 570–585.

Soloman, L. J., & Rothblum, E. D. (1984). Academic procrastination: Frequency and cognitive-be-havioral correlates. *Journal of Counseling Psychol-ogy, 31,* 503–509.

Southern Methodist University. (2006). *How is college different from high school?* Retrieved September 15, 2006, from http://www.smu.edu/alec/whyhighschool.html

Sprenger, M. (1999). *Learning and memory: The brain in action.* Alexandria, VA: Association for Super-vision and Curriculum Development.

Stark, J. S., Lowther, R. J., Bentley, M. P., Ryan, G. G., Martens, M. L., Genthon, P. A., et al. (1990). *Planning introductory college courses: Influ-ences on faculty.* Ann Arbor: National Center for Research to Improve Postsecondary Teaching and Learning, University of Michigan. (ERIC Docu-ment Reproduction Services No. 330 277 370).

Starke, M. C., Harth, M., & Sirianni, F. (2001). Re-tention, bonding, and academic achievement: Success of a first-year seminar. *Journal of the First-Year Experience & Students in Transition, 13*(2), 7–35.

Staudinger, U. M., & Baltes, P. B. (1994). Psychology of wisdom. In R. J. Sternberg (Ed.), *Encyclopedia of intelligence* (Vol. 1, pp. 143–152). New York: Macmillan.

Steel, P. (2003). *The nature of procrastination: A meta-analytic and theoretical review of self-regulatory fail-ure.* Retrieved June 28, 2006, from http://www.haskayne.ucalgary.ca/research/workingpapers

Steel, P., Brothen, T., & Wambach, C. (2001). Pro-crastination and personality, performance, and mood. *Personality & Individual Differences, 30,* 95–106.

Stein, B. S. (1978). Depth of processing reexamined: The effects of the precision of encoding and test-ing appropriateness. *Journal of Verbal Learning and Verbal Behavior, 17,* 165–174.

Sternberg, R. J. (2001). What is the common thread of creativity? *American Psychologist, 56*(4), 360–362.

Strommer, D. W. (1993). Not quite good enough: Drifting about in higher education. *AAHE Bul-letin, 45*(10), 14–15.

Sullivan, R. E. (1993, March 18). Greatly reduced ex-pectations. *Rolling Stone,* pp. 2–4.

Sundquist, J., & Winkleby, M. (2000, June). Country of birth, acculturation status and abdominal obe-sity in a national sample of Mexican-American women and men. *International Journal of Epide-miology, 29,* 470–477.

Susswein, R. (1995). College students and credit cards: A privilege earned? *Credit World, 83,* 21–23.

Svinicki, M. D., & Dixon, N. M. (1987). The Kolb model modified for classroom activities. *College Teaching, 35*(4), 141–146.

Szalavitz, M. (2003). Stand and deliver. *Psychology To-day,* pp. 50–54.

Taylor, S. E., Peplau, L. A., & Sears, D. O. (2006). *Social psychology* (12th ed.). Upper Saddle River, NJ: Pearson/Prentice Hall.

Teigen, K. H. (1994). Yerkes-Dodson—A law for all seasons. *Theory & Psychology, 4,* 525–547.

Pennsylvania State University. (2005). *How to avoid plagiarism.* Retrieved October 15, 2005, from http://tlt.its.psu/suggestions/cyberplag/cyber-plagexamples.html

Thomson, R. (1998). University of Vermont. In B. O. Barefoot, C. L. Warnock, M. P. Dickinson, S. E. Richardson, & M. R. Roberts (Eds.). (1998). *Exploring the evidence: Vol. 2. Reporting outcomes of first-year seminars* (Monograph No. 29, pp. 77–78). Columbia: National Resource Center for the First-Year Experience and Students in Transition, University of South Carolina.

Tice, D. M., & Baumeister, R. F. (1997). Longitudi-nal study of procrastination, performance, stress, and health: The costs and benefits of dawdling. *Psychological Science, 8,* 454–458.

Tinto, V. (1993). *Leaving college: Rethinking the causes and cures of student attrition* (2nd ed.). Chicago: University of Chicago Press.

Tinto, V. (1997). Classrooms as communities: Explor-ing the educational character of student persis-tence. *Journal of Higher Education, 68,* 599–623.

Tinto, V. (2000). Linking learning and leaving: Ex-ploring the role of the college classroom in stu-dent departure. In J. M. Braxton (Ed.), *Reworking the student departure puzzle* (pp. 81–94). Nashville: Vanderbilt University Press.

Tisdell, E. J. (2003). *Exploring spirituality and culture in adult and higher education*. San Francisco: Jossey-Bass.

Tobias, S. (1985). Test anxiety: Interference, defective skills, and cognitive capacity. *Educational Psychologist, 20*(3), 135–142.

Tomasho, R. (2009, April 22). Study tallies education gap's effect on GDP. *Wall Street Journal*.

Torrance, E. P. (1963). *Education and the creative potential*. Minneapolis: University of Minnesota Press.

Tyson, E. (2003). *Personal finance for dummies*. Indianapolis: IDG Books.

Underwood, B. J. (1983). *Attributes of memory*. Glenview, IL: Scott, Foresman.

University of New Hampshire Office of Residential Life. (2001). *The hate that hate produced*. Retrieved January 8, 2007, from http://www.unh.edu/residental-life/diversity/kn_article6.pdf

U.S. Bureau of Labor Statistics. (2005). *Number of jobs, labor market experience, and earnings growth: Results from a longitudinal survey*. Retrieved September 24, 2005, from http://www.bls.gov/news.release/nlsoy.toc.htm

U.S. Census Bureau. (2000). *Racial and ethnic classifications in Census 2000 and beyond*. Retrieved December 19, 2006, from http://census.gov/population/www/socdemo/race/racefactcb.html

U.S. Census Bureau. (2004). *The face of our population*. Retrieved December 12, 2006, from http://factfinder.census.gov/jsp/saff/SAFFInfojsp?_pageId=tp9_race_ethnicity

U.S. Census Bureau. (2008). *Bureau of Labor Statistics*. Washington, DC: Author.

U.S. Department of Health & Human Services. (2000). *Healthy people 2010: Understanding and improving health*. Washington, DC: Government Printing Office.

Van Dongen, H. P. A., Maislin, G., Mullington, J. M., & Dinges, D. F. (2003). The cumulative cost of additional wakefulness: Dose–response effects on neurobehavioral functions and sleep physiology from chronic sleep restriction and total sleep deprivation. *Sleep, 26*, 117–126.

Van Overwalle, F. I., Mervielde, I., & De Schuyer, J. (1995). Structural modeling of the relationships between attributional dimensions, emotions, and performance of college freshmen. *Cognition and Emotion, 9*(1), 59–85.

Viorst, J. (1998). *Necessary losses*. New York: Fireside.

Voelker, R. (2004). Stress, sleep loss, and substance abuse create potent recipe for college depression. *Journal of the American Medical Association, 291*, 2177–2179.

Vygotsky, L. S. (1978). Internalization of higher cognitive functions. In M. Cole, V. John-Steiner, S. Scribner, & E. Souberman (Eds. & Trans.), *Mind in society: The development of higher psychological processes* (pp. 52–57). Cambridge, MA: Harvard University Press.

Waddington, P. (1996). *Dying for information: An investigation into the effects of information overload in the USA and worldwide*. London: Reuters.

Wade, C., & Tavris, C. (1990). Thinking critically and creatively. *Skeptical Inquirer, 14*, 372–377.

Walker, C. M. (1996). Financial management, coping, and debt in households under financial strain. *Journal of Economic Psychology, 17*, 789–807.

Walsh, K. (2005). *Suggestions from more experienced classmates*. Retrieved June 12, 2006, from http://www.uni.edu/walsh/introtips.html

Walter, T. W., Knudsbig, G. M., & Smith, D. E. P. (2003). *Critical thinking: Building the basics* (2nd ed.). Belmont, CA: Wadsworth.

Webber, R. A. (1991). *Breaking your time barriers: Becoming a strategic time manager*. Englewood Cliffs, NJ: Prentice Hall.

Weinstein, C. F. (1994). Students at risk for academic failure. In K. W. Prichard & R. M. Sawyer (Eds.), *Handbook of college teaching: Theory and applications* (pp. 375–385). Westport, CT: Greenwood Press.

Weinstein, C. F., & Meyer, D. K. (1991). Cognitive learning strategies. In R. J. Menges & M. D. Svinicki (Eds.), *College teaching: From theory to practice* (New Directions for Teaching and Learning No. 45, pp. 15–26). San Francisco: Jossey-Bass.

Weinstein, C. E., & Underwood, V. L. (1985). Learning strategies: The how of learning. In J. W. Segal, S. F. Chapman, & R. Glaser (Eds.), *Thinking and learning skills* (pp. 241–258). Hillsdale, NJ: Erlbaum.

Wesley, J. C. (1994). Effects of ability, high school achievement, and procrastinatory behavior on college performance. *Educational & Psychological Measurement, 54*, 404–408.

Wheelright, J. (2005, March). Human, study thyself. *Discover*, pp. 39–45.

Wiederman, M. (2007). Why it's so hard to be happy. *Scientific American Mind, 18*(1), 36–43.

Wilkie, C. J., & Thompson, C. A. (1993). First-year reentry women's perceptions of their classroom experiences. *Journal of the Freshman Year Experience, 5*(2), 69–90.

Wilhite, S. (1990). Self-efficacy, locus of control, self-assessment of memory ability, and student activities as predictors of college course achievement. *Journal of Educational Psychology, 82*(4), 696–700.

Willingham, W. W. (1985). *Success in college: The role of personal qualities and academic ability.* New York: College Entrance Examination Board.

Winsor, J. L., Curtis, D. B., & Stephens, R. D. (1997). National preferences in business and communication education: A survey update. *JACA, 3* (September), 170–179.

Wolvin, A. D., & Coakley, X. X. (1993). *Perspectives on listening.* Norwood, NJ: Ablex Publishing.

Wright, D. J. (Ed.). (1987). *Responding to the needs of today's minority students.* New Directions for Student Services, No. 38. San Francisco: Jossey-Bass.

Wyckoff, S. C. (1999). The academic advising process in higher education: History, research, and improvement. *Recruitment & Retention in Higher Education, 13*(1), 1–3.

Yerkes, R. M., & Dodson, J. D. (1908). The relationship of strength and stimulus to rapidity of habit formation. *Journal of Neurological Psychology, 184,* 59–82.

Young, K. S. (1996, August). *Pathological Internet use: The emergence of a new clinical disorder.* Paper presented at the annual meeting of the American Psychological Association, Toronto, Ontario, Canada.

Zeidner, M. (1995). Adaptive coping with test situations: A review of the literature. *Educational Psychologist, 30*(3), 123–133.

Zimbardo, P. G., Johnson, R. L., & Weber, A. L. (2006). *Psychology: Core concepts* (5th ed.). Boston: Allyn & Bacon.

Zimmerman, B. J. (1995). Self-efficacy and educational development. In A. Bandura (Ed.), *Self-efficacy in changing societies.* New York: Cambridge University Press.

Zohar, D. (1998). An additive model of test anxiety: Role of exam-specific expectations. *Journal of Educational Psychology, 90,* 330-340.

Zull, J. E. (1998). The brain, the body, learning, and teaching. *National Teaching & Learning Forum, 7*(3), 1–5.

Zull, J. E. (2002). *The art of changing the brain: Enriching the practice of teaching by exploring the biology of learning.* Sterling, VA: Stylus.

Index